I believe in Christ, he is my King;
With all my heart to him I'll sing;
I'll raise my voice in praise and joy,
In grand amens my tongue employ.

I believe in Christ, he is God's Son;
On earth to dwell his soul did come;
He healed the sick, the dead he raised,
Good works were his, his name be praised.

I believe in Christ, O blessed name,
As Mary's Son he came to reign
'Mid mortal men, his earthly kin,
To save them from the woes of sin.

I believe in Christ, who marked the path,
Who did gain all his Father hath,
Who said to men: "Come follow me,
That ye, my friends, with God may be."

I believe in Christ—my Lord, my God—
My feet he plants on gospel sod;
I'll worship him with all my might;
He is the source of truth and light.

I believe in Christ, he ransoms me;
From Satan's grasp he sets me free,
And I shall live with joy and love
In his eternal courts above.

I believe in Christ, he stands supreme;
From him I'll gain my fondest dream;
And while I strive through grief and pain,
His voice is heard: "Ye shall obtain."

I believe in Christ; so come what may,
With him I'll stand in that great day
When on this earth he comes again,
To rule among the sons of men.

—Bruce R. McConkie

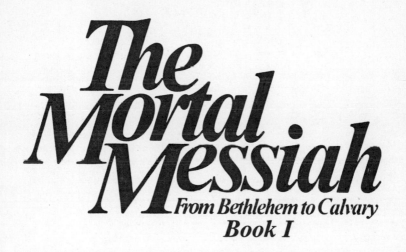

The Mortal Messiah
From Bethlehem to Calvary
Book I

Bruce R. McConkie

Deseret Book Company
Salt Lake City, Utah

Vol. 1 ISBN 0-87747-784-1 (hardbound)
ISBN 0-87579-403-3 (softbound)

Library of Congress Cataloging-in-Publication Data

McConkie, Bruce R.
   The mortal Messiah: from Bethlehem to Calvary.

   Includes index.
   1. Jesus Christ—Biography. 2. Christian biography—Palestine.
   3. Judaism—History—Post-exilic period, 586 B.C.–210 A.D.
   I. Title.
   BT301.2.M16   232.9'01   79-19606

Printed in the United States of America

10   9   8   7   6   5   4   3

THE MESSIANIC TRILOGY

The forerunner of this work is *The Promised Messiah: The First Coming of Christ,* which deals with the Messianic prophecies. This work, *The Mortal Messiah: From Bethlehem to Calvary,* is a Life of Christ published in four books. These four books contain the following:

BOOK I

Section I   *A Root Out of Dry Ground*
Section II   *Jesus' Years of Preparation*
Section III   *Jesus' Early Judean Ministry*

BOOK II

Section IV   *Jesus Begins the Great Galilean Ministry*
Section V   *The Twelve, The Sermon on The Mount, and Rising Pharisaic Opposition*
Section VI   *The Continuing Galilean Ministry*

BOOK III

Section VII   *The Galilean Ministry Reaches Its Peak*
Section VIII   *The Later Judean Ministry*
Section IX   *The Perean Ministry*
Section X   *From the Anointing to the Royal Reign*

BOOK IV

Section XI   *The Paschal Feast, The Private Prayers and Sermons, and Gethsemane*
Section XII   *The Trials, The Cross, and The Tomb*
Section XIII   *He Riseth; He Ministereth; He Ascendeth*

The concluding work in this whole series will be *The Millennial Messiah: The Second Coming of the Son of Man.*

ABBREVIATIONS

Scriptural references are abbreviated in a standard and self-identifying way. Other books are cited by author and title except for the following:

Commentary I	Bruce R. McConkie, *Doctrinal New Testament Commentary.* Vol. 1, *The Gospels.* Bookcraft, 1965.
Edersheim	Alfred Edersheim, *The Life and Times of Jesus the Messiah.* 1883.
Farrar	F. W. Farrar, *The Life of Christ.* London: Cassell & Co., Ltd., 1874.
Geikie	Cunningham Geikie, *The Life and Words of Christ.* 1886.
Hymns	*Hymns, The Church of Jesus Christ of Latter-day Saints.* 1948.
JST	Joseph Smith Translation (Inspired Version) of the Bible.
Mormon Doctrine	Bruce R. McConkie, *Mormon Doctrine,* 2nd ed. Bookcraft, 1966.
Sketches	Alfred Edersheim, *Sketches of Jewish Social Life in the Days of Christ.* 1876.
Talmage	James E. Talmage, *Jesus the Christ.* 1915.
Teachings	Joseph Fielding Smith, comp., *Teachings of the Prophet Joseph Smith.* 1938.
Temple	Alfred Edersheim, *The Temple: Its Ministry and Services As They Were at the Time of Jesus Christ.*

CONTENTS

Chapter 5

THE LAW OF MOSES 67

Chapter 6

JERUSALEM—THE HOLY CITY 83

Chapter 7

JEHOVAH'S HOLY HOUSES 98

Chapter 8

MOSAIC SACRIFICES IN JESUS' DAY 124

Chapter 9

JEWISH FEASTS IN JESUS' DAY............. 158

Chapter 10

JEWISH SYNAGOGUES IN JESUS' DAY 187

Chapter 11

JEWISH SABBATHS IN JESUS' DAY.............. 201

Chapter 12

JEWISH FAMILY LIFE IN JESUS' DAY 213

Chapter 13

JEWISH APOSTASY IN JESUS' DAY 228

SECTION III
JESUS' EARLY JUDEAN MINISTRY

Chapter 26

Chapter 27

Chapter 28

Chapter 29

Chapter 30

PREFACE

My original intent, as this opus and its companion volumes took form in my mind, was to write two volumes—one dealing with the Messianic prophecies and the First Coming of the Messiah; the other with the prophetic utterances and revealed realities relative to his Second Coming. I had not dared even to think of assuming the prerogative of writing an account of the life of the greatest Person ever to walk the dusty paths of planet Earth. After all, I reasoned, I already had in print a nearly nine-hundred-page doctrinal commentary on the four Gospels, which in the very nature of things dealt primarily with the doings and sayings of Him who is eternal as he dwelt among men in mortal guise.

I knew, of course, that no man has and no man can write a *Life of Christ* in the true sense of the word, for two very good and sufficient reasons:

1. The data to do so does not exist. The material is simply not available. We do not know how he spent his youth, who his friends were, what part he played in church and civic affairs, how he conducted himself within the framework of the Jewish family system, and hosts of other things. Though we know a great deal about the historical and social circumstances of his day, very little authentic information is available of his actual life from either secular or spiritual sources. What Matthew, Mark, Luke, and John put in their Gospel accounts was written as their testimony of a

small part of his divine doings. Personal items are scarcely mentioned. The Gospels contain only that portion of our Lord's words, and only those glimpses of selected acts and deeds, which the Spirit knew beforehand should be preserved for presentation to the unbelieving and skeptical masses of men into whose hands the New Testament would come. Even God will not pour more knowledge and light and intelligence and understanding into human souls than they are prepared to accept. Such would be and is contrary to his whole plan for the advancement and growth and ultimate perfection of his children.

2. No mortal man, no matter how gifted he may be in literary craftsmanship, and no matter how highly endowed he may be with that spiritual insight which puts the words and acts of men into a true eternal perspective—no mortal, I say, can write the biography of a God. A biography is but the projection through the eyes of a penman of what the writer *believes* were the acts and what he *feels* were the thoughts and emotions of another man who had like feelings with his own. How, then, can any mortal plumb the depths of the feelings, or understand in full the doings, of an Eternal Being? How can one of limited talent tell, in true perspective, the whole story of Him who has all talent, and tell it in such a way that other dustlike creatures will catch the vision and rejoice in the portrayal?

It is not mere chance that the ancient inspired writers did not write a *Life of Our Lord.* Even they could not have done so; and if they had been so magnificently and gloriously endowed as to be able to record and analyze the infinitely complex character of an Infinite and Eternal Being, still none of us, their fellow dust-low creatures, would have been qualified to understand to the full what was written. Indeed, such is the spiritual degeneracy that is spread out over carnal and fallen man, that many things that might have been written about him would have had an adverse effect upon the minds of the doubting souls destined to dwell on earth after his day.

Just as the sealed portion of the Book of Mormon cannot be understood by men until they exercise faith like unto the brother of Jared, so the real *Life of Our Lord* cannot be written, and could not be understood if it were written, until men attain the spiritual stature to stand the effulgent brilliance that would shine forth from such a work if all things relative to him and his mortal doings were set forth in pristine perfection. All of this means that the true *Life of Christ* must be written by the spirit of revelation and of prophecy, and cannot come forth until that millennial day when men, like the brother of Jared, have a perfect knowledge that God can show them all things. Only then will they be able to believe and rejoice in the heavenly account.

For our day and time, and for this dispensation of grace, all we can do is write a study relative to his life. We can take those slivers of knowledge of him that have been preserved to us, add to them the revealed truths made manifest through latter-day revelation, use our best literary skill and organizational ability, sift out the speculative fabrications of uninspired authors, and come up with a near-biography which, hopefully, will do credit to his holy name. Our present study relative to the life of him who was perfect—a study based on the best light and knowledge now available—will be far from perfect. But any deficiencies will be those of the intellect and not of the heart, for in our heart we know he was divine, and we desire to present him in such a light as to please him and his Father.

In addition to all this, I have a deep and profound respect for *Jesus the Christ,* the scholarly work of Elder James E. Talmage, one of my most prominent predecessors. Why, I thought, should I step into the most difficult of all fields of gospel writing—that of composing something akin to a *Life of Christ?* But as I pondered and prayed and put into words, in the first volume of this series, the true meaning of the many Messianic messages, as I gained a working knowledge of what the makers of words and the coiners of phrases in Christendom had presumed to write about him of whom they know so little, and as I envisioned more fully the faithless and uninspired nature of almost everything that worldly men have recorded about the marvelous works and message of him who is known to us by revelation, there came into my heart an overpowering desire to put into words, as best I might, for all to read, what we believe and know about the greatest life ever lived.

Further, I knew, as do all who have studied the sources and toiled through the voluminous tomes of many authors, that my friend and colleague who gave us *Jesus the Christ* did not attempt to bring forth a near-biography that partakes of as many elements of a life of Christ as is possible. His work, like my *Doctrinal New Testament Commentary—The Gospels,* is in large measure a commentary about and an explanation of the teachings of the Master. It follows the pattern of his day, interweaving with well-chosen words a true and sound perspective of those things with which he was privileged to deal. His work is profound and sound and should be studied by every member of the true Church. But I think I hear his voice, vocal and penetrating above those of all others qualified to speak in the specialized field here involved, saying, "Now is the time to build on the foundations I laid some seventy years ago, using the added knowledge that has since come by research and revelation, and to pen a companion volume to the one I was privileged to write."

Such in any event is the labor I have undertaken in this work—*The Mortal Messiah: From Bethlehem to Calvary.* As to its value, I say only that it is what it is, and it will stand or fall on its own merit; nor do I think what is here recorded is the beginning and the end. It too is but an opening door. Others who follow will find the errors and deficiencies that always and ever attend every mortal work, will correct them, and, building upon whatever foundations then exist, will write greater and better works on the same subject. But if perchance this work leads some soul—or, the Lord willing, many souls—to love and follow him of whom it speaks, it will have fulfilled the desires and hopes of the author, who himself knows and testifies of the divine Sonship and of the perfect ministry of the Mortal Messiah.

I am deeply indebted—more than I can express—to Velma Harvey, a most able and efficient secretary, for much wise counsel, for many thoughtful suggestions, and for handling the myriad matters presented in such a work as this.

SECTION I

A ROOT OUT OF DRY GROUND

A ROOT OUT OF DRY GROUND

"He shall grow up before him as a tender plant, and as a root out of a dry ground." (Isa. 53:2.)

Our Lord, King Messiah—born of Mary and begotten by Elohim—grew up before his Father as a Tender Plant; as a Vine of whose fruit men may eat and never hunger more; as a Tree from whose branches the fruit of eternal life may be plucked.

But he grew up also as a Root out of dry ground; as a Vine in arid and sterile soil; as a Tree for which there was little soil and sun and water in the dry garden where he had been planted by his Father.

Our Lord, King Messiah, grew up in the arid soil of a spiritually degenerate society—in a Holy City that had become like Egypt and Sodom; among a people who chose darkness rather than light because their deeds were evil; and in the midst of a people who had a form of godliness but denied the power thereof.

He grew up to sit on a throne honored only in memory; as part of a subject people who wore a Roman yoke and were ruled by an Idumean despot; as part of the only nation under heaven who would crucify their King.

He grew up in the arid and sterile soil of a Judaism where the priesthood was bought and sold; where his Father's house had become a den of thieves; where sacrifices and feasts and fasts and Sabbaths all testified of a then-unknown Jehovah.

As a prelude to studying his growth, we must analyze the soil in which he grew. If ever a divine and tender plant grew up in dry ground, it was he who one day would say, "Every plant, which my heavenly Father hath not planted, shall be rooted up." (Matt. 15:13.)

Chapter I

"COME . . . LEARN OF ME"

Come drink of the waters of life;
Come feast on the good word of God;
Come eat of the manna from heav'n;
Come bask in the light of the Lord.

Come hear him speak peace to the storm;
Come see him give sight to the blind;
Come watch him heal legs that are lame;
Come view him give life to the dead.

Come feel of his Spirit anew;
Come hear what he says to all men;
Come walk in the way he commands;
Come learn of the One who is God.

—*Bruce R. McConkie*

The Father Commands: "Hear Ye Him!"

"This is my beloved Son, in whom I am well pleased; hear ye him." (Matt. 17:5.)

The Shekinah, a visible manifestation of the Divine Presence, the bright and shining cloud—which rested upon Moses in the holy mount, and out of which a Voice spoke

3

from between the cherubim in the Holy of Holies—this sacred covering that surrounded the Presence of Deity, once more was manifest in Israel. A bright cloud, sent from heaven, overshadowed the angelic visitants who ministered to their mortal Kinsman, and a voice spake, the same voice that had said of old, "Thou art my Son; this day have I begotten thee." (Ps. 2:7.) The glory and power and Spirit, shining forth from the divine cloud, had come again, and the command was: *"Hear ye Him."*

This was the day of the Son, the dispensation of crucifixion and martyrdom, the hour of atonement. This was the day when the bright and shining cloud that shielded the Personage from men was to be lifted, and all men were to see God in the person of his Son. After four thousand weary years, as promised by all the holy prophets since the world began, the ransom was to be paid by One without sin. The Promised Messiah now ministered as the Mortal Messiah, and his Father commanded all men: *"Hear ye Him."*

Ancient Israel followed the cloud by day and the pillar of fire by night. Enoch hearkened to the voice from heaven, "Get ye upon the mount Simeon." There he beheld the heavens open, was clothed upon with glory, and "saw the Lord." (Moses 7:1-4.) Moses spent forty days amid the thunders and lightnings and fires of Sinai. There he received the holy law, written by the finger of God on tables of stone. Moriancumer talked with the Lord for three hours, and the voice came out of the cloud. (Ether 2.) It had ever been thus anciently—the Shekinah rested where the Lord's chosen people were; the power, glory, and Spirit of the Almighty was shown forth among those whom God had chosen out of the world; the Voice spake from the cloud, declaring truth, testifying, pointing the way. And now the Son himself, introduced by the Voice out of the cloud, dwelt among men, and they were commanded: *"Hear ye Him."*

"God, who at sundry times and in divers manners spake in time past unto the fathers by the prophets," so the Apostle announced, "hath in these last days spoken unto us by his

4

Son." (Heb. 1:1-2.) God spoke by and through the Son. The words of the Father fell from the lips of the Son. "My doctrine is not mine, but his that sent me," Jesus said. "If any man will do his will, he shall know of the doctrine, whether it be of God, or whether I speak of myself." (John 7:16-17.) That God whom it is life eternal to know was revealing himself through his Son. "He that hath seen me hath seen the Father" (John 14:9) was the divine pronouncement. Is it any wonder, then, when the Shekinah once again was seen on earth, that the Voice, speaking from the heavenly cloud of light surrounding the Divine Presence, proclaimed the heaven-sent message—*Hear ye Him!*

Who is this Jesus of whom the Father saith, "Hear ye him"? Whence came he, and of what import is his message?

Jesus our Lord—born in Bethlehem, crucified on Calvary—lived the only perfect life ever known on planet Earth, or, for that matter, on any of the worlds without number created by him and his Father.

He was and is the Firstborn, the first spirit child born to the Eternal Father. In that spirit realm of light and glory he advanced and progressed and became like the Father in power and might and dominion. He was and is the Great Jehovah. Under the Father he was and is the Creator of all things from the beginning, and he was chosen in the councils of eternity to be the Redeemer and Savior.

When the time came for him to gain his mortal body and undergo the probationary experiences of mortality, he was born on this earth. He came here to dwell as a mortal, subject to the testing experiences that are the common lot of all mankind. He lived and breathed as all men do; he ate and drank as his needs required; he wielded the carpenter's saw, toiled in the fields of grain, and slept on the barren Palestinian soil. His experiences were like those of his Israelite kinsmen. Upon him the rains fell; around him the snows swirled. He was hungry, cold, tired, sick, and afflicted, as all men are; and when he died, his eternal spirit left its tenement of clay, as is the case with all of Adam's race. He was a

5

man, a mortal man, a son of Adam, and God his Father saw fit to let him live as other men live, experience as they experience, sorrow and suffer as they do, and overcome as they must, if they are ever to return to the Divine Presence where joy and peace and eternal glory abound.

But he came from God and was born as his Son, inheriting from his Father the power of immortality. He came with the talents and abilities and spiritual endowments that he possessed in that eternal world where the spirit children of a gracious Father await the day of their mortal probation. He came with the spiritual talent to attune his soul to the Infinite so that he could think and speak and act in complete harmony with the mind and will of him whose Son he was. There was more than just a spark of divinity in his dust-created body. He was God's Son, the Only Begotten in the flesh. His native capacity exceeded that of any other person who ever lived. Not only could he alone work out the infinite and eternal atonement, because he possessed the power of immortality, but he alone could also do the other things that he did while in mortality—all because of his own preeminent preexistent stature, because of the talents and abilities he there possessed, and which were still his as he walked among mortal men.

Jesus our Lord was both a mortal man and a Divine Son. All men were his brethren and he was like them in appearance. Their ills and ailments were as his. But he alone was the Offspring of God in the flesh, and he alone came to earth with talents and insights that exceeded those of Adam and Enoch and Noah and Abraham. Though he was mortal, he retained his Godship. He was the only perfect Being ever to grace this lowly orb.

This Jesus of whom we now speak, and of whose mortal experiences we shall write in this work, was the greatest *man* who ever lived. In addition to the fact that he is "the Lord Omnipotent who reigneth, who was, and is from all eternity to all eternity," spoken of by King Benjamin (Mosiah 3:5), he is also the Suffering Servant of Isaiah (Isa. 53). Our challenge, as we attempt to paint a true picture of the Mortal Messiah, is to show him as a man; as a pilgrim far removed from his heavenly home; as the earthbound Christ, who lives and acts and is as other men—our challenge is to view him as a man, but with it all, a man of superlative talents and abilities, a man who reflected the light of heaven in every word and act.

"Though he were a Son," Paul tells us, as he confesses and certifies that our Lord is the Offspring of the Most High, "yet learned he obedience by the things which he suffered." That is, though God was his Father, he nonetheless was a mortal who suffered and struggled and obeyed. "And being made perfect," Paul continues, "he became the author of eternal salvation unto all them that obey him." (Heb. 5:8-9.) Thus, the Lord Jesus—having kept the whole law, having lived a perfect life, a life without sin—attained eternal perfection, a state of eternal glory like that of his Father. Because of his dual nature he became the Author (or, better, the Cause) of eternal salvation, meaning of both immortality and eternal life.

As to Jesus our Lord and the message he heralds to all who will hear, these things we know, and of them we are commanded to teach and testify:

1. That he who was born of Mary in Bethlehem of Judea; who dwelt and preached in Palestine; who healed the sick, opened the blind eyes, and caused the lame to leap; who stilled the storms and walked on the waters; who commanded the tomb-encased corpse to come forth, and it was done; who was condemned, scourged, and crucified; who died between two thieves at a place called Calvary; who came forth from a borrowed grave, on the third day, in glorious immortality—that this Jesus, who is both Christ and King, is, in fact, the Son of the living God.

2. That he who did all this did also, by virtue of his divine Sonship, work out the infinite and eternal atonement whereby all men are raised in immortality, while those who believe and obey come forth in the resurrection to inherit

eternal life; and that he, as the Word of God, the Spokesman of the Father, has and does present to the world the message of salvation, the plan of salvation, the gospel of Christ whereby this eternal life, the greatest of all the gifts of God, may be gained.

These things we know, for the Holy Spirit of God has revealed them to the spirit within us. We are living witnesses of him whose we are and by whom salvation comes. And we feel impelled to speak out, boldly, of him and his laws, and all that he has done for us, and all that he expects of us. This decision was not left to us: it is his will, and we are simply acting as his agent in teaching and testifying to all men everywhere those things which we verily believe and know to be true.

The Son Invites: "Come, . . . Learn of Me"

Jesus said: "Come, . . . learn of me" (Matt. 11:28-30)[1]— and learn we must, if we are ever to become like him and attain that kingdom where he and his Father dwell in celestial splendor.

"Learn of me!" Learn of the Lord Jesus Christ! Learn of him who is the Firstborn of the Father, the Great Jehovah, the Creator of worlds without number. Learn of him who is the God of Israel, the Promised Messiah, our Savior and Redeemer. Learn of him who dwelt in mortality for a scant thirty-four years; who set a perfect example for his brethren; who climaxed his earthly work in Gethsemane, at Golgotha, and before an open tomb.

Whence, then, comes our knowledge, and to what sources do we turn to learn truths about him whose name is Truth? As to his eternal existence and the things that he has done in ages past and will do in eons yet unborn, we have the Holy Scriptures and the inspired utterances of those whose Spirit-guided words come from the ultimate source of all truth. As to his ministry on planet earth, we have the four Gospels, the accounts in Third Nephi, sections 45 and 93 in the Doctrine and Covenants, and a few slivers of information in other parts of the Standard Works. As to all things connected with him, we should ponder and pray about that which is known, and then welcome the spirit of enlightenment and understanding that it is within our power to receive.

There is, of course, no such thing as a perfect biography of the Man Jesus, no such thing even as a sound and sane and proper biography. Neither I nor anyone else, with the knowledge presently available and with the literary craftsmanship with which writers of our generation have been blessed, could write such a work. Known facts about his mortal life are so fragmentary; the silence that broods over long periods of his earth life is so unbroken; what Matthew, Mark, Luke, and John chose to record was so selective and partial—that no one can even outline a chronological account of his life, or begin to show how his character and attributes became what they were. Recognized scholars have not so much as agreed upon a harmony of the four Gospels, nor can we expect them to do so with the data now available.

Biographies often reflect the feelings and sentiments, sometimes even the whims and idiosyncrasies, of those who write them. Authors are often prone to put their own proclivities and personality quirks into the pictures they paint of their subjects. Source materials, particularly for people long since departed to other realms, are often far from accurate. Tradition and speculation soon overshadow the fragments of reality that are known. How could a heavy tome on the life of Enoch or Ezra, on Melchizedek or Moriancumer, be other than a fictional accumulation of the fantasies of a fertile brain and a fluid pen? The known facts about any of these, and about Jethro and Joshua, about Joseph and Jeremiah, about Jesus himself, and about thousands of others who deserve an immortal remembrance in the hearts of succeeding generations, are so slight that any biography of the traditional sort must of necessity be largely imagination.

Unless and until more is known of Jesus and his life, it is

not only unwise but impossible to write a reality-based biographical dissertation about him. This work, thus, is not a biography in the traditional sense; it is not a life of our Lord of the sort that sectarians write; it is not a volume that puts words in the divine mouth, or assumes thoughts that may have been in his mind, or records with sinaitic finality emotions with which he may have been filled on great occasions. Insofar as finite limitations allow, it does not interlace the facts preserved in Holy Writ with the traditions of the fathers; it does not weave into the account the words of uninspired literary craftsmen, whose joy has always been to speculate what they would have done and therefore what Jesus did, in the various events of which we have knowledge; it does not draw out of the ethereal blue those personal fantasies—all of which taken together bring to full gestation and untimely birth the various biographies now extant about the greatest life ever lived.

This work is more of a commentary than a biography, more of an analysis of known events in his life than an exposition of his feelings and personality. Such biographical data, and such logical assumptions as fit in with his known character, can scarcely be avoided, nor is there any attempt so to do. There cannot help but be in this work, or in any work about any man written by any person, some things that are speculation and opinion. No biography, near-biography, or biography-type writing can possibly avoid this, and those who read any such compositions should be acutely aware that such is the case. Such awareness should be particularly keen when a devout person reads any biographical assumptions or recitations that deal with him who is our Lord.

In my judgment, those scriptural writers who have preserved for us the verities we do, in fact, know about him have so written their accounts as to omit, deliberately and designedly, nearly all of the personal items that would enable later biographers to portray his personality and personal affairs to the full. He is the Son of God; some things he had in common with his fellow mortals; other characteristics and abilities were his only; none of the rest of us have them, nor can we envision completely what they were or how they developed. We may suppose that an all-wise Father designed it so, and that he has permitted us to have available only those things with which we can equate and which are an example and an encouragement to us. We are not dealing with a mortal man in the full and unrestricted sense of the word when we write of him who inherited the power of immortality from that Man of Holiness who is the Immortal One. As he neared the end of his own Gospel account, the Beloved John said, "Many other signs truly did Jesus in the presence of his disciples, which are not written in this book: But these are written, that ye might believe that Jesus is the Christ, the Son of God; and that believing ye might have life through his name." (John 20:30-31.) Our approach and purpose will be the same as that of our ancient colleague.

We shall, accordingly, in this work talk about known family relations; known personality traits; known locales of labor and routes of travel; known facts about the character, perfections, and attributes that Jesus possessed; and beyond these limitations, we shall seek not to go. Much that is written will, of course, be in the nature of commentary; it will be akin to commentary, not the pure doctrinal commentary found in my *Doctrinal New Testament Commentary: The Gospels*, but commentary that teaches doctrines in the unique settings in which the utterances were given. We shall not strive to portray a rounded picture relative to each doctrine presented, but simply to expound and understand the portions of eternal truth that Jesus gave to the particular peoples who were then and there the hearers of his gracious words.

Doctrines and principles are the same under all circumstances. Truth is eternal. The principles of the everlasting gospel do not vary; they are the same in all ages and among all people. The Lord does not walk in crooked paths, nor vary from that which he hath said, nor alter the course in which men must walk to return to that far-off home whence

11

they came. All men, in all ages, in all parts of our planet, must believe and obey the same doctrines and ordinances to gain salvation.

But a knowledge of the circumstances and conditions under which Jesus expounded these principles of perfection to his fellow mortals will enable us more perfectly to perceive the profound nature of the truths themselves. What better setting is there for the proclamation, "I am the light of the world," than when the great golden lamp-stands in the temple are blazing forth their light as part of the Feast of Tabernacles? How better can he teach that he brings living water that quenches all thirst forever, and which is therefore a well springing up unto everlasting life, than when the woman of Samaria stoops to draw water for him from Jacob's Well? What teaching as to the nature and kind of bodies possessed by resurrected beings can equal that in the Upper Room, when he comes through the wall, eats food before his disciples, and permits them to feel the nail marks in his hands and feet and thrust their hands into the spear wound in his side? Truly a knowledge of the events in the life of Jesus enables us more fully to comprehend the doctrines he taught!

We have in our possession only a few brief words that fell from the lips of the Son of God while he dwelt in mortality. The time needed to read them is measured in minutes. And yet he spoke enough to fill libraries and to provide a lifetime of reading and more. We know from the Gospel accounts a few of the travels and troubles and trials of the Man who bore his Father's image and who did all things well. We know enough about him to envision what a perfect man should be and to have the hope of eternal life kindled in our souls. But "there are also many other things which Jesus did," says his intimate friend and confidant, the Beloved John, "the which, if they should be written every one, I suppose that even the world itself could not contain the books that should be written." (John 21:25.) Hyperbole? Perhaps. But regardless, what we have heard from His lips is but a stanza of a poetic gospel whose verses are without number; and what we have seen him do is but a glimpse of the acts and wonders that roll endlessly across the eternal screen where the acts of all beings are viewed.

To write a biography when only one-tenth of one percent of the background information is available would be foolhardy. To comment about and put into their perspective and relationship to us those choice and heaven-like gems that we do have is a work worthy of the mightiest pen, the keenest mind, and the deepest spiritual insight known to man. Someday a perfect biography will be forthcoming, written of course by the spirit of revelation. For the present we must content ourselves with what we have, and what we can envision, with the limited insight that is ours. Perhaps that in itself is a manifestation of the divine will. We have what we have, and we can comprehend what we can comprehend. If we knew more, it would be all to the good; yet, mayhap, we have all we are entitled to have and all we are capable of receiving.

We cannot but suppose that an Omnipotent wisdom has drawn a curtain of discreet silence over the childhood and youth of Mary's son; over the young manhood and growing experiences of him who was reared in Galilee and learned the carpenter's trade in Joseph's shop; over his family relationship and the endearing friendships that developing and maturing manhood so keenly cherishes; over the social and familial relationships that formed the basis of that Jewish culture in which an all-wise Father had sent him to dwell. Perhaps, after all, we have received all that we in our present state of spiritual maturity are prepared and qualified to receive. Perhaps, as we ponder what is recorded in this work, *The Mortal Messiah: From Bethlehem to Calvary*, we shall find enough to give us that guidance so devoutly desired and needed by those who love their Lord and who seek to impress his image upon their own countenances.

We do not have all gospel truths, but we do have the fulness of the everlasting gospel, meaning we have all of the laws, doctrines, principles, and ordinances needed to save and exalt us with a fulness of eternal glory hereafter. Similarly, we do not know all things about the life of our Lord, of the sayings of this greatest of the seers, or of the mighty works that he did in Judea and Perea and Galilee. But we do know enough about him to bask in the eternal light that proceeds from his presence, to see divinity inscribed on every feature and manifest in every act, and to know that if we heed his call, "Follow thou me" (2 Ne. 31:10), we can become like him and go where he is. With this assurance we are prepared to launch boldly into the glorious study at hand.

As we seek to learn of our Lord, we need guidance. He said: "Come unto me, all ye that labour and are heavy laden, and I will give you rest. Take my yoke upon you, and learn of me; for I am meek and lowly in heart: and ye shall find rest unto your souls. For my yoke is easy, and my burden is light." (Matt. 11:28-30.)

Learn of Him, whose roots sink deep as eternity! Learn what he was like while yet a spirit Son of an exalted Father. Learn of his valiance and progression in preexistence, of his creative enterprises, of the worlds without number that rolled into existence at his word. Learn of his power, might, and dominion in that day when he was chosen and became the Lamb slain from the foundation of the world. Learn of his foreordained ministry to redeem and to ransom and to save.

Learn of Him, of whom we know so little! Learn of the revelation of his holy gospel to the sons of men. Learn that all men everywhere, be they whosoever they are, whether Jew or Gentile, bond or free, black or white, all of the family of that Adam who begat us, all are to call upon God in the name of the Son forevermore. Learn that beginning with Adam, righteous mortals, by the revelations of the Holy Spirit to the spirits within them, have known of his divine Sonship. Learn that all of these Messianic ministers who preceded him in life have testified of his coming, and that all who have come thereafter have had the testimony of Jesus interwoven into the very fibers and sinews of their souls. Learn that it is he who appeared to the partriarchs, who is the God of Abraham and Israel, and who is the source of truth and light among all of us lowly creatures who dwell here below.

Learn of Him—the Man nobody knows! Learn that he was born of Mary in the City of David which is called Bethlehem. Learn that he received not of the fulness at the first, but grew from grace to grace, experiencing, feeling, undergoing all the needed probations of mortality. Learn that he was in all points tempted, like as we are, yet remaining without sin. Learn of the wondrous works that he wrought, how he healed earth's sin-sick souls by the power of his everlasting word. Learn that he sweat great drops of blood from every pore, so great was his anguish and sorrow for the sins of his people. Learn that he was lifted up upon the cross, crucified on Calvary, that he might thereby lay down his life, preparatory to taking it up again in immortal glory. Learn that he gained the victory over the grave, redeemed the faithful from their spiritual fall, and has now ascended up on high, where he sits on the right hand of the Father, reigning with almighty power. Learn that he has come again in our day to men whom he has called to be prophets, as of old, that he has set up his kingdom anew, and that in a not far distant day he shall return in all the glory of his Father's kingdom, to reign personally among us mortals for a thousand years.

All this learning, this weight of wondrous wisdom, this knowledge of truths beyond carnal comprehension, all is available to those who will pay the scholar's price. True it is that gospel scholarship is seldom sought in today's world, and that even many of those few who do so seek have little knowledge of the available source material or of how to read those volumes whose contents are known and understood only by the power of the Spirit.

"Understandest thou what thou readest?" inquired Philip

of the eunuch from the court of Candace. "How can I, except some man should guide me?" came the reply. (Acts 8:30-31.) Certain things men may learn for themselves, and that they are expected so to do by a divine providence, none can doubt. But after the alphabet has been learned, after fluency in reading has been acquired, after the source books have been identified by name and by title, still the seeker after spiritual truths must do his research subject to the eternal law which says, "The things of God knoweth no man, but the Spirit of God," and that "the natural man receiveth not the things of the Spirit of God: for they are foolishness unto him: neither can he know them, because they are spiritually discerned." (1 Cor. 2:11-14.)

Jesus Saith: "Come Unto Me"

Learn of Him! But do it in the way he has provided and by compliance with the laws that enable the desired knowledge to flow to the truth-seeking soul. How is this done, and whence comes that sure knowledge which is the testimony of him who is Lord of all?

"Come unto me," he says to all who labor in the libraries of the world. "Come unto me" is his invitation to all who are burdened with the weight of ignorance and intolerance. "Come unto me" and I will open the books; "Come unto me" and I will lift the gloom of darkness and uncertainty from your minds; "Come unto me" and I will remove the crushing weight of ignorance and doubt, and ye shall find rest to your souls.

"Come unto me" and "take my yoke upon you"—be as I am, join my Church, bear the burdens of my ministry, keep my commandments. "Come unto me" and the light of my everlasting word shall illumine your souls; "Come unto me" and ye shall receive the gift of the Holy Ghost, and he shall bear record to thee of the Father, and of me, and of all things that were and are and shall be, for he is a witness and a revealer of all truth.

"Come unto me" and receive my Spirit, and then shall ye have power to learn of me. This is the great and grand secret. This is the course that is provided for us and for all men, and it is provided in the wisdom of him who knoweth all things. This is the sole and only way to learn of Christ within the full sense and meaning of his tender and solicitous invitation. "No man can know that Jesus is the Lord, but by the Holy Ghost."[2] Little slivers of truth come to all who seek to know; occasional flashes of lightning give glimpses of the eternal realities that are hidden by the gloom and darkness of unbelief. But to learn and know those truths which reveal the Son of Man in his majesty and beauty and that prepare the truth seeker to be one with his Lord, such rays of the noonday sun shine forth only upon those who gain the enlightening companionship of the Holy Spirit.

It is with this understanding, then, that we open the eternal records and, having broken hearts and contrite spirits, begin to learn of our Lord. If we study, pray, ponder, and obey, as required by his eternal law, perchance it will then be with us as it was with Lehi: we shall see One descending out of the midst of heaven whose luster is above that of the sun at noonday. Perchance he will give us, as he gave Lehi, a book, bidding us also to read and learn the wonders of his ways. And then perchance, when we have read and seen for ourselves, we too will exclaim many great things unto him whose we are, such as:

"Great and marvelous are thy works, O Lord God Almighty! Thy throne is high in the heavens, and thy power, and goodness, and mercy are over all the inhabitants of the earth: and, because thou art merciful, thou wilt not suffer those who come unto thee that they shall perish!" (1 Ne. 1:14.)

Jesus Saith: "Follow Thou Me"

We all need our heroes, our patterns and guides. If we choose evil exemplars, we become evil ourselves because we

17

adopt their ways. Everyone imitates someone else; all of us learn what we know from other people. If all instruction and education ceased, if all patterns of living were taken away, civilization would cease in one generation, and all of earth's inhabitants would sink to a state of barbarism.

Providentially a gracious Father endows all his children with the Light of Christ, that righteous power and influence which proceeds forth from the presence of God to fill the immensity of space. Part of this enlightening spirit is the universal gift of conscience; it causes unlearned and untaught people to do what is right by instinct. But a gracious Father has also sent noble spirits and good men among all peoples to teach that measure of truth which they are able to bear, and to set such an example as their fellow mortals are capable of following. These are the prophets and seers, the poets and philosophers, the sages and wise men, the leaders and influential persons found among all nations and kindreds. And a gracious Father sent one Supreme Pattern and guide to be a light and an example for all men of all ages; he sent his Son. Christ is our Pattern, our Exemplar, the great Prototype of all that is good and right and edifying.

"What manner of men ought ye to be?" So asked our great Exemplar of his Nephite disciples. His own answer: "Verily I say unto you, even as I am." (3 Ne. 27:27.) Manifestly, if we emulate him so that his way of life becomes ours, we shall qualify for the same glory and exaltation that is his, for "when he shall appear, we shall be like him." (1 Jn. 3:2.)

In the final analysis, our purpose in learning of our Lord is to gain that knowledge, insight, and desire which will cause us to become like him—all in harmony with his divine promise: "Ye shall have fulness of joy; and ye shall sit down in the kingdom of my Father; yea, your joy shall be full, even as the Father hath given me fulness of joy; and ye shall be even as I am, and I am even as the Father; and the Father and I are one." (3 Ne. 28:10.)

NOTES

1. This invitation is always issued when the Lord has a people on earth. In every dispensation people have been invited to learn of Christ. For our day the invitation is: "Learn of me, and listen to my words; walk in the meekness of my Spirit, and you shall have peace in me. I am Jesus Christ; I came by the will of the Father, and I do his will." (D&C 19:23-24.)

2. This is Joseph Smith's inspired rendition of Paul's statement in 1 Corinthians 12:3. (*Teachings*, p. 223.)

Chapter 2

BEFORE BETHLEHEM

Our birth is but a sleep and a forgetting:
The Soul that rises with us, our life's Star,
    Hath had elsewhere its setting,
    And cometh from afar:
Not in entire forgetfulness,
And not in utter nakedness,
But trailing clouds of glory do we come
From God, who is our home.

—*William Wordsworth*[1]

Man—In the Beginning with God

Our blessed Lord, who as Mary's son dwelt among us for a short span, is truly the Man nobody knows. Those, in particular, whose knowledge of him is bounded by Bethlehem where he was born and Calvary where he died, have no intelligent way to put in a proper perspective even those slivers of light and knowledge which have been preserved for us by the Gospel authors. Before we even attempt to view and envision the events of his mortal life, we must have an acute awareness of certain eternal verities. These are:

1. *The Father is an exalted Person.*

It is a philosophical impossibility to believe that the Man

Jesus is the Son of God in the literal and full sense of the word if we suppose that his Father is a spirit essence or power that fills the immensity of space and is everywhere and nowhere in particular present, and if we believe that God is an immaterial, uncreated Being without body, parts, or passions, as the creeds of Christendom recite.[2] To know and understand Christ and his mission and ministry, we must know certain basic things about that Progenitor whence he sprang.

God himself is the First Man and the Father of all men. In the pure language, spoken by Adam, the name of the Father is *Man of Holiness*, which means he is a holy Man; and when the scriptures speak of Deity creating man in his own image, they are to be understood as literal renditions of that which in reality occurred. "God himself . . . is an exalted man, and sits enthroned in yonder heavens," the Prophet Joseph Smith said.[3] "The Father has a body of flesh and bones as tangible as man's" (D&C 130:22) is the scriptural assertion. When Paul says the Son is the brightness of his Father's glory, "and the express image of his person" (Heb. 1:3), he is certifying that the Risen Lord—who ate and drank with the apostles after he rose from the dead, and into whose riven side they had thrust their hands—had a resurrected body of the same sort and kind possessed by the exalted Father.

2. *Christ and all men are spirit children of the Father.*

God lives in the family unit. He is our Father in heaven—the literal and personal Father of the spirits of all men. He begat us; we are the offspring of Heavenly Parents; we have an Eternal Father and an Eternal Mother. We were born as spirits, and we dwelt in the presence of our Eternal Parents; we lived before our mortal birth. As spirits we were in all respects as we are now save only that we were not housed in mortal bodies as is the present circumstance. Christ was the Firstborn of all the heavenly host; Lucifer was a son of the morning; each of us came into being as conscious identities in our appointed order; and Christ is our Elder Brother.

3. *The spirit children of the Father were subject to his laws.*

In his infinite wisdom and goodness, the Eternal Father ordained laws by obedience to which his spirit children could advance and progress and eventually obtain the high reward of eternal life. These laws are the good news conveyed by God to his spirit progeny; they are the plan of salvation; they are the gospel of the Father. Paul called them "the gospel of God, . . . Concerning his Son Jesus Christ our Lord." (Rom. 1:1-3.) With reference to them, Joseph Smith said: "God himself, finding he was in the midst of spirits and glory, because he was more intelligent, saw proper to institute laws whereby the rest could have a privilege to advance like himself."[4]

Manifestly, there were no laws but God's laws in that eternal world; every law ordained and established by him was good; and obedience and conformity to any of his laws moved the obedient person (Christ included) along the path to glory and exaltation.

Similarly, failure to obey a given law denied such failing person the blessing and advancement that otherwise would have resulted, and disobedience imposed the penalties prescribed for such a rebellious course.

4. *All spirits were endowed with agency in preexistence.*

An all-wise Father endowed his spirit children with agency—the freedom and ability to choose good or evil—while they yet dwelt in his presence. Unless there are opposites—good and evil, virtue and vice, right and wrong—and unless intelligent beings are free to choose; free to obey or disobey; free to do good and work righteousness, or to walk in evil paths—unless this freedom exists, there can be no advancement and progression; no joy as contrasted with sorrow; no talents of one kind or another as contrasted with their absence; no eternal salvation as contrasted with eternal damnation. There can be no light unless there is darkness; no heat unless there is cold; no up unless there is down; no right unless there is left; no life unless there is death; and so on through all the realm of created and existent things. Opposites and agency are essential to existence and to progression. Without them there would be nothing.[5]

5. *Spirits developed an infinite variety and degree of talents while yet in preexistence.*

Being subject to law, and having their agency, all the spirits of men, while yet in the Eternal Presence, developed aptitudes, talents, capacities, and abilities of every sort, kind, and degree. During the long expanse of life which then was, an infinite variety of talents and abilities came into being. As the ages rolled, no two spirits remained alike. Mozart became a musician; Einstein centered his interest in mathematics; Michelangelo turned his attention to painting. Cain was a liar, a schemer, a rebel who maintained a close affinity to Lucifer. Abraham and Moses and all of the prophets sought and obtained the talent for spirituality. Mary and Eve were two of the greatest of all the spirit daughters of the Father. The whole house of Israel, known and segregated out from their fellows, was inclined toward spiritual things. And so it went through all the hosts of heaven, each individual developing such talents and abilities as his soul desired.

The Lord endowed us all with agency; he gave us laws that would enable us to advance and progress and become like him; and he counseled and exhorted us to pursue the course leading to glory and exaltation. He himself was the embodiment and personification of all good things. Every desirable characteristic and trait dwelt in him in its eternal fulness. All of his obedient children started to become like him in one way or another. There was as great a variety and degree of talent and ability among us there as there is among us here. Some excelled in one way, others in another. The Firstborn excelled all of us in all things.

6. *Spirit children have the capacity to become like their Eternal Father.*

We are members of the family of the Eternal Father. He is a glorified and exalted and eternal Being, having a resurrected body of flesh and bones. His name is God, and the kind of life he lives is God's life. His name is also Eternal, and the name of the kind of life he lives is eternal life. Eternal life is God's life, and God's life is eternal life. We are commanded to be perfect as he is perfect and to advance and progress until we become like him, or in other words, until we gain eternal life. Thus Joseph Smith said, "You have got to learn how to be Gods yourselves, and to be kings and priests to God, the same as all Gods have done before you, namely, by going from one small degree to another, and from a small capacity to a great one; from grace to grace, from exaltation to exaltation, until you attain to the resurrection of the dead, and are able to dwell in everlasting burnings, and to sit in glory, as do those who sit enthroned in everlasting power." (*Teachings*, pp. 346-47.) Christ our Lord has so obtained, thus enabling him to say to the faithful: "Ye shall be even as I am, and I am even as the Father." (3 Ne. 28:10.)

7. *Mortal life is an essential step leading to eternal life.*

According to the terms and conditions of the Father's plan, his spirit children must dwell on earth as mortals for two reasons:

a. To gain mortal bodies, bodies of flesh and bones, bodies subject to disease and death, bodies that could and would be raised in immortality, becoming bodies of flesh and bones, through an infinite and eternal atoning sacrifice;

b. To undergo a probationary, testing experience, one in which it would be determined whether each of the Father's spirit children would overcome the world, rise above carnal things, and love and serve that Being who made them, or whether they would live after the manner of the world, live as the generality of mankind do, and thus fail to gain eternal life.

Mortality paves the way for immortality, and eternal life is reserved for those who believe and obey. Is it any wonder, then, that when the great plan was presented to us in the councils of eternity, "the morning stars sang together, and all

24

the sons of God shouted for joy"? (Job 38:7.) The morning stars were those who were noble and great in preexistence, the Lord Jesus himself being chief among them and bearing the title "the bright and morning star" (Rev. 22:16), which brings us to the realization that a mortal probation was as essential for the Firstborn as for all those subsequently born among heaven's hosts.

8. *Mortal life is simply a projection of preexistent life.*

Birth and death are simply events that occur in the course of continuing life. We are born, which means the spirit passes from preexistence into a mortal body, there to dwell for a time and a season. We die, meaning the spirit steps out of its tenement of clay and enters a spirit world, there to await the day of the resurrection. Meanwhile the body returns to the dust whence it came, there to await that same day when mortality shall put on immortality and corruption shall put on incorruption.

When we die, our spirits continue to live. We take with us into the spirit realm every truth, every trait, every characteristic we enjoyed and possessed as mortals. And further: "Whatever principle of intelligence we attain unto in this life, it will rise with us in the resurrection. And if a person gains more knowledge and intelligence in this life through his diligence and obedience than another, he will have so much the advantage in the world to come." (D&C 130: 18-19.)

Similarly, when we pass from preexistence to mortality, we bring with us the traits and talents there developed. True, we forget what went before because we are here being tested, but the capacities and abilities that then were ours are yet resident within us. Mozart is still a musician; Einstein retains his mathematical abilities; Michelangelo his artistic talent; Abraham, Moses, and the prophets their spiritual talents and abilities. Cain still lies and schemes. And all men with their infinitely varied talents and personalities pick up the course of progression where they left it off when they left the heavenly realms.

25

Michael the archangel, standing second only to Christ among the spirits destined to dwell on earth, came to Eden's vales with all the sense, wisdom, and judgment that he had gained in preexistence. He came as a son of God, into an Edenic state from which he soon fell, bringing with him the desires, inclinations, aptitudes, and talents developed during long years of obedience in the Divine Presence. He came endowed with every gift and grace that rightfully was his. His life on earth was but a projection and a continuation of that life which was his before the foundations of his future abode had even been laid.

And as with Adam, so with all men: all bring with them what was then theirs; all build in mortality upon the foundation laid in premortality. Abraham, who by obedience and devotion became one of the noble and great in preexistence, came into mortality with every talent and capacity that then was his. He was foreordained to be the father of the faithful. "I know him," the Lord said of Abraham, "that he will command his children and his household after him, and they shall keep the way of the Lord, to do justice and judgment; that the Lord may bring upon Abraham that which he hath spoken of him." (Gen. 18:19.)

Jeremiah was chosen before he was born; before he came forth out of the womb, the Lord ordained him, and sanctified him, and called him to be a prophet; before he drew a mortal breath his mission was known and prepared— all because of the special talents and powers he came to have while yet a spirit being. (Jer. 1:5.)

And Christ our Lord, Firstborn of the Father, mightiest of all the spirit host, a Man like unto his Father, was also chosen and foreordained and anointed to come into mortality and do the very work that he then accomplished. Before he took upon himself flesh and blood he was the Great Jehovah, the Eternal One, Great I AM. He stood next to the Father, and became, at the Father's fiat, the Creator of all things from the beginning. Worlds without number rolled into their orbits at his word. He was the Word of God's power, the Messenger of salvation, the One who executed the divine will in all immensity. When such a life is projected from its eternal home into our mortal sphere, can anyone suppose that it could be other than the greatest life ever lived?

Jesus—God Before the World Was

Mortal life does not stand alone. It can only be understood when it is related to the premortality that went before and the immortality that will come after. If we know who Abraham and Jeremiah were in preexistence, we can understand the spiritual stature that was theirs while they dwelt on earth, while they lived apart from their heavenly associates, and we can also see how it is that they have now entered into their exaltation and, sitting upon thrones, are not angels but gods.[6]

And so it is with the greatest life ever lived. It was what it was because the Spirit housed in the body provided by Mary was the greatest of all the primeval hosts. Before Bethlehem, before the Holy Land, before the earth itself, before the universe and the whole sidereal heavens, before all things, was Christ our Lord. He who was to breath his first breath of mortal life in a little-known Judean village was the Eternal One whose goings forth had been from of old, from everlasting. Bethlehem was not the beginning. It was simply a way station along an eternal course. And he who found rest in a stable because there was no room in the inns was simply abiding with the animals for a moment as he rested from those creative enterprises by which he made the worlds and all things that in them are.

A Holy Being who was God yesterday remains as God today, and will continue in the same exalted state tomorrow. The course of the Gods is one eternal round; it does not vary. They are now as they were then, and they shall yet be as they have ever been. If it were not so they would not be exalted, for exaltation consists in being the same unchangeable being from everlasting to everlasting. Thus Paul said: "Jesus Christ the same yesterday, and to day, and for ever." (Heb. 13:8.) And Moroni, speaking of "the God of Abraham, and the God of Isaac, and the God of Jacob; . . . that same God who created the heavens and the earth, and all things that in them are," taught the same truth. He said: "God is the same yesterday, today, and forever, and in him there is no variableness neither shadow of changing." (Morm. 9:11, 9.) This unchanging, everlasting, eternal way of life—a way of life in which the same character, perfections, and attributes are always present—is the kind of life lived by both the Father and the Son, for they are one in powers and perfections.

Who, then, was Jesus before he was born of Mary to begin his mortal pilgrimage? Truly, he was God in the full sense of the word. He possessed all of the attributes of godliness in their fulness and perfection. He was perfect; he was like unto God. As the angelic visitant said to King Benjamin, he was "the Lord Omnipotent who reigneth, who was, and is from all eternity to all eternity," concerning whom the eternal decree was: "The time cometh, and is not far distant, that with power" he "shall come down from heaven among the children of men, and shall dwell in a tabernacle of clay." (Mosiah 3:5.)

"I was in the beginning with the Father, and am the Firstborn," he said to Joseph Smith. (D&C 93:21.) And of his high and exalted status—from the day of his birth as the First Son of his Father to the time he came forth in glorious immortality—Paul extols: He "is the image of the invisible God, the firstborn of every creature: For by him were all things created, that are in heaven, and that are in earth, visible and invisible, whether they be thrones, or dominions, or principalities, or powers: all things were created by him, and for him: And he is before all things, and by him all things consist. And he is the head of the body, the church: who is the beginning, the firstborn from the dead; that in all things he might have the preeminence. For it pleased the Father that in him should all fulness dwell." (Col. 1:15-19.) He was truly "like unto God." (Abr. 3:24.)

To Abraham and the ancients he revealed himself by the exalted and ineffable name, Jehovah—the Great I AM, the I AM THAT I AM, the Eternal One. He was the God of Israel who performed all the mighty works among that chosen race. But the thing about him which, above all else, crystallizes in our minds his high and exalted status and the infinite powers he possessed is the fact that he was the Creator of all things—this earth, all worlds, the universe, the sidereal heavens, worlds without number. By all this it is perfectly clear that our Lord prepared for his mortal probation by performing infinitely great acts through an eternity of time.

How long did Adam and Abraham and Jeremiah (and all men!) spend in preparing to take the test of a mortal probation? What ages and eons and eternities passed away while Christ dwelt in the Eternal Presence and did the work then assigned him? How can we measure infinite duration in finite terms? To such questions we have no definitive answers. Suffice it to say, the passage of time was infinite from man's viewpoint. We have an authentic account, which can be accepted as true, that life has been going on in this system for almost 2,555,000,000 years.[7] Presumably this system is the universe (or whatever scientific term is applicable) created by the Father through the instrumentality of the Son.

In attempting to give a concept of what is involved in the expression "worlds without number," the scripture says, "were it possible that man could number the particles of the earth, yea, millions of earths like this, it would not be a beginning to the number" of the Lord's creations. (Moses 7:30.) In terms of time, as we speak of time, the duration involved in such creative enterprises is beyond finite comprehension. Preexistence lasted for a duration beyond our power to understand, and during all the time then involved, the Firstborn and all those who came after him were

29

preparing to take the tests of this mortal probation. But in this case, he attained the status of God and exercised creative powers and was like his Father before he chose Bethlehem as the place of his birth.

These revealed truths about our Lord's premortal life have come to us so we will know and understand (among other things) that what he did in scarcely more than three decades of mortal life was not just chance. He was not an ordinary man. He was the great Creator housed in a tabernacle of clay. He was the Eternal Jehovah ministering among men. He was God's Almighty Son doing the things his Father sent him to do. He inherited from the Father of his mortal body the powers and characteristics of his Perfect Parent. He was placed in a position to excel all men. He was the God of Israel taking his place and receiving his lot and inheritance among that chosen people. He was the Only Begotten of the Father, the only Son born into mortality as the Offspring of an Immortal Being. He was both God and the Son of God. He was the Promised Messiah. No ordinary standards, no mortal measuring rods set forth his mortal stature and greatness. If we know and understand all these things we are in a position to learn of him as a mortal, as a Man among men, as a God housed in clay, as earth's Chief Citizen working out his own salvation, and as God's Son doing the things for his fellowmen that no other could ever do.

NOTES

1. "Ode: Intimations of Immortality." These words of the poet Wordsworth, well known among Latter-day Saints because of their inspired recitation of the doctrine of preexistence, a doctrine soon to be revealed to a latter-day prophet, were, interestingly, written in 1805, the very year of the birth of Joseph Smith, the prophet through whom the pure knowledge of preexistence was to come.

2. False creeds make false churches. There is no salvation in believing a lie. Every informed, inspired, and discerning person is revolted by the absurdities and scripture-defying pronouncements in the creeds of Christendom, whose chief function is to define and set forth the nature and kind of Being that God is. The same Lord Jesus who walked the dusty lanes of Palestine also appeared in glory, standing at the right hand of his Father, in a grove of trees in western New York, in the spring of 1820, to usher in the dispensation of the fulness of times. He then commanded his chief latter-day witness, Joseph Smith, to join none of the churches then upon the earth, because "they were all wrong," and "all their creeds were an abomination in his sight." (JS-H 1:17-19.) By way of illustration, let us note the following creedal concepts from the doctrinal foundation of the Church of England:

30

(a) From the "Articles of Religion," article I, entitled *Of Faith in the Holy Trinity:* "There is but one living and true God everlasting, without body, parts, or passions; of infinite power, wisdom, and goodness; the Maker, and Preserver of all things both visible and invisible. And in unity of this Godhead there be three Persons, of one substance, power, and eternity; the Father, the Son, and the Holy Ghost." (*Book of Common Prayer,* p. 685.)

(b) In *The Creed,* which is said or sung each time Holy Communion (the Lord's Supper) is administered, we find such assertions as: "Jesus Christ, . . . God of God, Light of Light, Very God of very God, Begotten not made, Being of one substance with the Father, . . . was incarnate by the Holy Ghost of the Virgin Mary." And: "The Holy Ghost, The Lord and giver of life." (Ibid., pp. 291-92.)

(c) In the *Apostles Creed,* which is said on thirty-nine Sundays each year, it is recited that "Jesus Christ . . . was conceived by the Holy Ghost." (Ibid., p. 52.)

(d) The *Creed of Saint Athanasius,* which is "sung or said . . . by the Minister and people standing," on Christmas, Easter, and a total of thirteen Sundays each year, and which is, if we may paraphrase Nephi's language, "most abominable above all other creeds" (1 Ne. 13:5), is here set forth in its entirety:

Whosoever would be saved: needeth before all things to hold fast the Catholick Faith.

Which Faith except a man keep whole and undefiled: without doubt he will perish eternally.

Now the Catholick Faith is this: that we worship one God in Trinity, and the Trinity in Unity;

Neither confusing the Persons: nor dividing the Substance.

For there is one Person of the Father, another of the Son: another of the Holy Ghost;

But the Godhead of the Father, and of the Son, and of the Holy Ghost is all one: the glory equal, the majesty co-eternal.

Such as the Father is, such is the Son: and such is the Holy Ghost;

The Father uncreated, the Son uncreated: the Holy Ghost uncreated;

The Father infinite, the Son infinite: the Holy Ghost infinite;

The Father eternal, the Son eternal: the Holy Ghost eternal;

And yet there are not three eternals: but one eternal;

As also there are not three uncreated, nor three infinites: but one infinite, and one uncreated.

So likewise the Father is almighty, the Son almighty: the Holy Ghost almighty;

And yet there are not three almighties: but one almighty.

So the Father is God, the Son God: the Holy Ghost God;

And yet there are not three Gods: but one God.

So the Father is Lord, the Son Lord: the Holy Ghost Lord;

And yet there are not three Lords: but one Lord.

For like as we are compelled by the Christian verity: to confess each Person by himself to be both God and Lord;

So are we forbidden by the Catholick Religion: to speak of three Gods or three Lords.

The Father is made of none: nor created, nor begotten.

The Son is of the Father alone: not made, nor created, but begotten.

The Holy Ghost is of the Father and the Son: not made, nor created, nor begotten, but proceeding.

There is therefore one Father, not three Fathers; one Son, not three Sons; one Holy Ghost, not three Holy Ghosts.

And in this Trinity there is no before or after: no greater or less;

But all three Persons are co-eternal together: and co-equal.

So that in all ways, as is aforesaid: both the Trinity is to be worshipped in Unity, and the Unity in Trinity.

He therefore that would be saved: let him thus think of the Trinity.

Furthermore it is necessary to eternal salvation: that he also believe faithfully the Incarnation of our Lord Jesus Christ.

Now the right Faith is that we believe and confess: that our Lord Jesus Christ, the Son of God, is both God and Man.

He is God, of the Substance of the Father, begotten before the worlds: and he is Man, of the Substance of his Mother, born in the world;

Perfect God: perfect Man, of reasoning soul and human flesh subsisting;

Equal to the Father as touching his Godhead: less than the Father as touching his Manhood.

Who although he be God and Man: yet he is not two, but is one Christ;

One, however, not by conversion of Godhead into flesh: but by taking of Manhood into God;

One altogether: not by confusion of Substance, but by unity of Person.

31

For as reasoning soul and flesh is one man: so God and Man is one Christ;
Who suffered for our salvation: descended into hell, rose again from the dead;
Ascended into heaven, sat down at the right hand of the Father: from whence he shall come to
    judge the quick and the dead.
At whose coming all men must rise again with their bodies: and shall give account for their own
    deeds.
And they that have done good will go into life eternal: they that have done evil into eternal fire.
This is the Catholick Faith: which except a man do faithfully and stedfastly believe, he cannot be
    saved.
Glory be to the Father, and to the Son: and to the Holy Ghost;
As it was in the beginning, is now, and ever shall be: world without end. Amen. (Ibid., pp. 68-71.)

It was of these creeds, and their kindred, as found in all the sects of Christendom and in one manner and form or another in all the churches of men, whether professing to be Christian or pagan, of which Jeremiah prophesied when he said that gathered Israel in the last days, having come again to know their God by revelation, would say: "Surely our fathers have inherited lies, vanity, and things wherein there is no profit. Shall a man make gods unto himself, and they are no gods?" (Jer. 16:10-21.)

3. This statement, as it fell from the lips of the seer of latter days, is found in the King Follett Discourse, the greatest sermon ever delivered by the Prophet Joseph Smith. The context is as follows: "God himself was once as we are now, and is an exalted man, and sits enthroned in yonder heavens! That is the great secret. If the veil were rent today, and the great God who holds this world in its orbit, and who upholds all worlds and all things by his power, was to make himself visible,—I say, if you were to see him today, you would see him like a man in form—like yourselves in all the person, image, and very form as a man; for Adam was created in the very fashion, image and likeness of God, and received instruction from, and walked, talked and conversed with him, as one man talks and communes with another." (Teachings, p. 345.)

4. Continuing this same thought, the Prophet also said: "The relationship we have with God places us in a situation to advance in knowledge. He has power to institute laws to instruct the weaker intelligences, that they may be exalted with himself, so that they might have one glory upon another, and all that knowledge, power, glory, and intelligence, which is requisite in order to save them." (Teachings, p. 354.)

5. Lehi's reasoning as to opposites and agency, as found in 2 Nephi 2, surpasses anything else of its kind in the whole realm of secular and scriptural writing. His conclusion is that without these things, "all things must have vanished away."

6. This concept that some of the children of our Father have already become gods is a sound doctrinal reality. In a measure and to a degree they have already become like Christ, who is the Prototype of all saved beings. As Paul expressed it, they have become "perfect" and have come "unto the measure of the stature of the fulness of Christ." (Eph. 4:13.) This high status is now enjoyed by all of the prophets and righteous saints who were with Christ in his resurrection. Abraham, Isaac, and Jacob, as examples and prototypes, whose attainments stand as a pattern of all others similarly situated, are specifically named by revelation as having already attained Godhood. (D&C 132:29-39.)

7. All of the prophets who have seen within the veil have known many things that were never preserved and passed on to their posterity and to the residue of men. Joseph Smith and the early brethren in this dispensation knew much that we do not know and will not know until we attain the same spiritual stature that was theirs. This matter of how long eternity has been going on in our portion of created things is one of these matters. The sliver of information that has been preserved for us is found in an epistle of W. W. Phelps, written on Christmas day, 1844, and published to the Church in the Times and Seasons. Brother Phelps speaks of "Jesus Christ, whose goings forth, as the prophets said, have been from of old, from eternity," in what is a clear allusion to Micah's prophecy that Bethlehem shall be the birthplace of our Lord. "Out of thee [Bethlehem Ephratah] shall come forth unto me that is to be ruler in Israel; whose goings forth have been from of old, from everlasting," the Lord said through that ancient prophet. (Micah 5:2.) Then, in an interpolative explanation of what is meant by "from eternity," or "from everlasting," Brother Phelps says, "And that eternity [the one during which Christ's doings have been known], agreeable

to the records found in the catacombs of Egypt, has been going on in this system [not this world], almost two thousand five hundred and fifty-five millions of years." (*Times and Seasons* 5:758.) That is to say, the papyrus from which the Prophet Joseph translated the Book of Abraham, to whom the Lord gave a knowledge of his infinite creations, also contained this expression relative to what apparently is the universe in which we live, which universe has been created by the Father through the instrumentality of the Son. The time mentioned has no reference, as some have falsely supposed, to the period of this earth's existence.

Chapter 3

THE PROMISED MESSIAH

Lo, I come: in the volume of the book it
is written of me, I delight to do thy will,
O my God: yea, thy law is within my
heart. (Ps. 40:7-8.)[1]

True Messianic Concepts

Our Lord—blessed be his name—was the Messiah in ages past ("I am Messiah, the King of Zion, the Rock of Heaven," he said to Enoch [Moses 7:53]). Ministering among men as Mary's son, he continued to act in all the glory and dignity of his Messianic might; and he yet serves in that same office, as John the Baptist witnessed when he conferred the Aaronic Priesthood upon mortals "in the name of Messiah." (D&C 13.)

I have written elsewhere, in *The Promised Messiah: The First Coming of Christ,* about the Messianic prophecies.[2] In a very real sense it is an introduction to this life of our Lord, *The Mortal Messiah: From Bethlehem to Calvary.* Knowing who the Mortal Messiah once was; knowing what he did in ages past; knowing what he was destined to do in the days of his mortal probation; knowing his present state of reenthroned glory and omnipotence as he sits with his Father on the blazing throne of God—a vision of all this puts us in a position to understand what he actually did when he dwelt among us lowly mortals. True Messianic concepts may well be summarized under three headings:

1. Who he was before the foundations of the earth were laid, and his position and standing in the eternal scheme of things;

2. What he was destined to do as a mortal to put into full operation the terms and conditions of the Father's plan; and

3. Various circumstances and events that were to occur incident to and in the course of his mortal pilgrimage.

As to his status, glory, and dominion in the midst of eternity, before the earth was made or mortal men were, we must come to know—

That there is a God in heaven who is infinite and eternal; who has a body of flesh and bones as tangible as man's, and who is in fact a resurrected, glorified, perfected, and exalted Man; who has all power, all might, and all dominion, and who knows all things; and who in the ultimate and full sense is the Creator, Upholder, and Preserver of all things, both this earth and all worlds, the sidereal heavens, and all things that in them are;

That the Great God, by whom all things are and for whom all things are created, is the personal and literal Father of the spirits of all men, of which number the Messiah was the Firstborn; and that our Primal Parent ordained and established the plan of salvation whereby all his spirit children, Christ included, had power to advance and progress and become like him;

That in the premortal sphere, by obedience to law, the Firstborn advanced and progressed and became like the Father in power and intelligence, and became, under the Father, the Creator of all things, meaning that he was the Executive Officer who brought to pass the Father's creative enterprises;

That the Messiah then was the Great Jehovah, the Eternal One, the Lord Omnipotent, and was God in his own right;

That when the Father presented his plan for the salvation of his children; when the nature and purpose of our mortal probation was set forth; when it was known that a

Redeemer would be needed to ransom men from temporal and spiritual death; and when the cry went forth, "Whom shall I send," the future Messiah stepped forth and said, "Here am I, send me" (Abr. 3:24-27; Moses 4:1-4)[3];

That he was then chosen and foreordained to be the Lamb slain from the foundation of the world; that he was then selected to be the Son of God, the Only Begotten in the flesh, the One Person who would come into mortality with the power of immortality, thus having power to work out the infinite and eternal atonement;

That the gospel of salvation was then named for him and he became the Savior and Redeemer, the God of Israel, the Holy One of Israel, the Word of God, the great Judge, the Lawgiver, the Father of the righteous of all ages.

If we come to know all those things which appertain to the premortal life and being of the Messiah—his position in the eternal scheme of things—then his mortal ministry takes on an entirely different perspective. What he did and was, as God, before the world was, is the basis for what he did and was, as a mortal, far removed from the throne and glory that once was his.

As to the crowning purpose of the mortal ministry of the second member of the Eternal Godhead, the ancient believers were well instructed. From Adam, the first man, to John, the last legal administrator of the old order, to a greater or lesser degree, depending on their faith and righteousness, the ancient saints knew—

That Adam, attended by his lovely consort Eve, fell from that state of immortality in which they lived when first clothed with flesh and bones; that they thereby became mortal and brought temporal and spiritual death into the world, for themselves and their posterity; and that in their mortal state they were able to bear the souls of men, thus providing bodies for the spirit children of the Father, and thus themselves becoming the parents of the human race;

That a Deliverer, a Savior, a Redeemer—a Messiah!— (who is Christ) must come to ransom men from the temporal

36

and spiritual death brought upon them by the fall of Adam; that the deliverance, the salvation, the redemption to be wrought by him would abolish death, bring immortality to all men, and make eternal life available to all the obedient;

That through this great redemption—this infinite and eternal atonement—the Messiah would reconcile fallen and sinful man to God; would mediate between man and his Maker; would intercede for the penitent before the Father's throne; would justify them, adopt them, free them from prison, and make them joint-heirs with himself of all the glory and dominion that are to be.

These realities relative to our status as the children of the Father; relative to the position of Christ in the eternal scheme of things; relative to the infinitely wondrous and eternally effective sacrifice he wrought—these realities are the heart and core of revealed religion. The Father created us and all things, and ordained and established his eternal plan, the gospel of God, so that we might become as he is. For this we worship and serve him with all our power. The Son redeemed us and put into operation the provisions of the Father's plan. And for this we worship and serve him also with all our hearts.

There are no concepts of revealed religion, no doctrines of the everlasting gospel, no views on any subject, that have ever entered the heart of man that compare, even in slight degree, with these Messiah-centered truths. These verities are the doctrine that salvation is in the Messiah; that by him redemption cometh; and that he is the resurrection and the life. His Father's name is Man of Holiness, and he was destined to be, and is, the Son of Man of Holiness, the great Deliverer, without whose atoning sacrifice the very purposes of creation would have vanished away.

As to the various circumstances and events of his mortal pilgrimage, which were foreknown and foretaught by the prophets who preceded him—as to these, their number and extent are sufficient to identify without question the One Life to which they apply. There have been, there are, and there will be other mortals of whose earthly missions small slivers of truth are manifest in advance. Joseph Smith and Moses were identified and foreknown by name centuries before they came to dwell on earth. Columbus and Cyrus had their work cut out for them long before their mortal probations, and because their labors were destined to affect the Lord's people, they were made known to prophets in advance. But the Man Jesus is the only one whose birth and life and ministry and death and resurrection were taught in such detail by the Messianic witnesses of old that it is almost as though his history was written in advance. Various of these Messianic utterances are analyzed in *The Promised Messiah: The First Coming of Christ,* and those applicable to this present work will be considered in the pages that follow. However, so that our approach in studying the only perfect life ever lived will be what it should be, we shall here recite enough to indicate the detail, extent, and import of those Messianic prophecies which deal with our Lord's mortal experiences.

Inspired men, hundreds and thousands of years before his birth, speaking by the power of the Holy Ghost, telling what God had revealed to them, taught and prophesied such things as these:

A mighty prophet would prepare the way before him. As the voice of one crying in the wilderness of unbelief, this forerunner would cry repentance and administer baptism in water to believing souls; and as the crowning act of his life, this prophet would baptize the Son of God, see the Holy Ghost descend upon him like a dove, and bear witness that he was the Lamb of God who should save the world.

The Promised Messiah would be conceived by the power of the Holy Ghost, God would be his Father, and his mother would be called Mary. She would be a virgin, pure, choice, favored above all womankind.

He would be born in Bethlehem. A new star and many other signs and wonders in heaven would herald the event, and it would occur six hundred years from the time Lehi left

38

Jerusalem. He would be the seed of Eve, a descendant of Noah, the seed of Abraham, a branch of Israel, the Son of David.

He was to bear the names Emmanuel, Jesus, Christ, Messiah, King, Lord, and God. He was to be the Redeemer and Savior, and the Holy One of Israel, who would live without sin. He was to be known as Jesus Christ, the Son of God, the Father of heaven and earth, the Creator of all things from the beginning.

He was to flee into Egypt and be called back to his homeland. He was to dwell in Nazareth and be called a Nazarene. He was to be baptized to fulfill all righteousness, and the ordinance would take place in Bethabara beyond Jordan, at which time the Holy Ghost would descend upon him in the sign of a dove.

He was to come down from heaven, dwell in a tabernacle of clay, work mighty miracles, heal the sick, raise the dead, cause the lame to walk and the blind to see, cure all manner of diseases, and cast out devils. He was to suffer temptations and pain, hunger, thirst, and fatigue, and in his greatest ordeal he would bleed great drops of blood from every po.e.

He was to teach the gospel, carry the lambs of his flock in his arms, speak in parables to the unbelieving, call twelve apostles and others, and send his message to the Gentiles. At a triumphal hour he was to ride into Jerusalem on an ass amid cries of "Hosanna to the Son of David."

He was to be persecuted for righteousness' sake; to bear the infirmities of the people; to be a man of sorrows and acquainted with grief; to be rejected by his people; to be betrayed for thirty pieces of silver by his own familiar friend; to be judged of men, lifted up upon a cross, and crucified by wicked hands; to die, be with the wicked in his death, find interment in a tomb of a wealthy person, rise again the third day, and bring to pass the resurrection of all men. No bone of his body was to be broken, though his flesh was to be pierced and nails were to be driven into his hands and feet. And so on and so on and so on.

To persons unacquainted with the Messianic prophecies, it may seem as though these words are a recitation made after the events, a recitation of what we now know to have occurred. They are, in fact, a partial summary only of some of the things the prophets foretold concerning him. This concept that his birth and life and ministry were all foreknown, foreordained, and foretaught is essential to an understanding of the things he did. Truly, he did not act of himself alone, but guided by the Spirit, he did ever those things which his Father directed.

Jewish Messianic Concepts

What were the Jewish concepts concerning that promised Prophet, that prophet who would be raised up by the Lord and given Messianic power, and who would be like unto Moses?

They should have been, in every respect and detail, the same as those of the saints who preceded them; and they would have been exactly the same concepts held by their righteous forebears if it had not been for the wickedness, rebellion, apostasy, and spiritual darkness that was almost everywhere present in the meridian of time. The Jewish Hebrews then dwelling in Canaan had the scriptures—"and they are they which testify of me." (John 5:39.)

It was a Jewish psalmist who prophesied that the Son would be begotten by God and worshipped by the people; that he would bear testimony of his Father in the congregation of the people; and that he would sit on his Father's right hand, as a priest forever, until all his enemies were overthrown. It was a Jewish prophet who said the Child, born of a virgin, would be the mighty God, the everlasting Father, the Prince of Peace, and that he would reign on David's throne. It was a Jewish prophet who proclaimed that the Lord Jehovah, in whom is everlasting strength, would live and die, and that his dead body would come forth from the grave. For that matter it was Moses, the man of God whom they revered, who set up the whole system of sacrificial offerings wherein the blood of animals—animals without spot or blemish—was shed in similitude of the coming sacrifice of the Lamb of God. It was a Jewish prophet who spoke of the Suffering Servant who would be despised and rejected; who would be a Man of Sorrows and acquainted with grief; who would bear our griefs, carry our sorrows, and be stricken, smitten, and afflicted by men; who would be wounded for our transgressions and bear the sins of many; who would heal us with his stripes; who would make his soul an offering for sin, and pour out his soul unto death; who would justify many, and make intercession for the transgressors; and so on and so on and so on.

All the Jewish prophets were Messianic prophets; many of their prophetic declarations were preserved in the scriptures then extant; and had that same Spirit which rested upon the prophets rested also upon the Jews of Jesus' day, then the people in that meridian period would have known the truth about their Messiah. They would have known that his kingdom was not of this world; that his mission was to bring life and immortality to light through the gospel; that he came to bring immortality and eternal life to men; that he was the resurrection and the life; and that his atoning sacrifice was the rock foundation upon which the house of salvation is built. That they did not know these things, and that such was not the case, brings us now to a consideration of what Jesus' contemporaries did in fact anticipate in the way of a Deliverer, and hence to an understanding of why they reacted to Jesus in the way the New Testament authors recite.

Israel became a kingdom when Samuel anointed Saul, in 1095 B.C., to rule and reign, in power and might, among and over the Lord's chosen people. Three decades later David received the same divine anointing. There then followed ten years of struggle and intrigue and war, culminating in the deaths of Saul and Jonathan. Thereupon, in 1055 B.C.—forty years after Saul had begun the process of imposing kingly designed burdens upon the people whose only previous King had been Jehovah himself—David ascended the throne of Judah; yet another seven years was to elapse before he became king and ruler of all Israel. But with the ascendancy of the son of Jesse, the Bethlehemite, to the throne of Israel, there was ushered in such a reign of power and might and dominion and supremacy as was scarcely known among the mighty nations of the day. Israel's enemies were defeated, slain, imprisoned, and made to serve their Hebrew masters. For forty years David's word was law and blood flowed when any dared oppose him. For another forty years Solomon, his son, reigned in such splendor and supremacy that for a thousand years the house of Jacob would look back with wonder and nationalistic pride at the kingdom and glory of their early rulers.

As king followed king, and war and bloodshed prevailed everywhere; as one king caused Israel to worship Jehovah, and the next commanded them to bow before Baal; as prophets came and went, and were persecuted and slain for the witness born in their Redeemer's name; as the kingdom of Israel, composed of ten of the tribes, went into Assyrian bondage in the days of Shalmanezer (about 721 B.C.); as the people of Judah, after Lehi left Jerusalem, were carried captive into Babylon by Nebuchadnezzar; as the Jews returned from Babylon under Zerubbabel in 536 B.C., and again under Ezra and Nehemiah nearly eighty years later; as all the wars and sorrows continued to sweep over Jewry, down to the days of Jesus; as all these things, and myriads more, came to pass during this long millennium of their history— yet the hope and expectancy of people always faced forward to a day of deliverance, to a Deliverer, to a Messiah.

In large measure and at many times, particularly from the day of Malachi, whose prophecies were forthcoming between 397 and 317 B.C., darkness prevailed in Israel. They had the scriptures; the priesthood remained; they kept the law of Moses to a degree; but their interests were upon the letter and not the spirit of the law. It comes, therefore, as no

surprise to find that all Israel in the days of Jesus were looking for a temporal Deliverer, for a Messiah born in the lineage of Abraham and David, who, sitting on the throne of
their greatest king, would free them from personal and national bondage and vanquish their enemies. They looked for
a preeminent Judahite ruler—for the scepter was not to depart from David's Judah until Shiloh came—who would
throw off the Roman yoke and scatter the legions of the
Caesars as David had caused the Philistines to flee when one
small pebble from his sling felled the mighty Goliath.

Such a Deliverer, such a Messiah, as they envisioned,
would not only restore the kingdom to Israel, but would also
return the dispersed of that great nation to their original
inheritance in their promised Canaan. All Israel again would
find residence on the soil that once was theirs. It would yet
be as when Joshua drove out the cursed races who worshipped Baal, who burned their children in the fires of
Moloch, and who sacrificed to devils. This glorious concept
of the gathering of Israel, proclaimed by all the prophets,
cherished by the downcast and downtrodden of Jacob for
generations, was truly part of their common Messianic hope.
So ingrained was it, and so assured were the chosen people
of its fulfillment in Messiah's day, that, as Edersheim ob-
serves, "Every devout Jew prayed, day by day: 'Proclaim by
Thy loud trumpet our deliverance, and *raise up a banner to
gather our dispersed, and gather us together from the four ends
of the earth.* Blessed be Thou, O Lord! *Who gatherest the
outcasts of Thy people Israel.*' That prayer included in its
generality also the lost ten tribes. So, for example, the
prophecy was rendered: 'They hasten hither, like a bird out
of Egypt,'—referring to Israel of old; 'and like a dove out of
the land of Assyria'—referring to the ten tribes. And thus
even these wanderers, so long lost, were to be reckoned in
the field of the Good Shepherd."[4]

This Jewish hope and full expectancy that their Messiah
would "recover the remnant of his people, which shall be
left, from Assyria, and from Egypt, and from Pathros, and

from Cush, and from Elam, and from Shinar, and from Hamath, and from the islands of the sea"; that he would "assemble the outcasts of Israel, and gather together the dispersed of Judah from the four corners of the earth"; and that they should "fly upon the shoulders of the Philistines," as they came (Isa. 11), was more than a vaporous dream of the night. It was the nationalistic hope that had kept them alive as a distinct people in spite of century after century of enslavement and slaughter. So fully was it a part of their religion, their worship, and their way of life that even the apostles of the Lamb, after they knew with a perfect knowledge that their Risen Lord was indeed the Promised Messiah; after they knew that his kingdom was not of this world; after they knew full well that he had no intention of throwing off the Roman yoke and of doing all the things their Jewish fellows supposed the Messiah would do—after all this, as they stood with him on Olivet, outside Jerusalem's walls, they asked that which was yet uppermost in their minds, the one great concern that still weighed in upon them: "Lord, wilt thou at this time restore again the kingdom to Israel?" His answer ended forever the Messianic hope that their era was the one appointed for the gathering of Israel, that the promised kingdom would be in their day. "It is not for you to know the times or the seasons, which the Father hath put in his own power," he replied. Their work was to be worldwide; it was to be of a scope and nature that even they had not yet envisioned; they were to preach the gospel to every creature; and there would yet be a future day, a millennial day, when the Millennial Messiah—"this same Jesus, which is taken up from you into heaven"— would come again to fulfill all that the prophets of old had promised. (Acts 1:6-11.)

Messiah's kingdom, in the full and complete sense of the word, was to be a millennial kingdom. Only then would the "living waters . . . go out from Jerusalem," according to the promise; only then would "the Lord" reign as "king over all the earth." (Zech. 14:8-9.) For their meridian-day Messiah was to be the Suffering Servant; the Teacher without peer; the Sinless One who would redeem and ransom and save; who would abolish death, and bring "life and immortality to light through the gospel" (2 Tim. 1:10); who would lay down his life, according to the flesh, and take it again, by the power of the Spirit, that all men might "be raised in immortality unto eternal life, even as many as would believe" (D&C 29:43).

He truly shall yet reign as King of kings and Lord of lords, and "the kingdoms of this world" shall "become the kingdoms of our Lord, and of his Christ." (Rev. 11:15.) But all the hopes of temporal rule, when he *first* came among men, were false and groundless. "My kingdom is not of this world: if my kingdom were of this world, then would my servants fight" (John 18:36), was his mortal proclamation. The day when he shall reign on the throne of David, slay the Goliaths of the world, and drive the Philistines from Israel's door is reserved for his *second* appearance. All the hopes of Jewish Israel that their Promised Messiah, like Moses and David, would free their lands, as it were, from the "modern" Canaanites, Hittites, Amorites, Perizzites, Hivites, and Jebusites were to fade away. Neither the wealth and wisdom of Solomon nor the might and glory of David were then to be restored, nor was Israel to gather in from her long dispersion to the standard he would then raise.

'What think ye of the Messiah,' Jesus asked certain Pharisees. "Whose son is he?" Their reply, using words that were but a summary of what was in the minds of the generality of the people, acclaimed: 'He is the son of David; he shall free us from our captors; he shall brake the hated Gentile yoke; he shall gather in our dispersed brethren; we shall become a mighty nation again.' But Jesus spoke not of the millennial kingdom, which was millenniums away; their concern should have been centered in his meridian ministry, which brought salvation to them. "Whose son is he?" If the Mortal Messiah was to be a temporal ruler only, how then was he God's Son, as even David attested in proclaiming that one Lord said to another Lord, 'Sit thou on my right hand, until that future day when all things spoken by all the prophets concerning thee and all Israel shall be fulfilled.' Is it any wonder that "no man was able to answer him a word, neither durst any man from that day forth ask him any more questions"? (Matt. 22:41-46.)

And yet we must not generalize to the point of assuming there were none among the Jews who knew and understood the mission and ministry of the Anointed One who would deliver and redeem. Our Lord—called *Christ* in the Greek and *Messiah* or *Messias* in the Hebrew—was known and recognized and worshipped by many of his Jewish kinsmen while he yet dwelt among them. There is no doubt that "all the people"—chanting in a frenzy of hate and derision, "His blood be on us, and on our children" as Pilate sought to free the Prisoner (Matt. 27:24-26)—were representative of the thought and feeling of a nation. But within the nation, and among the diverse parties and sects, there were those who loved light more than darkness, and who sought blessings from him of whom the hate-filled mob cried, "Crucify him, crucify him." (Luke 23:21.)

There were those who had sufficient spiritual insight to know that the Messiah was the Great Jehovah, and that born of woman he would deliver fallen men from their corrupt and carnal state and make them fit candidates for eternal salvation. Elisabeth, the Levite wife, while her womb contained the Messiah's forerunner, acclaimed Mary as the mother of the Lord. (Luke 1:41-45.) Simeon, a just and devout Jew who waited for the Consolation of Israel, learned from the Holy Ghost that he should not see death until he had seen the Lord's Messiah; and it became his blessed privilege to take the Child Jesus in his arms and to bless him and to prophesy of his mission in Israel. (Luke 2:25-35.) Anna the Jewess, a prophetess mighty in faith and good works, also saw and believed and testified. (Luke 2:36-38.) John the Baptist, our Lord's Jewish forerunner, answering the priests and Levites who asked, "Who art thou," replied,

"I am not the Christ"; and then of that Messiah whose shoe's latchet he felt unworthy to unloose, the Baptist testified, "Behold the Lamb of God, which taketh away the sin of the world." (John 1:19-36.)

Andrew, a Jew, brother to Simon Peter, introduced Peter himself to the gospel with the salutation, "We have found the Messias." (John 1:37-41.) Jewish Philip bore a like witness, and Jewish Nathanael, speaking to the Messiah mouth to mouth, affirmed, "Rabbi, thou art the Son of God; thou art the King of Israel." (John 1:41-51.) Peter, Jewish to the hilt, as were all the Twelve, testified before his fellow apostles and to the Lord Jesus: 'Thou art the Messiah, the Son of the Living God,' after which witness Jesus began to show the disciples how he should suffer and die and rise again the third day. (Matt. 16:13-21.) Martha, as Jewish as mortal women can be, who with her sister Mary knew that had Jesus been present, their brother Lazarus would not have died, spoke for herself and her Jewish sister in saying: 'I believe that thou art the Messiah, the Son of God, which should come into the world.' (John 11:1-46.)

All these and many others are named as Messianic witnesses in Holy Writ. Such accounts are but samples and illustrations. Among the Jewish people there were many who understood the scriptures, who knew their true meanings, and who believed in him of whom they testify. Indeed, it was "a very great multitude" of Jewish believers, on the occasion of our Lord's triumphal entry into Jerusalem, who cried out to their Messiah, 'Save, we beseech thee,' "Hosanna to the Son of David," and whose witness was: "Blessed is he that cometh in the name of the Lord; Hosanna in the highest." (Matt. 21:1-11.) And it was Jewish converts who became living torches on Roman walls; whose flesh was torn by wild beasts in orgies of slaughter in Roman arenas; whose bodies were hewn and slashed with gladiatorial swords; who welcomed crucifixion and death rather than bring dishonor to the Messianic name that they as Christians chose to bear. Whatever we may say of the Messianic hopes and knowledge of the generality of the Jews, the basic reality remains unchanged that there were those who believed, and that all men had power to believe, and would have believed, had they not chosen darkness rather than light because their deeds were evil.

NOTES

1. These Messianic words, as first spoken by David, are in a context that marvelously summarizes the nature of Messiah's ministry. Of the coming Christ the Psalmist said: "Sacrifice and offering thou didst not desire; mine ears hast thou opened: burnt offering and sin offering hast thou not required. Then said I, Lo, I come: in the volume of the book it is written of me, I delight to do thy will, O my God: yea, thy law is within my heart. I have preached righteousness in the great congregation: lo, I have not refrained my lips, O Lord, thou knowest. I have not hid thy righteousness within my heart; I have declared thy faithfulness and thy salvation: I have not concealed thy lovingkindness and thy truth from the great congregation. . . . Let all those that seek thee rejoice and be glad in thee: let such as love thy salvation say continually, The Lord be magnified." (Psalm 40:6-10, 16.)

That these words foretold the Messiah's approach in presenting the message of his Father is perfectly clear. Their use by Paul in his theological discourse to the Hebrews dramatizes that the Messiah came to end sacrifices and center the attention of all true believers in the sacrifice he made of his own body. In showing how Israel's ancient sacrifices were "a shadow of good things to come" and would in due course be done away, Paul uses the Psalmic words here involved in this way: "When he [the Messiah] cometh into the world, he saith, Sacrifice and offering thou wouldest not, but a body hast thou prepared me: In burnt offerings and sacrifices for sin thou hast had no pleasure. Then said I, Lo, I come (in the volume of the book it is written of me,) to do thy will, O God."

Paul then shows that the first sacrifices, those offered anciently, were done away when God established the second, the sacrifice of the body of his Son. Of the will and purpose of Deity in so ordaining, the inspired record says: "By the which will we are sanctified through the offering of the body of Jesus Christ once for all." (Heb. 10:1-10.)

2. For twice as many years as the two thousand of the so-called Christian era, believing persons looked forward for salvation to the then future atonement of the Messiah. Even as we now look back with rejoicing to what has been done by Deity, our forebears looked forward in joyful anticipation to what he would do in the day of his mortality. To envision how he deals with men, it is of surpassing import to know the Messianic teachings and promises given the saints during the first four thousand years of the earth's temporal continuance. To summarize the truths in this field, as they were revealed to and known by those who lived before our Lord placed himself in the hands of men, is the purpose of *The Promised Messiah: The First Coming of Christ* (Deseret Book, 1978).

3. One of the saddest examples of a misconceived and twisted knowledge of an otherwise glorious concept is the all-too-common heresy that there were two plans of salvation; that the Father (presumptively at a loss to know what to do) asked others for proposals; that Christ offered a plan involving agency and Lucifer proposed a plan denying agency; that the Father chose between them; and that Lucifer, his plan being rejected, rebelled, and then there was war in heaven.

Even a cursory knowledge of the overall scheme of things reassures spiritually discerning persons that all things center in the Father; that the plan of salvation which he designed was to save his children, Christ included; and that neither Christ nor Lucifer could of themselves save anyone. As Jesus said: "The Son can do nothing of himself. . . . I can of mine own self do nothing." (John 5:19, 30.)

There is, of course, a sense in which we may refer to Lucifer's proposed modifications of the Father's plan as Lucifer's plan, and Christ made the Father's plan his own by adoption. But what is basically important in this respect is to know that the power to save is vested in the Father, and that he originated, ordained, created, and established his own plan; that he announced it to his children; and that he then asked for a volunteer to be the Redeemer, the Deliverer, the Messiah, who would put the eternal plan of the Eternal Father into eternal operation.

4. Edersheim 1:78. Italics added. In another passage Edersheim says: "Perhaps the most valuable element in Rabbinic commentation on Messianic times is that in which, as so frequently, it is explained, that all the miracles and deliverances of Israel's past would be re-enacted, only in a much wider manner, in the days of the Messiah. . . . It is in this sense that we would understand the two sayings of the Talmud: 'All the prophets prophesied only of the days of the Messiah,' and 'The world was created only for the Messiah.' " (Edersheim 1:162 63.)

FOUR MILLENNIUMS OF TRUE WORSHIP

Thou shalt worship the Lord thy God,
and him only shalt thou serve.
(Luke 4:8.)[1]

True Worship Before the Flood

True and heaven-sent worship has been found on earth from the day of the first man to the present moment whenever and wherever men have been willing to hearken to their Maker. Christianity did not originate in the so-called Christian era. Our Lord did not bring it for the first time when he came to dwell on earth. Pure religion and approved worship have been with us from the beginning.

In the beginning that God who created man, male and female, in his own likeness and image; in the beginning the Eternal Father, by whom all things are, and who placed his son, Adam, and his daughter, Eve, in Eden; in the beginning the great Creator whose Beloved and Chosen Son was foreordained to be the Redeemer and Savior; in the beginning this Holy Being, as it was his right to do, commanded all men "that they should love and serve him, the only living and true God, and that he should be the only being whom they should worship." (D&C 20:18-19.)

The divine decree—"Thou shalt love the Lord thy God with all thy heart, with all thy might, mind, and strength; and in the name of Jesus Christ thou shalt serve him" (D&C

59:5) —is as old as the human race. An angelic ministrant, speaking by the power of the Holy Ghost, delivered to Adam the heaven-sent word: "Thou shalt do all that thou doest in the name of the Son, and thou shalt repent and call upon God in the name of the Son forevermore." (Moses 5:8.) Line upon line and precept upon precept, our first father was counseled from on high until he gained the fulness of the everlasting gospel, which gospel is the good news, the glad tidings, that all men may be saved if they keep the commandments of the Lord.

True worship consists in obeying the laws and ordinances of the gospel. It consists in believing in Christ, in joining the true Church, in being born again, in keeping the commandments after baptism, in acquiring the attributes of godliness, in doing all the things that must be done to gain eternal life in our Father's kingdom. True worship consists in emulating the thoughts and words and deeds of the Holy Messiah, so that men, following him and becoming like him, may reign with him in everlasting glory. True worship is the chief and major concern of man. God speaks, revelations are forthcoming, apostles and prophets labor out their days, the gifts of the Spirit are poured out upon the faithful, miracles are wrought, and the hand of the Lord is seen in all things—all to the end that men may worship the Father in spirit and in truth.

True worship is always and everlastingly the same. Truth does not vary, and God does not change. We are saved today by obedience to the same eternal laws that have saved men in all ages past and that will save them in all ages future.[2] The Author and Finisher of our faith is the same yesterday, today, and forever. In him there is no variableness, neither shadow of turning. Salvation always comes by obedience to the laws and ordinances of the everlasting gospel, the gospel that has existed with God from all eternity and that will continue to crown his unchangeable goodness toward his creatures forever.

Some have supposed that God dealt differently with the

ancient patriarchs than he did with men in the Christian era, or that he requires more of us in this age of supposed enlightenment than he did of those in the early ages of man's life on earth. Nothing could be further from the truth. Some of the mightiest and noblest spirits of all the hosts of heaven were sent to earth in the early gospel dispensations. Michael, known in his mortal ministry as Adam, in preexistence stood next to the Lord Jehovah himself in power, might, dominion, and intelligence; and Gabriel, who dwelt among men as Noah, was but a hair's breadth behind the first man in possession of godly graces. We can scarcely conceive of the high spiritual endowments of Enoch and all his city, true saints who qualified to flee the bounds of this earth and dwell in an appointed heaven without tasting death.

Let us look at each of the great patriarchs who presided as high priests over the Lord's people during the 1,656 years from the fall of Adam to the flood of Noah. These noble and great souls worshipped the Father in spirit and in truth and, with the hosts of faithful saints in each of their days, have long since gone on to glory and exaltation in the mansions that are prepared. For instance:

Adam, standing as the presiding high priest over all the earth for all ages, offered sacrifices of the firstlings of his flocks in similitude of the sacrifice of the Only Begotten of the Father.

Seth, who was like unto Adam in all things and could only be distinguished from him by their differences in age, performed baptisms by immersion for the remission of sins.

Enos laid on hands for the gift of the Holy Ghost and confirmed believing and obedient persons as members of the Church of Jesus Christ as it was then constituted.

Cainan conferred the holy priesthood upon his fellow mortals and ordained them to offices in that holy order which is without beginning of days or end of years.

Mahalaleel entered that order of the priesthood which is named the new and everlasting covenant of marriage and taught his children to go and do likewise.

Jared preached the gospel, prophesied of the coming Messiah, and testified that salvation was and is and is to come in and through the atoning blood of Christ, the Lord Omnipotent.

Enoch received revelations and visions, saw the Lord, and kept the law of Christ so fully and completely that he and all his city were translated.

Methuselah saw the future, prophesied by the power of the Holy Ghost, and dwelt in righteousness on earth for more years than any of the descendants of Adam of whom we have record.

Lamech enjoyed the gifts of the Spirit and rejoiced in that testimony of Jesus which is the spirit of prophecy.

Noah, going forth as a legal administrator and holding the same priesthood possessed by Enoch and his forebears, taught faith in the Lord Jesus Christ, repentance, baptism, and the receipt of the Holy Ghost, telling his wicked and adulterous generation that unless they accepted the gospel, the floods would come in upon them and misery would be their doom.

All these—and they comprise the patriarchal chain from Adam to Noah—and the saints over whom they presided in their days had the fulness of the everlasting gospel and dwelt in righteousness upon earth all the days of their appointed probation.[3] Souls were just as precious in that day as in any day, and a gracious God gave his laws to all who would accept them.

True Worship from Noah to Moses

When father Noah entered the ark, he took the holy priesthood with him. When the rains descended and the floods came; when the fountains of the mighty deep broke forth, sweeping from the earth all living things save those that were in the ark; when the Lord cleansed and baptized the very earth itself, the man Noah was a mighty prophet, a preacher of righteousness, a legal administrator who represented his God. Noah entered the ark as a member of the Church of Jesus Christ, as a saint in the congregation of Zion, and when he stepped forth onto dry ground one year and seventeen days later, there was no change in his status. He was still the Lord's agent; he still held the priesthood; the gospel was still on earth. True worship continued.

One of Noah's first acts after the flood was to build an altar and offer sacrifices in similitude of the coming sacrifice of the Lamb of God. After his day the gospel continued as it had after Adam's day. Each was the father of all living in his day, and their faithful descendants hearkened to their words and continued to worship Him who is eternal. Thus, pure religion was preserved through the flood, and men continued to work out their salvation as they had before the wicked and ungodly were destroyed in earth's one great deluge.

Our knowledge of prophets and peoples who had the gospel between Noah and Moses is somewhat sketchy. According to the best chronologies, from the flood in 2348 B.C. to the exodus from Egypt in 1491 B.C., there were 857 intervening years. We do know that whenever any person or group of people possessed the higher priesthood, they had the fulness of the gospel and were therefore worshipping the Lord according to the approved pattern.[4] We know that from the flood to the birth of Abraham was 352 years, during which time there were ten generations of men. These were: Noah, Shem, Arphaxad, Salah, Eber, Peleg, Reu, Serug, Nahor, Terah, and Abram (who became Abraham). How many of these remained true and faithful to the covenant of salvation made with their fathers we do not know. Terah, the father of Abraham, lived under apostate conditions and worshipped false gods. After Abraham came Isaac, Jacob, Joseph, Ephraim and Manasseh, and the children of Israel in general, who as a nation were burdened by Egyptian bondage, and among whom Moses was born in 1571 B.C.

It would appear that the gospel continued to operate to some degree, perhaps only in a fragmentary form, among

the enslaved descendants of Jacob, in spite of the enticements of Egypt and the cruel overlordship and persecutions
imposed by their Egyptian rulers. It is true that Moses received his priesthood from a non-Israelite source, but when
he came to deliver his nation from Pharaoh, the record
speaks of others who were elders of Israel and who well may
have been priesthood bearers. It describes a people who,
though in bondage, had an effective organization of their
own, and it tells how they demanded of Pharaoh the privilege of journeying into the wilderness so they might offer
sacrifices to Jehovah. It would seem that they had preserved
at least some of the teachings of their fathers, and that some
degree of true worship continued among them. In any event
there were those on earth among whom the priesthood and
true worship had remained. Abraham received the priesthood from Melchizedek, "who received it through the lineage of his fathers, even till Noah." (D&C 84:14.)[5] Thus
there is a direct priesthood line from Adam to Abraham
without a break.

There were also in the days of Abraham other nations
and peoples of whom we know nothing—except that they
dwelt on earth and worshipped the true God—who also held
the priesthood. Through these nations the priesthood
descended to Jethro, who conferred it upon his son-in-law
Moses. The revealed account speaks of one Esaias, of whose
ministry we know nothing, except that he received the priesthood under the hand of God (meaning, apparently, by special dispensation); that he lived in the days of Abraham and
was blessed by him; and that he conferred the priesthood
upon Gad. From Gad it descended by successive and authoritative conferrals to Jeremy, Elihu, Caleb, and Jethro,
and then to the great lawgiver, Moses. (D&C 84:6-15.)

From such inspired writings as have been preserved to
us, we are led to believe that the high points of true worship
from the assuaging of the flood to the ministry of Moses occurred under the leadership of Melchizedek and in the days
of Abraham, Isaac, Jacob, and Joseph. This man Mel-

chizedek, than whom none of the ancients were greater, reigned as king in Shiloam, which is Salem, and which we suppose was Jeru-Salem. His people had all gone astray, reveling in unrighteousness and every form of evil. By faith and mighty works Melchizedek reclaimed them, brought them back to the cause of Christ, established peace among them, and was called by them the prince of peace, the king of heaven, and the king of peace. When but a child he feared God, stopped the mouths of lions, and quenched the violence of fire. His people wrought righteousness and sought the blessing of translation and to find an inheritance in Enoch's city. He it was, as priest of the Most High God, who conferred the priesthood upon Abraham, who blessed the father of the faithful, and who received tithes from him. Because he was such a great high priest, the Church in ancient days, to avoid the too-frequent repetition of the name of the divine Son, called the priesthood itself in his name: *The Melchizedek Priesthood.* That there have been few high points in history to compare with the pinnacles of pure worship attained in the days of Melchizedek none can doubt.[6]

Abraham is everywhere revered as the father of the faithful and the friend of God. Whatever patriarchal lines may have been for the first 2,008 years of man's life on this earth, with the advent of Abraham in 1996 B.C., the Lord centered all things in his friend from Ur. From that day onward as long as time should roll or the earth should stand, the decree was that faithful spirits (in the main), those who would believe God and work righteousness, would come to earth as Abraham's seed. Those not of his literal bloodline who accept the gospel are adopted into his family, become his seed, and rise up and bless him as their father. With Abraham, and then with Isaac, and then with Jacob, the Lord made the covenant that their seed would continue, both in the world and out of the world, as innumerable as the sand upon the seashore or as the stars in heaven for multitude. This is the promise of eternal increase that is made in connection with celestial marriage, and that has been restored in modern times. It was restored by Elias and Elijah: by Elias, "who committed the dispensation of the gospel of Abraham," under which commission all who enter into celestial marriage receive the promise that in them and in their seed after them shall all generations be blessed; and by Elijah, who brought back the sealing power so that once again legal administrators could seal on earth and have it bound eternally in the heavens.[7]

These are in fact "the promises made to the fathers" that have been planted "in the hearts of the children." (D&C 2:1-3.) "I give unto thee a promise," Jehovah said to Abraham, that "in thy seed after thee (that is to say, the literal seed, or the seed of the body) shall all the families of the earth be blessed, even with the blessings of the Gospel, which are the blessings of salvation, even of life eternal." (Abr. 2:11.) Eternal life grows out of celestial marriage, out of the continuation of the family unit in eternity, and out of the inheritance of eternal increase. And thus, of all those who enter this order of matrimony, our revelation says: "This promise"—the promise of eternal increase, the promise of exaltation, the promise made to Abraham, the promise that has been planted in the hearts of all faithful members of the Church in this day—"This promise is yours also, because ye are of Abraham, and the promise was made unto Abraham." With reference to the promise, the Lord then says, "By this law is the continuation of the works of my Father, wherein he glorifieth himself," and then he adds this divine exhortation: "Go ye, therefore, and do the works of Abraham; enter ye into my law and ye shall be saved." (D&C 132:31-32.)

Joseph, the son of Jacob, who was sold by his envious and conniving brothers to the Ishmaelites for twenty pieces of silver (appropriately a lesser price than the thirty pieces of silver given Judas for betraying Jesus), was by them sold in Egypt to Potiphar, captain of Pharaoh's guard. This Joseph, who is described as being like his latter-day counterpart of the same name—Joseph Smith, Jr., who heads our dispensation—became one of the greatest prophets. His prophecies deal primarily with Moses, who was to deliver Israel from Egypt; with the Nephites and Lamanites, his descendants, who were to inhabit an American promised land; and with Joseph Smith and the restoration of the gospel in the latter days. (2 Ne. 3-4; JST, Gen. 50.)

Thus, only one conclusion can be reached for the period from Noah to Moses: heaven-sent worship was on earth, and pure religion ruled in the hearts of the saints.

True Worship in Ancient Israel

True worship among the chosen people rose to the heights and dropped to the depths during the fifteen hundred years of Israelite history that preceded the ministry of the Mortal Messiah. There were times when the house of Jacob climbed Sinai and found God; times when they were conquered by the world in the valley of Megiddo; times when they wandered through the wilderness of Idumea in search of truth; times when, without living water to drink, they perished in the deserts of Edom.

Nor did all Israel always travel together in one course. Worship among them was as varied as life itself; all degrees and kinds of conduct were shown forth at one time or another. Some of our fathers worshipped the Lord with a pure heart and a contrite spirit; others bowed before Baal, burned their children in the fires of Moloch, and found more pleasure in the deceptions of Jezebel than in the exhortations of Elijah. There were faithful maidens who could persuade a Naaman to dip seven times in Jordan and come up free from leprosy, according to the word of Elisha the man of God; and there were also selfish and grasping Gehazis who sought to enrich themselves by selling the gifts of God, and upon whom the leprosy of sin was permanently attached.

There were prophets and there were evil men among the Lord's people. Moses spoke with the Lord face to face, as a man speaketh with his friend, while Korah, Dathan, and Abiram, preferring the fleshpots of Egypt to the austerity of the gospel, led a rebellion against the great lawgiver. And there was opposition from without the fold as well as from within. Nehemiah rebuilt the walls of Jerusalem with a sword in one hand and a trowel in the other as Sanballat and the Arabians mocked and opposed at every turn. It was no easier to come off triumphant in the warfare of life in those days than it is in these; Israel's whole history was one of trial and testing. When they served the Lord, they prospered; when they rebelled, evil and desolation and death attended them.

Israel grew from a small group of some 70 souls into a great nation while sojourning in Egypt. When they came out of bondage there were 600,000, and more, men of war in age from twenty years old and upwards. Counting wives and children and others, the Israelites who went through the Red Sea—while the waters congealed as a wall on the right hand and on the left—numbered in the millions. We suppose they had retained fragments and portions of their ancient religion, portions of that which came down to them from the patriarchs, in spite of their enslavement by the Pharaohs. But it seems clear that the fulness of the gospel, at least in its beauty and perfection, came to them anew under the hands of Moses. Because Moses held the higher or Melchizedek Priesthood, he had the fulness of the gospel: he could thereby lay on hands for the gift of the Holy Ghost and confer upon men the power to sanctify their souls; he could thereby perform celestial marriages, which open the door to eternal life; and he could thereby seal people up unto eternal life with callings and elections made sure, so that they had an absolute guarantee of arising in the resurrection in a state of glory and honor and immortality and eternal life.

When Israel, as a people and as a whole, failed to live in harmony with the law of Christ as contained in the fulness of his everlasting gospel, the Lord "in his wrath" withdrew the fulness of his law from them. Because "they hardened their hearts" and would not "enter into his rest while in the wilderness, which rest is the fulness of his glory, . . . he took Moses out of their midst, and the Holy Priesthood also." (D&C 84:19-28.) That is, he took the Melchizedek Priesthood, which administers the gospel, out of their midst in the sense that it did not continue and pass from one priesthood holder to another in the normal and usual sense of the word. The keys of the priesthood were taken away with Moses so that any future priesthood ordinations required special divine authorization. But in place of the higher priesthood the Lord gave a lesser order, and in place of the fulness of the gospel he gave a preparatory gospel—the law of carnal commandments, the law of Moses—to serve as a schoolmaster to bring them, after a long day of trial and testing, back to the law of Christ in its fulness.[8] There is the fulness of the gospel, and there is the preparatory gospel. There is the full law of Christ, and there is a partial law of Christ. The Mosaic system was the partial law, a portion of the mind and will of Jehovah, a strict and severe testing arrangement that would qualify those who obeyed its terms and conditions to receive the eternal fulness when the Messiah came to deliver and to restore it.

Whenever any individual or any selected groups in Israel qualified for more light and greater blessings than were found in the law of Moses, the Lord gave them the law of Christ in its fulness. Such was the case among the Nephites for six hundred continuous years. They kept the law of Moses "because of the commandments," even though it had "become dead" unto them. But they also had the Melchizedek Priesthood and the fulness of the gospel. They believed in Christ and were "reconciled to God," and all things were theirs. (2 Ne. 25:23-27; Alma 13.) We know this same state of superior enlightenment existed at many other times and places in Israel. There were at many times, and may have been at all times, prophets and righteous men in Israel who held this higher order of priesthood. Joseph

Smith said, "All the prophets had the Melchizedek Priesthood and were ordained by God himself" (*Teachings*, p. 181), meaning they received that holy order by special dispensation. Elijah, for instance, was the very prophet chosen to bring back the keys of the sealing power in our day. (*Teachings*, pp. 172, 330, 335-41.)

With the advent of a lesser law in Israel, there came also a lesser priesthood to administer the inferior order. Aaron and his sons, and the Levites in general, received the Aaronic or Levitical order. By the power and authority of this preparatory priesthood—this priesthood of Elias which is a forerunner to prepare the way for the higher order—all of the ordinances and rites and performances of the Mosaic system were administered from the days of Aaron to the coming of John. It was the priesthood that governed Israel temporally whenever they were willing to submit to the rule of Deity, and the high priests who governed in their religious affairs were high priests of the Aaronic order.

Messiah's advent brought back again the Melchizedek Priesthood and placed it over the kingdom so that future direction and governance came from that source. With the restoration of the higher priesthood came the restoration of the higher law. Again men had the everlasting fulness. Again they could perfect their souls and enter into that rest which is the fulness of the glory of the Lord. As Paul stated to his Hebrew brethren, brethren who knew and practiced priesthood performances and understood the need for proper authority in all that they did: "If therefore perfection were by the Levitical priesthood, (for under it the people received the law,) what further need was there that another priest should rise after the order of Melchisedec, and not be called after the order of Aaron?" He is here showing how Christ, who was "called of God an high priest after the order of Melchisedec," brought back the gospel to replace the law of Moses. "For the priesthood being changed," he continues, "there is made of necessity a change also of the law." (Heb. 5:10; 7:11-12.)

Our conclusion, then, is that during all her long, wearisome, wandering history, Israel (or at least portions of that chosen race) worshipped the Lord in the true and proper sense of the word, either as possessors of the fulness of the gospel or while in subjection to the inferior and lesser order, which nonetheless came from God and was founded upon as many true principles as the people were willing to accept.

True Worship Among the Jews

In evaluating both the presence and the practice of true worship among the Jews, we must walk lightly and tread in winding paths, paths that are poorly marked and difficult to discern, paths that crisscross in a maze of diverse and differing directions. Many of the Jews in that day followed the form of true worship. They had the revealed pattern before them, and they adhered to it rigidly, with a fixity of purpose seldom seen among any people. A few of them enjoyed also the true spirit that is appointed to be the companion of true worship. But among their leaders and spreading out among the generality of the people, their worship embraced only the form of godliness. They went through the rituals and performances; they overstepped the mark in many things, Sabbath observance being chief among them; and they perverted and twisted so many basic principles that the Spirit of the Lord could not find lodgment in their souls. But with it all, the light still burned in some quarters in Israel; sacrifices were still offered by legal administrators upon divinely consecrated altars; the temple was still the Father's house, however much they had made it a den of thieves; and there were those prepared to receive their Messiah when he came even though the clamoring crowds chanted their cries of crucifixion.

Our Lord's conversation with the woman of Samaria at Jacob's Well gives a clear insight into the quality and kind of worship then extant. The woman—who was living in adultery and devoid of the true spirit of inspiration, and who was concerned more with form than with substance, as was the case with that whole adulterous society of ritualistic worshippers, yet who perceived Jesus to be a prophet—said: "Our fathers worshipped in this mountain; and ye say, that in Jerusalem is the place where men ought to worship."

Knowing that it is not where, but who and how we worship that counts; knowing that the whole Jerusalem-centered system of ritualistic performances would soon be fulfilled; knowing that his Jewish compatriots would soon be scattered to the four winds, Jesus replied: "Woman, believe me, the hour cometh, when ye shall neither in this mountain, nor yet at Jerusalem, worship the Father." These words began to put the subject back into perspective; it is the Father in whom true worship centers. Then came the prophetic words: "Ye worship ye know not what: we know what we worship: for salvation is of the Jews." (John 4:5-22.) The Samaritans had lost the knowledge of God, but it had been retained by the Jews. They knew that God was their Father, and the sweet incenses burned in their ordinances ascended to him.

If an inspired, modern-day Mormon, placed in a like situation, had been speaking today—not to a Samaritan but to a sectarian who believed the creeds of Christendom, creeds that convert the true God into a confused spirit nothingness that fills immensity—the forthcoming words might have been: 'Ye worship ye know not what: we know what we worship: for salvation is of the Latter-day Saints.'

"We know what we worship!" A true knowledge of God is the true foundation upon which true worship and true religion rest. Other peoples anciently worshipped gods of wood and stone fashioned by men's hands. The Greeks placed a stone Diana in a majestic temple, above Mars Hill, in their Athenian acropolis. Before this statue and in this pagan temple, itself one of the architectural marvels of the world, they performed such acts of worship and generated such feelings of adoration as one can develop for an inanimate work of art.[9] In contrast the Jews knew their God was a personal being, a glorified and exalted Man, an Eternal Father.

Many modern Christians worship a Trinity defined as being three Gods in one; as a spirit essence that fills the immensity of space; as a power and influence that has neither body, parts, nor passions; and is in fact as impersonal as Diana and all her kindred images. No doubt they generate such feelings of reverence, awe, and adoration as one can for such an impersonal nothingness. In contrast, the Latter-day Saints worship the God of the Jews.

Having announced that the Jews knew what they worshipped, meaning they were operating within the framework of true worship, our Lord said: "Salvation is of the Jews." That is to say, the Jews knew God was their Father; they looked forward to a Jewish Messiah and Deliverer who would reign forever on the throne of Jewish David; they had the holy scriptures, the words of the prophets, the guideposts for the lives of men; and they followed the law of Moses, the highest revealed standards then had among men. Salvation was available only to those who lived by pure and perfect Jewish standards, the standards set forth by the prophets.

Then came the perfect counsel that was needed for that day and for ours: "But the hour cometh, and now is, when the true worshippers shall worship the Father in spirit and in truth: for the Father seeketh such to worship him." And for an accurate rendition of the actual words then spoken, we now turn to the Joseph Smith Translation: "For unto such hath God promised his Spirit," the account says, "And they who worship him, must worship in spirit and in truth." (John 4:23; JST, John 4:26.) And therein lay the problem. Though the door was open that would have enabled them to worship the Father in spirit and in truth, and to receive thereby the sanctifying influence of the Holy Ghost in their lives, most of the Jews failed so to do. To them the Mortal Messiah—and no man could come unto the Father but by him—was a stumbling block. Because they rejected him and his mission, true worship ceased and the whole nation, scattered and peeled, meted out and trodden down, became a hiss and a byword wherever they sought to lay their heads.

But, for our present purposes, suffice it to say that true worship was found on earth during all of the first four millenniums of that mortality which began with Adam's fall. For four thousand years—nearly a million and a half days—the mind and will of the Lord had been manifest among men. Over two hundred thousand weekly Sabbaths had passed, each providing an occasion and an opportunity to deal more particularly with spiritual things. Prophets and preachers of righteousness had given as much of the mind and will of the Lord as men in their various days would receive. All things from the beginning had pointed to one supreme and transcendent event: the coming and mortal ministry of the Eternal Messiah.

NOTES

1. These words, quoted from a source not now found in the Bible, were spoken by Jesus to the arch-tempter when that evil spirit sought the soul of him who "was in all points tempted like as we are, yet [who remained] without sin." (Heb. 4:15.) It is evident they were part of some text then extant, and it is even more evident that they constitute the perfect summary of the real and true meaning of the whole body of revealed writ. Man was created so that he might worship the Lord because by so doing fallen mortals become as their Eternal Progenitor.

2. Joseph Smith spoke at extended length, on numerous occasions, reasoning along the same lines as here set forth, to show that the Lord "set the ordinances to be the same forever and ever." (*Teachings*, p. 168.) One brief reference to these teachings will here suffice: "The gospel has always been the same; the ordinances to fulfill its requirements, the same, and the officers to officiate, the same; and the signs and fruits resulting from the promises, the same; therefore, as Noah was a preacher of righteousness he must have been baptized and ordained to the priesthood by the laying on of the hands, etc." (*Teachings*, p. 264.)

3. One of the high points in the ministerial and worshipful experiences of the ancient patriarchs occurred in 3077 B.C., three years before Adam's spirit took leave of his mortal tenement. On that occasion, Adam "called Seth, Enos, Cainan, Mahalaleel, Jared, Enoch, and Methuselah, who were all high priests, with the residue of his posterity who were righteous, into the valley of Adam-ondi-Ahman, and there bestowed upon them his last blessing." Lamech, who was born in 3130 B.C., certainly would have been included in the unnamed "posterity." It was on this occasion that "the Lord [Christ] appeared unto them, and they rose up and blessed Adam, and called him Michael, the prince, the archangel. And the Lord administered comfort unto Adam, and said unto him: I have set thee to be at the head; a multitude of nations shall come of thee, and thou art a prince over them forever. And Adam stood up in the midst of the congregation; and, notwithstanding he was bowed down with age, being full of the Holy Ghost, predicted whatsoever should befall his posterity unto the latest generation." (D&C 107:53-56.) This certainly was one of the crowning worship services of all history, a service in which the righteous saints assembled to pay their devotions; and the Lord Jesus Christ himself, more than three millenniums before his mortal birth, came to speak to the people and to bless the great head of the human race.

4. "This greater priesthood administereth the gospel and holdeth the key of the

mysteries of the kingdom," our revelation says. Also: This "priesthood continueth in the church of God in all generations." (D&C 84:17-19.) These statements, as their context shows, refer to the authority, organization, and doctrine found on earth from Adam to Moses. Thus, whenever the Melchizedek Priesthood is found among men, there also is the Church of Jesus Christ and the fulness of the gospel; and wherever the gospel and the Church are found, there also is the priesthood. Any one of these is inseparable from each of the others. It is a knowledge of this and other similar truths that enables us to know, from the very sketchy and fragmentary accounts available to us, what the ancient saints actually possessed.

5. These words of scripture seem to say that there was more than one generation between Melchizedek and Noah, which means that the tradition from apocryphal sources that Melchizedek was Shem the son of Noah cannot be true.

6. Alma 13:14-19; D&C 84:13-14; 107:1-4; JST, Gen. 14:17-40; Heb. 7:1-4; 11:33-34; *Teachings*, pp. 322-23. Our King James Version of the Bible speaks of Melchizedek as being "without father, without mother, without descent, having neither beginning of days, nor end of life; but made like unto the Son of God; abideth a priest continually" (Heb. 7:3-4), as though he were some unique and mystical character apart from the races of men. The Joseph Smith Translation perfects the obviously imperfect King James passage in this way: "For this Melchizedek was ordained a priest after the order of the Son of God, which order was without father, without mother, without descent, having neither beginning of days, nor end of life. And all those who are ordained unto this priesthood are made like unto the Son of God, abiding a priest continually." (JST, Heb. 7:3.) In this connection it should be noted that the Joseph Smith Translation renditions in the fourteenth chapter of Genesis recite some of the greatest and most glorious concepts in any revelation relative to this "order of the Son of God," this Melchizedek Priesthood as we call it. (JST, Gen. 14:17-40.)

7. D&C 110:12-16; 132:29-32; Abr. 2:6-11; Gen. 17:1-4; 23:15-18; 26:1-5; 28:10-15.

8. Galatians 3. This chapter, contrary to the views that prevail in modern Christendom, shows how Abraham had the gospel, how in the day of Moses the lesser law "was added because of transgressions," how this law was to continue until the Messiah came, and how "the law was our schoolmaster to bring us unto Christ."

9. It was of this temple and this statue, in all their artistry and magnificence, that Paul said to the Epicurean and Stoic philosophers: "God that made the world and all things therein, seeing that he is Lord of heaven and earth, dwelleth not in temples made with hands; Neither is worshipped with men's hands, as though he needed any thing, seeing he giveth to all life, and breath, and all things." (Acts 17:24-25.) Would it be amiss to give a modern paraphrase of Paul's words, a paraphrase pointed not at those who worship Diana, but at those who suppose that "God is a spirit," as the King James Version erroneously says in the Jacob's Well passage? Would it be amiss if the passage said: "God that made the world and all things therein, seeing that he is Lord of heaven and earth, is not a congeries of laws floating like a fog in the universe; he is not the unclothed, indivisible, uncreated, impersonal spirit essence defined in the creeds of Christendom; for what adoration and what true worship (including the essential element of emulation) can there be for impersonal laws, as though man should pray: O thou great law of gravity grant me this my petition"?

Chapter 5

THE LAW OF MOSES

My servant Moses . . . who is faithful
in all mine house. With him will I speak
mouth to mouth, even apparently,
and not in dark speeches; and the
similitude of the Lord shall he behold. . . .
(Num. 12:7-8.)

And there arose not a prophet since in
Israel like unto Moses, whom the Lord
knew face to face, In all signs and
wonders, which the Lord sent him to do.
(Deut. 34:10-11.)[1]

Jesus Lived the Law of Moses

We cannot portray, with any degree of sense and wisdom, the deeds done by the Mortal Messiah, nor can we envision the true meaning of much that he taught, unless we know what was involved in the law and system that was given to men to prepare the way for his coming. That system was the law of Moses—the law, on the one hand, that for fifteen hundred burdensome years had been the whip and the scourge in the hands of the Almighty to bring recalcitrant Israel repeatedly back to their proper standards; the law, on the other hand, that had shown forth bright rays of divine light for that blessed millennium and a half during which men were privileged to live in harmony with its uplifting standards.

Jesus was born among a people and in a home where the law of Moses was the rule and standard by which all things were measured. During his young and maturing years he was taught its precepts; he learned all that appertained to it; and he conformed in every respect to its rituals and provisions. When he was eight days old he was circumcised, according to the law, so that the mark of Moses, the man of God, and of Abraham, the friend of God, might ever thereafter be found in his flesh. When the days of Mary's purification according to the law of Moses were accomplished, she and Joseph took the newborn baby to the temple to present him to the Lord. At the age of twelve he became a son of the law, attended the regular feasts, and began to assume the responsibilities of the maturing males of the chosen race. It was at that age, at the Feast of the Passover, that he confounded the wise men in the temple and made to Mary the famous statement "Wist ye not that I must be about my Father's business" (Luke 2:49), indicating that even then the divine truth had come to him that he was one set apart from his fellows because God was his Father.

We can rest assured that our Lord was present many times when the morning and evening sacrifices were offered; that he went up to Jerusalem to keep the Feast of Tabernacles and to worship in the holy convocations that were recurring times of rejoicing under the Mosaic system; that he rejoiced with his kindred on the Day of Atonement and made it an occasion to draw near to his Father; that he went many times to the temple, which he revered as his Father's house, to ponder and pray and worship. To the growing boy, the eager and inquiring youth, the maturing man, and the teaching Rabbi, the law that had so long been a light to the paths of his forebears was also a light to his.

We must gaze back to the day of Moses and of Aaron; we must look upon the performances and ordinances of the Levitical law, during the fifteen hundred years it was in force in Israel; we must hear the voices of the prophets and teachers who were subject to the Mosaic system; we must know what the ancients had and were—all this if we are to catch the true vision of what Jesus was; if we are to learn why he taught as he did; if we are to understand why he reacted as he did to both friend and foe. This we shall do as we lay the foundation for the study of his life.

The Divinity of the Law of Moses

It is axiomatic, an obvious truism, that all things have their opposites and that nothing can be understood or known except as it relates to other similar or diverse things. The beauties and blessings of one system of conduct or of one way of life can only be envisioned to the full when both compared and contrasted with other systems or ways in the same field. We must both compare and contrast the law of Moses with the gospel of Christ, and each of them with other lesser systems of worship, if we are to see how the Mosaic system fits into the eternal scheme of things.

To have the whole picture before us, we might well divide individuals, groups, races, and nations into four classes or types:

1. *There are those whose consciences are seared with a hot iron, who rebel against light and decency, who revel in unrighteousness, and who seek to live and rule in outright wickedness.*

Such are the Gadianton robbers of the Nephites, the marauding bands of ancient Palestine, and the thieves and robbers of every society. Such are the Genghis Khans, the Caesars, and the war lords of China and other nations whose lives consist of plundering, ravaging, and destroying. Such are the ancient mystery religions, the sex-centered worship of Ashtoreth, and the witchcraft, necromancy, astrology, and outright Satan worship of both ancient and modern peoples. Such also are the empire-building nations of history— Egyptians, Assyrians, Babylonians, Persians, Greeks, Romans, Barbarians, many of the kingdoms and empires of Europe and Asia, the anti-Christs among the Jaredites, and the degenerate Lamanites of Hebrew descent: all these are peoples and nations led by godless wretches whose aim is to enslave and rule their fellowmen. All these are without God in the world: their course is one of carnality and evil; they are not neutral in the warfare between good and evil; they affirmatively defy the good and espouse the evil. Their religion is the religion of Satan; they serve on his errand and further his purposes. They are purely and simply in opposition to all that is good and decent among men. To put them in perspective, theologically speaking, we might say that all these are the telestial mortals among us.

2. *There are those who seek to do good and to live by standards of decency and integrity; who heed the voice of conscience; who believe that a man's word should be his bond; and who maintain that men should organize and govern themselves so as to better their social circumstances and assure to each person freedom of conscience and the rights to life, liberty, and the pursuit of happiness.*

Such are the ideals at least of the great religions of the world—Christian, Jewish, Islam, Buddhism, Confucianism, Shintoism, or what have you—all seek to better and uplift man; all seek to assure him of whatever they conceive salvation to be. Such are the temperance societies, the welfare organizations, the freedom foundations, the schools and universities among free peoples. Such also are the benevolent dictatorships, the kindly monarchies, and the republics of both the Old and New Worlds.

None of these is pure religion; none embraces within its fold true worship; but all are founded, in general, on right principles; all operate for the betterment and uplift of fallen man.

Theologically speaking, these might be said to be terrestrial in nature. They are good for man; they advance him in the scale of progression; they help the downtrodden and better the status of those in need. But they can neither save nor exalt a human soul; they neither embrace nor follow a course of pure and perfect worship.

3. *Above these peoples and nations come those who have the preparatory gospel—the law of Moses!—the principles of revealed truth that put them in the course leading to eternal life in our Father's kingdom.*

Such was the righteous portion of the house of Israel from the day of Moses to the coming of John; such was the righteous or Nephite portion of father Lehi's seed on the American continent. Be it known that not all Israel kept the law of Moses. There were clusters and groups and whole tribes and nations that for generations at a time wallowed in dire and awful apostasy and denied themselves the blessings that might have been theirs. And be it known that not all of father Lehi's children walked in the path charted for them by their noble parent. Laman and Lemuel and their seed (with some notable exceptions) sought that which was evil and kept not the law of Moses.

But what we must have clearly before us is that the law of Moses as such was a higher and more perfect order of worship than any system of worship other than the fulness of the everlasting gospel. That is to say, the law of Moses was a higher and better and more nearly perfect system of worship than modern Catholic and sectarian Christianity, to say nothing of the fact that it surpassed Mohammedanism, Buddhism, and all other forms of worship. This is so because those who lived the law of Moses had revelation, were led by prophets, held the priesthood, and did the things that started them in the direction of the celestial kingdom. This superiority of the law of Moses will become apparent as we set forth the principles and practices upon which it was based. Theologically speaking, those who received and lived the law of Moses might be said to have been walking in a celestial course, to have been taking some of the initial steps leading to eternal life, to have been preparing themselves for that eternal fulness out of which eternal life comes.

4. *Finally we come to those who have the fulness of the everlasting gospel; who have the law of Christ in all its beauty and perfection; who are the true saints, the saints of the living God; who hold the holy priesthood; who enjoy the gift of the Holy Ghost; who have been born again and are in process of sanctifying their souls; who have the gifts of the Spirit; who receive revelations and see within the veil; who work miracles, open blind eyes, unstop deaf ears, and cause lame men to leap; and who have power to seal righteous souls up to eternal life in the everlasting realms of Him who is Eternal.*

Such are the citizens of the true kingdom, in whatever age is involved; such are members of the only true and living church on earth, in whatever age is involved; such are the faithful among the Latter-day Saints. Theologically speaking, those who believe and obey the everlasting fulness of saving truth might be said to be earth's celestial souls, souls who will receive back again in the resurrection the same body that was a natural body, which perfected body will be able to stand the glory of a celestial kingdom.

Moses and Christ—Their Laws Compared

We shall now compare the law of Moses with the fulness of the gospel. In doing so we must be aware that both of them come from God and are the laws of Christ.

We say, and our scriptures so certify, that there are two gospels, two laws, two revealed systems that Jehovah has given his people. One gospel is called the everlasting gospel, the fulness of the gospel, the gospel of Christ. It is the plan of salvation, by conformity to which man can gain the fulness of reward in that kingdom which is everlasting. The other gospel is the preparatory gospel, the partial gospel, the lesser gospel. It is the law of Moses by conformity to which men qualify, either in this life or the next, to receive that eternal fulness out of which eternal life grows. Both gospels are good news from God (as the very word *gospel* signifies), but one is greater than the other: one contains sufficient power and knowledge to save and exalt here and now, while the other prepares men to receive that future fulness which alone gives the guarantee of salvation.

We say, and our scriptures also so certify, that there are two priesthoods, two systems that authorize man to represent his Maker and to act in his place and stead in ministering salvation to mortals. One priesthood is the priesthood after the order of the Son of God; it is the Melchizedek Priesthood, the higher or greater priesthood, the holy order, the priesthood that administers the fulness of the gospel and has power to seal men up unto eternal life. The other priesthood is the Aaronic Priesthood, the Levitical Priesthood, the lower or lesser priesthood, the priesthood that administers the law of Moses.

Joseph Smith was asked, "Was the Priesthood of Melchizedek taken away when Moses died?" He replied: "All Priesthood is Melchizedek, but there are different portions or degrees of it. That portion which brought Moses to speak with God face to face was taken away; but that which brought the ministry of angels remained." (*Teachings*, pp. 180-81.) In other words, there is only one priesthood, but it comes in degrees; it is given partially or it is conferred in its fulness; it comes as the order of Aaron or as the order of Melchizedek. In this same sense, there is only one gospel, one law, one system of salvation, and it comes in degrees. It is all the law of Christ. Salvation comes from no other source. He gives to men as much of his law as they are able to bear. If they can only bear up under the burdens of the lesser system, the schooling system, the preparatory gospel, that is all they receive. Men are given according to their desires and their deeds.

Even today with the fulness of the gospel we have not received all of the light and knowledge that Enoch and many of the ancients possessed. We do, of course, have all the keys and powers ever had by any peoples and hence are able to assure worthy people of the fulness of reward in our Father's kingdom. Historically, the fulness of the gospel and the fulness of the priesthood came first; the law of Moses and the partial priesthood came second. The law of Moses was added to the gospel and the lesser priesthood was added to the greater. There are restrictions and limitations in the lesser system that are not present in the gospel itself. All of the saints from Adam to Moses had the fulness of the priesthood and the fulness of the law of Christ. Those from Moses to John had the lesser orders, the lesser priesthood and the lesser gospel, except of course when groups and portions of the people (such as the Nephites) qualified for the higher law and power.

To gain the celestial kingdom, the Lord says: Ye must be "sanctified through the law which I have given unto you, even the law of Christ," which law is the fulness of the gospel. The revealed word specifies that those who "abide the law of a terrestrial kingdom" shall obtain a terrestrial glory, and that those who "abide the law of a telestial kingdom" shall obtain a telestial glory. No such requirement is set forth for gaining a celestial glory. Instead, the revelation says that those who so obtain must be *able* to abide the law of a celestial kingdom." (D&C 88:21-24.) In other words, salvation in the celestial kingdom will come to all who are *able* to live the full law of Christ, even though they did not have opportunity so to do in the course of a mortal probation. Thus, all those who kept the law of Moses, who lived the law of the preparatory gospel to the full, thus establishing that they were able to live the Lord's law, will in due course gain a celestial inheritance. All of the great and eternal truths found in the law of Moses are also part and portion of the fulness of the gospel, in the same sense that all of the powers of the Aaronic Priesthood are embraced within the Melchizedek Priesthood.

It should come as no surprise to learn that the law of Moses includes such basic and eternal verities as these:

Under the law, the people had "the first and great commandment," which is, "Thou shalt love the Lord thy God with all thy heart, and with all thy soul, and with all thy mind"; they had also the second great commandment, which is "like unto" the first: "Thou shalt love thy neighbour as thyself." So spake Jesus in answer to the query, "Which is the great commandment in the law?" And having so stated, our Lord added, "On these two commandments hang all the law and the prophets." (Matt. 22:35-40.) That is to say, all of the gospel of salvation, all of the ancient law given to Moses, all of the prophetic counsel of all the inspired men of all the ages—all of it is anchored and grounded upon these two eternal verities: love of the true God and love of one's fellowmen.

The words used to codify these laws did not originate with the Lord Jesus during his mortal ministry. The two commandments were not an outpouring of his superior wisdom; they were not a new and superlative summary of the mind and will of the Lord; they were, rather, a direct quotation from the law of Moses. Moses said them and Jesus quoted them. It was Moses who said: "Hear, O Israel: The Lord our God is one Lord: And thou shalt love the Lord thy God with all thine heart, and with all thy soul, and with all thy might"; and having so said, it was Moses who commanded Israel to teach these words diligently unto their children, to talk of them as they sat in their houses and as they walked by the way, when they lay down and when they rose up, and also that they should bind them for a sign upon their hands, let them be continually before their eyes, and write them upon the posts of their houses and the gates to their dwelling places. (Deut. 6:4-9.) And it was Moses who said, in the Lord's name, "Thou shalt love thy neighbour as thyself." (Lev. 19:18.) It is indeed difficult to conceive how a greater emphasis could have been put on these basic truths than was placed upon them by Moses, the man of God.

We have stated that those who kept the law of Moses were heirs of eternal life, an eternal verity that Jesus confirmed in this conversation. Our Lord was asked,

"Master, what shall I do to inherit eternal life?" He responded: "What is written in the law? how readest thou?" which is tantamount to saying, 'If you want eternal life, keep the law of Moses.' His interrogator replied: "Thou shalt love the Lord thy God with all thy heart, and with all thy soul, and with all thy strength, and with all thy mind; and thy neighbour as thyself." If there was anything that all Israel knew about the law of Moses and the teachings of all the prophets, it was that to gain salvation, they must love their God and their fellowmen. And so Jesus affirmed: "Thou hast answered right: this do, and thou shalt live." 'Keep these commandments which came through Moses, and thou shalt have eternal life.' It was at this point that our Lord's tempter, desiring to justify himself, asked, "Who is my neighbour?" and the Master Teacher replied with the parable of the good Samaritan. (Luke 10:25-37.)

Upon the foundation of the first and second commandments, we place the Ten Commandments, that Israelite code of revealed law that is so highly esteemed that it has become the basic legal code for nearly all those who accept the Christian way of life. The Lord revealed the Ten Commandments to Moses twice, the first time as part of the gospel, the second time as part of the law of Moses, with the only substantive difference between the two revealed accounts being the reason for keeping the Sabbath day holy. Under the gospel the Sabbath day commemorated the creation; under the Mosaic system, the deliverance from Egypt with a mighty hand and a stretched-out arm.

The Ten Commandments—decreeing as they do that the saints shall have no gods before the Lord; that they shall neither make nor worship any graven images; that they shall not take the name of God in vain; that they shall keep holy the Sabbath; that they shall honor their father and mother; that they shall not kill, nor commit adultery, nor steal, nor bear false witness, nor covet—all of these are part of the law of Moses as they are part of the gospel.[2] And it was to these commandments that Jesus turned to give answer to the query, "Good Master, what good thing shall I do, that I may have eternal life?" Having replied, "If thou wilt enter into life, keep the commandments," and then being asked, "Which?" Jesus particularized by saying: "Thou shalt do no murder, Thou shalt not commit adultery, Thou shalt not steal, Thou shalt not bear false witness, Honour thy father and thy mother: and, Thou shalt love thy neighbour as thyself." (Matt. 19:16-19.) And thus again the witness is born that by keeping the law of Moses men go forward on the charted course toward eternal life.

As an integral part of the whole law of Moses; as an essential part of every rite and performance of the Mosaic system; as a spoken or implied part of every commandment given to Israel; as a unifying thread woven into the whole tapestry of their society; as a divine decree, echoing and reechoing like the thunders of Sinai—stands the great Mosaic message: Keep the commandments. Keep the commandments and be blessed; disobey and be cursed. The repetitively stated Nephite declaration—"Inasmuch as ye shall keep my commandments ye shall prosper in the land; but inasmuch as ye will not keep my commandments ye shall be cut off from my presence" (2 Ne. 1:20)—was but an echo of what Moses and the prophets had been telling Israel for generations.

"And now, Israel," Moses proclaimed, "what doth the Lord thy God require of thee, but to fear the Lord thy God, to walk in all his ways, and to love him, and to serve the Lord thy God with all thy heart and with all thy soul, To keep the commandments of the Lord, and his statutes, which I command thee this day for thy good?" Thereupon Moses acclaims the might and glory of the Lord, recounts some of his wondrous works, and says: "Therefore thou shalt love the Lord thy God, and keep his charge, and his statutes, and his judgments, and his commandments, alway." The blessings to accrue by obedience and the curses to befall from disobedience are then enumerated in graphic detail. (Deut. 10:12-22; 11; 27; 28.)

Perhaps nothing shows the divine approval enjoyed by ancient Israel—and therefore the divine nature of their law, by obedience to which they gained such great things—than the endless miracles and wonders wrought among them by the power of God. The Lord by his angel went before the camps of Israel in a cloud by day and a pillar of fire by night, that they might know he was near and had a personal interest in preserving them. (Ex. 13:20-22; 14:19-24; 23:20-25; Deut. 1:33.) Lest they perish in the wilderness for want of food, the Lord, for forty years, rained bread from heaven upon them. This manna—by which no other people before or since has ever been fed, coming as it did by the opening of the heavens—certified to all who tasted its delicious flavor that as man doth not live by bread alone, even so his spiritual life depends upon receiving every word that proceedeth out of the mouth of God. Temporal food and spiritual food come from the same source, and both are essential to the full and complete life of the soul. (Ex. 16:1-36; Deut. 8:1-4.)

What indicates divine approval more than the receipt of personal and continuing revelation? Under the Mosaic system, direct revelation was given; the voice of a living, personal, speaking God was heard; angels ministered to men. God was not, as he is in Christendom today, an unknown spirit essence; he was a living reality. Many of these revelations came to the high priest of the Aaronic order, by means of the Urim and Thummim, which he carried in the breastplate of judgment when he went in before the Lord. (Ex. 28:30.)

As a result of the sacrificial offerings of Aaron and his sons and the consequent devotion and worship of the people, the Lord Jehovah promised to dwell among the children of Israel and to be their God, thus leading to that close personal relationship which existed between the Lord and his people when he dwelt personally in Zion. (Ex. 29:38-46; Moses 7:16.)

All of this—and much more that could be set forth—

shows the greatness and dignity of the law of Moses. This law was no mean or low system, either of theology or of ethics. That it exceeded what is had among sectarian Christians today is shown by the fact that the Lord wrought miracles and poured out wonders upon its faithful adherents. What Moses had was ennobling and uplifting. It was part of the law of Christ. Its essence and tenor is summed up perfectly in the words of Micah: "What doth the Lord require of thee, but to do justly, and to love mercy, and to walk humbly with thy God?" (Micah 6:8.)

Moses and Christ—Their Laws Contrasted

By obedience to his law, by heeding his voice, by keeping his gospel covenant, Israel had power to become "a peculiar treasure" unto the Lord above all people, to become "a kingdom of priests, and an holy nation." (Ex. 19:5-6; Deut. 7:6; 14:1-2.) This they failed to do. The gospel offered to them was not "mixed with faith in them that heard it." (Heb. 4:2.) In its place came the law of Moses, a law that was "added because of transgressions." (Gal. 3:19.) As Abinadi expresses it, "They were a stiffnecked people, quick to do iniquity, and slow to remember the Lord their God; Therefore there was a law given them, yea, a law of performances and of ordinances, a law which they were to observe strictly from day to day, to keep them in remembrance of God and their duty towards him." (Mosiah 13:29-30.)

As we have seen, many of the great and eternal truths of the gospel remained and were the rock foundation upon which the law was built. Men were still to worship and serve the Lord; they were still to love their neighbors as themselves; and the Ten Commandments retained their efficacy, virtue, and force; but under the law of Moses severe penalties were added for disobedience. The element of fear as well as of love became a dominant incentive in doing the things that must be done if salvation is to be won. Under the law of the gospel men are commanded to honor the Sabbath

79

day and keep it holy. If they keep this commandment, they are blessed; if they heed it not, the promised blessings pass them by. But under the law of Moses a penalty was added for dishonoring the Sabbath, and that penalty was death. Extreme? Severe? So it would seem to us, but the Lord was taking a nation of bondsmen and slaves and turning them into kings and priests. It required strict obedience to his laws, and the sooner the rebels were sloughed off the sooner the whole nation would walk in paths of righteousness.

There are, in fact, a great host of offenses, set forth primarily in Exodus and Leviticus, for which the law decreed either excommunication or death as the penalty. Israelites were excommunicated, for instance, for eating any manner of fat from oxen, sheep, or goats, or for eating the blood of birds or beasts. The death penalty was imposed for murder, adultery, and various sexual perversions; it was decreed for blasphemy, witchcraft, and sacrificing to false gods; even those who either cursed or smote father or mother, and the sons of Aaron who drank wine or strong drink before entering the tabernacle of the congregation, were to be put to death. The whole tone and tenor of the Mosaic system may be summed up in the decree: "Thou shalt give life for life, Eye for eye, tooth for tooth, hand for hand, foot for foot, Burning for burning, wound for wound, stripe for stripe." (Ex. 21:23-25.) An illustration of the severity with which the divine decrees were applied anciently is seen in the slaying of Nadab and Abihu by the Lord. "There went out fire from the Lord, and devoured them," the account says, because they offered "strange fire" upon the altar; that is, these sons of Aaron performed a sacrificial ordinance of their own devising. (Lev. 10:1-2.)[3]

The contrast between the benevolent influence exerted by Christianity and the severe near-compulsion of the law of Moses is nowhere better illustrated than in the sayings of Jesus. Coming as he did to lift Israel from the level of the law to the high standard of the gospel, it was our Lord's wont to say: "Ye have heard that it was said by them of old time," such and such, "But I say unto you," this and this. In this way he extended the ancient definition of adultery to include looking upon a woman in lust; he condemned the ancient practice of giving "a writing of divorcement," and set forth a marital standard that is higher than the one even now required in the Church, a standard that labels as adultery and fornication the marrying of certain divorced persons. He revoked the power to swear oaths and in place of the ancient law, "An eye for an eye, a tooth for a tooth," he counseled, "That ye resist not evil: but whosoever shall smite thee on thy right cheek, turn to him the other also." And the Mosaic standard, "Thou shalt love thy neighbour, and hate thine enemy," became "Love your enemies, bless them that curse you, do good to them that hate you, and pray for them which despitefully use you, and persecute you." (Matt. 5.)

Our conclusion, then, is:

1. That the law of Moses is superior to every law except the gospel;

2. That those who lived its terms and conditions thereby charted a course leading to eternal life;

3. That it prepares men for the fulness of revealed truth; and

4. That the gospel itself is far greater than the ancient law of Moses.

NOTES

1. We must not lose sight of the high and exalted place of Moses in the divine program. He ranks with Adam and Enoch; he has the spiritual stature of Noah and Abraham; and he stands with Melchizedek and Moriancumer in faith and devotion. How fitting it is that the law that was to govern the Lord's people for one-fourth of the entire period from the fall of man to the Second Coming of the Messiah should come through this son of Amram and Jochebed. It is no wonder that Holy Writ speaks of him in words like these: "Moses was caught up into an exceedingly high mountain, And he saw God face to face, and he talked with him, and the glory of God was upon Moses; therefore Moses could endure his presence. And God spake unto Moses, saying: Behold, . . . thou art my son; wherefore look, and I will show thee the workmanship of mine hands. . . . And I have a work for thee, Moses, my son; and thou art in the similitude of mine Only Begotten." (Moses 1:1-6.)

2. The account in Exodus (Ex. 20:1-17) sets forth the Ten Commandments as part of the gospel. The account in Deuteronomy (Deut. 5:1-21), given later and written anew by the finger of God on a second set of tablets of stone, is the account that governed those under the law of Moses. It is of more than passing interest that the direction to Israel to keep the Sabbath in commemoration of the day of their deliverance from Egypt had the

effect of changing the day of the week on which the Sabbath was kept each succeeding year. Christmas comes on a different day of the week each year for us, and so did the weekly Sabbaths in ancient Israel: A full consideration of this is found in *Sunday—The True Sabbath of God* by Samuel Walter Gamble, a Methodist minister.

3. The death of these priests for performing an unauthorized ordinance gives us insight into how the Lord deals with those of his people, at least, who do that which he has not authorized them to do. Certainly in principle, and to some degree the same condemnation, in a spiritual sense, rests upon all ministers who perform unauthorized ordinances.

Chapter 6

JERUSALEM—THE HOLY CITY

Beautiful for situation, the joy of the
whole earth, is mount Zion, . . . the city
of the great King. God is known in
her palaces. . . . Jerusalem . . . the
city of the great King.
(Ps. 48:2-3; Matt. 5:35.)[1]

Enoch's Zion—the City of Holiness

Holy cities, sacred sites, dwelling places set apart—symbols of celestial rest—such are the capital cities of the saints in all ages. Always the Lord has a Zion, a Jerusalem, a City of Holiness, a place from which his word and his law can go forth; a place to which all men can look to receive guidance from on high; a place where apostles and prophets give counsel to their fellowmen; a place where living oracles commune with the Infinite and speak forth his mind and announce his will. In every age the Lord gathers his people; in every age the saints come together to worship the Father in the name of the Son; in every age there is a capital city, a city of refuge, a City of Holiness, a Zion of God—a sacred site from which he can send forth his word and govern his people. Such is Jerusalem—Old Jerusalem, New Jerusalem, Jerusalem of the ages.

Up to now, through all of earth's long years, there has been one time, one time only, when the Lord's system of capital cities has worked perfectly. Such was in the day of Enoch, the seventh from Adam. In that holy day, so faithful were the saints that the Lord, the Great Jehovah, "came and dwelt with his people," even as he will in the millennial era that is to be. In that holy day, the saints "dwelt in righteousness," even as they shall when the Lord comes again to dwell among mortals. "And the Lord called his people ZION, because they were of one heart and one mind, and dwelt in righteousness; and there were no poor among them. And Enoch . . . built a city that was called the City of Holiness, even ZION. . . . And Enoch and all his people walked with God, and he dwelt in the midst of Zion; and it came to pass that Zion was not, for God received it up into his own bosom; and from thence went forth the saying, ZION IS FLED." (Moses 7:16-21, 69.)

Zion is taken up into heaven! And "this is Zion—THE PURE IN HEART," and the pure in heart shall see God. (D&C 97:16-21.) The Lord's people—and it is the people who were named Zion—went where he was; the inhabitants of the City of Holiness ascended up on high; their purity and perfection prepared them for the divine presence.

Thereafter, from the time when the people whose name was Zion were translated until the day of the great deluge, the converted saints had no earthly city to which they could gather. And so, as the divine record recites, for "generation upon generation" the faithful saints were translated and taken up into heaven to associate with others of like spiritual caliber in that Zion which God had taken into his own bosom. "The Holy Ghost fell on many," the account says, "and they were caught up by the powers of heaven into Zion." (Moses 7:24-27.)

Righteous men, after the flood—knowing what had happened to their faithful counterparts before the flood; knowing that those who held the holy priesthood had "power, by faith, . . . to stand in the presence of God"; knowing that if

God had gathered some into a translated realm, he might be prevailed upon to gather others also—"men having this faith, coming up unto this order of God, were translated and taken up into heaven." (JST, Gen. 14:25-32.)

Melchizedek Creates His Zion—Ancient Jerusalem

Righteous men, after the flood, not only sought an inheritance in Enoch's Zion, but also began the process of building their own City of Holiness on earth; and this brings us to the first scriptural mention of Salem, of Jeru-Salem, of Jerusalem. In reciting what Enoch and his people had gained through faith and by the power of the priesthood, the scripture says: "And now, Melchizedek was a priest of this order; therefore he obtained peace in Salem, and was called the Prince of peace. And his people wrought righteousness, and obtained heaven, and sought for the city of Enoch which God had before taken, separating it from the earth, having reserved it unto the latter days, or the end of the world. . . . And this Melchizedek, having thus established righteousness, was called the king of heaven by his people, or, in other words, the King of peace." (JST, Gen. 14:33-36.)

Abraham, who received his priesthood from Melchizedek, was one of those who sought for the heavenly city. "He looked for a city," Paul says, "which hath foundations, whose builder and maker is God." Isaac and Jacob, heirs of the promises made to Abraham, also sought an inheritance in the heavenly city. But it was not their privilege so to obtain.

Theirs was a different mortal mission; and though they declared "plainly" that they sought such a reward, yet they knew it was not to be, and "confessed that they were strangers and pilgrims on the earth." Their reward was postponed to a future day, for God "hath prepared for them a city," as he has for all those who serve him with like faith and zeal. (Heb. 11:8-16.)

In the true and full sense of the word *Zion* and *Jerusalem* are probably synonymous terms. Enoch built Zion, a City of Holiness, and Melchizedek, reigning as king and ministering as priest of the Most High God, sought to make Jerusalem, his capital city, into another Zion. As we have seen, Melchizedek himself was called by his people the Prince of peace, the King of peace, and the King of heaven, for Jerusalem had become a heaven to them. And interestingly, according to the linguistic scholars and specialists, Salem means *peace*, and Jerusalem means *city of peace*, or *sacred Salem*, and Isaiah's designation of Jerusalem as the holy city is said to mean, literally translated, the *city of holiness*.[2]

That Jerusalem came nearer in Melchizedek's day to becoming in truth and in fact a Zion of God than it has in any of its long and tumultuous history is perfectly clear. Indeed, after Melchizedek's day we lose track of what transpired in and relative to this sacred spot, which had started out to be an abode for the righteous, and we know little more of its history until Israelite times. Joshua found the city in the hands of the Jebusites, and he and others who followed made war upon its inhabitants, but it was not until David's day that it became an Israelite city. David made it his capital; Solomon built the temple in it; the ark of God rested there; the Shekinah rested in the Holy of Holies; the whole system of Levitical sacrifices centered in its hallowed areas; and it was called Zion, or Mount Zion. Isaiah called it the Holy City, and the Psalmist proclaimed: "In Judah is God known: his name is great in Israel. In Salem also is his tabernacle, and his dwelling place in Zion." (Ps. 76:1-2.) Jerusalem had become and ever thereafter would remain the center of Israelite and Jewish worship. Truly, as it is written: "The Lord loveth the gates of Zion more than all the dwellings of Jacob. Glorious things are spoken of thee, O city of God. . . . And of Zion it shall be said, This and that man was born in her: and the highest himself shall establish her. The Lord shall count, when he writeth up the people, that this man was born there." (Ps. 87.)

The Jewish Jerusalem of Jesus' Day

Out of all this there arose a general concept and feeling, both in ancient Israel and in Jewish Israel, that the place of worship was almost as important as the very God to whom reverential adoration was given. The chosen people came to feel that the place where the great altar was built, the land whereon the temple stood, and the city wherein these sacred structures were found were as essential to true worship as the very manner and form in which they paid their devotions to the Most High. Jacob's descendants were almost as concerned about where they worshipped as with who received their devotions and how they were extended. Jehovah was the God of Jerusalem; Jerusalem, with its temple, was the focal point of all their religious devotions; it was Jehovah himself who had so decreed; and whenever Israel, either those of old or the Jews of Jesus' day, were in line of their duty, they turned to their capital city for spiritual refreshment.

It was no idle expression when, near Sychar at Jacob's Well, the woman of Samaria, recognizing Jesus as the Jew that he was, said: "Our fathers worshipped in this mountain; and ye say, that in Jerusalem is the place where men ought to worship." Nor was the reply of the Incarnate Jehovah—who once centered the worship of his people in the Holy City, but who would soon fulfill his ancient law and command all men to worship the Father in spirit and in truth in all places—nor was his reply anything short of an endorsement of the existing practice and a prophetic pronouncement as to the future, when he said: "Woman, believe me, the hour cometh, when ye shall neither in this mountain, nor yet at Jerusalem, worship the Father." (John 4:5-25.)

This city where the Jews worshipped in the day of Jesus, and from which holy place true worship was soon to go forth to all cities in all lands, is not an unknown quantity. We know what life was like within its precincts. Our knowledge comes from reliable sources, both secular and profane. Written accounts and archeological unearthings are numerous and authentic. We may not be able to paint as complete and detailed a picture as we can of, say, Korea's Seoul, or Thailand's Bangkok, or Indonesia's Djakarta—all cities that are far removed and socially distinct from our western civilization—but we have no trouble piecing enough together to envision with a certainty that borders on complete knowledge the way people lived in that day, both in Jerusalem and in all Palestine.

We know their way of worship and system of religious rites; their governmental structure and the names and duties of their legislative, executive, and judicial officers; their social structure, including their customs, practices, mores, legends, and folklore. We know their business practices, their commercial customs, their monetary system, the trades they plied, the crops they grew. We know the kind of houses they lived in, the sources of their water, the way they disposed of their garbage and refuse, and the degree of sanitation that prevailed among them. We know about their architectural abilities, their palaces and public buildings, the walls that surrounded their cities, and the gates by which they came and went. We know enough about the roads they built so that we can imagine ourselves traveling on them; enough about their beasts of burden and modes of transportation so that we could duplicate them; enough about their weapons and system of warfare to depict them in paintings and replay them in dramas. We know the diseases with which they were afflicted, the state of their healing arts, their quarantine regulations, the general status of their health, and how they buried their dead. We know what foods they ate, what beverages they drank, how they cooked, the clothes they wore, and the jewelry with which they adorned themselves. We know the language they spoke, the degree of their literary craftsmanship, the educational standards of all classes, and the effect upon them of Greek and Roman and other Gentile cultures. These and a host of related matters all were preserved in the records of the past and have been set forth for us by competent and able historians. They will be considered by us as occasions require.

Blessed Canaan, sacred spot, land of the ancient saints, has as its capital city Jerusalem, the city of Jewish delight; the Holy Land is crowned with the Holy City. Stretched out as a garden of choice land, this Canaan of old, this Palestine of the Hebrews, provided the trade routes between the great nations of antiquity. Toward the south and west lay Egypt and the fertile valley of the Nile; to the north and east lay the rich stretches of Mesopotamia and the Tigris and Euphrates rivers—the Nile pouring its life-giving fluids into the Mediterranean Sea, and the great rivers of Mesopotamia joining hands to feed the Persian Gulf. Palestine was anchored, as it were, to all the wealth of Egypt and her Pharaohs, on the one hand, and to the kingdoms that held sway, from time to time, in Syria, Assyria, and Babylonia, on the other hand. It was to be expected—nay, it was inevitable, greed and conquest being what they are—that the armies of these lands and kingdoms would invade the places where Moses had placed the house of Jacob.

Palestine was truly a land flowing with milk and honey. It had been such in the days of Abraham and Melchizedek; its wealth had been tapped by the Amorites and Hittites and assorted Gentile tribes in the pre-Israelite days; and it was still to be found in abundance when Joshua and Caleb and their fellow spies crossed over Jordan to survey the land. During all of Israel's long history, ten thousand shepherds led their sheep beside still waters in fruitful valleys, while their cattle browsed and fattened on a thousand hills. And it was through these same valleys and over these same hills that the armies of Assyria, of Babylon, and of Egypt ravaged and pillaged from generation to generation as envious Gentiles coveted the wealth and crops of Jehovah's people.

It was a land sanctified by a sacrificial struggle on Mount Moriah; by a bush that burned and was not consumed; by a voice that commanded, "Put off thy shoes from off thy feet, for the place whereon thou standest is holy ground" (Ex. 3:5); by the faith of a widow in Zarepath whose son rose from the dead because she hearkened to the words of a Tishbite prophet. It was a land choice and favored, a promised land, a land selected and saved as a habitation for Israel. And Jerusalem was its crowning jewel.

Jerusalem itself is a mountain city, a city founded amid and upon the Judean hills, a city built upon the mountains. When, in due course, the true saints build the promised temple there, then the scripture will be fulfilled that says that Judah shall "flee unto Jerusalem, unto the mountains of the Lord's house." (D&C 133:13.) It was founded upon land awarded by lot to Benjamin, although adjacent Bethlehem was part of the inheritance of Judah.

Deep ravines on three sides made it easy to defend in olden times. On the east is the valley of Kidron, or valley of Jehoshaphat. Over the brook Kidron are the Garden of Gethsemane, the Mount of Olives, and the road to Bethany and Jericho. There also was the ancient village of Siloam. On the south is the valley of Hinnom, one of the most evil spots in a land that should have been holy.[3] Another ravine, the Tyropoeon Valley, is on the west. Mount Zion is probably the hill just south of the southwest corner of the city wall.[4] And the place of greatest interest within those sacred walls was the Temple of Herod.

In the days of Jesus, the walled portion of the city encompassed some three hundred acres of houses and streets and markets and shops. Perhaps 200,000 to 250,000 Palestinians dwelt within its walls and immediate environs. Tacitus speaks of a population of 600,000; at the time of the Passover this number rose to between 2,000,000 and 3,000,000. Ecclesiastically speaking, persons living outside the walls were counted as inhabitants of the city, and at Passover time great numbers of Jews camped outside the city proper, but within the limits of a Sabbath day's journey. Josephus says that 1,100,000 men perished in Jerusalem when Titus and the legions from Rome wrought vengeance upon the nation that crucified their King. But whatever the actual number of its inhabitants, Jerusalem of the Jews, in Jesus' day, was truly a city of greatness and magnificence.

Among its citizens were artisans of every kind. In its shops and at its bazaars could be purchased goods from every nation. Its palaces, academies, and synagogues were places of renown, and the learned and mighty of all nations could tread its streets with the same satisfaction found in Rome or any of the great metropolises of the day. But in addition to all that was had elsewhere, Jerusalem was the center of such true religion and heaven-approved worship as was then found on earth.

Contrasting its then state with that which prevailed a millennium before, when David and Solomon had first made it an Israelite capital, Edersheim says: "If the dust of ten centuries could have been wiped from the eyelids of those sleepers, and one of them who thronged Jerusalem in the highday of its glory, during the reign of King Solomon, had returned to its streets, he would scarcely have recognized the once familiar city. Then, as now, a Jewish king reigned, who bore undivided rule over the whole land; then, as now, the city was filled with riches and adorned with palaces and architectural monument; then, as now, Jerusalem was crowded with strangers from all lands. Solomon and Herod were each the last Jewish king over the Land of Promise; Solomon and Herod, each, built the Temple. But with the son of David began, and with the Idumean ended, 'the kingdom'; or rather, having fulfilled its mission, it gave place to the spiritual world-kingdom of 'David's greater Son.' The sceptre departed from Judah to where the nations were to gather under its sway. And the Temple which Solomon built was the first. In it the Shekhinah dwelt visibly. The Temple which Herod reared was the last. The ruins of its burning, which the torch of the Romans had kindled, were never to be restored. Herod was not the antitype, he was the Barabbas, of David's Royal Son." (Edersheim 1:111.)

However, our chief concerns are not in the social, governmental, and cultural conditions of Jewish life in the meridian of time, important as these are to an understanding of the Life we are to consider. It is not the palaces and markets, not the kings and soldiers, not the schools and pedagogy that will set the stage for Messiah's ministry. His work will deal with the things of the Spirit. Our chief interest, then, is in the spiritual state of the people, their religious life, their understanding of the Messianic message delivered to them by the ancient prophets, and—above all!—their personal spiritual stature and the degree to which they kept the commandments and were in a condition to receive the guidance of the Holy Spirit.

That they were dull of hearing and slow to perceive the truth was proclaimed by the Lord Jesus as he spoke in irony and in sorrow of the city where he came to reign as King but was rejected by his own. "It cannot be that a prophet perish out of Jerusalem," he said. "O Jerusalem, Jerusalem, which killest the prophets, and stonest them that are sent unto thee; how often would I have gathered thy children together, as a hen doth gather her brood under her wings, and ye would not! Behold, your house is left unto you desolate." (Luke 13:31-35.)

And again: "He beheld the city, and wept over it, Saying, If thou hadst known, even thou, at least in this thy day, the things which belong unto thy peace! but now they are hid from thine eyes. For the days shall come upon thee, that thine enemies shall cast a trench about thee, and compass thee round, and keep thee in on every side, And shall lay thee even with the ground, and thy children within thee; and they shall not leave in thee one stone upon another; because thou knewest not the time of thy visitation." (Luke 19:41-45.)

The depths to which Jerusalem had sunk are seen in the words of the Beloved John, who, identifying it as "the great city, . . . where also our Lord was crucified," said that "spiritually [it] is called Sodom and Egypt." (Rev. 11:8.)

The Jerusalem of the Future

"Jerusalem shall be trodden down of the Gentiles," Jesus said, "until the times of the Gentiles be fulfilled." (Luke 21:24.)[5] Jerusalem—glorious and perfect in the days of Abraham and Melchizedek; Jerusalem—like Enoch's Zion for a time and a season some four thousand years ago; Jerusalem—then lost to our sight for a millennium, and until David took it from the Jebusites; Jerusalem—in Israelite hands for another millennium; Jerusalem—where kings reigned and prophets preached for a thousand Israelite years; Jerusalem —where our Lord ministered, was rejected by his own, and found death upon the cross; Jerusalem—a city of saints and a city of devils: this Jerusalem, Jesus says, "shall be trodden down of the Gentiles!"

And so for two millenniums the Gentiles have held sway in Jehovah's Jerusalem. Completely destroyed by Titus in A.D. 70, it was restored by Hadrian in A.D. 135 and became a Roman colony. He erected a temple to Jupiter Capitolinus on the very site where once the temple to Jehovah had stood. Two centuries later, in 336, wicked Constantine, an evil emperor who made apostasy and false worship reputable, erected a so-called Christian church on the supposed site of the holy sepulchre. Thereafter the sacred soil passed from the hands of apostate Christians into the hands of apostate pagans; it was retaken by the Crusaders in 1099, retaken by "nonbelievers" in 1187, and passed back and forth among various groups of them until 1917, when it was taken by British troops under General Allenby. The modern walls were built in 1542; on the site of Solomon's Temple now stands the Muslim temple known as the Dome of the Rock. Christians, Mohammedans, and Jews now dwell together under a tenuous and oft-interrupted peace, and the Holy City continues to be trodden down of the Gentiles. And, be it noted, even Jews are Gentiles when they believe not the truth.

But it shall not ever be thus. Darkness flees before light.

A new day is dawning. Already, in the language of Isaiah of old, the cry is going forth: "Awake, awake; put on thy strength, O Zion; put on thy beautiful garments, O Jerusalem, the holy city." What does it mean for Zion to put on her strength, and to what people was Isaiah making reference? Joseph Smith answers: "He had reference to those whom God should call in the last days, who should hold the power of priesthood to bring again Zion, and the redemption of Israel; and to put on her strength is to put on the authority of the priesthood, which she, Zion, has a right to by lineage; also to return to that power which she had lost." And when that day comes, again in Isaiah's language, "there shall no more come into [Jerusalem] the uncircumcised and the unclean," for it will be a day of righteousness, a day when men shall be cleansed in the waters of baptism.

Addressing himself further to the city he loved, Isaiah says: "Shake thyself from the dust; arise, and sit down, O Jerusalem: loose thyself from the bands of thy neck, O captive daughter of Zion." Question: "What are we to understand by Zion loosing herself from the bands of her neck?" The Prophet's answer: "We are to understand that the scattered remnants are exhorted to return to the Lord from whence they have fallen; which if they do, the promise of the Lord is that he will speak to them, or give them revelation. . . . The bands of her neck are the curses of God upon her, or the remnants of Israel in their scattered condition among the Gentiles."

As to what shall transpire relative to Israel and Jerusalem in the promised day of restoration, Isaiah says in the Lord's name: "My people shall know my name; therefore they shall know in that day that I am he that doth speak: behold, it is I." Jehovah shall be known again. Revelation shall commence anew. "How beautiful upon the mountains are the feet of him that bringeth good tidings, that publisheth peace; that bringeth good tidings of good, that publisheth salvation; that saith unto Zion, Thy God reigneth! Thy watchmen shall lift up the voice; with the voice together shall they sing: for they shall see eye to eye, when the Lord shall bring again Zion. Break forth into joy, sing together, ye waste places of Jerusalem: for the Lord hath comforted his people, he hath redeemed Jerusalem." (Isa. 52:1-10; D&C 113:7-10.)

In the great day of restoration—a day that has commenced, but in which many things yet remain to be restored—there will finally be two world capitals, both called Zion, both called Jerusalem. One shall be the seat of government, the other the spiritual capital of the world, " for out of Zion shall go forth the law, and the word of the Lord from Jerusalem." (Isa. 2:1-5.) That is to say, Jerusalem of old shall be restored, built up anew in glory and beauty, according to the promises, and also, another Jerusalem, a New Jerusalem, shall be established. Moroni tells us "of the New Jerusalem, which should come down out of heaven," and of "the holy sanctuary of the Lord." He says that Ether wrote both of this New Jerusalem, which should be upon the American continent, and of the restoration of the Jerusalem in the Old World, the one whence Lehi came. "And there shall be a new heaven and a new earth," the account says; "and they shall be like unto the old save the old have passed away, and all things have become new. And then cometh the New Jerusalem; and blessed are they who dwell therein, for it is they whose garments are white through the blood of the Lamb. . . . And then also cometh the Jerusalem of old; and the inhabitants thereof, blessed are they, for they have been washed in the blood of the Lamb; and they are they who were scattered and gathered in from the four quarters of the earth, and from the north countries, and are partakers of the fulfilling of the covenant which God made with their father, Abraham." (Ether 13:1-12; 3 Ne. 20:22; 21:23-24.)

That the New Jerusalem, the latter-day Zion, the Zion to which Enoch and his city shall return, shall be in Jackson County, Missouri, has been set forth plainly in latter-day revelation. (D&C 84:1-4.) Of this millennial Zion, the New Testament apostle says: "And I saw a new heaven and a new earth: for the first heaven and the first earth were passed away; and there was no more sea. And I John saw the holy city, new Jerusalem, coming down from God out of heaven, prepared as a bride adorned for her husband. And I heard a great voice out of heaven saying, Behold, the tabernacle of God is with men, and he will dwell with them, and they shall be his people, and God himself shall be with them, and be their God. And God shall wipe away all tears from their eyes; and there shall be no more death, neither sorrow, nor crying, neither shall there be any more pain: for the former things are passed away." (Rev. 21:1-4.)

To complete our vision of the concept of holy cities, as the New Testament account records, there will also be a day, a celestial day, when this earth becomes a heaven in the full, complete, and eternal sense, when the celestial New Jerusalem shall be with men. It was John, also, who saw this "holy Jerusalem, descending out of heaven from God, Having the glory of God." This is the city having twelve gates and twelve foundations, "and in them the names of the twelve apostles of the Lamb." This is the city with streets of pure gold, "as it were transparent glass." Of it John says: "And I saw no temple therein: for the Lord God Almighty and the Lamb are the temple of it. And the city had no need of the sun, neither of the moon, to shine in it: for the glory of God did lighten it, and the Lamb is the light thereof. And the nations of them which are saved shall walk in the light of it: and the kings of the earth do bring their glory and honour into it. And the gates of it shall not be shut at all by day: for there shall be no night there. And they shall bring the glory and honour of the nations into it. And there shall in no wise enter into it any thing that defileth, neither whatsoever worketh abomination, or maketh a lie: but they which are written in the Lamb's book of life." (Rev. 21:10-27.)

NOTES

1. The Great King is the Lord—the Lord Jehovah, the Lord Jesus.
2. These word usages, which so closely parallel divine terminology where Zion itself is

concerned, are set forth in the article on Jerusalem in *The New Bible Dictionary*, p. 615.

3. The valley of Hinnom was the scene of some of the most horrifying and abominable practices ever to defile Israel. It was here that Solomon built places for the worship of Molech; it was here that infant sacrifices were sponsored by those wicked kings, Ahaz and Manasseh; it was here that Josiah spread human bones and other corruptions; it was here (in Jesus' day) that garbage, dead animals, and human corpses were burned. This valley was both the cesspool of Jerusalem and the place where continuing fires burned the refuse of the city, giving rise to the use of the term *Ge Hinnom* or *Gehenna,* or land of Hinnom, as the symbol for the eternal fires of hell.

4. This same name, Mount Zion—as it is associated with the New Jerusalem—is the place where the Lamb shall stand at his Second coming with 144,000 high priests; it is located in Jackson County, Missouri. (Rev. 14:1; D&C 133:17-25.)

5. The times of the Gentiles is that time or era, that expanse of time or years, during which the gospel goes to the Gentiles on a preferential basis. In Jesus' day the gospel was offered first to his Jewish kinsmen; only later was it preached in Gentile ears. In our day it has been restored to Gentiles, meaning to non-Jewish people—people, however, who are of the house of Israel. It now is being taught on a preferential basis to Gentiles or non-Jewish people, for, as Paul said, "blindness in part is happened to Israel, until the fulness of the Gentiles be come in." (Rom. 11:25.)

The restoration of the gospel foreshadows the end of the Gentile era and the ushering in of the Jewish era. Our revelations say that after the remnant of Jerusalem's Jews have been scattered in all nations, an event that has long since occurred, "they shall be gathered again." They are, however, to remain in their scattered state "until the times of the Gentiles be fulfilled. . . . And when the times of the Gentiles is come in, a light shall break forth among them that sit in darkness, and it shall be the fulness of my gospel. But they [the generality of the scattered Jews] receive it not; for they perceive not the light, and they turn their hearts from me because of the precepts of men. And in that generation shall the times of the Gentiles be fulfilled." (D&C 45:24-29.) That the Jews, a few of them, are now beginning to believe the restored gospel and are returning to their true Messiah is well known. The times of the Gentiles shall soon be fulfilled, and the times of the Jews once again shall come into being.

Chapter 7

JEHOVAH'S HOLY HOUSES

The Lord, whom ye seek, shall
suddenly come to his temple.
(Mal. 3:1.)[1]

The Law of Temple Worship

What is a temple? It is a house of the Lord; a house for
Deity that is built on earth; a house prepared by the saints as
a dwelling place for the Most High, in the most literal sense
of the word; a house where a personal God personally
comes. It is a holy sanctuary, set apart from the world,
wherein the saints of God prepare to meet their Lord; where
the pure in heart shall see God, according to the promises;
where those teachings are given and those ordinances
performed which prepare the saints for that eternal life
which consists of dwelling with the Father and being like
him and his Son. The teachings and ordinances here involved embrace the mysteries of the kingdom and are not
now and never have been heralded to the world, nor can
they be understood except by those who worship the Father
in spirit and in truth, and who have attained that spiritual
stature which enables men to know God and Jesus Christ,
whom he hath sent.

When the Lord comes from heaven to the earth, as he

does more frequently than is supposed, where does he make his visitations? Those whom he visits know the answer; he comes to one of his houses. Whenever the Great Jehovah visits his people, he comes, suddenly as it were, to his temple. If he has occasion to come when he has no house on earth, his visit is made on a mountain, in a grove, in a wilderness area, or at some location apart from the tumults and contentions of carnal men; and in that event the place of his appearance becomes a temporary temple, a site used by him in place of the house his people would normally have prepared.

Why have temples? They are built by the tithing and sacrifice of the Lord's people; they are dedicated and given to him; they become his earthly houses; in them the mysteries of the kingdom are revealed; in them the pure in heart see God; in them men are sealed up unto eternal life— all to the end that man may become as his Maker, and live and reign forever in the heavenly Jerusalem, as part of the general assembly and Church of the Firstborn, where God and Christ are the judge of all. Of temples the Lord says: "Therein are the keys of the holy priesthood ordained, that you may receive honor and glory." In them, he says, his saints shall receive washings, anointings, baptisms, revelations, oracles, conversations, statutes, judgments, endowments, and sealings. In them are held solemn assemblies. In them the fulness of the priesthood is received and the patriarchal order conferred upon men. In them the family unit is made eternal. Because of them life eternal is available. With temples men can be exalted; without them there is no exaltation. (D&C 124:28-40; 131:1-4; 132:1-33.)

When and where have there been temples on earth? We know the answer to this question in principle, but we do not know the specific times and places. Our revelation on temples tells us that the blessings conferred through their use are essential to the "foundation of Zion," that is, to the setting up of congregations of saints who shall be pure in heart; that through their use, "glory, honor, and endowment" shall be conferred upon all the inhabitants of Zion; and that these blessings are to come only "by the ordinance of my holy house, which my people are *always* commanded to build unto my holy name." (D&C 124:39. Italics added.) That is to say, whenever the Lord has had a people on earth, from the days of Adam to the present moment, he has always commanded them to build temples so that they could be taught how to gain eternal life, and so that all of the ordinances of salvation and exaltation could be performed for and on their behalf.

Temples constructed before the flood of Noah were obviously destroyed in that great deluge; those built by the Jaredites and Nephites are buried in the jungles and lost in the wildernesses of the Americas; apostate versions of true temples are being uncovered by archeologists in many places, including perhaps the pyramids of Egypt and the Americas; but such slivers of truth about ancient temples as the world now has are found in the accounts relative to Israel's tabernacle and the subsequent houses of the Lord built in Jerusalem. It is of them we shall now speak more particularly.

Temples in Ancient Israel

One of the first things Israel did when freed from Egyptian bondage was to set up a tent or tabernacle as a house or place where Moses and Aaron and the elders of the people could commune with Jehovah. This tabernacle—in reality a portable temple—became more elaborate as rapidly as the seed of Jacob gained the means and had the time to perfect its construction. Detailed directions came to Moses by revelation as to the materials to be used, the ornamentation for its curtains and parts, and the manner and form of worship attending its use.

The tabernacle complex consisted of a large rectangular court in the western part of which stood a small building or tabernacle. In the eastern part of the court were an altar for the offering of sacrifices and a laver for priestly washings. All Israel had access to the court wherein these burnt offerings were made. The tabernacle proper was divided into two parts, the holy place and the most holy place, or Holy of Holies; and the Holy of Holies was separated from the holy place by the veil of the temple. A curtain or screen also hung at the entrance to the holy place. The tabernacle proper was made of delicate tapestries decorated with cherubim and spread on wooden frames covered with gold. In the holy place there was the altar of incense, the golden candlestick, and the table of shewbread. In the Holy of Holies was placed the ark of the covenant with its mercy seat and with the two golden-winged cherubim at the sides.

All that was part of, or placed in, or performed in the tabernacle was symbolical of Christ and his atoning sacrifice. The sacrifices on the great altar in the court were performed in similitude of the coming sacrifice of the Lamb of God, and each detailed step in their performance bore record in one way or another of something concerning the infinite sacrifice of Israel's Promised Messiah. Light from the seven candles on the golden candlestick shone forth as a reminder of him who is the Light of the world; clouds of odors rising from the altar of incense were as the prayers of the saints before the throne of God ("golden vials full of odours, which are the prayers of the saints," John says in Rev. 5:8); and the shewbread, the bread on display, the bread of the Presence, bore record that there in the temple was found the Presence of God. These loaves of bread, twelve in number, one for each of the tribes of Israel, spread out on "the table of the bread of the Presence," were both an acknowledgment that Jehovah gave life and nourishment to Israel and a witness that Israel was grateful for the goodness of their God to them.

But it was in the Holy of Holies that the most perfect symbolism was found. There was placed the ark of the covenant, a chest of acacia wood in which rested the stone tablets on which were written the Ten Commandments. The presence of these sacred stones, the commandments having been written by the finger of God, was a constant reminder to Israel of their covenant to worship and serve him who had delivered them from bondage, and that they should have no God before him. On top of the ark rested the mercy seat, a cover of pure gold, symbolizing to the mind that because of the atonement yet to be wrought, repentant souls would find mercy before the eternal throne. The mercy seat, serving as it were as the throne of God, was a symbol of his forgiveness and of his goodness and grace in providing mercy through his atonement. Once each year, on the Day of Atonement, the high priest entered the Holy of Holies, thus testifying anew to all the people that mercy might be theirs through the great propitiatory sacrifice that was to be. And the two cherubim—overshadowing the mercy seat with their wings—bore record that the ark itself was the very throne of God set up among his people and that Jehovah did in fact dwell in his house and was among them.

Once the tabernacle was prepared according to the divine plan; once this sacred sanctuary was set up as a house of the Lord; once a holy temple was again available in Israel—then Jehovah honored his word and used the sacred building and the holy place and the Holy of Holies as his own earthly house. To this place he came down to commune with Moses and give commandments to his people. When Moses, for instance, complained, saying, "I am not able to bear all this people alone, because it is too heavy for me," the Lord replied: "Gather unto me seventy men of the elders of Israel, whom thou knowest to be the elders of the people, and officers over them; and bring them unto the tabernacle of the congregation, that they may stand there with thee. And I will come down and talk with thee there: and I will take of the spirit which is upon thee, and will put it upon them; and they shall bear the burden of the people with thee, that thou bear it not thyself alone." As was his wont, Moses hearkened to the voice of his Lord. He "went out, and told the people the words of the Lord, and gathered the seventy men of the elders of the people, and set them round about the tabernacle. And the Lord came down in a cloud, and spake unto him, and took of the spirit that was upon him, and gave it unto the seventy elders: and it came to pass, that, when the spirit rested upon them, they prophesied, and did not cease." (Num. 11.)[2]

Truly, in that day, the Shekinah rested in the Holy of Holies, and God was with his people.

As far as we know, all temples in Israel from Moses to Solomon were of the portable-tabernacle type. But after David had secured and established the temporal kingdom, with all the power and prestige of an oriental court, he collected the materials so that his son Solomon could build a house to Jehovah. That house—Solomon's Temple—patterned after the tabernacle of the congregation and used for the same purposes, was one of the earth's then most magnificent and costly buildings. The courtyard contained the sacrificial altar, thirty feet square and fifteen feet high, and the molten sea, a bronze basin, fifteen feet in diameter and seven and a half feet in height, resting on the backs of twelve oxen, one for each tribe, as is the case also in all modern temples. That this sea was a baptismal font for the living is perfectly clear, even as its modern counterparts are fonts or seas wherein baptisms are performed for the dead.[3] The holy place and the Holy of Holies contained the same items that once were found in the same sacred places in the tabernacle, except that Solomon's Temple had ten golden candlesticks rather than the one in the Temple of Moses. The Urim and Thummim was kept in the Holy of Holies in Solomon's Temple, which may also have been the case in the older and less ornate building after which it was patterned. And, of course, the divine presence, the Shekinah, yet rested where it had of old, insomuch that "fire came down from heaven, and consumed the burnt offering and the sacrifices; and the glory of the Lord filled the house," and the Lord appeared to Solomon in a dream. (2 Chron. 7.)

Solomon's Temple was destroyed by the Babylonians

under Nebuchadnezzar, shortly after Lehi left Jerusalem. It was rebuilt some seventy years later by Zerubbabel and was dedicated in 516 B.C. However, there never again was that same rich and plenteous outpouring of Divine grace that once had set Israel apart from all peoples. Zerubbabel's Temple did not contain the ark of the covenant and the tablets of the Decalogue; the mercy seat was no more; and the cherubim no longer bore visible testimony that the throne of God was in the midst of his people. All these things had been lost; and the Urim and Thummim, the ultimate symbol of divine grace—for by it revelations came—had been taken away. The spirit of prophecy, the fire from heaven, the cloud surrounding the Divine Presence were seldom seen in those and later days.

Ordinances of the House of the Lord

We do not have a complete knowledge of what ordinances were performed in ancient temples, and if we did it would not be our privilege to delineate the doings of our brethren of old with any degree of particularity. Nor, for that matter, can we set forth the things that transpire in modern temples. Ordinances performed in the Lord's sanctuaries, though not secret, are of such a sacred nature as to be reserved for the eyes and ears and hearts of those only whose attained spiritual maturity prepares them to receive the mysteries of the kingdom. Temple ordinances, whether ancient or modern, are not published to the world; their sacred nature witnesses that they should not be bandied about by brutish persons; that which is spiritual and sacred must not be held up to mockery, or be made the object of raillery by carnal men.

We can, however, speak in general terms of what is done in temples; we can name the ordinances and tell their purpose and intent; and we can quote from the scriptures such passages as speak in guarded and reserved terms of those things which are reserved for the faithful only. And based on what has been revealed and is preserved to us and on what we know about the purpose and use of latter-day temples, we can reach some reasonable conclusions as to what was involved in their ancient usage.

We know that Mosaic temples were used for the offering of sacrifices and various related performances of the law of carnal commandments. It is clear that the molten sea was for baptisms and that the laver was for ritualistic washings. In commanding his saints of latter days to build him a house, the Lord asked: "How shall your washings be acceptable unto me, except ye perform them in a house which ye have built to my name?" Then he said: "For, for this cause [that Israel's washings might be acceptable] I commanded Moses that he should build a tabernacle, that they should bear it with them in the wilderness, and [for the same reason] to build a house in the land of promise." Then the Lord speaks of anointings, endowments, and other temple ordinances— all in a context that shows that what we now have is patterned after the rites and ceremonies of our ancestors. (D&C 124:37-41.)

Isaiah's call to ancient Israel—"Wash you, make you clean; put away the evil of your doings from before mine eyes; cease to do evil; Learn to do well"—was an invitation to partake of and implement the cleansing ordinances of the temple. (Isa. 1:16-17.) The Lord's promise to gathered Israel in the latter days—"Then will I sprinkle clean water upon you, and ye shall be clean: from all your filthiness, and from all your idols, will I cleanse you"—has reference to the same things as do the words of revelation that say: "Cleanse your hands and your feet before me, that I may make you clean; That I may testify unto your Father, and your God, and my God, that you are clean from the blood of this wicked generation." (Ezek. 36:25; D&C 88:74-75.)

Joseph Smith tells us that "all things" pertaining to our dispensation "should be conducted precisely in accordance with the preceding dispensations," and that the Lord "set the ordinances to be the same forever and ever." He says the same ordinances are revealed anew in one dispensation after another. (*Teachings,* p. 168.) We know that celestial marriage is the crowning ordinance of the house of the Lord today and assume it must have been so also in days gone by. For instance, "David's wives and concubines were given unto him of me, by the hand of Nathan, my servant, and others of the prophets who had the keys of this power," the Lord says. (D&C 132:39.) This same thing would have been true relative to the marriage discipline among all the faithful of Israel. We cannot, therefore, escape the conclusion that then, as now, temples were the places where those higher ordinances were performed which lead to glory and honor everlasting.

Herod's Temple

This is the temple Jesus knew. It is the one in which Gabriel and Zacharias conversed relative to him who should prepare the way before the Lord. It is the one in which Jesus was taken as an infant. Here at the age of twelve he confounded the wise men. From it he drove the moneychangers, and in its courts his voice was raised day after day as he acclaimed in word and by deed his own divine Sonship. It was of this house that he spoke when he said that not one stone should be left upon another. It was an integral part of his life and played a major role in his death. False witnesses swore he had said he would destroy the temple and raise it again in three days. It was the seat of the Great Sanhedrin that condemned him to death, and its veil, separating the holy place from the Holy of Holies, was the one rent from top to bottom when he voluntarily gave up the ghost and went to preach to the spirits in prison. And to it, after his demise, Peter and John resorted when they commanded the man, lame from his mother's womb, to rise up and walk; and when he found he could do so, he leaped for joy, praising God.

This temple—the last divinely approved sanctuary of the

Jewish dispensation—was refurbished by Herod the Great commencing in 20 B.C. It had been built in the days of Ezra, and was defiled and cleansed again in the days of the Maccabees, and was raised to new heights of grandeur. Its construction was still going forward when Jesus blessed its courts with his presence, and it was not completed in every respect until A.D. 64, just six years before its destruction. Built on a larger and grander scale than anything of the past, as far as the building itself was concerned, it yet never gained a fraction of the spiritual preeminence of its predecessors. The Shekinah—the visible manifestation of the presence of the Lord—never filled its Holy of Holies and the divine cloud never overshadowed its courts. Angels did minister before its altars, visions were seen by some of its priests, and the spirit of prophecy rested upon some who worshipped within its portals. But the great divine outpouring of grace and goodness and miracles that so filled the houses of Moses and Solomon, and to a lesser extent that of Zerubbabel, were absent. Jesus himself foretold its destruction, and his words were made a living reality by the flames and venom of Rome in A.D. 70—thus ending Jewish sacrifices and their form of temple worship forever.

Herod's Temple[4]—built by as evil and corrupt a tyrant as ever wore a crown—was an enlargement and a perfection of those houses of the Lord after which it was patterned. Solomon's Temple, though magnificent and costly, was small in comparison; and the Temple of Zerubbabel, larger but less elaborate than that of Solomon, was far from the magnificent masterpiece built by the Jewish Idumean who bore the title "king of the Jews." In its construction, which had gone on for forty-six years by the time of Jesus' ministry, a thousand vehicles transported the stone, a thousand priests supervised the work, and ten thousand skilled laborers wrought wonders with the costly materials. Built of marble and gold, the house of worship itself probably surpassed any of the architectural marvels of that or any day. Certainly Rome and Greece and Egypt had nothing to compare with

107

it. And a Jewish proverb kept alive their tradition: "He that has not seen the Temple of Herod, has never known what beauty is."

To all of this there attaches a certain fitness of things as well as a touch of irony. This was the temple where the Son of God ministered—and what is more fitting than for temple building to reach its pinnacle in the day when his voice was heard within its walls? But this was also a temple built by an evil ruler—a Jew, yes, but an Idumean Jew, one who was half Idumean and half Samaritan, one whose lineage was impure, one who was apparently a descendant of Edom who is Esau—whose interest was not to serve Jehovah and see true rites performed, but to court popularity with the people and to satisfy an almost lustful desire to build monuments of splendor and renown. And yet, perhaps, there is even a certain fitness about this, for the very temple that he built in wickedness and that was turned into a den of thieves by those who used it was in its final destruction, when not one stone was left upon another, left to serve as a symbol of the destruction of all the evils of those who crucified their Lord.

Temples, of course, whether made by righteous or evil hands, do not of themselves establish the truth or falsity of the religious systems under which they flourish. The Parthenon—the chief temple of Athena on the Acropolis at Athens, where her gold and ivory statue sat anciently—was also one of the architectural marvels of the ages. But it was the very building of which Paul spoke, having reference to the pagan idol housed therein, when on Mars' Hill he said: "God that made the world and all things therein, seeing that he is Lord of heaven and earth, dwelleth not in temples made with hands; Neither is worshipped with men's hands, as though he needed any thing, seeing he giveth to all life, and breath, and all things." (Acts 17:22-31.) Temples as such do not prove the divinity of a system of religion, but without them there is no true order of worship. When built among those who have the priesthood and who enjoy the spirit of revelation, they are in fact the Lord's houses, and when such peoples are true and faithful—and such was not the case among the Jews of Jesus' day—the Divine Presence rests upon and the Person of the Lord is seen within these holy houses.

Herod's Temple was a true temple. It bore the stamp of divine approval, and true ordinances, performed by legal administrators who had been called of God as was Aaron, were performed in its courts, on its altars, and in the Holy of Holics itself. The priests who ministered in this house of the Lord held the Aaronic or Levitical Priesthood, and on occasional instances, as when Gabriel visited Zacharias, they saw within the veil. The problem of worship among the Jews was not the lack of a temple; it was not that they had departed from the true ordinances; it was not that baptism and sacrifices were unknown among them. They had the form and knew the manner in which they should worship. Their problem was one of substance: they had the form of godliness, but they denied the power thereof; they were wading through ritualistic performances whose true meanings they no longer comprehended. That faith, hope, charity, and love which prepares men for the acceptance of revealed truth no longer was found in sufficient measure to enable them to see in Jesus their true Messiah, in spite of the fact that all the ordinances of Herod's Temple bore record of this Man from Galilee.

But the temple itself, the foundations, walls, and courts, the altars, fires, and veils—all these were as they should be. The ark of the covenant with its mercy seat, the stone tablets whereon the Decalogue was written, the Urim and Thummim, and the cherubim overshadowing the throne of God, as it were—all these were absent. But so had they been in the divinely approved Temple of Zerubbabel. If there was a brazen sea, or its equivalent, for baptisms, we do not know it. Probably there was not, as witness the need for the son of Zacharias to baptize in Jordan near Bethabara. Yet the sacrificial ordinances could and did go forward, as properly they should have done; the holy incense still ascended to the

Lord; and the holy lights still shone forth from the candles in the holy place.

Drawings of the temple, based on recorded accounts and archeological unearthings, agree in general as to the arrangements of the walls, gates, porches, courts, and altars. However, all independent researchers have come up with differing views on many points, and all are faced with problems they cannot solve. No doubt this is as it should be, and there is no reason to suppose that the things of God—the washings, anointings, endowments, sealings, marriages, "conversations," and the like, which our revelations tell us were performed in the temples of old—shall ever be discovered by the wisdom of men.

According to the best data available, the wall surrounding the temple grounds—and the wall and everything therein, in the full sense of the word, is accounted to be the temple—was 5,085 feet long, just 195 feet short of a full mile. Some stones in these walls measured from 20 to 40 feet in length and weighed more than a hundred tons each. Within the nearly and approximately rectangular space so enclosed, scores and hundreds of thousands of worshippers at a time could easily and conveniently assemble. The number 210,000 is given as the attendance figure for those assembling to worship in the great court at one time. The four principal gates to the temple area were in the west wall, where the Tyropoeon Valley lies. There was also one gate on the north, and another on the east, where the Kidron Valley runs, and there were two on the south.

Just inside the four walls were porches, that is, cloisters or halls. Over this porch area was a flat roof, supported by three rows of Corinthian pillars, each pillar being cut from a single block of marble, and each being $37\frac{1}{2}$ feet high. The Royal Porch on the south was supported by 160 pillars arranged in four rows of 40 pillars each. Solomon's Porch was on the east. In all of the porches it was the custom for the people to meet and have gospel discussions, and there may even have been benches or seats in them. In one of them the young Jesus, when but twelve years of age, was found by Joseph and Mary disputing with the doctors and wise men; in all of them our Lord taught his doctrine from time to time; and Solomon's Porch is singled out by name as the place, during the Feast of Dedication, where he affirmed in plainness the doctrine of the divine Sonship, saying, "I and my Father are one." (John 10:30.) It was in these sacred porches—cloisters or halls, if you will—where the early saints met, "continuing daily with one accord in the temple, . . . Praising God," and seeking to learn and do his will. (Acts 2:46-47.) The porches themselves, architecturally speaking, were among the finest features of the temple, and spiritually speaking, were the centers—for the true significance of the sacrificial ordinances was in large part lost—where most of the temple-truth came forth that was taught in Jesus' day.

Within the walls and their porches was the court of the Gentiles, an area, paved with marble, to which all people were welcome, both Jew and Gentile. Proper reverence and decorum were expected of all, and there were signs, in Greek and Latin, warning Gentiles not to enter the temple building itself on pain of death. It was in this public court that oxen, sheep, and doves were sold for sacrificial purposes, and from it our Lord, in anger, drove those who he said had turned his Father's house into a den of thieves.

As to the temple building proper, it contained the court of women with its chests for charitable contributions, in which place Jesus probably made his comments about the widow's mite. It contained the court of Israel and of the priests, in which stood the great altar of unhewn stones, which was 48 feet square at the bottom and 36 feet at the top, and which rose 15 feet in height. In the temple also was the holy place, containing the table of the shewbread, the golden candlestick, and the altar of incense. And finally, with a veil separating it from the holy place, in it stood the Holy of Holies, a sanctuary 30 feet square, a sanctuary now empty except for a large stone—occupying the place where

111

the ark, the mercy seat, and the cherubim should have been—and on which stone the high priest sprinkled the blood each year on the Day of Atonement. In overall dimensions the temple proper, including the steps and a "porch" on each side, was 150 feet square. Its foundations rested on immense blocks of white marble covered with gold, each block being, according to Josephus, $67\frac{1}{2}$ by 9 feet. The abbreviated recitations here given, though sufficient for our purposes, cannot begin to set forth the grandeur and magnificence and the architectural perfections of this holy house, a house that was truly one of the greatest buildings of any age and that also was truly a house of the Lord.

It is one thing to have a temple building of grandeur and architectural perfection, one built of all the costly materials that the wealth of kingdoms can produce, and quite another to have one in which the Spirit of God dwells in full measure. Though both may be houses of and for the Almighty, one far exceeds the other in eternal worth and glory as Edersheim so aptly says: "To the devout and earnest Jew the second Temple must, 'in comparison of' 'the house in her first glory,' have indeed appeared 'as nothing.' True, in architectural splendour the second, as restored by Herod, far surpassed the first Temple. But, unless faith had recognized in Jesus of Nazareth 'the Desire of all nations,' who should 'fill this house with glory,' it would have been difficult to draw other than sad comparisons. Confessedly, the real elements of Temple-glory no longer existed. The Holy of Holies was quite empty, the ark of the covenant, with the cherubim, the tables of the law, the book of the covenant, Aaron's rod that budded, and the pot of manna, were no longer in the sanctuary. The fire that had descended from heaven upon the altar was extinct. What was far more solemn, the visible presence of God in the Shechinah was wanting. Nor could the will of God be now ascertained through the Urim and Thummim, nor even the high-priest be anointed with the holy oil, its very composition being unknown." (*Temple*, pp. 61-62.) And thus is it ever when the Lord's people fail to walk faithfully in the light they have received. Though they continue to enjoy all their lessened spiritual capacity permits, that which once was theirs and which might still rest in power upon them is withheld.

For fifteen hundred years—while wandering in the wilderness near the borders of their promised land; while walking in the course set by their inspired judges; while wearing the yoke forged upon them by their despotic kings; while faced with Assyrian overlordship or led captive into Babylon; while freed from bondage and returned to Jerusalem's hills; while faced with the tyranny of Antiochus Epiphanes, or suffering through the era of the Maccabees; while plundered by Rome or ruled by Antipater, the Idumean, and all the Herods that sprang from him; and even while the very Son of God ministered among them— for all those long years the temple was the center of Jewish religion.

To the temple every devout person turned for spiritual refreshment, and from it streams of living water flowed. To it the hosts of Israel came to celebrate their great religious feasts. In its courts sacrifices were made, sins were forgiven, and souls were sanctified. Within its porches the truths of salvation were taught; and within its walls the faithful assembled to renew their covenants and offer their vows and sacraments to the Most High. On its altars legal administrators burned the offerings that were slain in similitude of the sacrifice of the Son of God. Behind its veil and in its Holy of Holies, once each year, the high priest made atonement for the sins of the people, and on occasion fire descended from heaven to consume the offerings on its altars, and the Divine Presence, the Shekinah, dwelt visibly between the cherubim. There is no way of overstating or overdramatizing the place and power of the temple in the lives of the Jewish people.

"Wherever a Roman, a Greek, or an Asiatic might wander, he could take his gods with him, or find rites kindred to his own. It was far otherwise with the Jew. He had only one Temple, that in Jerusalem; only one God, Him who had once throned there between the Cherubim, and Who was still King over Zion. That Temple was the only place where a God-appointed, pure priesthood could offer acceptable sacrifices, whether for forgiveness of sin, or for fellowship with God. Here, in the impenetrable gloom of the innermost sanctuary, which the High-Priest alone might enter once a year for most solemn expiation, had stood the Ark, the leader of the people into the Land of Promise, and the footstool on which the Shechinah had rested. From that golden altar rose the sweet cloud of incense, symbol of Israel's accepted prayers; that seven-branched candlestick shed its perpetual light, indicative of the brightness of God's Covenant Presence; on that table, as it were before the face of Jehovah, was laid, week by week, 'the Bread of the Face,' a constant sacrificial meal which Israel offered unto God, and wherewith God in turn fed His chosen priesthood. On the great blood-sprinkled altar of sacrifice smoked the daily and festive burnt-offerings, brought by all Israel, and for all Israel, wherever scattered; while the vast courts of the Temple were thronged not only by native Palestinians, but literally by 'Jews out of every nation under heaven.' Around this Temple gathered the sacred memories of the past; to it clung the yet brighter hopes of the future. The history of Israel and all their prospects were intertwined with their religion; so that it may be said that without their religion they had no history, and without their history no religion. Thus, history, patriotism, religion, and hope alike pointed to Jerusalem and the Temple as the centre of Israel's unity." (Edersheim 1:3-4.)

But all this was soon to end. True sacrificial ordinances could be performed only in similitude of the Eternal Sacrifice which was to be. When the Lamb of God—the Eternal Paschal Lamb—permitted himself to be sacrificed for the sins of the world, the need for sacrificial similitudes pointing to and pre-figuring his atoning sacrifice were no longer needed. And when the need for sacrifices ceased, the need for sacrificial altars and sacrificial sites ceased also. All the temples of all the ages up to then had been constructed as sanctuaries in which burnt offerings should be made. They were the true centers of worship for the ancient saints, but their purposes were now accomplished and their usefulness as sacrificial sanctuaries was at an end. The temples of the future, the houses of the Lord which were yet to be, the holy sanctuaries to which the saints of the future would turn, these would be constructed according to the needs of the new dispensation.

And so it was that Herod's Temple died—not in peace and serenity surrounded by children and loved ones; not with the calmness and assurance that attends the passing of the faithful; not with the hope of a better life that lives in the hearts of the saints—but Herod's Temple died in agony; died of internal corruption and pain; died with a sword at its throat and while ravaged by wild beasts; died with the burning conscience that foresees the sulfurous fires of gehenna; died in terror under the hand of Titus. And it was even denied a decent burial: in its expiring agonies its sanctuaries were looted, its gold and treasures became the booty of war, and, according to the promises, not one stone was left upon another. If a stele of stone had been placed on the once sacred ground—the ground where the struggle for life brought only death—it would have borne some such inscription as this: "Slain in A.D. 70—Along with 1,100,000 of the men of Israel, whose worship center it was—By Roman Gentiles—As befits a heavenly house that had been desecrated and turned into a den of thieves by those in whose custody it had been placed."

Jewish Temples of the Future

The Jewish Temple—named for hated Herod, an Idumean Jew, one of the most dissolute and evil rulers ever to work iniquity among the chosen people—was utterly destroyed, as well it should have been, in that day when

115

Jerusalem began to be trodden down of the Gentiles. But when the fulness of the Gentiles is come in, and the Jews once again believe in the true Messiah and worship the Father in his name, there will once again be a temple in Jerusalem—a temple named for their beloved Lord, Jesus of Nazareth, a Galilean Jew, the only perfect Man of all the chosen race.

Herod's Temple became dust because the Jewish nation, whose house of worship it was, rejected their Messiah and chose to walk in their own wayward course. A house of the Lord—the Lord Jesus Christ, the Messiah of the Jews—shall rise again in Jerusalem, perhaps on the very site where the ancient holy house stood, because the remnants of Judah shall accept their King, believe his gospel, and walk in his paths. A holy temple, the house of the Lord—a sacred sanctuary with its Holy of Holies where the Divine Presence, the Shekinah of old, shall once more be manifest to Israel— shall be built in Old Jerusalem. It shall be built by the Jews: Jews who believe in Christ; Jews who are converted to the truth; Jews who are members of The Church of Jesus Christ of Latter-day Saints; Jews who hold again the powers and priesthoods possessed by their ancestors. The keys and powers whereby temples are built vest in the President of the Church, the presiding high priest among the Lord's latter-day people. These keys, first conferred by angelic minis-trants—Moses, Elijah, Elias, and others—upon Joseph Smith and Oliver Cowdery, have come down in direct suc-cession and rest upon and are exercised by the prophet of God on earth, the one who, as it were, wears the mantle of Joseph Smith. And so it is that the Jews shall build their temple, and the Jews who do it will be Mormons; they will be Jews who are the converted and baptized saints of the lat-ter days.

In a discourse on the Second Coming of Christ, given April 6, 1843, the Prophet Joseph Smith said: "Judah must return, Jerusalem must be rebuilt, and the temple, and water come out from under the temple, and the waters of the Dead

Sea be healed. It will take some time to rebuild the walls of the city and the temple, &c.; and all this must be done before the Son of Man will make His appearance." (*Teachings,* p. 286.) In a revelation to Joseph Smith, given November 3, 1831, the Lord said: "Let them . . . who are among the Gentiles flee unto Zion," which was then being established in America. "And let them who be of Judah flee unto Jerusalem, unto the mountains of the Lord's house." (D&C 133:12-13.) That is to say, let the Jews gather in their own Jerusalem, a city built upon four hills or mountains, a city in whose mountains they shall build the house of the Lord in due course.[5]

These modern prophetic words, about the return of Judah and the building of a temple in Jerusalem, make allusion to other ancient prophetic words that set forth with great clarity that the Jews shall yet build such a house in Old Jerusalem. We shall now note what three of the prophets of Judah—Malachi, Zechariah, and Ezekiel—have said in this respect.

Malachi, in speaking of the Second Coming of the Messiah, asks: "Who may abide the day of his coming? and who shall stand when he appeareth?" Of that glorious day this ancient prophet then says of the Lord: "He shall sit as a refiner and purifier of silver: and he shall purify the sons of Levi, and purge them as gold and silver, that they may offer unto the Lord an offering in righteousness. Then shall the offering of Judah and Jerusalem be pleasant unto the Lord, as in the days of old, and as in former years." (Mal. 3:1-6.) Shall the sons of Levi, those ancient Levitical ministers, offer sacrifices again, at the Second Coming, "as in the days of old, and as in former years"? We shall speak more particularly of this in the next chapter as we analyze the Mosaic system of sacrifices that was to operate in the day of Jesus. For our present purposes we need only observe that when John the Baptist conferred the Aaronic Priesthood again upon mortals, he alluded to these very words of Malachi by saying that this newly restored Aaronic order "shall never be taken again from the earth, until the sons of Levi do offer again an offering unto the Lord in righteousness." (D&C 13:1.)

Zechariah, also speaking of our Lord's return in power and great glory—"the Lord my God shall come, and all the saints with thee"—said: "And it shall be in that day, that living waters shall go out from Jerusalem; half of them toward the former [eastern] sea, and half of them toward the hinder [western] sea: in summer and in winter shall it be. And the Lord shall be king over all the earth: in that day shall there be one Lord, and his name one." This is the millennial day when the Lord reigns personally upon the earth, and when, as the Prophet said, "water" shall "come out from under the temple." Zechariah continues: "And it shall come to pass, that every one that is left of all the nations which came against Jerusalem [most of the people will have been destroyed in the wars and desolations incident to the Second Coming] shall even go up from year to year to worship the King, the Lord of hosts, and to keep the feast of tabernacles," which feast, anciently, was centered in and around the temple and its ceremonies. Also, Zechariah says—and here we have mention both of the temple and of sacrifices— "In that day shall there be upon the bells of the horses, HOLINESS UNTO THE LORD; and the pots in the Lord's house [the temple] shall be like the bowls before the altar. Yea, every pot in Jerusalem and in Judah [he is speaking of Old Jerusalem and the land of Judah, not the American New Jerusalem] shall be holiness unto the Lord of hosts: and all they that sacrifice [are not these the sons of Levi?] shall come and take of them, and seethe therein: and in that day there shall be no more the Canaanite in the house of the Lord of hosts." (Zech. 14.) With reference to this last restriction as to who may enter the house of the Lord, it should be remembered that anciently anyone was free to enter the court of the Gentiles, a permission that will be revoked in that millennial day when all are converted to the truth.

Ezekiel has much more to say about Judah's latter-day

house than either of his fellow prophets, or perhaps than all of Israel's other prophets combined. Twelve of the forty-eight chapters in the book of Ezekiel deal with the general subject here involved. In chapter 37 is the glorious vision of the resurrection in which Israel's dry bones come out of their graves; breath enters each person; sinews and flesh and skin take on a newness of life; the whole house of Israel lives again; they arise, stand upon their feet, and march as a very great army; and then—in resurrected glory—they inherit the land promised to Abraham and his seed forever. Associated with this is the coming forth of the Stick of Joseph—the Book of Mormon—in the hands of latter-day Ephraim, to join with the Stick of Judah—the Bible—the two volumes of holy scripture being destined to take the message of salvation to all Israel.

Then, as Ezekiel records, the Lord says: "Behold, I will take the children of Israel from among the heathen, whither they be gone, and will gather them on every side, and bring them into their own land." They shall return to their ancient Palestine, the very land where the feet of their fathers were planted.

"And I will make them one nation in the land upon the mountains of Israel; and one king shall be king to them all: and they shall be no more two nations, neither shall they be divided into two kingdoms any more at all." Rehoboam shall not reign in Judah and Jeroboam in Ephraim. They shall have one King, the Lord of hosts, who reigns personally upon the earth; the day of the divided kingdom, of two nations of the chosen people, shall cease. Israel shall be one.

"Neither shall they defile themselves any more with their idols, nor with their detestable things, nor with any of their transgressions: but I will save them out of all their dwellingplaces, wherein they have sinned, and will cleanse them: so shall they be my people, and I will be their God." At long last, after worshipping false gods, the gods of the creeds; after following the evil and detestable practices of carnal

119

men; after being in an apostate and degenerate state for centuries—their ancient Lord will save them. They will be cleansed by baptism; once again they will be the Lord's people, and he will be their God.

"And David my servant shall be king over them; and they all shall have one shepherd: they shall also walk in my judgments, and observe my statutes, and do them. And they shall dwell in the land that I have given unto Jacob my servant, wherein your fathers have dwelt; and they shall dwell therein, even they, and their children, and their children's children for ever: and my servant David shall be their prince for ever." What shall happen to Israel, both Judah and Ephraim? They shall be one nation and have one King, even David, who is Christ, and he shall reign over them forever. He is the one Lord and the one Shepherd over all the earth. They shall walk in his statues and in his judgments; they shall keep his commandments and live his gospel precepts. And where shall they dwell? In the land given unto Jacob, old Canaan, the Jewish Palestine, the Holy Land where also our Lord lived during mortality. And how long shall they abide there? They and their children, and their children's children, shall dwell there forever. The meek shall inherit the earth. This is not to say that there are not other lands of promise, and that the American land of Joseph shall not become the inheritance of Nephites and that portion of latter-day Israel, in the main, which is now in the restored kingdom; but it is to say that the Israel of Ezekiel's day, which was Jewish, shall dwell in the land of old Jerusalem, where their temple will be built.

"Moreover I will make a covenant of peace with them; it shall be an everlasting covenant with them: and I will place them, and multiply them, and will set my sanctuary in the midst of them for evermore. My tabernacle also shall be with them: yea, I will be their God, and they shall be my people. And the heathen shall know that I the Lord do sanctify Israel, when my sanctuary shall be in the midst of them for evermore." The covenant of peace, the everlasting covenant, is the gospel—the gospel of the Lord Jesus Christ, the gospel restored through Joseph Smith and his associates. It contains that plan of salvation which requires the building of temples so that all the ordinances of salvation and exaltation may be performed for the living and the dead. In the very nature of things the Lord's sanctuary, his temple, will stand in the midst of his congregations; otherwise they would not be his people. We have, then, an express prophecy of the building of the Lord's sanctuary, not alone in Jackson County where the New Jerusalem will be built, but in Old Jerusalem, in the land of Judah, among and for the people who descended from those who worshipped there in Solomon's Temple, in Zerubbabel's Temple, and in Herod's Temple.

Having laid this foundation relative to the conversion and glory of latter-day Israel, with particular emphasis upon the Jewish portion of that people, Ezekiel, in chapters 38 and 39, tells of the wars and desolations incident to the Second Coming. Then in chapters 40 through 48 he devotes himself to the details, and they are most specific, of what has come to be called Ezekiel's Temple. Worldly scholars, not knowing the purposes of the Lord where his people are concerned; not understanding the doctrine of the gathering of Israel in the last days; not being aware that the gospel was to be restored in the latter days; not knowing that temples are essential to the salvation of men no matter what age they live in—worldly scholars have assumed that Ezekiel's Temple was not and will not be built. The truth is that its construction lies ahead. No doubt some of the recitations relative to it are figurative, though it is clear that some sacrificial ordinances are yet to be performed.

It is clear that Ezekiel's Temple, to be built by the Jews in Jerusalem, is destined for millennial use. In chapter 43, for instance, the Lord calls it, specifically, "the place of my throne, and the place of the soles of my feet, where I will dwell in the midst of the children of Israel for ever." That is to say, it will be the place of his throne during the Millennium when he dwells among the house of Israel, and it was

121

the place where the soles of his feet trod when he dwelt on earth as a mortal. In this same chapter he says his house shall be built "upon the top of the mountain." In chapter 47 we find the statements to which the Prophet alluded when he said the water would "come out from under the temple, and the waters of the Dead Sea be healed." Ezekiel's language is: "Waters issued out from under the threshold of the house eastward. . . . These waters issue out toward the east country, and go down into the desert, and go into the sea: which being brought forth into the sea, the waters shall be healed." Ezekiel's concluding expression, relative to Old Jerusalem where the temple shall stand, is: "And the name of the city from that day shall be, The Lord is there."

NOTES

1. When the Lord comes—be it in time's meridian, at his Second Coming, or whensoever—he always comes to his temple, for temples are his dwelling places on earth. Accordingly, Malachi's Messianic utterance, though part of a recitation of what is to be in latter days, when only those who are prepared shall "abide the day of his coming," has application also, in principle, to his mortal ministry. The Lord Jehovah came to his temple in Jerusalem; came to cleanse and purify it, at least to the extent of casting out the money-changers and evil men who were making merchandise therein; even as he shall come to cleanse the earth and destroy the wicked when he comes again to his temple to usher in the millennial era.

2. The episode here recited is, of course, the calling of the Seventy, and their responsibility, then as now, was "to act in the name of the Lord," under proper direction, "in building up the church and regulating all the affairs of the same." (D&C 107:34.)

3. There was no baptism for the dead until after the visit of the slain Messiah to the spirits in prison and his proclamation of liberty to the captives there imprisoned. Baptism for the living, as is becoming increasingly clear even in apostate Christendom, has prevailed among mortals in all ages, including those which antedated the ministry of John the Baptist.

4. The part played by Herod's Temple in the social, cultural, and religious life of the Jews of Jerusalem, those of Palestine, and those scattered abroad is seen in these words of Edersheim: "The Temple itself," he says, "which, from a small building, little larger than an ordinary church, in the time of Solomon, had become that great and glorious House which excited the admiration of the foreigner, and kindled the enthusiasm of every son of Israel. At the time of Christ it had been already forty-six years in building, and workmen were still, and for a long time, engaged on it. But what a heterogeneous crowd thronged its porches and courts! Hellenists; scattered wanderers from the most distant parts of the earth—east, west, north, and south; Galileans, quick of temper and uncouth of Jewish speech; Judeans and Jerusalemites; white-robed Priests and Levites; Temple officials; broad-phylacteried, wide-fringed Pharisees, and courtly, ironical Sadducees; and, in the outer court, curious Gentiles! Some had come to worship; others to pay vows, or bring offerings, or to seek purification; some to meet friends, and discourse on religious subjects in those colonnaded porches, which ran round the Sanctuary; or else to have their questions answered, or their causes heard and decided, by the smaller Sanhedrin of twenty-

three, that sat in the entering of the gate or by the Great Sanhedrin. The latter no longer occupied the Hall of Hewn Stones, Gazith, but met in some chamber attached to those 'shops' or booths, on the Temple Mount, which belonged to the High-Priestly family of Ananias, and where such profitable trade was driven by those who, in their cupidity and covetousness, were worthy successors of the sons of Eli. In the Court of the Gentiles (or in its porches) sat the official money-changers, who for a fixed discount changed all foreign coins into those of the Sanctuary. Here also was that great mart for sacrificial animals, and all that was requisite for offerings. How the simple, earnest country people, who came to pay vows, or bring offerings for purifying, must have wondered, and felt oppressed in that atmosphere of strangely blended religious rigorism and utter worldliness; and how they must have been taxed, imposed upon, and treated with utmost curtness, nay, rudeness, by those who laughed at their boorishness, and despised them as cursed, ignorant country people, little better than heathens, or, for that matter, than brute beasts. Here also there lay about a crowd of noisy beggars, unsightly from disease, and clamorous for help. And close by passed the luxurious scion of the High-Priestly families; the proud, intensely self-conscious Teacher of the Law, respectfully followed by his disciples; and the quick-witted, subtle Scribe. These were men who, on Sabbaths and feast-days, would come out on the Temple terrace to teach the people, or condescend to answer their questions; who in the Synagogues would hold their puzzled hearers spell-bound by their traditional lore and subtle argumentation, or tickle the fancy of the entranced multitude, that thronged every available space, by their ingenious frivolities, their marvellous legends, or their clever sayings; but who would, if occasion required, quell an opponent by well-poised questions, or crush him beneath the sheer weight of authority. Yet others were there who, despite the utterly lowering influence which the frivolities of the prevalent religion, and the elaborate trifling of its endless observances, must have exercised on the moral and religious feelings of all—perhaps, because of them—turned aside, and looked back with loving gaze to the spiritual promises of the past, and forward with longing expectancy to the near 'consolation of Israel,' waiting for it in prayerful fellowship, and with bright, heaven-granted gleams of its dawning lift amidst the encircling gloom." (Edersheim 1:114-15.)

5. There will also be, of course, a latter-day temple in the New Jerusalem on the American continent. (D&C 84:1-5.)

Chapter 8

MOSAIC SACRIFICES IN JESUS' DAY

Why dost thou offer sacrifices unto the
Lord? (Moses 5:6.)

Gospel Sacrifices—Past and Future

All things bear record of Christ—things which are in heaven above, and in the earth beneath, and in the waters under the earth—all bear record of the Lord; of his creative power; of his redeeming grace; of his goodness and mercy unto us. From the dead dust of the deserts to the living light of the heavenly luminaries; from the amoeba in its primordial ooze to the sons of God who reign in immortal glory; from the lowest to the highest, and from the least unto the greatest—things, both animate and inanimate, bear record of Him whose we are and by whom we have life and breath and all things.

All gospel ordinances, all the religious rites revealed from heaven, all of the performances and formalisms of the law of Moses—all bear witness of Christ, all are ordained in such a way, all are performed in such a manner as to symbolize something about him and his ministry. And those ordinances and performances which teach the truths relative to his infinite and eternal atonement are the most important and perfect of them all. The three ordinances that excel in this respect are baptism, the sacrament, and sacrifice, with the sacrificial rites setting forth the best similitudes of the three.

Baptisms, in all ages, are performed by immersion in water in similitude of the death, burial, and resurrection of Christ. When baptized persons are buried with Christ in baptism, they die as to the carnal things of this world. When they come forth from their watery grave, it is with a newness of life; they are, as it were, "resurrected" to a continuing mortal life of righteousness. The elements of water, blood, and spirit, which were present in the atonement, are also the elements that are present in every baptism. Thus, every baptismal ordinance centers attention in the atonement, in the very atonement by virtue of which the ordinance of baptism gains efficacy, virtue, and force.

The sacramental emblems, the bread and wine or water, are administered by Aaronic authority in similitude of and in remembrance of the broken flesh and spilt blood of our Redeemer. By this sacred ordinance the saints of God renew the covenant previously made in the waters of baptism; by it they covenant anew to keep the commandments and are promised, in return, the companionship of the Holy Spirit in this life and eternal life in the realms ahead. And, similarly, when proper sacrifices were made—and throughout Israelite history these were also performed by Aaronic authority and were in similitude of the atoning sacrifice of the Son—they also were occasions for renewing the covenant of salvation that had been made in the waters of baptism. Sacrifices before the coming of the Messiah and the sacramental ordinance thereafter each served the same purpose in the great and eternal scheme of things.

Sacrifices were first performed as gospel ordinances. They antedated Moses and his law; they were administered by Melchizedek authority; and Adam was the first legal administrator to use the similitudes involved. He and Eve were commanded by the Lord "that they should worship the Lord their God, and should offer the firstlings of their flocks,

for an offering unto the Lord." Manifestly this commandment contained the divine instructions as to how and in what
manner the newly revealed ordinances should be performed;
and when Adam, acting pursuant to revelation, conformed
to the divine will, an angel descended and asked: "Why dost
thou offer sacrifices unto the Lord?" Adam replied: "I know
not, save the Lord commanded me." Thereupon the angel
revealed the great underlying principle that pertains to all
true sacrificial ordinances: "This thing is a similitude of the
sacrifice of the Only Begotten of the Father, which is full of
grace and truth. Wherefore, thou shalt do all that thou doest
in the name of the Son, and thou shalt repent and call upon
God in the name of the Son forevermore." (Moses 5:5-8.)

From that Adamic day until our Lord shed his own
blood in sacrifice for the sins of the world, the sacrificial
system remained in force among his people. Whenever and
wherever there were legal administrators who had the truth,
sacrifices were offered that prefigured the coming sacrifice of
the Lamb of God. So fundamental and basic were these ordinances to the true system of worship, and so ingrained
were they in every devout person, that they continued
among apostate groups. Even though men changed the ordinances and broke the everlasting covenant, most of them still
retained sacrifices and burnt offerings in one form or
another. Not knowing that the true sacrificial system was
first revealed to the first man; not knowing that it continued
without variation among faithful people; and not knowing
that it was then imitated in one perverted form or another
among apostate peoples, it has been assumed, falsely, that it
is a performance that each evolving nation has developed for
itself. Edersheim, interestingly, is not far from the truth
when he sets forth the view that sacrificial performances
came by instinct to Adam's seed. "We might argue from
their universality," he says, "that, along with the acknowledgment of a Divine power, the dim remembrance of
a happy past, and the hope of a happier future, sacrifices
belonged to the primeval traditions which mankind

inherited from Paradise. To sacrifice seems as 'natural' to man as to pray; the one indicates what he feels about himself, the other what he feels about God. The one means a felt need of propitiation; the other a felt sense of dependence." (*Temple,* pp. 106-7.)

But the fact is that sacrificial offerings were revealed gospel ordinances. For over twenty-five hundred years, from Adam to Moses, all those who had the gospel also offered sacrifices. When the Mosaic law was added to the gospel system, then for nearly fifteen hundred years these ordinances—changed, expanded upon, and set forth in meticulous detail—were performed as part of the Mosaic system.

When the Lamb of God, in Gethsemane and at Golgotha, worked out the infinite and eternal atonement and permitted himself to be slain for the sins of the world, it was intended that the sacrificial ordinances prefiguring that most transcendent of all events should cease. No one has set forth why this was destined to be with the clarity and plainness found in the words of the prophet Amulek. "According to the great plan of the Eternal God," he said, "there must be an atonement made, or else all mankind must unavoidably perish. . . . It is expedient that there should be a great and last sacrifice; yea, not a sacrifice of man, neither of beast, neither of any manner of fowl; for it shall not be a human sacrifice; but it must be an infinite and eternal sacrifice. . . . and then shall there be, or it is expedient there should be, a stop to the shedding of blood; then shall the law of Moses be fulfilled; yea, it shall be all fulfilled, every jot and tittle, and none shall have passed away. And behold, this is the whole meaning of the law, every whit pointing to that great and last sacrifice; and that great and last sacrifice will be the Son of God, yea, infinite and eternal." (Alma 34:9-14.)

Appearing in resurrected glory to his Nephite kinsmen, our Lord affirmed the end of the old order and announced the beginning of the new one. "By me redemption cometh," he said, "and in me is the law of Moses fulfilled. . . . And ye shall offer up unto me no more the shedding of blood." It is the Lord Jesus who is the Lord Jehovah who is speaking, which means that the sacrifices of old were offered to Christ. "Yea, your sacrifices and your burnt offerings shall be done away, for I will accept none of your sacrifices and your burnt offerings. And ye shall offer for a sacrifice unto me a broken heart and a contrite spirit." (3 Ne. 9:17-20.)

It was during this American ministry that our Lord instituted in the New World, as he had done in Jerusalem and the Old World, the sacramental ordinance in which broken bread was eaten in remembrance of his body, and wine was drunk in remembrance of his blood. From that blessed day onward the sacrament replaced sacrifices except that as part of the restitution of all things—and then on a limited basis only—blood sacrifices will be offered again. It was of these future sacrificial ordinances that Malachi prophesied, in a setting descriptive of the Second Coming of the Son of Man, that the returning Lord would "purify the sons of Levi, . . . that they may offer unto the Lord an offering in righteousness." Of this offering, to be made in "Judah and Jerusalem," the prophecy says it shall be "pleasant unto the Lord, as in the days of old, and as in former years." (Mal. 3:1-5.) It was to these sacrifices that Ezekiel alluded when he set forth the nature and use of the temple yet to be built in Jerusalem. And so that they might be performed by Levites who once again were legal administrators, John the Baptist, a Levite whose right it was to offer sacrifices anciently, and who was in fact the last Levitical priest to hold the keys of the ministry, brought back the ancient order of Aaron, saying to Joseph Smith and Oliver Cowdery, as he did so, that "this shall never be taken again from the earth, until the sons of Levi do offer again an offering unto the Lord in righteousness." (D&C 13.)[1]

The Sacrifices in Herod's Temple

In this our day—which we, in our self-conceived conceit, are pleased to designate as an age of enlightenment and intellectual achievement—we look with some revulsion upon religious rites that call for the slaying of lambs and fowl and the sprinkling of their blood in a particular and specified way. In our modern sophistication we suppose we have risen above the seeming barbarism of those sacrificial ordinances which called for the slaying of oxen and sheep and red heifers; which called for a scapegoat to carry the sins of the people into a wilderness area; and which imposed the stench and dung and filth of dying beasts upon those who sought to commune with Deity in holy places. We are pleased to replace the daily sacrifices with the weekly sacramental ordinances; to partake of the emblems of his broken flesh and spilt blood rather than to burn the firstlings of our flocks upon altars of stone; to renew the covenant made in the waters of baptism by partaking of bread and water in the quiet of a chapel rather than by burning the flesh of animals amid the death noises and bleating that accompanied sacrificial ordinances.

But whatever our oversophisticated sensitivities lead us to assume, the facts remain that sacrifices were instituted by the mild and merciful Jesus; that they were set forth, in a manner and in a form, to bear witness of his atoning sacrifice; that they were as essential to the salvation of men anciently as the sacrament is to ours today; and that they were performed with divine authority, by legal administrators, for the whole of that four thousand years which extended from the day the first man was cast out of his garden home to the day when our Lord's forerunner baptized in Jordan near Bethabara. In contrast there have been only two or three hundred years during which legal administrators, empowered from on high, have performed sacramental ordinances that were in fact binding on earth and sealed in the heavens.

Unless we have more than a superficial knowledge of what was involved in the sacrificial ordinances; unless we know why and how the Lord dealt with his people through this type of formalism; unless we catch the vision of the si-

129

militudes of sacrifice—and in many respects they are better than those found in the sacrament—we can never understand the life and ministry of the Man Jesus as fully as we should. And we are now speaking not just of a dim and general awareness that sacrifices are performed in similitude of the sacrifice of the Son of God, who is full of grace and truth, but of an awareness of enough of the details and rituals to envision how and in what manner they bore testimony of him whose life we study.

We need not extract from the writings of Moses, the man of God, all that is set forth relative to sacrificial performances. Volumes might be written in exposition of what the ancient lawgiver recorded, to say nothing of the manner in which his counsel was followed or perverted, as the case may be, both in Israel and among those who knew not the Mosaic system. We shall, rather, turn to the sacrificial offerings that the Jews made on the great altar in the holy temple in Jerusalem at the time of Jesus. These are the ordinances Jesus learned as he grew up in his Jewish home. They are the ones that should have introduced his Jewish brethren to their Lord and King. Unfortunately for most of his brethren, however, they had lost the true and correct understanding of the sacred rites. Though they performed by rote and to the best of their ability what had come down to them from their fathers; though they were strict and vigilant in conforming to the divine will as they understood it—and the ordinances themselves were virtually identical with those of former days—the unfortunate reality was that they had only the form and not the substance. They had a form of godliness, but were far removed from the eternal power that should have been present; the true meaning and intent of the rites did not register in their sin-filled hearts.

There are, of course, many commentaries, plus shelves of dry tomes, that deal with the sacrificial systems of old. We shall limit our quotations, however, to one author, Alfred Edersheim, a sectarian of faith and understanding who wrote a century ago and who had the sense and insight to recognize Jesus as the Messiah and to seek to extol him for what he in fact was, God's own Son. In his scholarly work *The Temple—Its Ministry and Services as They Were at the Time of Christ*, he exhibits a remarkably sound view of the principles and doctrines underlying the law of sacrifice, a view that is especially commendable since he did not have the Book of Mormon and latter-day revelation to keep him on the true course. As to the procedures and intricate mechanics of the ritualistic performances themselves, they can be deciphered by any competent scholar who will dredge his way through the surprisingly voluminous Jewish source material.

We shall now speak, in an abbreviated and digested way, of both the doctrine and the performances; of the law of sacrifice itself and the sacrificial rites based thereon; of the principles that are eternal and of the procedures that change with the variant circumstances. As to the procedures, those mentioned are the ones operative in Herod's Temple in Jesus' day. With deliberate intent we shall not record a hundredth—nay, not a thousandth—part of the unbelievably complex rituals and formalisms.

First we will note the order and meaning of those Mosaic rites that are sacrificial in nature. One basic principle is set out in these words: "The sacrifices of the Old Testament were *symbolical* and *typical.* An outward observance without any real inward meaning is only a ceremony. But a rite which has a present spiritual meaning is a *symbol;* and if, besides, it also points to a future reality, conveying at the same time, by anticipation, the blessing that is yet to appear, it is a *type.* Thus the Old Testament sacrifices were not only symbols, nor yet merely predictions by fact (as prophecy is a prediction by words), but they already conveyed to the believing Israelite the blessing that was to flow from the future reality to which they pointed." (*Temple*, p. 106. Italiacs added.) That is to say, believing Israel then knew, and believing Israel of old had always known, that in the symbolical and typical ordinances performed by their authorized priests

131

there was immediate forgiveness, mediation, and that at-one-ment with God which is part of atonement.

Another basic concept is given thus: "The fundamental idea of sacrifice in the Old Testament is that of substitution, which again seems to imply everything else—atonement and redemption, vicarious punishment and forgiveness." (*Temple,* p. 107.) Sacrificial ordinances were performed by "a mediatorial priesthood," a conclusion that accords with the revealed word to Joseph Smith that Moses "was ordained by the hand of angels to be a mediator of this first covenant, (the law.)" (JST, Gal. 3:19-20.) "All this was *symbolical* (of man's need, God's mercy, and his covenant), and *typical,* till He should come to whom it all pointed, and who had all along given reality to it; He whose Priesthood was perfect, and who on a perfect altar brought a perfect sacrifice, once for all—a perfect Substitute, and a perfect Mediator." (*Temple,* p. 108.)

One other basic concept must be set forth. When Israel became the Lord's people, it was by covenant. The Lord revealed his mind and his will to Moses. "And Moses came and told the people all the words of the Lord, and all the judgments: and all the people answered with one voice, and said, All the words which the Lord hath said will we do." Then Moses wrote all the words in a book, built an altar and offered sacrifices, took the blood of the oxen, and sprinkled half of it on the altar and half on the people. Then he said: "Behold the blood of the covenant, which the Lord hath made with you concerning all these words." (Ex. 24.) Israel was thus in fellowship with their God; they had attained at-one-ment. The sacrificial system then became the arrangement whereby this covenant could be renewed and the chosen people could reinstate themselves in grace whenever they fell therefrom. "On the ground of this covenant-sacrifice all others rested. These were, then, either sacrifices of communion with God, or else intended to restore that communion when it had been disturbed or dimmed through sin and trespass: sacrifices *in* communion, or *for* communion with God. To the former class belong the burnt- and the peace-offerings; to the latter, the sin- and trespass-offerings." (*Temple,* p. 108.)

Sacrifices were of two kinds—bloody and unbloody, the latter group including meat and drink offerings, the first sheaf at the Passover, the two loaves at Pentecost, and the shewbread. Bloody sacrifices were made with oxen, sheep, goats, turtledoves, and young pigeons. There were eleven occasions for public sacrifices and five for private sacrifices;[2] some were said to be most holy, others less holy. Always they were made with something that belonged to the offerer. All animal sacrifices were to be free of blemishes, and salt was always added as a symbol of incorruption. The sacrificial animals were always slain by the priests, and "the death of the sacrifice was only a means towards an end, that end being the shedding and sprinkling of the blood, by which the atonement was really made."

When men offered private sacrifices the formalities included, in most instances, the laying on of hands on the animal while sins were confessed and a prayer offered. Words of the prayer were to this effect: "I entreat, O Jehovah: I have sinned, I have done perversely, I have rebelled, I have committed (naming the sin, trespass, or, in the case of a burnt-offering, the breach of positive or negative command); but I return in repentance, and let this be for my atonement." (*Temples,* pp. 109-15.)

Did the Jewish worshippers in the day of Jesus know that their sacrificial ordinances were part of an atoning process? That the blood of animals was being shed so they could gain forgiveness of sins? That the animal or fowl—slain for the sins of men, as it were—was but a substitute, a symbol, a type of him who should bear the sins of all men? The answers are in the affirmative. Contrary to what is found in some sweeping and superficial pronouncements, the fact is that they did know and they did understand; at least the knowledge was had by many of them, for Jewry, as is the case with Christendom, was fragmented and there were many divergent views on all basic doctrines. However, the Messianic problem in Jesus' day was one of the Person to whom the similitudes pointed rather than the fact of their so doing. As to the fact that the principles themselves were known and understood by the spiritually literate among them, there are many quotations from rabbinical and related sources that say such things as:

"The soul of every creature is bound up in its blood; therefore I gave it to atone for the soul of man—that one soul should come and atone for the other."

"One soul is substitute for the other."

"I gave the soul for you on the altar, that the soul of the animal should be an atonement for the soul of the man."

"The offerer, as it were, puts away his sins from himself, and transfers them upon the living animal."

"As often as any one sins with his soul, whether from haste or malice, he puts away his sin from himself, and places it upon the head of his sacrifice, and it is an atonement for him."

"After the prayer of confession (connected with the imposition of hands) the sins of the children of Israel lay on the sacrifice (of the Day of Atonement)."

"Properly speaking, the blood of the sinner should have been shed, and his body burned, as those of the sacrifices. But the Holy One—blessed be He!—accepted our sacrifice from us as redemption and atonement. Behold the full grace which Jehovah—blessed be He!—has shown to man! In His compassion and in the fulness of His grace He accepted the soul of the animal instead of his soul, that through it there might be an atonement."

"He that brought a sacrifice [was] required to come to the knowledge that that sacrifice was his redemption." (*Temple*, pp. 119-20.)

Having set forth the doctrine that sacrifices were offered—(1) as a means of maintaining communion with Deity; as a renewed seal of man's acceptance of the covenant God made with Moses; as a reaffirmation on the part of the Lord's people that they would keep his statutes and judgments (and burnt offerings and peace offerings were for these purposes); and (2) that they were "intended to restore that communion when it had been dimmed or disturbed"; that through them an atonement was made for sin; that they were the recurring means of receiving freedom from the burdens of iniquity (and sin offerings and trespass offerings were for these purposes)—we now come to a consideration of these four types of sacrifices:

1. *The burnt offering.*

This offering symbolized "the entire surrender unto God, whether of the individual or of the congregation, and His acceptance thereof." It was a "sacrifice of devotion and service. Thus day by day it formed the regular morning and evening service in the Temple, while on the sabbaths, new moons, and festivals additional burnt-offerings followed the ordinary worship. There the covenant people brought the covenant-sacrifice, and the multitude of offerings indicated, as it were, the fulness, richness, and joyousness of their self-surrender." (*Temple,* pp. 126-27.)

2. *The sin offering.*

"This is the most important of all sacrifices [from an individual standpoint]. It made atonement for the *person* of the offender, whereas the trespass-offering only atoned for one special offence. Hence sin-offerings were brought on festive occasions for the whole people, but never trespass-offerings. In fact, the trespass-offering may be regarded as representing ransom for a special wrong, while the sin-offering symbolized general redemption. Both sacrifices applied only to sins 'through ignorance,' in opposition to those done 'presumptuously' (or 'with a high hand'). For the latter the law provided no atonement, but held out 'a certain fearful looking for of judgment, and fiery indignation.' . . . In reference both to sin- and to trespass-offerings, the Rabbinical principle must be kept in view—that they only atoned in case of real repentance. . . . Neither oil nor frankincense were to be brought with a sin-offering. There was nothing joyous about it. It represented a terrible necessity, for which God, in his wondrous grace, had made provision." (*Temple,* pp. 128-30.)

One rare and unusual sin offering must be noted. It was of a red heifer, one pure in color "upon which never came yoke," and it was to cleanse any in Israel from "Levitical defilement," from "defilement by the dead." The chief thing distinguishing it from all other sacrifices was "that it was a sacrifice offered once for all (at least so long as its ashes lasted); that its blood was sprinkled, not on the altar, but outside the camp towards the sanctuary; and that it was wholly burnt, along with cedarwood, as the symbol of imperishable existence, [with] hyssop, as that of purification from corruption, and [with] 'scarlet,' which from its colour was the emblem of life. Thus the sacrifice of highest life, brought as a sin offering, and, so far as possible, once for all, was in its turn accompanied by the symbols of imperishable existence, freedom from corruption, and fulness of life, so as yet more to intensify its significance. But even this is not all. The gathered ashes with running water were sprinkled on the third and seventh days on that which was to be purified. Assuredly, if death meant 'the wages of sin,' this purification pointed, in all its details, to 'the gift of God,' which is 'eternal life,' through the sacrifice of Him in whom is the fulness of life." (*Temple,* p. 349.)

3. *The trespass offering.*

This was offered to clear a person from specific instances of wrongdoing, "for certain transgressions committed through ignorance, or else, according to Jewish tradition, where a man afterwards voluntarily confessed himself guilty." (*Temple,* p. 133.)

4. *The peace offering.*

"The most joyous of all sacrifices was the peace-offering, or, as from its derivation it might also be rendered, the offering of completion. This was, indeed, a season of happy fellowship with the Covenant God, in which He condescended to become Israel's Guest at the sacrificial meal, even as He was always their Host. . . . It is this sacrifice which is so frequently referred to in the Book of Psalms as the grateful homage of a soul justified and accepted before God." (*Temple,* p. 134.) Appropriately, for instance, Solomon at the dedication of the temple offered 22,000 oxen and 120,000 sheep as a peace offering. (1 Kgs. 8:63.)

There is much to say about sacrifices as they were from Moses to Zacharias, who begat John, nearly all of which is beyond the scope and need of this work. We cannot, however, leave this portion of our study without referring to the Day of Atonement; the day when all Israel was commanded to look to the Lord for remission of sins; the day when the high priest, who sat in Aaron's seat, mediated between Israel and their King—all according to the directions given by Moses, the man of God. "The most solemn of all sacrifices were those of the Day of Atonement, when the high-priest, arrayed in his linen garments, stood before the Lord Himself within the Most Holy Place to make an atonement." (*Temple,* p. 132.) On this day, once each year, the high priest entered the Holy of Holies, spoke the ineffable name, sprinkled the blood of the covenant, and performed the expiatory rites by which the Lord's people were cleansed from sin.

Without going into all the preparations for and complexities of the performances undertaken on the Day of Atonement—and they were complex, numerous, and burdensome—but simply as a means of getting a feeling relative to sacrifice as such, let us set forth a portion of what transpired on this day of days. "From Numbers 29:7-11 it appears that the offerings on the Day of Atonement were really of a threefold kind—*'the continual burnt offering,'* that is, the daily morning and evening sacrifices, with their meat- and drink-offerings; *the festive sacrifices of the day,* consisting for the high-priest and the priesthood, of 'a ram for a burnt-offering,' and for the people of one young bullock, one ram, and seven lambs of the first year (with their meat-offerings) for a burnt-sacrifice, and one kid of the goats for a sin-offering; and, thirdly, and chiefly, *the peculiar expiatory sacrifices of the day,* which were a young bullock as a sin-offering for the high-priest, his house, and the sons of Aaron, and another sin-offering for the people, consisting of two goats, one of which was to be killed and its blood sprinkled, as directed, while the other was to be sent away into the wilderness, bearing 'all the iniquities of the children of Israel, and all their transgressions in all their sins' which had been confessed 'over him,' and laid upon him by the high priest." (*Temple,* p. 306.)

As to the sin offering for himself, and the uttering of the ineffable name, Edersheim says of the high priest: "He then laid both his hands upon the head of the bullock, and confessed as follows:—'Ah, JEHOVAH! I have committed iniquity; I have transgressed; I have sinned—I and my house. Oh, then, JEHOVAH, I entreat Thee, cover over (atone for, let there be atonement for) the iniquities, the transgressions, and the sins which I have committed, transgressed, and sinned before Thee, I and my house—even as it is written in the law of Moses, Thy servant: "For, on that day will He cover over (atone) for you to make you clean; from all your transgressions before JEHOVAH ye shall be cleansed." ' It will be noticed that in this solemn confession the name JEHOVAH occurred three times. Other three times was it pronounced in the confession which the high priest made over the same bullock for the priesthood; a seventh time was it uttered when he cast the lot as to which of the two goats was to be 'for JEHOVAH;' and once again he spoke it three times in the confession over the so-called 'scape-goat' which bore the sins of the people. All these *ten* times the high-priest pronounced the very name of JEHOVAH, and, as he spoke it, those who stood near cast themselves with their faces on the ground, while the multitude responded: 'Blessed be the Name; the glory of His kingdom is for ever and ever.' "

Thereafter the two goats were brought forth, the lots were cast, and one was chosen to bear the inscription, "la-

JEHOVAH," for Jehovah, the other "la-Azazel," for Azazel (an expression translated "scapegoat" in our Bible). The goat bearing the name of Jehovah was sacrificed; the one chosen as the scapegoat, after all the sins of the people were placed upon him, was to be set free in a wilderness place to carry off the sins and iniquities of the Lord's people. In the course of the various sacrifices the high priest sprinkled the blood of the bullock and the goat according to the ritualistic pattern. (*Temple,* pp. 310-16.)

"By these expiatory sprinklings the high priest had cleansed the sanctuary in all its parts from the defilement of the priesthood and the worshippers. The Most Holy Place, the veil, the Holy Place, the altar of incense, and the altar of burnt-offering were now clean alike, so far as the priesthood and as the people were concerned; and in their relationship to the sanctuary both priests and worshippers were atoned for. So far as the law could give it, there was now again free access for all; or, to put it otherwise, the continuance of typical sacrificial communion with God was once more restored and secured. Had it not been for these services, it would have been impossible for priests and people to offer sacrifices, and so to obtain the forgiveness of sins, or to have fellowship with God. But the consciences were not yet free from a sense of personal guilt and sin. That remained to be done through the 'scape-goat.' . . .

"Most solemn as the services had hitherto been, the worshippers would chiefly think with awe of the high-priest going into the immediate presence of God, coming out thence alive, and securing for them by the blood the continuance of the Old Testament privileges of sacrifices and of access unto God through them. What now took place concerned them, if possible, even more nearly. Their own personal guilt and sins were now to be removed from them, and that in a symbolical rite, at one and the same time the most mysterious and the most significant of all. All this while the 'scape-goat,' with the 'scarlet tongue,' telling of the guilt it was to bear, had stood looking eastwards, confronting the people, and waiting for the terrible load which it was to carry away 'unto a land not inhabited.' Laying both his hands on the head of this goat, the high-priest now confessed and pleaded: 'Ah, JEHOVAH! they have committed iniquity; they have transgressed; they have sinned—Thy people, the house of Israel. Oh, then, JEHOVAH! cover over (atone for), I intreat Thee, upon their iniquities, their transgressions, and their sins, which they have wickedly committed, transgressed, and sinned before Thee—Thy people, the house of Israel. As it is written in the law of Moses, Thy servant, saying: "For on that day shall it be covered over (atoned) for you, to make you clean from all your sins before JEHOVAH ye shall be cleansed." ' And while the prostrate multitude worshipped at the name of Jehovah, the high-priest turned his face towards them as he uttered the last words, '*Ye shall be cleansed!*' as if to declare to them the absolution and remission of their sins." (*Temple,* pp. 316-18.)

Sacrifices—Both Mortal and Eternal

Our Lord was born to die. He came into the world to die upon the cross for the sins of the world. The Lamb of God came to be sacrificed. He came to shed his blood on an eternal altar not made with hands. He came to sprinkle his redeeming blood upon his saints so they might be pure and spotless before him. Did he kneel by a rock—a natural altar—as he sweat great drops of blood in Gethsemane? Was the blood of the Lamb of God sprinkled upon an earthly altar and in a Most Holy Place, as it were? Perhaps; but be that as it may, the eternal reality is that he came to die; he came as a Lamb slain from the foundation of the world as it were, to shed his blood for his brethren. He came to bear their sins, to carry them as Azazel to a land apart. He came as the great and Eternal High Priest to rend the veil of the temple, that all men might enter the Holy of Holies and dwell forever in the Divine Presence. He came as the living Paschal Lamb to put a divine seal upon all the sacrifices, all the burnt offerings, all the sin offerings, all the trespass offerings, all the peace offerings ever offered by either Melchizedek or Aaronic authority since the world began. He came to fulfill the law that he himself had given to Moses, to bring redemption, to atone for the sins of the world. He came as the Lamb of God. He was appointed unto death, and all else incident to his mortal probation was truly incidental.

Did he speak as no man before or since has ever spoken? Was he the Master Teacher, the greatest Rabbi of them all? Did the lame leap when he spoke? the blind eyes see when he willed it? the deaf hear at a whisper from him? Did the decaying and stinking corpse of his friend from Bethany live again because he said, "Lazarus, come forth"? Did wondrous words and wondrous works flow from him as a stream? Was his life perfect in all respects as befits the Holy One of Israel? So be it. All this, and more, is as it is. Never was there such a man as this man. But underlying it all, like a great foundation upon which a Holy Temple is built, is the eternal reality that the chief and foremost achievement in the life of God's Son was his death—his death as a sacrifice for sin, the death in which he made his soul an offering for sin.

We shall trace his travels as best we may. We shall hear his words to the extent our ears are open. We shall rejoice with the sick souls who rise in health from their cots of pain. We shall partake of his feelings as he is glorified by his Father on the Holy Mount, and as he sorrows for the sins of his people. We shall weep with him over doomed Jerusalem. We shall seek to think what he thought, to speak as he spoke, to act as he acted, to feel as he felt—such of necessity must be in studying his life. But underlying it all will be the spoken and unspoken message: He came to die; he must go up to Jerusalem, and suffer many things, and be killed, and be raised again the third day; he must lay down his life of himself because his Father wills it; and he must make his soul an offering for sin, for he is the Lamb of God.

Whatever else he did is all to the good. It prepares men

for the one supreme act of his life. Because he spoke and lived as he did, men are able to believe he was the Son of God; and because he was the Son of God, his atoning sacrifice has efficacy, virtue, and force in time and in eternity.

That we may now have an acute awareness of how our Lord's eternal sacrifice crowned all the sacrifices of the past; that we may know how the types and shadows of the Mosaic system took on form and substance in Christ; that we may see how the work of the mediator of the old covenant ended, and how that of the Mediator of the new covenant began, we shall turn to our theological friend, Paul. He wrote to the Hebrews. His message was that Christ came in fulfillment of the Mosaic sacrificial system; that the old covenant was now fulfilled; and that all Israel and all men must now look to the great and Eternal High Priest if they are to enter into the eternal Holy of Holies and dwell with God and Christ and the prophets and apostles of all the ages.

Paul's epistle to the Hebrews takes on a whole new meaning when it is read and studied with an understanding of the sacrificial system and the temple rites that prevailed in the day of Jesus. Our apostolic friend begins his epistle—as it is the nature and disposition of a true apostle to do—by announcing that the Great Elohim, the God to whom the Hebrews prayed in times past, sent his Son into the world; that the Son was in the express image of the Father's person; and that he came as promised in the holy scriptures. The Son is identified by name as the Man Jesus—the Captain of their salvation, who came to destroy death—who "took on him the seed of Abraham," so that "in all things" being "made like unto his brethren, . . . he might be a merciful and faithful high priest in things pertaining to God, to make reconciliation for the sins of the people. For in that he himself hath suffered being tempted, he is able to succour them that are tempted." (Heb. 2:16-18.) As we have seen, the high priests in Israel, on the Day of Atonement and at other times, through their sacrificial offerings made "reconciliation for the sins of the people." That is, by the shedding and sprinkling of the blood of bullocks and goats an atonement was wrought and the sins of the people were forgiven. It is this same prerogative that Paul is now claiming for another of Abraham's seed.

With this introduction Paul issues this invitation to his Hebrew brethren: "Consider the Apostle and High Priest of our profession, Christ Jesus." (Heb. 3:1.) That is, even as the high priests in Israel made reconciliation for the sins of the people, let us now consider the High Priest of the gospel, of our profession, of the new covenant, and see wherein he also made reconciliation through his blood for the sins of men. Paul then sets forth how and why Christ's position was greater than that of Moses, the man of God, and tells how their fathers, lacking faith, rejected Jehovah's gospel and were not able, under the law, to enter into the rest of the Lord, which rest is the fulness of his glory.

Having shown from the scriptures that Israel did not and could not enter the Lord's rest under the law, Paul then turns to Christ as the means of so obtaining. "Seeing then that we have a great high priest," he says, "that is passed into the heavens, Jesus the Son of God, let us hold fast our profession." Let us hold fast to Christ and his gospel, for he has entered into the heavens and can guide us in so doing, which thing the high priests of the Aaronic order could not do. "For we have not an high priest which cannot be touched with the feeling of our infirmities; but was in all points tempted like as we are, yet without sin." Our High Priest, the High Priest of the gospel, having suffered, having felt infirmities, having been tempted in all points like as we are, he will understand our like situation and make intercession for us. "Let us therefore come boldly unto the throne of grace" as the high priests of old turned to the Holy of Holies wherein was the throne of God with its mercy seat, "that we may obtain mercy, and find grace to help in time of need." (Heb. 4:14-16.)

With the principle now set forth that the new gospel

covenant—"our profession"—has also its High Priest; that the new religion has come to supplant the old, which former system was a type and shadow of things to come; that the High Priest of the new order is Christ Jesus who has ascended into heaven—Paul makes a pointed comparison of the mortal offerings of the Aaronic high priests and the eternal offering of the High Priest who came after the order of Melchizedek. "For every high priest taken from among men," he says, having reference to the high priests of the Aaronic order who served on the Day of Atonement and at other times, "is ordained for men in things pertaining to God, that he may offer both gifts and sacrifices for sins." The sacrifices offered by the ancient legal administrators were for the remission of sins. Like baptism and the sacrament, they had cleansing power; sin and iniquity were burned away upon the altars where they were offered. If it had not been so, what a direful and calamitous state rebellious and sinful Israel would have been in.

But such was God's gracious system; and of a high priest who had such a delegation of authority, Paul continues, such a one "can have compassion on the ignorant, and on them that are out of the way; for that he himself also is compassed with infirmity." Transgressions made in ignorance and those for which there was full repentance were forgiven through the sacrifices. "And by reason hereof," by reason of his own infirmities and sins, such a high priest "ought, as for the people, so also for himself, to offer for sins." We have seen that the high priest went first into the Holy of Holies to cleanse himself and thereafter to cleanse the people so that it would be, as with the priest, so with the people.

"And no man taketh this honour unto himself, but he that is called of God, as was Aaron." None but God can forgive sins; any man, of himself, who attempts such a high spiritual labor fails. Either God does it or he authorizes someone to act on his behalf. Anciently the one so authorized was Aaron, and those thereafter endowed with this priestly power were those who were called as had been their worthy ancestor. Hence Paul's need to establish the authority of the Son of God himself to act in the sin-remitting capacity here involved. "So also Christ glorified not himself to be made an high priest." He did not assume the prerogative of ministering in that high and exalted status; the power to make reconciliation and forgive sins did not originate with him; it was conferred upon him by his Father, as Paul shows by quoting these words spoken to Christ by the Father: "Thou art my Son, to day have I begotten thee. As he saith also in another place, Thou art a priest for ever after the order of Melchisedec."

And so we have an Eternal High Priest, one whose priesthood and service continue forever. The old high priests of the Aaronic order served, each in turn, for a time and a season. Each entered the Holy of Holies on one day each year during their tenure in the high and holy office that was theirs. But now there is an Eternal High Priest, who came after the order of Melchizedek; he continueth ever. Of him the account testifies: "In the days of his flesh," while he dwelt in mortality and before he became immortal, "when he had offered up prayers and supplications with strong crying and tears unto him that was able to save him from death"—when, as an Intercessor, he had prayed for his brethren; when, on his own behalf, he had pleaded that if it were possible, he might not drink the bitter cup, as he took upon himself the sins of the world—"and was heard in that he feared." That is, the Father heard the prayer and declined to remove the cup. The answer was: "Though he were a Son, yet learned he obedience by the things which he suffered." 'Though he were a Son yet he learned of obedience its terrible costs and glorious rewards by the things which he suffered, for he knew how to obey.' In agony he drank the dregs of the bitter cup, sweat great drops of blood from every pore, suffered more than it is possible for man to suffer except it be unto death, and thereby performed the appointed sacrificial labor. "And being made perfect, he became the author [the cause] of eternal salvation unto all them that obey him," and the Messianic promise was fulfilled relative to him, being "called of God an high priest after the order of Melchisedec." (Heb. 5:1-10.)

At this point in his Spirit-guided epistle to the Hebrews—to those who practiced the sacrificial ordinances and who did know or should have known their significance—Paul says there are many things he would like to tell them of the Eternal High Priest if they were not "dull of hearing." (Heb. 5:11.) He does exhort the Hebrew saints to "go on unto perfection" and not to turn back from their newly found profession, lest "they crucify to themselves the Son of God afresh, and put him to an open shame," thus becoming sons of perdition. He says God is not unmindful of their "labour of love" as they have "ministered to the saints," and he exhorts them to endure "unto the end."

Then he turns back to their ancient Hebrew history; speaks of Abraham, whom they revered, and of the promises of the Lord to him; tells how Abraham was promised, with an oath, that he and his seed, including all who become his seed by faith, repentance, and baptism, should be blessed forever—"even with the blessings of the Gospel, which are the blessings of salvation, even of life eternal" (Abr. 2:10-11)[3]—and then he exhorts the Hebrews to "lay hold upon the hope set before us: Which hope we have as an anchor of the soul, both sure and stedfast, and which entereth into that within the veil; Whither the forerunner is for us entered, even Jesus, made an high priest for ever after the order of Melchisedec." (Heb. 6:1-20.) Paul's exhortation is that the Hebrews should lay hold upon the hope of eternal life promised them as the seed of Abraham. This hope, he says, will be an anchor to their souls and will prepare them to enter within the veil—to pass through the veil of the temple, even as it is in temples today, in similitude of entering the presence of God—which is made possible because of the sacrifice of the Eternal High Priest, Jesus our Forerunner, who as a priest forever after the order of Melchizedek has already passed through the veil.

In this setting, as the Hebrew readers think on Abraham—their patriarch, progenitor, and friend—Paul turns their minds to one who presided over the father of the faithful and to whom their great progenitor was in subjection. He speaks of the man Melchizedek, "who met Abraham returning from the slaughter of the kings, and blessed him." He speaks of the priesthood of the man Melchizedek, a priesthood that that mighty man conferred upon Abraham, and that preceded and is greater than the priestly powers given later to Aaron and his seed. "For this Melchizedek was ordained a priest after the order of the Son of God, which order was without father, without mother, without descent, having neither beginning of days, nor end of life. And all those who are ordained unto this priesthood are made like unto the Son of God, abiding a priest continually." (JST, Heb. 7:1-3.)

Then follows an argument that cannot be gainsaid. It is that Melchizedek and Abraham held an eternal priesthood that was not confined to any one lineage and was not gained by Levitical descent. This priesthood is the power whereby men gain endless life, which is eternal life, which is exaltation within the veil. It preceded the Levitical order, which order came because of father and mother and was conferred only upon those who descended from Aaron and Levi. In contrast to the higher order, as he had already shown, this lesser priesthood did not prepare men to enter the rest of the Lord; and also, while this Levitical priesthood was in active operation, yet Messianic prophecies were made that another Priest would rise after the order of Melchizedek. Paul's argument is that since perfection came not by the Levitical priesthood which administered the law of Moses, and since there was to be another Priest come after the higher order of Melchizedek, it follows that with the change of priesthood there would be a change of the law also, and that the new law was the gospel. He notes that Christ, who came "after the similitude of Melchisedec," was not of the tribe of Levi but of Judah; that he received his priesthood with an oath, which was not the case with the Levitical priests; and that the oath was a declaration in the Lord's name that he, Jesus, would be a priest forever, that is, that his priesthood would continue in time and in eternity. "By so much was Jesus made a surety of a better testament," Paul says.

Then our apostolic author gets back to the matter of sacrifices and temple ordinances. "And they [the Aaronic high priests of Levitical descent] truly were many priests, because they were not suffered to continue by reason of death." They were born and died, they came and went, one succeeded another, as is the common lot of mortals as pertaining to all the positions to be filled in this life. "But this man [Jesus, who received the Melchizedek Priesthood, which is not confined to those of the lineage of Levi], because he continueth ever, hath an unchangeable priesthood. Wherefore he is able also to save them to the uttermost that come unto God by him, seeing he ever liveth to make intercession for them." And even at this time the intercessory prayers continue to ascend to the Father, as the Eternal High Priest pleads: "Father, behold the sufferings and death of him who did no sin, in whom thou wast well pleased; behold the blood of thy Son which was shed, the blood of him whom thou gavest that thyself might be glorified; Wherefore, Father, spare these my brethren that believe on my name, that they may come unto me and have everlasting life." (D&C 45:4-5.) Paul continues: "For such an high priest became us, who is holy, harmless, undefiled, separate from sinners, and made higher than the heavens; Who needeth not daily, as those high priests, to offer up sacrifice, first for his own sins, and then for the people's: for this he did once, when he offered up himself. For the law maketh men high priests which have infirmity; but the word of the oath, which was since the law, maketh the Son, who is consecrated for evermore." (Heb. 7.)

Thus far Paul has taught the principles involved. He has shown that Israel failed to enter into eternal glory through the law alone. He has shown that salvation did not come by the law of Moses alone. He has shown that the Messianic High Priest was needed to sacrifice himself for the sins of the people. Now he is prepared to show how each performance of the Mosaic sacrificial system bore record of and pointed to the great and eternal sacrifice of the promised High Priest. "We have such an high priest," he says, "who is set on the right hand of the throne of the Majesty in the heavens." He is "a minister of the sanctuary, and of the true tabernacle, which the Lord pitched, and not man." There is, as it were, an eternal sanctuary, an eternal tabernacle in the heavens above, after which the tabernacle of Moses was patterned; the one was temporal, the other spiritual. "For every high priest is ordained to offer gifts and sacrifices: wherefore it is of necessity that this man have somewhat also to offer. For if he were on earth, he should not be a priest [for he was not of the house of Levi], seeing that there are priests that offer gifts according to the law." But, be it noted, these Levitical priests, these sons of Aaron, these mortal ministers who receive their priesthood because of lineage, who gain their power because of father and mother, as it were, these priests "serve unto the example and shadow of heavenly things, as Moses was admonished of God when he was about to make the tabernacle: for, See, saith he, that thou make all things according to the pattern shewed to thee in the mount." All that Moses ordained in the way of sacrificial performances; all that had been done in Israel in this respect for fifteen hundred years; all the oxen and sheep and goats that had been given as gifts to the Lord to be slain on his altars; all the offerings burned on these altars; all the blood shed and sprinkled in the rituals of the law—all of these things were but a shadow of what was to be; all of them typified and bore record of the Eternal High Priest. Manifestly the tabernacles and the temples in which they were performed must be built according to the heavenly pattern.

And now, because the Eternal High Priest has made his sacrifice, he has "obtained a more excellent ministry, by how much also he is the mediator of a better covenant [the gospel], which was established upon better promises. For if that first covenant [the law of Moses] had been faultless, then should no place have been sought for the second." At this point our inspired writer quotes Jeremiah's prophetic assurance that the Lord would make a new covenant with the house of Israel—a gospel covenant to replace the law— and that part of the new covenant was the promise: "I will be merciful to their unrighteousness, and their sins and their iniquities will I remember no more." (Heb. 8.)

As of the Mosaic covenant, whose terms and conditions were kept in force by Aaron's priestly sons, it is written: "Then verily the first covenant had also ordinances of divine service." The Lord's hand was in what came to Moses; his law was of divine origin. And this covenant had also "a worldly sanctuary. For there was a tabernacle made; the first, wherein was the candlestick, and the table, and the shewbread; which is called the sanctuary." This was the Holy Place, set off from the courts by a covering or veil; and the same arrangement prevailed in the temple of Jesus' day. "And after the second veil [which was in reality the veil of the temple], the tabernacle which is called the Holiest of all [the Holy of Holies]; Which had the golden censer, and the ark of the covenant overlaid round about with gold, wherein was the golden pot that had manna, and Aaron's rod that budded, and the tables of the covenant." The ark, the manna, Aaron's rod, the tables whereon the Decalogue was written, and the Urim and Thummim—none of these remained in Herod's Temple, the Holy of Holies containing only a rock whereon the high priest sprinkled the blood on the Day of Atonement. "And over it [the ark, stand] the cherubims of glory shadowing the mercyseat; of which we cannot now speak particularly." (Paul is here limiting himself as to what he will write openly about those sacred things which go on in temples.)

"Now when these things were thus ordained," when all these things were in order, "the priests went always [continually, from day to day] into the first tabernacle [the Holy

Place], accomplishing the service of God. But into the second [the Holy of Holies] went the high priest alone once every year [on the Day of Atonement], not without blood, which he offered for himself, and for the errors of the people." The blood of the bullock and the goat were sprinkled in the Holy of Holies as the earthly high priest atoned for the sins of the people.

With the sacrificial services of the temple thus summarized, and with specific mention being made of the sprinkling of the blood in the Holy of Holies on the Day of Atonement, Paul now says: "The Holy Ghost this signifying, that the way into the holiest of all was not yet made manifest, while as the first tabernacle was yet standing: Which was a figure for the time then present, in which were offered both gifts and sacrifices, that could not make him that did the service perfect, as pertaining to the conscience; Which stood only in meats and drinks, and divers washings, and carnal ordinances, imposed on them until the time of reformation." That is to say: The Holy Ghost bore record—to Paul, to Moses, to all who would hear—that all of these Mosaic performances were but a figure, a type and a shadow, a similitude of what was to be. They of themselves and standing alone did not admit Israel into the Holiest Place, which is heaven itself. The sacrificial service was not to be perfected until Christ's atonement was brought to pass, and all of the offerings, washings, and divers ordinances simply pointed toward the time of reformation, the time when Christ would come with the new covenant, at which time these sacrifices and performances would be done away. (Heb. 9:1-10.)

Now our apostolic friend turns from what was in Moses' day to what Jesus did to fulfill the law and bring in "the time of reformation." "But Christ being come an high priest of good things to come," he says, "by a greater and more perfect tabernacle, not made with hands, that is to say, not of this building; Neither by the blood of goats and calves, but by his own blood he entered in once into the holy place, having obtained eternal redemption for us." As the earthly high priests, once each year, entered into the Holy of Holies to cleanse the people with the blood of their sacrifices, so Christ, once for all, entered the eternal Holy of Holies and through the shedding of his own blood made forgiveness of sins possible for all men. "For if the blood of bulls and of goats, and the ashes of an heifer sprinkling the unclean, sanctifieth to the purifying of the flesh [this is the red heifer whose ashes were sprinkled upon those defiled by contact with death]: How much more shall the blood of Christ, who through the eternal Spirit offered himself without spot to God, purge your conscience from dead works to serve the living God?"

"And for this cause," because of our Lord's atonement, "he is the mediator of the new testament [covenant], that by means of death [his own], for the redemption of the transgressions that were under the first testament [covenant]"—that is, Christ's death gave efficacy and validity to the sacrificial performances made under the Mosaic system; if he had not been slain for the sins of the world there would have been no forgiveness as a result of the ordinances performed by the high priests of the Aaronic order; and, hence, through his atonement "they which are called," whether in Moses' day or in his own, "receive the promise of eternal inheritance." All men in all ages are saved through the atoning blood of Christ the Lord Omnipotent; any ordinance in any age, past, present, or future, is efficacious only because of that atonement and in no other way.

"For where a testament [covenant] is," Paul continues, "there must also of necessity be the death of the testator. For a testament [covenant] is of force after men are dead: otherwise it is of no strength at all while the testator liveth." The gospel covenant was not and could not be put into force and operation without the death of Christ. Except for his atoning sacrifice there would be neither immortality nor eternal life. If there were no atonement, there would be no forgiveness of sins, no reconciliation with God, no validity to baptism, no eternal marriage, no sanctified souls. If there were no atonement, the purposes of creation would have failed. The gospel covenant would have had "no strength at all" without the death of the testator.

"Whereupon neither the first testament [the old covenant made with Moses] was dedicated without blood. For when Moses had spoken every precept to all the people according to the law, he took the blood of calves and of goats, with water, and scarlet wool, and hyssop, and sprinkled both the book, and all the people, Saying, This is the blood of the testament [covenant] which God hath enjoined unto you. Moreover he sprinkled with blood both the tabernacle, and all the vessels of the ministry. And almost all things are by the law purged with blood; and without shedding of blood is no remission." How perfectly did Jehovah make blood sacrifices the type of the sacrifice that he himself should make for the cleansing and purifying of those who believe in him!

"It was therefore necessary that the patterns of things in the heavens should be purified with these; but the heavenly things themselves with better sacrifices than these." That is to say, the tabernacle and all its appurtenances, patterned as they were after what was in heaven, were purified by the sprinkling of blood; but they who shall dwell in heaven itself must be purified with an eternal sacrifice, that of Christ. "For Christ is not entered into the holy places made with hands, which are the figures of the true; but into heaven itself, now to appear in the presence of God for us." Our Lord did not enter the Holy Place and the Holy of Holies in offering his sacrifice—these places are only figures of the true heavenly tabernacle; but he entered into heaven itself there to make intercession forever for us.

"Nor yet that he should offer himself often, as the high priest entereth into the holy place every year with blood of others; For then must he often have suffered since the foundation of the world: but now once in the end of the world hath he appeared to put away sin by the sacrifice of himself.

And as it is appointed unto men once to die, but after this the judgment: So Christ was once offered to bear the sins of many; and unto them that look for him shall he appear the second time without sin unto salvation. For the law having a shadow of good things to come, and not the very image of the things, can never with those sacrifices which they offered year by year continually make the comers thereunto perfect." Again the announcement is made that perfection does not come by the Levitical priesthood, for its ordinances were only a shadow of what was to be. "For then would they not have ceased to be offered? because that the worshippers once purged should have had no more conscience of sins. But in those sacrifices there is a remembrance again made of sins every year. For it is not possible that the blood of bulls and of goats should take away sins." (Heb. 9:11-10:2.)

At this point Paul quotes a Messianic prophecy that contrasts the sacrifices of the law with the sacrifice of the "body" prepared for the Messiah, and explains that the Lord taketh away the old sacrifices "that he may establish the second. By the which will we are sanctified through the offering of the body of Jesus Christ once for all. And every priest standeth daily ministering and offering oftentimes the same sacrifices, which can never take away sins: But this man, after he had offered one sacrifice for sins for ever, sat down on the right hand of God; From henceforth expecting till his enemies be made his footstool. For by one offering he hath perfected for ever them that are sanctified."

Lest any reader should think that the apostle was simply drawing interesting analogies or comparing systems which by chance had analogous patterns, Paul says that the Holy Ghost was a witness of the truth of his interpretations. He refers again to Jeremiah's prophecy about the new covenant whereby sins and iniquities will no longer be remembered and then says: "Now where remission of these is, there is no more offering for sin." (Heb. 10:3-18.)

After all these explanations, not a few of which are repetitious in nature, the author of the epistle to the Hebrews applies the doctrine taught to his hearers with these words of exhortation: "Having therefore, brethren, boldness to enter into the holiest by the blood of Jesus, By a new and living way, which he hath consecrated for us, through the veil, that is to say, his flesh; And having an high priest over the house of God; Let us draw near with a true heart in full assurance of faith, having our hearts sprinkled from an evil conscience, and our bodies washed with pure water. Let us hold fast the profession of our faith without wavering."

Coupled with this exhortation is a warning that "if we sin wilfully after that we have received the knowledge of the truth, there remaineth no more sacrifice for sins, But a certain fearful looking for of judgment and fiery indignation, which shall devour the adversaries. He that despised Moses' law died without mercy under two or three witnesses: Of how much sorer punishment, suppose ye, shall he be thought worthy, who hath trodden under foot the Son of God, and hath counted the blood of the covenant, wherewith he was sanctified, an unholy thing, and hath done despite unto the Spirit of grace?" (Heb. 10:19-29.)

There follows the great discourse on faith, some further exhortations and promises of eternal reward, and then a return to the purpose of the epistle, that of proving to the Hebrews, by their own sacrificial performances, that Jesus is the Lamb of God whose atoning sacrifice taketh away the sins of the world. "We have an altar, whereof they have no right to eat which serve the tabernacle. For the bodies of those beasts, whose blood is brought into the sanctuary by the high priest for sin, are burned without the camp. Wherefore Jesus also, that he might sanctify the people with his own blood, suffered without the gate. Let us go forth therefore unto him without the camp, bearing his reproach. For here have we no continuing city, but we seek one to come. By him therefore let us offer the sacrifice of praise to God continually, that is, the fruit of our lips giving thanks to his name. But to do good and to communicate forget not: for with such sacrifices God is well pleased." (Heb. 11-13.)

It may seem, in a life of Christ, that we have been unnecessarily prolix and have gone into too much detail relative to the sacrifices of Jesus' day, as well as to their purpose and meaning. To the contrary, this very omission is one of the great deficiencies of most of what is written about our Lord in modern times. Paul thought it of sufficient moment to give forth such statements as we have now quoted, and the reality is that no one can really understand our Lord's life and sayings without a knowledge of the religious system in which he was reared and which was designed to introduce him and bear record of his ministry. The law of sacrifice is the introduction of the Lord Jesus Christ to the world.

It was a desolating day when Herod's Temple died. It was a sad and sorrowful day for the Jews when sacrifices ceased, for with their passing went also the last vestige of the true religious performances that prevailed among them. Without these they had left less than a shell of godliness. Had they turned to the Eternal Temple and to the Eternal Sacrifice, all would have been well with them, but as it is, we can only say, with Peter: "Repent ye therefore, and be converted, that your sins may be blotted out, when the times of refreshing shall come from the presence of the Lord; And he shall send Jesus Christ, which before was preached unto you: Whom the heaven must receive until the times of restitution of all things, which God hath spoken by the mouth of all his holy prophets since the world began." (Acts 3:19-21.) The times of restitution commenced in the spring of 1820, and the times of refreshing, when the earth shall be renewed and receive its paradisiacal glory, are not far distant.

NOTES

1. In speaking of the restoration of all things, as promised by all the holy prophets since the world began, and after quoting Malachi's promise that the Lord, at his Second Coming, would purify the sons of Levi so that once again they could and would offer anew unto him their ancient sacrifices, the Prophet Joseph Smith said: "It is generally supposed that sacrifice was entirely done away when the Great Sacrifice [i.e.,] the sacrifice of the Lord Jesus was offered up, and that there will be no necessity for the ordinance of sacrifice in [the] future; but those who assert this are certainly not acquainted with the duties, privileges and authority of the Priesthood, or with the Prophets." The authority of the priest-

hood here referred to is the thing that John the Baptist brought back on May 15, 1829, and the knowledge of what the prophets have left us includes, among other things, the teachings of Malachi, Zechariah, and Ezekiel as these are set forth in chapter 7 herein.

Joseph Smith continues: "The offering of sacrifice has ever been connected and forms a part of the duties of the Priesthood. It began with the Priesthood, and will be continued until after the coming of Christ, from generation to generation. We frequently have mention made of the offering of sacrifice by the servants of the Most High in ancient days, prior to the law of Moses; which ordinances will be continued when the Priesthood is restored with all its authority, power and blessings." The frequent references to sacrifices performed by Melchizedek authority include those of Adam, Abraham and the patriarchs, and all those performed among the American Hebrews known as Nephites, for among them there were no Levites and the detailed performances of the law of Moses, such as the daily sacrifice, were not undertaken. The restoration of the priesthood to perform, once again, the type of ordinances that were part of the ancient gospel dispensations has reference to the revelation of all things incident to these holy performances, which restoration is still future.

"These sacrifices, as well as every ordinance belonging to the Priesthood, will, when the Temple of the Lord shall be built, and the sons of Levi be purified, be fully restored and attended to in all their powers, ramifications, and blessings. This ever did and ever will exist when the powers of the Melchizedek Priesthood are sufficiently manifest; else how can the restitution of all things spoken of by the Holy Prophets are brought to pass. It is not to be understood that the law of Moses will be established again with all its rites and variety of ceremonies; this has never been spoken of by the prophets; but those things which existed prior to Moses' day, namely, sacrifice, will be continued.

"It may be asked by some, what necessity for sacrifice, since the Great Sacrifice was offered? In answer to which, if repentance, baptism, and faith existed prior to the days of Christ, what necessity for them since that time?" (*Teachings*, pp. 172-73.)

2. The *public sacrifices* were "the daily sacrifices; the additional for the Sabbath; for the New Moon; the Passover sacrifices; the lamb when the sheaf was waved; the Pentecostal sacrifices; those brought with the two first loaves; New Year's; Atonement Day sacrifices; those on the first day of, and those on the octave of 'Tabernacles.' *Private sacrifices* they classify as those on account of sins by word or deed; those on account of what concerned the body (such as various defilements); those on account of property (firstlings, tithes); those on account of festive seasons; and those on account of vows or promises." (*Temple*, p. 111.)

3. It should be noted that all who receive the gospel are called by Abraham's name and are accounted his seed.

Chapter 9

JEWISH FEASTS IN JESUS' DAY

> When he was come into Galilee, the
> Galileans received him, having seen all
> the things that he did at Jerusalem at
> the feast: for they also went unto the
> feast. . . . After this there was a feast of
> the Jews; and Jesus went up to
> Jerusalem. (John 4:45; 5:1.)

The Nature of Jewish Feasts

Jesus used the Jewish feasts as the ideal and perfect occasions to proclaim his divine Sonship, to dramatize the great and eternal truths concerning himself in such ways that they never would be forgotten, and to work miracles and bless his fellowmen. We may suppose also that he used them as occasions of personal worship and communion with his Father, for such was the very purpose for which they had been established, and it was his wont, as a Jew, to keep his own law, until the time that he himself fulfilled and revoked it.

Many sweet and lovely episodes of his life occurred at the feasts. Some of his most profound doctrine was taught to the worshipful throngs who assembled to keep the feasts; and miracles, beyond compare, were wrought by his hands at those solemn and sacred times. The Jewish feasts were part of the life of Jesus. We see him at the Feast of the Passover, when but twelve years of age, confounding the wise and the learned. He was there because "his parents went to Jerusalem every year at the feast of the passover." (Luke 2:41-52.) We hear him tell Peter and John to prepare the Passover so that he and the Twelve could eat thereof. We hear his brethren—Mary's other sons, who did not then believe—chide him with the challenge to go to the Feast of Tabernacles and work further miracles, and we hear his reply that they should go now and he will come later. We see the Jews, astonished at his absence, seeking him at the feast. About the midst of the feast, we find him teaching in the temple; and then, "In the last day, that great day of the feast," as the priest takes water from the stream of Siloam, in a golden vessel, and pours it upon the altar, we hear his dramatic pronouncement: "If any man thirst, let him come unto me, and drink. He that believeth on me, as the scripture hath said, out of his belly shall flow rivers of living water." (John 7:1-39.)

As we place Jesus in the setting of the Jewish feasts, where he so logically is found and so naturally fits; as we envision that these feasts were part of the great schooling system, part of the way of worship of devout Jews, and were, therefore, imposed upon Jesus by his guardians and by the social pressure of his day; as we realize that he was acquainted with them and participated in their rituals, we must keep foremost in our thoughts the central performances undertaken at them. All of the feasts were occasions for the offering of sacrifices: public sacrifices for the spiritual well-being and salvation of the whole congregation, and private sacrifices for the forgiveness of personal sins and the reconciliation of true worshippers with their God. Sacrificial offerings; offerings made on the great altar, thirty by thirty feet square at the top; sacrifices in which blood was shed as a symbol of reconciliation; sacrifices made in similitude of Him who mingled with the festive throngs at those very feasts, seeking to do them good, while their rulers sought to do him ill—these were the center of Jewish religious worship. They were ordinances of salvation, and without them, as far as that day was concerned, men could not gain an inheritance with Him who dwells behind the veil.

There were three great feasts—the Feast of the Passover, the Feast of Pentecost, and the Feast of Tabernacles. All Israelite males were commanded to appear three times a year before the Lord in his sanctuary, meaning that attendance at these three feasts was obligatory, and all were to go up to Jerusalem to worship the King, the Lord of Hosts, to purify themselves before him, and to carry back to their various cities and farms the spirit of festive worship in which they had participated. Women were welcome—and we find Mary accompanying Joseph, at least when their twelve-year-old son taught in the temple—though they were not required to attend.

These feasts, in ancient times, had a great unifying effect upon the people, both religiously, politically, and socially. Without them the self-willed tribes might have divided themselves into a dozen kingdoms, each going its own way, to the destruction of Israel as a people and as a nation. By the time of Jesus, however, it was no longer possible for all males—scattered among many nations, as they were—to go up three times a year to the City of God. Instead twenty-four courses of lay attendants were appointed to stand in the temple as representatives of all the people; attendance at the feasts became something that could be delegated, as it were.

These great feasts were times for festive offerings, a form of private sacrifices, as distinguished from the public sacrifices for the whole congregation. They were occasions for making freewill offerings for the poor and the Levites. At them and at other feasts there was a holy convocation, or gathering together for sacred purposes; there was rest, either from all work or from all servile work, as the case may be; and certain special sacrifices, depending upon the occasion, were offered for the whole congregation.

We shall now make such reference as must needs be to

the feasts here named and to the others—the Feast of Esther or Purim, and the Feast of the Dedication of the Temple— that also played a vital part in Jewish worship.

The Feast of the Passover

By Feast of the Passover we mean the Passover itself, which fell on the 14th of Nisan, and also the Feast of Un- leavened Bread, which lasted from Nisan 15 through 21. Though separate feasts, they were considered to be one, and they both commemorated the Exodus from Egyptian bond- age. Our chief interest in them, as we study the life of our Lord, is to learn why and how and in what manner they were kept by the Jews in Jesus' day, and for that matter how the Lord Jesus himself kept this greatest of all Jewish feasts. This latter we shall set forth more particularly when we recline with Jesus and the Twelve, in a place apart from the throngs, to eat the Paschal Supper, and see how naturally and easily the sacrament of the Lord's Supper grew out of it.

But as to the Passover proper, and as to the Feast of Un- leavened Bread, which was part and portion of the over-all festival—what were they, whence and why did they come, and what purpose did they serve? Without question the Passover season was the most joyous and glorious time of Jewish and Israelitish worship. Israel was born when Jacob's name was changed and when that faithful patriarch began to have seed. Her numbers were a mere seventy when she saved herself from famine by going down into Egypt. There she prospered until there arose a new king who knew not Jo- seph. Then came slavery, bondage, toil. Then were her male children slain and her young men scourged. Then did they find their own straw to make the bricks for Pharaoh's palaces and cities. Then were they downtrodden physically, socially, culturally, spiritually. Now, after four centuries, numbering more than two million souls, they cried mightily unto the Lord for deliverance. And the Great I AM, the God of Abraham, Isaac, and Jacob, their fathers, sent them a Moses.

Miracles were wrought; plagues were poured out; Pharaoh hardened his heart; the burdens on Jacob's seed increased; until finally, in their dire extremity, the Lord in his wrath chose to slay the firstborn of Pharaoh who sat on his throne, the firstborn of the governors who hated his people, the firstborn of the taskmasters whose whips cut the flesh of the chosen seed, the firstborn in every Egyptian family in all the land, and the firstborn of all their cattle. Let these hosts die, he decreed, and die they did, for they had defied God and said by the mouth of Pharaoh, 'Who is Jehovah that I and my people should give heed unto him?'

Then, in his mercy and goodness, lest the destroying angel slay any of the chosen seed, the Lord provided a Passover, a way of escape for his people. Later, in the wilderness, as their priestly rituals were perfected, he added to this the Feast of Unleavened Bread. That all Israel might know and remember and ponder that the Lord Jehovah, who delivered them from Egyptian bondage, was their Messiah, their Christ and the One who would shed his blood for the sins of the world, the angel of death was commanded to pass over the houses on whose doors and lintels the blood of a sacrificial lamb had been sprinkled. Israel was to be saved by the blood of the lamb.

In each Israelite house a young lamb or kid, a male of the first year and one without blemish, was selected and slain. The head of each house, using a sprig of hyssop, sprinkled blood on the doorposts and on the lintel; the lamb or kid was roasted whole; not a bone was broken; and it was eaten, in haste, along with unleavened bread and bitter herbs.

No uncircumcised male, none in whose flesh the symbol of the Abrahamic covenant was not found, was to partake, but each male who did partake was to stand with his loins girt, his staff in his hand, and his shoes on his feet. Any of the uneaten flesh was to be burned. In later generations this Egyptian Passover became a permanent Passover with such changes and perfections in the ritualistic arrangements as better suited the accustomed and established order of religious services.

Israel was a people, the Lord's people, from the day Jacob and Leah had Reuben. She became a nation, a dependent nation, while dwelling in Goshen and living under Egyptian sovereignty, and she went into bondage and slavery when the fortunes of war put Egypt in unfriendly hands. But she was born as a free nation when Jehovah removed the heavy hand of Egypt, and she was redeemed from a state of slavery when the Great Jehovah led her through the Red Sea—first into a wilderness, and then into a fruitful land flowing with milk and honey. Israel became a free people, a free nation, a new kingdom on that first Passover night, and ever thereafter the Passover festivities were a birthday celebration, but—and this was the whole center and heart of the occasion—a celebration in which Christ and his redeeming ministry were brought over and over again to the attention of all those who subjected themselves to the rituals of this chief feast.

In the day of Jesus, both public and private sacrifices were made, and the paschal lambs were slain for each family or group, each of such units containing from ten to twenty persons. Jesus and the Twelve made up a group of thirteen, which dropped to an even twelve when evil Judas withdrew. When Nero sat in Caesar's seat a count was made of the number of lambs slain in Jerusalem at one Passover: the total, 256,000. On the basis of a minimum of ten in each group, this meant a Passover population for the holy city of 2,560,000. Josephus placed it that year at 2,700,200, and there were times when the assembled hosts numbered not less than 3,000,000.

Rabbi Gamaliel, the teacher of Paul, said: "Whoever does not explain three things in the Passover has not fulfilled the duty incumbent on him. These three things are: the Passover lamb, the unleavened bread, and the bitter herbs. *The Passover lamb* means that God passed over the blood-sprinkled place on the houses of our fathers in Egypt; *the un-*

leavened bread means that our fathers were delivered out of Egypt (in haste); and *the bitter herbs* mean that the Egyptians made bitter the lives of our fathers in Egypt." (*Temple*, p. 237.)

Paul, who was taught from on high as well as being the pupil of Gamaliel, knew more about the Passover than did his rabbinical instructor. In administering a severe rebuke to the sinning saints of Corinth, the apostle says: "Your glorying is not good." Then he asks: "Know ye not that a little leaven leaveneth the whole lump?" That is, if you have in your heart the spirit of the gospel, it will influence you to pursue a course of righteousness, but if you still have in your heart the spirit of the world, your conduct will be after the manner of the world. "Purge out therefore the old leaven"— forsake the world and cast away the evil inclinations of your souls—"that ye may be a new lump"—that ye may be born again, be a new creature of the Holy Ghost, live in a newness of life—"as ye are unleavened"—that is, live in righteousness because ye are no longer leavened with the unrighteousness of the world. "For even Christ our passover is sacrificed for us," meaning that all this is possible because the Eternal Paschal Lamb has wrought the atoning sacrifice for us. "Therefore let us keep the feast, not with old leaven, neither with the leaven of malice and wickedness; but with the unleavened bread of sincerity and truth." (1 Cor. 5:6-8.) With the offering of the Eternal Sacrifice the Passover ceases except in the sense that the true saints adopt the true principles upon which it was based, and so purge the leaven of wickedness out of their souls and eat forever of the unleavened bread of truth and righteousness.

The Feast of Unleavened Bread was an occasion in Israel for joy and rejoicing. The bread itself was called "the bread of affliction," to remind Israel of the sorrows and sufferings of their Egyptian bondage (Deut. 12:1-8), but the emphasis was not upon the afflictions of the past but upon the joys of the present and the future. Israel had been delivered from bondage through the Passover, and the eating of unleavened

164

bread for seven days did more to remind them that the fulness of the earth was now theirs than to unduly emphasize the afflictions that once were theirs.

On the first day of the feast (the second day of the Passover) there was a holy convocation, and the first ripe sheaf of grain was presented to the Lord. It was the feast of spring, with all the joy and rebirth that goes with the season. On each day of the feast, following the regular morning sacrifice, burnt offerings were made wherein the people surrendered their will to the will of the Lord, and sin offerings were made as an atonement for their sins. On the concluding day there was a solemn assembly. All in all it is difficult to imagine how a festive period could have been devised, under the Mosaic system, that would have done more to bring spirituality and blessings into the lives of the people than did the performances and worship of the Passover period. And that the Lord participated in them to the full we shall set forth in due course.[1]

Everything connected with the Passover period, from Nisan 14 through 21, is so dramatic, so filled with symbolism, so designed to center the attention of the Lord's people in the great and eternal truths of salvation that even today, when the Passover is past and we no longer need, to the extent our forebears did, to ponder its place in the plan of salvation, we are still prone to use its happenings to teach various related truths and principles. Thoughtful Christians may well reason, as many of them have, along such lines as these:

The Passover is a type of deliverance from the slavery of sin; from the bondage of the world; from the Pharaohs of greed and power and lust. It is the passing over of the angel of spiritual death so that the darkness of unbelief is replaced by the light of the gospel. It is a deliverance from the doom we deserve for our sins; from the spiritual death that awaits the wicked; from the outer darkness of Egypt and Sodom and Sheol—because the blood of Christ has been applied to us by faith. By sprinkling our Lord's blood upon the doorposts of our hearts and upon the lintels of our souls, we set our dwellings apart from the world; we make open and visible confession of our allegiance to Him whose blood has eternal saving power; we set ourselves apart from the Egyptians, the Sodomites, and the seekers after Sheol; and we place ourselves with the believing portion of mankind. As each family group ate their paschal lamb and drank of the cup of blessing, so must we eat the flesh and drink the blood of the Lord Jesus. As the Passover was useless unless eaten, so must we live godly lives in Christ, and openly certify our love for him by keeping his commandments. As it was eaten with bitter herbs, so must we eat our Passover with the bitter herbs of confession and repentance. As ancient Israel ate their Passover girt for a journey, shod with sandals, with a staff in their hands, so must modern Israel dress for their journey; so must they clothe themselves with the robes of righteousness, as they journey from Idumea to Zion, from Babylon to Palestine. As they, in the face of all the power and influence of Egypt, prepared to follow Moses wherever he led them, so must we follow our modern Moses through the Red Sea of doubt, into the wilderness of trials, and finally over the Jordan to that Promised Land where Abraham, Isaac, and Jacob and all the saints now dwell, there to rest in glory.

Truly the saints today can slay their own paschal lambs, eat their own unleavened bread, keep their own Passover, and serve Him whom their forebears served during that millennium and a half when the original Feast of the Passover was kept with joy and rejoicing!

The Feast of Pentecost

Pentecost had its beginning in the Passover, and the Passover had its ending, seven weeks later, in Pentecost; the two feasts are tied together, with the one growing out of the other. At the Passover, on the first day of the Feast of Unleavened Bread, Israel presented the Passover sheaf to the

Lord. With ritualistic ceremony they harvested the first of the barley crop, threshed the heads of grain, parched the grain, and ground it into fine flour. One omer (just over five pints) of fine flour was chosen, and oil and frankincense were added; the mixture was then waved before the Lord, and a portion was burned on the altar. This was the beginning of the harvest, which would be climaxed fifty days later at Pentecost. The Passover began on Nisan 14 (early April) with the beginning of the harvest of barley, and Pentecost came on Sivan 6 (about the end of May) with the start of the harvest of wheat. They were the harvest festivals of Israel.

On the day of Pentecost—called also the Feast of Harvest, the Day of First Fruits, and the Feast of Weeks— Israel was to hold a holy convocation and do no servile work. All males were to appear before the Lord in his sanctuary, and the appointed sacrifices and offerings were to be made. The order of worship and the performances attending it are generally conceded to be as follows:

1. On the days preceding the feast, the pilgrim bands— "Jews, devout men, out of every nation under heaven" (Acts 2:5)—joyously assembled at Jerusalem, at the Holy City, the City of the Great King, the site of the Lord's House. What a glorious thing it is for the faithful to go up to Zion, the city of their God!

2. Also before the appointed day, attended by the appointed ceremonial recitations and performances, sheaves of wheat were reaped and the grain was harvested, parched, ground into flour, and sifted through twelve sieves. The night before, the two wave loaves, each of leavened bread and weighing together more than ten pounds, were baked.

3. The great altar was cleansed, all things were arranged for the rites to follow, and about midnight the temple gates were opened so the priests could examine the animals brought by the people for burnt offerings and for peace offerings.

4. With the dawn came the regular morning sacrifice and the assembling of great throngs of worshippers at the temple.

Devout Jews took seriously Jehovah's decree that the adult males of his kingdom should appear before him in his sanctuary three times each year.

5. Then came the appointed festive offerings. These were, first, one kid of the goats, for a sin offering, made with proper imposition of hands, confession of sin, and sprinkling of blood; and then, the burnt offerings, consisting of two young bullocks, one ram, and seven lambs of the first year, along with their appropriate meat offerings.

6. At this point, the Levites chanted the Hallel, Psalms 113 to 118, to the accompaniment of a flute and the singing voices of Levite children, and the people either repeated or responded to the psalms of praise as they did at the Feast of the Passover.

7. "Then came the peculiar offering of the day—that of the two wave-loaves, with their accompanying sacrifices. These consisted of seven lambs of the first year, without blemish, one young bullock, and two rams for a burnt-offering, with their appropriate meat-offerings; and then 'one kid of the goats for a sin-offering, and two lambs of the first year for a sacrifice of peace-offerings.' " These are not to be confused with the festive offerings. The two lambs were waved, while yet alive, along with the wave loaves, and their principal parts were again waved after being slain.

8. "After the ceremony of the wave-loaves, the people brought their own freewill-offerings, each as the Lord had prospered him—the afternoon and evening being spent in the festive meal, to which the stranger, the poor, and the Levite were bidden as the Lord's welcome guests."

9. There was of course the evening sacrifice, and in practice, because of the great number of freewill offerings, it generally took up to a week to offer them all. (*Temple*, pp. 249-67.)

Jewish tradition, having apparent foundation in fact, held that as the Passover commemorated the deliverance from Egypt, so Pentecost commemorated the wondrous outpouring of divine grace that occurred fifty days later when with his own finger—the same finger that had touched the sixteen stones for Moriancumer—the Great Jehovah wrote his law on tablets of stone and gave them to Moses the man of God. What is more to the point is that our Lord was crucified as part of the Passover, and that the Holy Spirit of God came in power on the Day of Pentecost. For forty days after his resurrection Jesus continued to minister among the Twelve as a resurrected Being. Then he ascended to his Father, leaving them with instructions to tarry in Jerusalem until they were endowed with power from on high. Ten days later, "when the day of Pentecost was fully come," the apostles, with Matthias now one of their number, and perhaps other believers, "were all with one accord in one place. And suddenly there came a sound from heaven as of a rushing mighty wind, and it filled all the house where they were sitting."

Were they in the temple at the time, and was the house where they were sitting one of the porches where Jesus had so often sat to teach and expound? Opinions may vary, but such is not improbable. The "house," wherever it was, was open to the public, for great hosts—of whom three thousand were converted and baptized—rushed to hear and see and feel the miracle. How many houses there were, aside from the house of the Lord, where three or ten or scores of thousands could readily assemble is open to question. Further, the place where Jerusalem's throngs were found on a feast day was in the great court that surrounded the holy sanctuary. But an even more compelling question is: Where else would the Jewish apostles and their followers have gone on a Jewish feast day than to the Lord's holy sanctuary? They, as yet—for the gift of the Holy Ghost had not taken hold of their minds—felt subject to the law that called for every male to appear before the Lord in his sanctuary on that day. Would they have been keeping the commandment and standing in the line of their duty, as they then understood it, or would they have been elsewhere, plotting, as it were, against what they had always known to be the established order? For that matter, it was their wont, on all days, to make the temple their center of worship. Habits change gradually. Jesus and the Twelve had worshipped in the temple while the Lord dwelt among them. Each one of them, time after time, had made the required appearance at the appointed place.

Further, after Jesus "was parted from them, and carried up into heaven," the Twelve "worshipped him, and returned to Jerusalem with great joy: And were continually in the temple, praising and blessing God." (Luke 24:49-53.) And even after the Day of Pentecost, their numbers swelled by the three thousand Pentecostal baptisms, the record says: "And they, continuing daily with one accord in the temple, and breaking bread from house to house, did eat their meat with gladness and singleness of heart, Praising God, and having favour with all the people." (Acts 2:46-47.) Later still, Peter and John, while walking through the gate called Beautiful, healed the man lame from his mother's womb, causing the "Gentile" mobs, then in the court of the Gentiles, to cause their arrest and imprisonment. Indeed, we might well ask: If fire was to come down from heaven again, as it had done in Solomon's Temple, where else would it come than to the house used by the Lord as his own?

But wherever the miracle occurred, it was the ushering in of the day of miracles and revelation that always attends the true saints. For, "there appeared unto them cloven tongues like as of fire, and it sat upon each of them." It was as though the fires on the stony altars of the dying dispensation were now ignited in the mellowed hearts of the Saints. "And they were all filled with the Holy Ghost, and began to speak with other tongues, as the Spirit gave them utterance. . . . Now when this was noised abroad, the multitude came together, and were confounded, because that every man heard them speak in his own language." The apostles spoke in Aramaic, with their Galilean and Palestinian dialects, and all men, be they whosoever they might be and speaking whatsoever language was theirs, heard and understood.

"And they were all amazed and marvelled, saying one to another, Behold, are not all these which speak Galileans? And how hear we every man in our own tongue, wherein we were born?" (Acts 2:1-13.) How fitting it was that, while the sacrificial fires yet burned on the altar of sacrifice, living fire should come down from heaven to burn forever in the hearts of those who were to sacrifice their lives in the cause of truth and righteousness.

The Feast of Tabernacles

Taking our cues and quotations from Edersheim (*Temple,* pp. 268-87), but tempering his views with the added light and knowledge revealed in the dispensation of the fulness of times, we shall now turn to the Feast of Tabernacles, "the most joyous of all festive seasons in Israel." As we have heretofore seen, this is the one great Jewish-Israelitish feast that was not abolished forever when He who gave the law also fulfilled that which had come from Him. As the prophets have said, it shall be celebrated again during the Millennium, when the sons of Levi, in purity and worthiness, at the direction of the Melchizedek authority that governs the Church of God in all ages, shall offer again an offering unto the Lord in righteousness. Our present major concern, however, is to see how and in what manner this feast bore record of Jesus and to see how he himself used it during his mortal ministry to show the people what witness they were in fact bearing through its sacred and holy rituals.

Of Passover, Pentecost, and Tabernacles—the three annual festive occasions when Jehovah commanded all male Israelites to appear before him in his holy sanctuary in Jerusalem, and not to come empty handed—it is appropriately said: "If the beginning of the harvest had pointed back to the birth of Israel in their Exodus from Egypt, and forward to the true Passover-sacrifice in the future; if the corn-harvest was connected with the giving of the law on Mount Sinai in the past, and the outpouring of the Holy

Spirit on the Day of Pentecost; the harvest-thanksgiving of the Feast of Tabernacles reminded Israel, on the one hand, of their dwelling in booths in the wilderness, while, on the other hand, it pointed to the final harvest when Israel's mission should be completed, and all nations gathered unto the Lord." (*Temple,* p. 269.)

Thus the Feast of Tabernacles is called also the Feast of Booths, for Israel dwelt in booths or huts when she first came out of Egypt, and the Feast of Ingathering, for by Tishri 15, when the seven-day feast began (the September-October period), the whole harvest, with its corn and wine and oil, had been stored for the winter ahead. To envision how Jewish Israel worshipped in the days of Jesus, it will be instructive to summarize what was done at this feast. As with all feasts, it was a period of worship and spiritual refreshment, a time to renew covenants and return unto the Lord with full purpose of heart. In this case, however, the feast began four days after the Day of Atonement, "in which the sin of Israel had been removed, and its covenant relation to God restored. Thus a sanctified nation could keep a holy feast of harvest joy unto the Lord, just as in the truest sense it will be in that day," spoken of by the prophets, when "every one that is left of all the nations . . . shall even go up from year to year to worship the King, the Lord of hosts, and to keep the feast of tabernacles," when millennial righteousness will be such that "Holiness unto the Lord" will be inscribed on almost all things. (Zech. 14:16-21; *Temple,* pp. 271-72.)

Joyous festivities marked the Feast of Tabernacles; the "ingathering" spirit prevailed; without their harvests Israel would perish for want of bread; and famine was a constant threat. How natural that they should rejoice in what the Lord had given them—from the soil and the rain and the sun! And how natural that Jehovah would expect of them thanksgiving and rejoicing for the bounties that flowed from his hands! Thus we hear him say: "Thou shalt observe the feast of tabernacles seven days, after that thou hast gathered in thy corn and thy wine: And thou shalt rejoice in thy feast, thou, and thy son, and thy daughter, and thy manservant, and thy maidservant, and the Levite, the stranger, and the fatherless, and the widow, that are within thy gates." Why? "Because the Lord thy God shall bless thee in all thine increase, and in all the works of thine hands, therefore thou shalt surely rejoice." Then, as to the three great feasts—Passover, Pentecost, and Tabernacles—the Lord said of all who went up to Jerusalem to keep them: "And they shall not appear before the Lord empty: Every man shall give as he is able, according to the blessing of the Lord thy God which he hath given thee." (Deut. 16:13-17.) And at these festive occasions, both those who gave and those who received would have occasion to rejoice. "Votive, freewill, and peace-offerings would mark their gratitude to God, and at the meal which ensued the poor, the stranger, the Levite, and the homeless would be welcome guests, for the Lord's sake." (*Temple*, p. 272.)

In the day of Jesus, as had been the case since the day of Moses, all male Israel, at Tabernacle-time, left their houses of wood and stone and dwelt in huts or booths made of the boughs of living trees. For one week, except in very heavy rain, they ate, slept, prayed, studied, and lived in these temporary abodes. Women, the sick and their attendants, slaves, infants dependent on their mothers, and some away on pious duties were exempt. "When ye have gathered in the fruit of the land," was the decree the Lord had given them, "ye shall keep a feast unto the Lord seven days: on the first day shall be a sabbath, and on the eighth day shall be a sabbath." The eighth day, the Octave of the feast, was, strictly speaking, not part of the feast itself, but served as an added day of worship. "And ye shall take you on the first day the boughs of goodly trees, branches of palm trees, and the boughs of thick trees, and willows of the brook; and ye shall rejoice before the Lord your God seven days." The use of these boughs and branches in the rejoicing rites shall be set forth shortly. "And ye shall keep it a feast unto the Lord seven days in the year. It shall be a statute for ever in your generations: ye shall celebrate it in the seventh month. Ye shall dwell in booths seven days; all that are Israelites born shall dwell in booths: That your generations may know that I made the children of Israel to dwell in booths, when I brought them out of the land of Egypt: I am the Lord your God." (Lev. 23:39-43.) Surely there were those among them who realized thereby, not alone that their tent-type life in escaping from Egypt was a temporary arrangement as they traveled en route to a promised land, but that all men are strangers and pilgrims on earth, en route to a more enduring abode, a home, not made with hands, that is eternal in the heavens.

We have heretofore dealt, sufficiently for our needs—in connection with Passover and with Pentecost and with Mosaic sacrificial performances as such—with the sacrificial system of worship. We are aware of how sins are forgiven, how covenants are made, how vows are kept, how God is blessed and glorified, and how spiritual refreshment comes through sacrificial offerings. We need here merely point out the unique and peculiar nature of the sacrifices required at the Feast of Tabernacles, and to remind ourselves that sacrifices as such—whether public or private, and whether offered as burnt offerings, sin offerings, trespass offerings, or peace offerings—were at the heart and core of ritualistic religion in those days.

Burnt offerings—the sacrifices of devotion and service, which symbolized the entire surrender of the people to Jehovah and his acceptance of them—were more numerous during the Feast of Tabernacles than at any of the other festivals. On each of the seven days, two rams and 14 lambs were offered; on the first day 13 bullocks were also offered, with this number being diminished by one each day, so that seven only were offered on the seventh day. Thus 182 burnt offerings, each with its proper meat and drink offering, sent their sweet savor up to Jehovah during this period. In addition, one kid was offered for a sin offering on each day; and on the Octave day, seven lambs, one ram, and one bullock were offered as burnt offerings, plus one kid as a sin offering. All of these were in addition to the continual burnt offerings, their meat and drink offerings, and all of the private offerings of the hosts of devout worshippers. Our purpose in setting this forth is simply to show that the Feast of Tabernacles should have been and was the great period both of thanksgiving and of rededication.

Now let us go back to "the boughs of goodly trees, branches of palm trees, and the boughs of thick trees, and willows of the brook," which the people were to take and use as they rejoiced before the Lord. In the day of Jesus—and we must assume such was the case from the beginning of the feast—these were carried in the hands of the people. Since the use to which they were put is the same as that of the white handkerchiefs, when the Hosanna Shout is given at temple dedications and certain other solemn assemblies in latter-day Israel, we shall note particularly the rabbinical regulations relative to them. "The Rabbis ruled, that 'the fruit of the goodly trees' meant the *aethrog,* or citron, and 'the boughs of thick trees' the myrtle, provided it had 'not more berries than leaves.' The *aethrogs* must be without blemish or deficiency of any kind; the palm branches at least three handbreadths high, and fit to be shaken; and each branch fresh, entire, unpolluted, and not taken from any idolatrous grove. Every worshipper carried the *aethrog* in his left hand, and in his right the *lulav,* or palm, with myrtle and willow branch on either side of it, tied together on the outside with its own kind, though in the inside it might be fastened even with gold thread. There can be no doubt that the *lulav* was intended to remind Israel of the different stages of their wilderness journey, as represented by the different vegetation—the palm branches recalling the valley and plains, the 'boughs of thick trees,' the bushes on the mountain heights, and the willows those brooks from which God had given his people drink; while the *aethrog* was to remind them of the fruits of the good land which the Lord had given them. The *lulav* was used in the Temple on each of the seven festive days, even children, if they were able to shake it, being bound to carry one."

The use of these *lulavs* was in this manner: On each of the seven days of the feast, "while the morning sacrifice was being prepared, a priest, accompanied by a joyous procession with music, went down to the Pool of Siloam, whence he drew water into a golden pitcher." Amid much pageantry this water was carried back to the great altar; and when the wine of the drink offering was poured out, so was the water from Siloam, as part of an elaborate ceremony. "As soon as the wine and the water were being poured out, the temple music began, and the 'Hallel' was sung. . . . When the choir came to these words, 'O give thanks to the Lord,' and again when they sang, 'O work then now salvation, Jehovah;' and once more at the close, 'O give thanks unto the Lord,' all the worshippers shook their *lulavs* towards the altar. When, therefore, the multitudes from Jerusalem, on meeting Jesus, 'cut down branches from the trees, and strewed them in the way, and . . . cried, saying, O then, work now salvation to the Son of David!' they applied, in reference to Christ, what was regarded as one of the chief ceremonies of the Feast of Tabernacles, praying that God would from 'the highest' heavens manifest and send that salvation in connection with the Son of David, which was symbolised by the pouring out of the water." (*Temple*, pp. 274-79.)

In the cries of praise and adoration—given each day for seven days, as the temple throngs waved their palm branches toward the great altar, and consisting of a three-times-repeated expression of glorious exultation—we see the pattern for the Hosanna Shout as it has been revealed anew and is now given, also on special and sacred occasions. In our day, while waving white handkerchiefs with each word or phrase of praise, united Israel exults:

> *Hosanna, Hosanna, Hosanna,*
> *To God and the Lamb;*

> *Hosanna, Hosanna, Hosanna,*
> *To God and the Lamb;*
> *Hosanna, Hosanna, Hosanna,*
> *To God and the Lamb;*
> *Amen, Amen, Amen!*

However, at the Feast of Tabernacles, in addition to the daily Hosanna Shout, which followed and grew out of the offering of the daily sacrifice, there was yet another shout—a Great Hosanna, a Hosanna of Hosannas—which was given on one day only, following the festive sacrifices, and on "that great day of the feast." The setting for the Great Hosanna was the ceremonial circuiting of the altar by those appointed so to do. "On every one of the seven days the priests formed in procession, and made the circuit of the altar, singing: 'O then, now work salvation, Jehovah! O Jehovah, give prosperity!' But on the seventh, 'that great day of the feast,' they made the circuit of the altar seven times, remembering how the walls of Jericho had fallen in similar circumstances, and anticipating how, by the direct interposition of God, the walls of heathenism would fall before Jehovah, and the land lie open for his people to go in and possess it." This time, on the day called by the Rabbis "Day of the Great Hosanna," "Day of Willows," and "Day of Beating the Branches," amid their cries of praise to Jehovah, the worshipping throngs waved their *lulavs* with such vigor that "all the leaves were shaken off the willow boughs, and the palm branches beaten in pieces by the side of the altar." Such was the climactic moment of the Hosanna Shout in the Feast of Tabernacles. (*Temple*, pp. 280-81.)

Similitudes of the Feast of Tabernacles

There are in the Feast of Tabernacles more ceremonies that center in Christ, more similitudes that tell of his life and ministry, and more types and shadows that testify of him and his redeeming sacrifice than in any of the other feasts. In a general sense, the Feast of Tabernacles has all that the other feasts had, and a great deal more that is unique, distinctive, and reserved for this most joyous of all festive occasions.

The chief and most important symbolism in all the feasts was that shown forth through the sacrificial ordinances. These bore record of the coming sacrifice of the Lamb of God and taught the people how redemption came and how sins were to be remitted by the sprinkling of his blood. At the Feast of Tabernacles the number of public sacrifices was multiplied, and we may suppose that in practice—because the Day of Atonement had just cleansed and sanctified the people, and because of the especially joyous nature of the feast—there were more private sacrifices, more votive offerings, more freewill offerings than at any other time.

We are aware of the reasons Israel dwelt in booths at this season and of their rejoicing over the harvests reaped; and we see in these things a type of man's pilgrimage through the wilderness of the world and of the eternal rejoicing that will attend the harvest of the souls of men. We have noted how the Hosanna Shout spoke praise to Jehovah and how its very words were interpreted by the multitudes to apply to the Son of David as he made his triumphal entry into Jerusalem as they spread palm branches in the way. We need not pursue further what is clear to all who are spiritually literate, except to show how two of the special ceremonies of the feast bore record of Christ and were used by him to dramatize and announce the fulfillment of the figures found in them. One of these is the pouring out of the water, which preceded the Hosanna Shout, and the other is the illumination of the temple. Both of these ceremonies are said to be post-Mosaic and post-Exilic, that is, to have been added after the day of the great lawgiver and after the return from Babylon. This may be true; if so, it is an indication of continuing revelation to the Lord's people; or, it may be that the rites, though not mentioned in Holy Writ, were part of the ceremonies from the beginning. In any event they were a vital part of valid and approved performances in the day of Jesus. He was acquainted with them and used them for his own purposes.

As we have seen, the priests poured the water from Siloam on the altar after the daily morning sacrifice and before the festive offerings, and as a prelude to the waving of palm branches in the Hosanna Shout. Of this pouring of the water it is said: "Its main and real application was to the future outpouring of the Holy Spirit, as predicted—probably in allusion to this very rite—by Isaiah the prophet. Thus the Talmud says distinctly: 'Why is the name of it called, The drawing out of water? Because of the pouring out of the Holy Spirit, according to what is said: "With joy shall ye draw water out of the wells of salvation." ' Hence, also, the feast and the peculiar joyousness of it are alike designated as those of 'the drawing out of water;' for, according to the same Rabbinical authorities, the Holy Spirit dwells in man only through joy."

Now with this concept before us—that Israel by the power of the Spirit was to draw waters from the wells of salvation, and that such was symbolized by the rite then in progress—and with the Hosanna Shout ringing in our ears, let us see what happened in the life of Jesus on the seventh day of the feast. "It was on that day, after the priest had returned from Siloam with his golden pitcher, and for the last time poured its contents to the base of the altar; after the 'Hallel' had been sung to the sound of the flute, the people responding and worshipping as the priests three times drew the threefold blasts from their silver trumpets—just when the interest of the people had been raised to its highest pitch, that, from amidst the mass of worshippers, who were waving towards the altar quite a forest of leafy branches as the last words of Psalm 118 were chanted—a voice was raised which resounded through the Temple, startled the multitude, and carried fear and hatred to the hearts of their leaders. It was Jesus, who 'stood and cried, saying, If any man thirst, let him come unto me, and drink.' Then by faith in him should each one truly become like the Pool of Siloam, and from his inmost being, 'flow rivers of living water.' 'This spake he of the Spirit, which they that believe on him should receive.' (John 7:37-39.) Thus the significance of the rite, in which they had just taken part, was not only fully explained, but the mode of its fulfilment pointed out." (*Temple,* pp. 279-81.)

At the close of the first day of the feast—amid hymns and songs of praise; with instrumental music accompanying and trumpets blowing repeated blasts; as dancers held flaming torches in their hands; and amid pageantry that was itself ritualistic—four of the sons of Levi lighted the four great golden candelabras. "The light shining out of the Temple into the darkness around, and lighting up every court in Jerusalem, must have been intended as a symbol not only of the Shechinah which once filled the Temple, but of that 'great light' which 'the people that walked in darkness' were to see, and which was to shine 'upon them that dwell in the land of the shadow of death.' " (*Temple,* p. 285.) Surely, Master Teacher that he was, the shining forth of this light from the temple was the occasion for Jesus, at that very feast, to say: "I am the light of the world: he that followeth me shall not walk in darkness, but shall have the light of life." (John 8:12.)

So much for the similitudes of the past. But what of the future? The Feast of Tabernacles is both past and future. What wondrous types and figures, what sacred similitudes and symbolisms, will yet be given at the Feast of Tabernacles that is to be? Surely, whatever they are—fitted to the then-existing needs, as they will be—they will testify of a Lord who came, of a Christ who is risen, and of a King who reigns. And it is not without significance that when the Beloved John saw in vision the hosts of Israel and of all men worshipping God in millennial peace and in celestial glory, he saw a renewed scene, before the throne of God, of what had been prefigured around the altar in Herod's Temple. "After this I beheld, and, lo, a great multitude, which no man could number, of all nations, and kindreds, and people, and tongues, stood before the throne, and before the Lamb, clothed with white robes, and palms in their hands; And cried with a loud voice, saying, Salvation to our God which sitteth upon the throne, and unto the Lamb." These are they who are "before the throne of God, and serve him day and night in his temple." And "the Lamb which is in the midst of the throne shall feed them, and shall lead them unto living fountains of waters." (Rev. 7.)

Other Feasts, Fasts, and Formalities

Passover, Pentecost, and Tabernacles—each with its sacred symbolism; each with its redeeming power; each serving as a shadow of better things to come—these were the three great feasts of Jewish Israel, the triennial times when all adult males were to appear before the Lord, in the holy sanctuary, and there renew their covenants and receive anew a remission of their sins. But if there are greater feasts, there must needs be lesser ones: there cannot be the blazing light of the sun at its zenith unless there is also the lesser light of the dawning day or the calming glow of an approaching twilight, and what we must not forget is that the lesser light also guides our footsteps and the lesser feasts also feed our souls.

Each New Moon—of which there were twelve or thirteen each year, as the case may be[2]—was a festive day marked by the offering of special sacrifices,[3] the blowing of trumpets, and a joyous spirit of rededication. It was also an occasion for state banquets, for family feasts, and one, like the Sabbath, when trade and handicraft work ceased. It was with the Day of the New Moon as it was with all else that Israel had: by offering in sacrifice the firstlings of their flocks and the firstfruits of their harvests, all of their flocks and the whole of their harvests became holy before the Lord; and so by sanctifying the first day of the month, the whole lunar period became one of rejoicing and thanksgiving. Religion was truly a way of life with Jewish Israel; their whole course of conduct was religious in nature, worshipful in character, and Jehovah-centered in fact.

"Scarcely any other festive season could have left so continuous an impress on the religious life of Israel as the 'New Moons.' Recurring at the beginning of every month, and marking it, the solemn proclamation of the day, by—'It is sanctified,' was intended to give a hallowed character to each month, while the blowing of the priests' trumpets and the special sacrifices brought, would summon, as it were, the Lord's host to offer their tribute unto their exalted King, and thus bring themselves into 'remembrance' before Him. . . .

"In the law of God only these two things are enjoined in the observance of the 'New Moon'—the 'blowing of trumpets' and special festive sacrifices. Of old the 'blowing of trumpets' had been the signal for Israel's host on their march through the wilderness, as it afterwards summoned them to warfare, and proclaimed or marked days of public rejoicing, and feasts, as well as the 'beginnings of their months.' The object of it is expressly stated to have been 'for a memorial,' that they might 'be remembered before Jehovah,' it being specially added: 'I am Jehovah your God.' It was, so to speak, the host of God assembled, waiting for their Leader; the people of God united to proclaim their King. At the blast of the priests' trumpets they ranged themselves, as it were, under his banner and before his throne, and this symbolical confession and proclamation of him as 'Jehovah their God,' brought them before him to be 'remembered' and 'saved.' And so every season of 'blowing the trumpets,' whether at New Moons, at the Feast of Trumpets or New Year's Day, at other festivals, in the Sabbatical and Year of Jubilee, or in the time of war, was a public acknowledgment of Jehovah as King. Accordingly we find the same symbols adopted in the figurative language of the New Testament. As of old the sound of the trumpet summoned the congregation before the Lord at the door of the Tabernacle, so 'His elect' shall be summoned by the sound of the trumpet in the day of Christ's coming, and not only the living, but those also who had 'slept'—'the dead in Christ.' Similarly, the heavenly hosts are marshalled to the war of successive judgments, till, as 'the seventh angel sounded,' Christ is proclaimed King Universal: 'The kingdoms of this world are become the kingdoms of our Lord, and of his Christ, and he shall reign for ever and ever.' "[4]

On the first day of the seventh month, *Tishri,* the New Moon festival became the Feast of Trumpets, or the Day of Blowing of Trumpets, when horns and trumpets were blown—not merely during the offering of sacrifices as on the regular New Moon festivals, but all day long in Jerusalem, when additional sacrifices were prescribed,[5] and when a holy convocation was held. This was New Year's Day, the first day of the civil year. It preceded the Day of Atonement by ten days, during which time the people were expected to repent, as a condition precedent to the remission of sins that came when the high priest made an atonement for them and sprinkled the redeeming blood in the Holy of Holies.

In the day of Jesus there were three other festive seasons that are not mentioned in the law of Moses, but that were an established part of the worship system to which our Lord was subject. These feasts, brought into being by the spirit of inspiration as it had rested upon the recognized leaders of the people, were established to commemorate great historical events rather than to typify gospel truths. Hence, no special rites and sacrifices were prescribed.

The Feast of Purim commemorated the preservation of the Jews in Persia from the massacre planned by Haman in the days of Esther and Ahasuerus. It lasted two days and included the reading of the book of Esther, the cursing of Haman and all idolaters, and the blessing of Mordecai and all Israelites. It was an occasion of great merriment and rejoicing, and is believed by some to be the "feast of the Jews" to which Jesus went when he healed "the impotent man" at the pool of Bethesda. (John 5:1-9.)[6]

The Feast of Dedication commemorated the cleansing and rededication of Zerubbabel's Temple in 164 B.C., when Judas Maccabaeus freed the Jews from Syro-Grecian domination. It was patterned after the Feast of Tabernacles to the extent that it lasted eight days, included the illumination of the temple, the singing of the Hallel on each day, and the waving of palm branches toward the altar in the Hosanna Shout. It was during this feast that the Lord Jesus, having healed the man who was blind from birth, having announced himself as the Good Shepherd, and having taught plainly that he would die for the people, made the great proclamation: "I and my Father are one." (John 9, 10.)

There were eight times each year when selected families were privileged to bring wood to the temple for sacrificial use, and a ninth, the Feast of Wood Offering, when all the people—"even proselytes, slaves, Nethinim, and bastards, but notably the priests and Levites"—were so privileged. "On this occasion (as on the Day of Atonement) the maidens went dressed in white, to dance and sing in the vineyards around Jerusalem, when an opportunity was offered to young men to select their companions for life." (*Temple,* pp. 336-38.)

Feasting is one form of worship and fasting another; both are so ordained as to bring the Lord's people into communion with him, so that he can bless them for their goodness and purity of heart. From Adam's day to ours, whenever and wherever the true saints have dwelt on earth, the law of the fast has been interwoven into their system of worship. If we had the records of all the dispensations from the beginning, we would find in them the same type of recitation found in the Nephite scripture: "And the church did meet together oft, to fast and to pray, and to speak one with another concerning the welfare of their souls." (Moro. 6:5.)

And so it was with the Jews in the day of Jesus. Fasting was a basic and integral part of their way of worship. The Day of Atonement was a fast day; so also was the first day of the Feast of Purim, which was called the Fast of Esther. Besides these two, there were four other great fasts: one, "in memory of the taking of Jerusalem by Nebuchadnezzar and the interruption of the daily sacrifice"; another, "kept on account of the destruction of the first (and afterwards of the second) Temple"; still another, "in memory of the slaughter of Gedaliah and his associates at Mizpah," as set out in Jeremiah 41; and fourth, commemorating the day on which "the siege of Jerusalem by Nebuchadnezzar commenced." Further: "It was customary to fast *twice a week,* between the Paschal week and Pentecost, and between the Feast of Tabernacles and that of the Dedication of the Temple. The days appointed for this purpose were the Monday and the Thursday of each week—because, according to tradition, Moses went up Mount Sinai the second time to receive the Tables of the Law on a Thursday, and came down again on a Monday." (*Temple,* pp. 339-40.) From Passover to Pentecost was seven weeks, and from Tabernacles to Dedication was about ten weeks, the two periods thus adding about thirty-four fast days to the Jewish calendar of fasts, bringing to a total of about forty the number of formal fast days in each year. In addition there were such private fasts for private purposes as devout persons felt they should hold, all of which adds up to a far heavier fasting schedule than is commonly followed in the true Church as it is now constituted.

When the whole sacrificial system, plus the ritualistic formalities of the various feasts, plus the rituals attending the formal fasts are all viewed together, we have a reasonably comprehensive picture of at least the formal side of Jewish worship in our Lord's day. We have heretofore summarized their rites and formalisms where sacrifices and feasts are concerned. These words relative to fasts complete the picture: "On public fasts, the practice was to bring the ark which contained the rolls of the law from the synagogue into the streets, and to strew ashes upon it. The people all appeared covered with sackcloth and ashes. Ashes were publicly strewn on the heads of the elders and judges. Then one more venerable than the rest would address the people, his sermon being based on such an admonition as this: 'My brethren, it is not said of the men of Nineveh, that God had respect to their sackcloth or their fasting, but that "God saw their works, that they turned from their evil way." Similarly, it is written in the "traditions" of the prophets: "Rend your heart, and not your garments, and turn unto Jehovah your God." ' An aged man, whose heart and home 'God had emptied,' that he might give himself wholly to prayer, was chosen to lead the devotions. Confession of sin and prayer mingled with the penitential Psalms. In Jerusalem they gathered at the eastern gate, and seven times as the voice of prayer ceased, they bade the priests 'blow!' and they blew with horns and their priests' trumpets. In other towns, they only blew horns. After prayer, the people retired to the cemeteries to mourn and weep. In order to be a proper fast, it must be continued from one sundown till after the next, when the stars appeared, and for about twenty-six hours the most rigid abstinence from all food and drink was enjoined." (*Temple,* pp. 340-41.)

Our Lord fasted for forty days at the beginning of his ministry, although he and his disciples deliberately did not conform to the burdensome and ritualistic fasting formalities of the day. Instead, in some of the strong language he was wont to use, he condemned the hypocritical and self-seeking level to which the fasting of his day had degenerated.

NOTES

1. See chapters 22, 29, 30, and 95 through 101 in this work, *The Mortal Messiah.*

2. Israel's calendar was lunar, and the advent of each New Moon—a determination made by observing the lunar phases—became a matter of great moment to them. The calendar was kept in balance by inserting a thirteenth month in the year from time to time. The mean duration of the Jewish month was 29 days, 12 hours, 44 minutes, and $3\frac{1}{2}$ seconds; the year itself consisted of 354 days, 8 hours, 48 minutes, and 38 seconds. In a nineteen-year period it took the insertion of seven lunar months to keep the calendar in accordance with the Julian.

3. In addition to the daily sacrifice, the offering included two bullocks, a ram, and seven lambs as a burnt offering, with meat offerings and drink offerings, and a kid as a sin offering. (Num. 28:11-15.) And as on all festive occasions there were also the private offerings of the people.

4. *Temple,* pp. 288-91; Num. 10:1-10; 28:11-15; Matt. 24:31; 1 Cor. 15:52; 1 Thess. 4:16; Rev. 8:2; 10:7; 11:15.

5. In addition to the daily sacrifice and the eleven victims offered at all other New Moon festivals, a young bullock, a ram, and seven lambs of the first year were offered with their accustomed meat offerings, and a kid for a sin offering. (Num. 29:1-6.)

6. In chapter 38 we take the view, as does President J. Reuben Clark, that it was the Feast of the Passover. Elder James E. Talmage skirts the issue and expresses no view one way or the other.

186

Chapter 10

JEWISH SYNAGOGUES IN JESUS' DAY

Organize yourselves; prepare every
needful thing; and establish a house,
even a house of prayer, a house of
fasting, a house of faith, a house
of learning, a house of glory, a house of
order, a house of God; That your
incomings may be in the name of the
Lord; that your outgoings may be in the
name of the Lord; that all your
salutations may be in the name of the
Lord, with uplifted hands unto
the Most High. (D&C 88:119-120.)[1]

The Law of Synagogue Worship

What is a synagogue? In the proper and true and full
sense, it is a congregation of saints who worship the Father,
in the name of the Son, by the power of the Holy Spirit. It is
a congregation of people, of true believers; an assemblage of
the saints, of those who have received the truths of heaven
by revelation and are trying to apply them to their lives. Just
as Zion is the pure in heart, so the synagogue is the saints of
God. Zion is people, and the synagogue is people.

But Zion is also a place, one where the pure in heart congregate; and a synagogue is also a place, a house of worship, a building where the worshippers of the true God assemble to pay their devotions to the Most High. In the very nature of things, the term *synagogue* came to refer to the building in which the Lord's people assembled to praise his name and seek his grace. It became a house of worship comparable to the ward meetinghouses and the stake tabernacles found in latter-day Israel. When the people who are Zion lose their purity in heart, and when the congregation that is a true synagogue departs from the faith, all that is left is the house or place where they communed with their Maker. The Spirit may depart, but the building remains. It is looked upon as the synagogue and is so considered by all who see it. Such were the synagogues of which the New Testament speaks.

The word *synagogue* itself is of Greek origin and means to bring together or assemble; it is used in the Septuagint for the Assembly of Israel. It is thus the scriptural designation given, especially from exilic times, to the congregations of true believers, although there have been synagogues or congregations or assemblies of saints from the beginning. Adam assembled his righteous posterity in the valley of Adam-ondi-Ahman, possibly in a house built to hold them; Enoch and others of the preachers of righteousness who lived before the flood presided over congregations of true saints; and Shem, Melchizedek, Abraham, and others of the patriarchs did likewise after the day when the earth was cleansed by water. Moses and the prophets, Aaron and his sons, and various of the Levites and other Israelites continued so to do all down through Jewish history.

We do not know what kinds of temples the saints had before the flood. Our knowledge is limited to the fact that the gospel and its ordinances are always the same, and are always administered in the same way and according to the same terms and conditions; that those who lived anciently were as much entitled to endowments and sealings and washings and anointings and conversations in holy places as we are; and that the Lord has told us that he always, and in all ages, commands his people to build a house to his "holy name." (D&C 124:39.)

Similarly, we do not know what kinds of buildings were used as synagogues before the flood, or during patriarchal times, or while Israel dwelt in Egypt, or during the period of the First Commonwealth, which extended from the Exodus to the Babylonian captivity. Since there were congregations of true worshippers in those days, it follows that they built, as directed by the spirit of inspiration, such facilities as fitted their needs. We do know from secular and archeological sources that synagogues were built during the entire period of the Second Commonwealth, which extended from the captivity of the Jews in Babylonia to the destruction of their temple in A.D. 70. The Book of Mormon tells us that the Nephites had temples and sanctuaries and synagogues "which were built after the manner of the Jews." (2 Ne. 26:26; Alma 16:13.) It is clear from this, since Lehi and Ishmael and their families left Jerusalem just before that great city was overrun by Nebuchadnezzar, that there were synagogues in Jewish Israel before that people was taken into Babylonia. Jews since the destruction of their temple have, of course, continued to build and use synagogues.

Based on the records of the past, and knowing the divinely approved practice of the true Church in modern times, we conclude that synagogues are essential to salvation; that is to say, the Lord's people always and ever must build holy houses in which they can worship him whose they are. Otherwise the great blessings of the gospel will not flow to them in such an abundant measure as to prepare them for celestial rest.

The Manner of Worship in Jewish Synagogues

Whatever the nature of synagogues may have been for the first four thousand years of planet Earth's temporal continuance, our present interest is in what they were like and

189

how they were used in the day the Mortal Messiah dwelt among men. Pure religion, as it once came from the Eternal Fountain, had long since been muddied with the silt and dross of disobedient men; and the synagogues, where streams of living water should have flown, had become stagnant pools full of filth and disease.

These synagogues—those in Judea and Galilee and Perea and in all the places where Jewish Israel dwelt in the first decades of the Christian era—were built in prominent places: on the highest ground, at the corners of streets, or at the entrance to chief squares. Sacred symbols, such as the seven-branched candlestick or a pot of manna, were often carved on the lintels. The synagogues contained seating room for the worshippers, an ark or chest containing the rolls of the law, and a platform with a pulpit or lectern. They were consecrated by prayer, and rules of decorum were imposed upon worshippers, including decency and cleanliness of dress and reverence in demeanor. The church buildings of the early Christians were patterned after them. It is said that there were between 460 and 480 synagogues in Jerusalem at the time it was burned by the torch of Titus. Assuming a normal city population of 600,000, this means somewhat more than 1250 worshippers for each synagogue, a not improbable circumstance.

Synagogues were not used for the offering of sacrifices, but they were used for nearly all other forms of worship—for prayers, funerals, weddings, circumcisions, musical presentations, scriptural readings, sermons, and lectures, as schools for young children, and as places of general assembly and social intercourse. It is apparent from several New Testament accounts that they sometimes were the centers of religious contention and debates. Judicial bodies met in them, and penalties of beating and scourging were carried out within their walls.

Synagogue worship did not fall into a rigid mold. There was a needed elasticity in the approved services, and the ruler of the synagogue exercised the prerogative of altering the services as special needs arose, of inviting whom he would to offer prayers, and of calling on such guest readers and preachers as he chose. It was then as it is now: the over-all objective was the teaching of the people; then, as now, the purpose was to learn the Lord's law and to gain the encouragement needed to keep his commandments. The basic pattern of synagogue worship in the day of Jesus, and thus the one with which he was familiar and in which he participated, was as follows:

1. *Two opening prayers or "benedictions" were offered.* Those in use two thousand years ago were:

"I. Blessed be Thou, O Lord, King of the world, Who formest the light and createst the darkness, Who makest peace and createst everything; Who, in mercy, givest light to the earth and to those who dwell upon it, and in Thy goodness day by day and every day renewest the works of creation. Blessed be the Lord our God for the glory of His handiwork and for the light-giving lights which He has made for His praise. Selah! Blessed be the Lord our God, Who hath formed the lights."

"II. With great love hast Thou loved us, O Lord our God, and with much overflowing pity hast Thou pitied us, our Father and our King. For the sake of our fathers who trusted in Thee, and Thou taughtest them the statutes of life, have mercy upon us and teach us. Enlighten our eyes in Thy law; cause our hearts to cleave to Thy commandments; unite our hearts to love and fear Thy name, and we shall not be put to shame, world without end. For Thou art a God Who preparest salvation, and us hast Thou chosen from among all nations and tongues, and hast in truth brought us near to Thy great Name—Selah—that we may lovingly praise Thee and Thy Oneness. Blessed be the Lord Who in love chose His people Israel." (*Sketches,* pp. 269-70.)

2. *Then came the Shema.* This consisted of the reading of three passages of scripture from Deuteronomy and Numbers that were considered credal in nature; that is, they expressed the basic belief of the Jews concerning the Lord and their

relationship to him, and the need on their part to keep his statutes and judgments as a condition precedent to the receipt of his blessings. The initial word in the passage that begins "Hear, O Israel," is *Shema;* hence the name applied to the scriptures involved. The three passages were:

"Hear, O Israel: The Lord our God is one Lord: And thou shalt love the Lord thy God with all thine heart, and with all thy soul, and with all thy might. And these words, which I command thee this day, shall be in thine heart: And thou shalt teach them diligently unto thy children, and shalt talk of them when thou sittest in thine house, and when thou walkest by the way, and when thou liest down, and when thou risest up. And thou shalt bind them for a sign upon thine hand, and they shall be as frontlets between thine eyes. And thou shalt write them upon the posts of thy house, and on thy gates." (Deut. 6:4-9.)

"And it shall come to pass, if ye shall hearken diligently unto my commandments which I command you this day, to love the Lord your God, and to serve him with all your heart and with all your soul, That I will give you the rain of your land in his due season, the first rain and the latter rain, that thou mayest gather in thy corn, and thy wine, and thine oil. And I will send grass in thy fields for thy cattle, that thou mayest eat and be full. Take heed to yourselves, that your heart be not deceived, and ye turn aside, and serve other gods, and worship them; And then the Lord's wrath be kindled against you, and he shut up the heaven, that there be no rain, and that the land yield not her fruit; and lest ye perish quickly from off the good land which the Lord giveth you. Therefore shall ye lay up these my words in your heart and in your soul, and bind them for a sign upon your hand, that they may be as frontlets between your eyes. And ye shall teach them your children, speaking of them when thou sittest in thine house, and whcn thou walkest by the way, when thou liest down, and when thou risest up. And thou shalt write them upon the door posts of thine house, and upon thy gates: That your days may be multiplied, and the days of your children, in the land which the Lord sware unto your fathers to give them, as the days of heaven upon the earth." (Deut. 11:13-21.)

"And the Lord spake unto Moses, saying, Speak unto the children of Israel, and bid them that they make them fringes in the borders of their garments throughout their generations, and that they put upon the fringe of the borders a ribband of blue: And it shall be unto you for a fringe, that ye may look upon it, and remember all the commandments of the Lord, and do them; and that ye seek not after your own heart and your own eyes, after which ye use to go a whoring: That ye may remember, and do all my commandments, and be holy unto your God. I am the Lord your God, which brought you out of the land of Egypt, to be your God: I am the Lord your God." (Num. 15:37-41.)

3. *Next came the prayers after the Shema.*

"True it is, that Thou art Jehovah our God and the God of our fathers, our King and the King of our fathers, our Saviour and the Saviour of our fathers, our Creator, the Rock of our salvation, our Help and our Deliverer. Thy name is from everlasting, and there is no God beside Thee. A new song did they that were delivered sing to Thy Name by the seashore; together did all praise and own Thee King, and say, Jehovah shall reign world without end! Blessed be the Lord Who saveth Israel!"

Next: "O Lord our God! cause us to lie down in peace, and raise us up again to life, O our King! Spread over us the tabernacle of Thy peace; strengthen us before Thee in Thy good counsel, and deliver us for Thy Name's sake. Be Thou for protection round about us; keep far from us the enemy, the pestilence, the sword, famine, and affliction. Keep Satan from before and from behind us, and hide us in the shadow of Thy wings, for Thou art a God Who helpest and deliverest us; and Thou, O God, art a gracious and merciful King. Keep Thou our going out and our coming in, for life and for peace, from henceforth and for ever." (*Sketches,* p. 271.)

4. *Then came nineteen eulogies, benedictions, or supplications.* The first three and the last three—and we shall quote these six—were fixed and formalized in the day of Jesus. In his day other petitions, extemporaneous in nature, were inserted between the two groups of three, thus giving rise to the endless repetitions and long prayers so offensive to our Lord. The six formal eulogies were as follows:

"I. 'Blessed be the Lord our God and the God of our fathers, the God of Abraham, the God of Isaac, and the God of Jacob; the great, the mighty, and the terrible God; the Most High God, Who showeth mercy and kindness, Who createth all things, Who remembereth the gracious promises to the fathers, and bringeth a Saviour to their children's children, for His own Name's sake, in love. O King, Helper, Saviour, and Shield! Blessed art Thou, O Jehovah, the Shield of Abraham.'

"II. 'Thou, O Lord, art mighty for ever; Thou, Who quickenest the dead, art mighty to save. In Thy mercy Thou preservest the living; Thou quickenest the dead; in Thine abundant pity Thou bearest up those who fall, and healest those who are diseased, and loosest those who are bound, and fulfillest Thy faithful word to those who sleep in the dust. Who is like unto Thee, Lord of strength, and who can be compared to Thee, Who killest and makest alive, and causest salvation to spring forth? And faithful art Thou to give life unto the dead. Blessed be Thou, Jehovah, Who quickenest the dead!"

"III. 'Thou art holy, and Thy Name is holy; and the holy ones praise Thee every day. Selah! Blessed art Thou, Jehovah God, the Holy One!' "

At this point there were thirteen other eulogies, and then the following three:

"XVII. 'Take gracious pleasure, O Jehovah our God, in Thy people Israel, and in their prayers. Accept the burnt-offerings of Israel, and their prayers, with Thy good pleasure; and may the services of Thy people Israel be ever acceptable unto Thee. And oh that our eyes may see it, as

Thou turnest in mercy to Zion! Blessed be Thou, O Jehovah, Who restoreth His Shechinah to Zion!'

"XVIII. 'We praise Thee, because Thou art Jehovah our God, and the God of our fathers, for ever and ever. Thou art the Rock of our life, the Shield of our salvation, from generation to generation. We laud Thee, and declare Thy praise for our lives which are kept within Thine hand, and for our souls which are committed unto Thee, and for Thy wonders which are with us every day, and Thy wondrous deeds and Thy goodnesses, which are at all seasons—evening, morning, and mid-day. Thou gracious One, Whose compassions never end; Thou pitying One, Whose grace never ceaseth—for ever do we put our trust in Thee! And for all this Thy Name, O our King, be blessed and extolled always, for ever and ever! And all living bless Thee—Selah—and praise Thy Name in truth, O God, our Salvation and our Help. Blessed art Thou, Jehovah; Thy Name is the gracious One, to Whom praise is due.'

"XIX. 'Oh bestow on Thy people Israel great peace, for ever; for Thou art King and Lord of all peace, and it is good in Thine eyes to bless Thy people Israel with praise at all times and in every hour. Blessed art Thou, Jehovah, Who blesseth His people Israel with peace." (*Sketches,* pp. 273-75.)

All of these prayers were given by one person, with the congregation responding by an "Amen." The normal procedure was for the one appointed to give the prayers and recite the Shema also to be the one who read from the prophets. If this procedure was followed in Capernaum on that Sabbath when our Lord read the prophecy of Isaiah relative to Himself and announced its fulfillment in Him, then Jesus himself gave, on that occasion, the foregoing prayers. A careful analysis will show many things in these prayers that were fulfilled in the mortal ministry of him of whom we testify.

5. *At this point the Aaronic blessing was pronounced,* either by a priest or by someone appointed to represent him.

This blessing was:

"The Lord bless thee, and keep thee: The Lord make his face shine upon thee, and be gracious unto thee: The Lord lift up his countenance upon thee, and give thee peace." (Num. 6:24-26.)

6. *Then came the reading of the law.* That is, selected readings were taken from the Pentateuch, composed of the five books of Moses, which was considered to be the law. On the Sabbath seven persons were called upon to read from the law, and on other days a lesser number. The first and the last reader also offered a benediction.

7. *Next came a lesson from the prophets,* meaning that someone read from and expounded upon a selected prophetic passage. This is what our Lord did when in Capernaum he opened the book and found in Isaiah the passage pertaining to himself, which he then read and expounded.

8. *Finally, there was a sermon or address.* No doubt this was the portion of the service when Jesus and Paul and the early disciples found occasion to preach Christ, and that salvation which comes through him, to the Jewish worshippers in the synagogues of Palestine, Ephesus, Corinth, and elsewhere.

How Jesus Used Jewish Synagogues

There can be little room for doubt that the Lord Jesus while a child went to school in a synagogue in Nazareth. We know he grew up in subjection to Mary and Joseph, and synagogue schooling was a way of life for all of the young and rising generation. Nor can there be any doubt that during his formative and maturing years our Lord worshipped in various synagogues, even as he also went to Jerusalem and mingled with the worshipping throngs in the temple courts at Passover time. He was a Jew, brought up in subjection to Jewish law and Jewish tradition, and these included making the synagogue a living part of one's being.

We do know that from the day he began his ministry

until he voluntarily laid down his life, the temple and the various synagogues became his bases of operation. In them he taught and read and preached; in them he testified, exhorted, and rebuked; in them he healed the sick and wrought endless miracles; in them the Divine Light was shown forth with a heavenly radiance that left no place for the shadows of darkness then enshrouding a fallen nation.

Our New Testament accounts themselves do not recite the mode and manner of worship carried out in the synagogues in our Lord's day in the Land of Jesus; nor is it needful that they should do so. Those to whom the Gospels and the Acts of the Apostles were first written were already familiar with the songs and sermons, with the prayers and preachments, and with the rites and readings presented so repetitiously in those Jewish houses of worship and learning. What we have recounted in this respect has come from non-scriptural but authentic sources. Our scriptures simply say that the Savior taught or healed or read or preached in the synagogues, and it is left for us to conclude—and there is no alternative but to do so—that his doings and sayings within the sacred walls of necessity fitted into the regular order supervised by the rulers of the synagogues and with which those then and there assembled were familiar.

He taught in the synagogues because that is where people went to be taught, to hear sermons, and to learn how and in what manner they might draw near to Jehovah. And he healed the sick in the synagogues because that is where devout people, people with faith to be healed, came to seek blessings from the Source of all that is good. Those who first received the scriptural words of the apostles Matthew and John and of the disciples Mark and Luke would expect to read that Jesus taught and healed in the synagogues because those were the places where such things should have been done in the society and under the circumstances then prevailing.

When the day of Jesus' ministry arrived, he was first baptized by John in Jordan. There the Holy Ghost descended in quiet serenity like a dove. Then he was led of the Spirit into the wilderness, where he fasted for forty days, was tempted of the devil, and overcame the world as it were. Then he was ready to preach; then he was ready to heal.

As Matthew records it: "From that time Jesus began to preach. . . . And Jesus went about all Galilee, teaching in their synagogues, and preaching the gospel of the kingdom, and healing all manner of sickness and all manner of disease among the people." (Matt. 4:17-23.) Also: "And Jesus went about all the cities and villages, teaching in their synagogues, and preaching the gospel of the kingdom, and healing every sickness and every disease among the people." (Matt. 9:35; 13:54-58; Mark 6:1-6.)

Mark says our Lord called Zebedee's sons from their nets, and that he and they went straightway into Capernaum, where Jesus "on the sabbath day . . . entered into the synagogue, and taught. . . . And there was in their synagogue a man with an unclean spirit," which evil spirit forsook his ill-gotten abode at Jesus' word. Thereafter, "he preached in their synagogues throughout all Galilee, and cast out devils." (Mark 1:16-39; Luke 4:31-44.)

Luke gives this account of the commencement of his ministry: "And he taught in their synagogues, being glorified of all. And he came to Nazareth, where he had been brought up: and, as his custom was, he went into the synagogue on the sabbath day, and stood up for to read." This day in Nazareth was the one on which he announced his divine Sonship by saying in the synagogue that he came in fulfillment of Isaiah's great Messianic prophecy about preaching the gospel, healing the brokenhearted, and setting the captive free. (Luke 4:15-30.) And so it was that day in and day out, Sabbath after Sabbath, throughout his whole ministry, he sought out congregations of hearers, who were assembled, as was the norm of the day, in places where preachments should be given, and he there gave food and drink to those who hungered and thirsted after righteousness.

It was in a synagogue on the Sabbath that he was asked,

"Is it lawful to heal on the sabbath days?" to which he responded, "It is lawful to do well on the sabbath days"; then, so that his answer would be forever implanted in the hearts of his hearers, he said to one with a withered hand, "Stretch forth thine hand," and he doing so was healed instantly. (Matt. 12:9-13; Luke 13:9-17.) It was in a synagogue in Capernaum, upon whose lintel archeologists have found carved a pot of manna, that he preached his great sermon on the bread of life, showing that the manna given to their fathers was but a type of the living bread that should come down from heaven, "that a man may eat thereof, and not die." (John 6:50.) We need not say more along this line except to note that, when questioned by the high priest, Jesus answered, "I spake openly to the world; I ever taught in the synagogue, and in the temple, whither the Jews always resort." (John 18:19-20.)

Until the day of Jesus, except for the temple itself, Jewish synagogues were the only divinely approved houses of worship in the Old World. But as the Jewish people began the process of rejecting their Jewish Messiah, the true spirit of worship began to withdraw itself from those houses in which the revealed truths of the past had been taught with at least a measurable degree of understanding. As the people became polarized—a few believing in Jesus, the great masses rejecting his divine Messiahship—the Pharisees and rulers of the synagogues decreed that all who believed in Christ "should be put out of the synagogue." (John 9:22; 12:42-43; 16:2.) The schooling, the social intercourse, the religious teachings of the people—these were to be denied them.

In process of time the synagogues became houses of hate and persecution rather than houses of learning and true worship. Jesus told the Twelve and other true believers: "Beware of men: for they will deliver you up to the councils, and they will scourge you in their synagogues." (Matt. 10:17; 23:34; Mark 13:9.) In those sacred spots where sermons had attested to the saving power of the Promised Messiah, cries of anguish would now be heard from the lips of true believers as the scourgers' lash cut their flesh. Paul himself, "breathing out threatenings and slaughter against the disciples of the Lord," took letters from the high priest addressed to the rulers of the synagogues in Damascus, reciting "that if he found any of this way, whether they were men or women, he might bring them bound unto Jerusalem." (Acts 9:1-2.) In an open confession of his sins, Paul later said, "Lord . . . I imprisoned and beat in every synagogue them that believed on thee." (Acts 22:19; 26:11.) By rejecting Jesus and opposing the truth, the congregation of Israel became the congregation of unbelief, of hatred, of evil, of Lucifer. They became, as the scripture recites, "the synagogue of Satan." (Rev. 2:9; 3:9.)

NOTES

1. These words appertain to the building of the Kirtland Temple, which temple was a synagogue; that is to say, the Kirtland Temple was not a temple in the full and true sense of the word; it was not a sanctuary set apart from the world; it was not designed for the performance of those endowments, ordinances, and sealings which open the door to eternal salvation for the living and the dead—for, in the day of its building, these things had not yet been revealed in this dispensation. The Lord's House in Kirtland was a temple in the sense that it was a House of the Lord, one to which he and his servants came, but it was also, in a manner of speaking, a synagogue, meaning a House of the Lord where true worshippers came to worship the Father in Spirit and in truth.

Chapter 11

JEWISH SABBATHS IN JESUS' DAY

The sabbath was made for man, and
not man for the sabbath: Therefore the
Son of man is Lord also
of the sabbath. . . .

Is it lawful to do good on the sabbath
days, or to do evil? to save life, or to
kill? (Mark 2:27-28; 3:4.)

The Law of Sabbath Worship

We do not overstate our case when we say that the
Jewish system of Sabbath observance that prevailed in the
day of Jesus was ritualistic, degenerate, and almost unbelievably absurd, a system filled with fanatical restrictions.
Nor do we think that this is a conclusion upon which
reasonable minds can differ, once the facts are in and the
evidence is weighed.

Their system of Sabbath worship clearly shows how a
great and important concept can be preserved even though it
is twisted and perverted in the hands of uninspired teachers.
To see why our Jewish brethren in the meridian of time
placed such emphasis on Sabbath observance, we need but
record the true order of such worship that has prevailed

among the Lord's people from the beginning. This we have done, in brief form, in chapter 21 of *The Promised Messiah: The First Coming of Christ.* For our purposes now, as a prelude to a recitation of what prevailed in our Lord's day, we shall simply summarize some of the basic principles.

Those whose souls are touched by the Holy Spirit and who understand the hand-dealings of the Almighty with his earthly children know that Sabbath observance is essential to salvation, and that those who keep this day holy, in the manner and way Deity designed, shall be guided along the path leading to salvation in the celestial kingdom of heaven. Again, we are not overstating the case, nor are we reaching a conclusion without scriptural warrant.

The Lord our Heavenly Father created us; ordained the plan and system whereunder we could advance and progress and become like him; placed us in this mortal sphere, where we are subject to all of the lusts and passions of the flesh; and decreed that if we would overcome the world and live godly lives in spite of earth and hell, he would save us in his everlasting presence. While here, we must deal with temporal things and be subject to Satan's enticements. Unless we somehow manage to turn from worldly matters and put first in our lives the things of God's kingdom, we shall fail the test and lose our souls.

We need help, constant help—help from day to day, help all the time. Such is given through the gospel and by the Holy Spirit. And the Sabbath day is one of the chief arrangements whereby this spiritual help is made available. That Holy Being who prepared the test we are now taking, in his infinite wisdom, knew—and so arranged—that if we would devote one day in seven exclusively to spiritual things, we would have power to conduct ourselves in such a way as to save our souls. Hence came the Sabbath.

The true Sabbath is a day of worship, a day for spiritual refreshment, a day to learn the laws of the Lord, a day to renew our covenants, a day to pay our devotions to the Most High. The true Sabbath is a day to remember the Lord and his goodness to us, a day to read and ponder his holy word, a day to confess our sins, a day to strengthen each other, and to visit the fatherless and the widows in their affliction. The true Sabbath is a day of preaching and testifying, a day of fasting and prayer, a day of rejoicing and thanksgiving, a day to partake of the good things of the Spirit and to sanctify our souls. The true Sabbath is essential to salvation, and those who use it to the full, according to the divine intent, shall attain celestial rest.

In the very nature of things, true Sabbath worship precludes worldly activities. Hence on that day we rest from all servile work; we lay our temporal pursuits aside for the moment; we refrain from recreational activities; we let our crops and our herds fend for themselves and our shops and our factories remain closed and idle; we leave the fish in the streams and the golf clubs in the locker room. Except for the preparation of modest meals, or the pulling of the ox from the mire, as it were, on this the Lord's day, we do no other things except to worship the Lord in spirit and in truth. Such was the law of the Sabbath among the ancestors of the Jews, and such is that law among us.

It should come as no surprise, then, to find this law singled out as a sign between the Lord and his people. Its proper observance always has identified and always will identify the true saints, and its desecration and improper observance always has revealed and always will reveal those who are not the Lord's people and who are not feeding their souls spiritually according to the plan of the great Creator.

It should come as no surprise to find the Lord, by the mouth of Moses, decreeing death to those who desecrate his holy day, or to hear him promise Israel that if they would hallow the Sabbath, "As I commanded your fathers . . . Then shall there enter into the gates of this city kings and princes sitting upon the throne of David, riding in chariots and on horses, they, and their princes, the men of Judah, and the inhabitants of Jerusalem: and this city shall remain for ever." (Jer. 17:20-27.)

We need not, for our present purposes, pursue further the matter of the true law of the Sabbath. It suffices for us to know that few things in the gospel are more important, and for us to be aware of the original philosophy that preceded the perversions of Jesus' day. The Sabbath as such was no less important among the Jews in that day than it had ever been. If properly kept, it could have led to the fulness of the blessings of the gospel. That those then living in the fading light of the past still knew, in principle, that it was important beyond expression is perfectly clear from the records of the day. The issue is that they chose to keep and observe its law in such a way that their very observance was itself a desecration.

The Jews and Their Sabbath

Jewish worship in the day of Jesus—with its inordinate emphasis on formalisms, on rituals, on performances, on the letter rather than the spirit of the law—revolved around four centers:

1. *The temple,* Jehovah's holy house, the place where Deity revealed himself, and to which he called all Israel to come and serve and worship him;

2. *Sacrificial offerings* performed in similitude of the sacrifice of the Promised Messiah, performed as types and shadows of the sacrifice of the Eternal High Priest, who, entering himself within the heavenly veil, was able to lead all others into the Divine Presence;

3. Those *feasts or festivals* when the faithful, in person or represented by delegates, appeared before the Lord in Jerusalem, at the temple, to worship, sacrifice, and receive a renewed outpouring of divine grace; and

4. *Sabbath observance,* which included attendance at worship services in the synagogues, plus conformity to the rabbinically imposed restrictions of rest, which turned what should have been a day of spiritual refreshment into one of drudgery and unneeded and often unheeded self-denial.

As to the temple—it was still the Lord's house, though it had been defiled in large measure by wicked men, so much so that the Divine Presence no longer rested between the cherubim in the Holy of Holies.

As to sacrifice—they were still performed by Aaronic authority, though the priestly administrators and the people generally no longer saw in them the great spiritual symbolisms that made them such an important part of the worship of their fathers.

As to the feasts—they still assembled Israel to the city of the Great King, where true worship and divinely approved ordinances could be performed, but they had degenerated into occasions of revelry and debate, and the worship that should have attended them left much to be desired.

As to Sabbath observance—this was a field in which all Jewry had gone wild, a true principle, out of which a sane practice should have grown but which was so altered, twisted, and perverted that what should have been a holy day had become a blasphemous mockery. The synagogue services had some merit, to which reference has been made in chapter 10, but all else that then attended these dehallowed days came from beneath and not from above.

"Ye Shall Do No Servile Work Therein"

Of his holy day—"the sabbath of the Lord thy God"—Jehovah commanded: "In it thou shalt not do any work, thou, nor thy son, nor thy daughter, thy manservant, nor thy maidservant, nor thy cattle, nor thy stranger that is within thy gates." (Ex. 20:10.)

Such was the divine decree, but the practical problem was—what is work? What physical acts might be done by members of the chosen race, or their slaves, or their cattle, without incurring the wrath of Him who was jealous of his name and who visited the iniquity of the fathers upon the children unto the third and fourth generation among those that hated him?

205

Sowing and reaping are clearly work. But suppose only a few seeds are scattered on unploughed land, is such an act sinful? If oxen bear a yoke and pull a plough, it is work, but if they only carry the weight of a rope, what then? Is it permissible to set a broken arm, to give medicine to sick persons, or for a lame man to use his crutches? Can an author write a page, a single line, or even one letter from the alphabet? Is it permissible to read, or walk, or boil water, or what have you, and if so, how limited or extensive may the exertions be? If a man stumbles and falls, must he lie prone until the Sabbath's end? How heavy a burden may he bear without breaking the divine decree? These and ten thousand other tickish, petty questions occupied the time of the brightest minds in all Jewry, and the answers they gave and the rules they adopted can scarcely be believed.

Jewish law in Jesus' day forbade thirty-nine chief or principal types of work. These were: (1) sowing, (2) ploughing, (3) reaping, (4) binding sheaves, (5) threshing, (6) winnowing, (7) sifting (selecting), (8) grinding, (9) sifting in a sieve, (10) kneading, (11) baking—all of which restrictions had to do with the preparation of bread; (12) shearing the wool, (13) washing it, (14) beating it, (15) dyeing it, (16) spinning, (17) putting it on the weaver's beam, (18) making two thrum threads, (19) weaving two threads, (20) separating two threads, (21) making a knot, (22) undoing a knot, (23) sewing two stitches, (24) tearing in order to sew two stitches—all of which restrictions had to do with dress; (25) catching deer, (26) killing, (27) skinning, (28) salting it, (29) preparing its skin, (30) scraping off its hair, (31) cutting it up, (32) writing two letters, (33) scraping in order to write two letters—all of which are connected with hunting and writing; (34) building, (35) pulling down, (36) extinguishing fire, (37) lighting fire, (38) beating with the hammer, and (39) carrying from one possession into the other—all of which appertain to the work necessary for a private house. Each of these thirty-nine principal prohibitions contained within itself numerous related items that were banned on the Sabbath day.

Jewish tractates of Jesus' day set forth chapter after chapter of detailed explanations and illustrations relative to these thirty-nine principal types of prohibited work. For instance: Scattering two seeds was sowing; sweeping away or breaking a single clod was ploughing; plucking one blade of grass was sin; watering fruit or removing a withered leaf was forbidden; picking fruit, or even lifting it from the ground, was reaping; cutting a mushroom was a double sin, one both of harvesting and of sowing, for a new one would grow in place of the old; fishing, or anything that put an end to life, ranked with harvesting; rubbing ears of corn together, or anything else connected with food, was classed as binding of sheaves.

"If a woman were to roll wheat to take away the husks, she would be guilty of sifting with a sieve. If she were rubbing the ends of the stalks, she would be guilty of threshing. If she were cleansing what adheres to the side of a stalk, she would be guilty of sifting. If she were bruising the stalk, she would be guilty of grinding. If she were throwing it up in her hands, she would be guilty of winnowing. Distinctions like the following are made: A radish may be dipped into salt, but not left in it too long, since this would be to make pickle. A new dress might be put on, irrespective of the danger that in so doing it might be torn. Mud on the dress might be crushed in the hand and shaken off, but the dress must not be rubbed (for fear of affecting the material). If a person took a bath, opinions are divided, whether the whole body should be dried at once, or limb after limb. If water had fallen on the dress, some allowed the dress to be shaken but not wrung; others, to be wrung but not shaken. One Rabbi allowed to spit into the handkerchief, and that although it may necessitate the compressing of what had been wetted; but there is a grave discussion whether it was lawful to spit on the ground, and then to rub it with the foot, because thereby the earth may be scratched. It may, however, be done on stones. In the labour of grinding would be included such an act as crushing salt. To sweep, or to water the ground, would involve the same sin as beating out the corn. To lay on a plaster would be a grievous sin; to scratch out a big letter, leaving room for two small ones, would be a sin, but to write one big letter occupying the room of two small letters was no sin. To change one letter to another might imply a double sin. And so on through endless details!" (Edersheim 2:783.)

What constituted a burden that might not be carried on the Sabbath day? By the mouth of Jeremiah the Lord had said: "Take heed to yourselves, and bear no burden on the sabbath day, nor bring it in by the gates of Jerusalem: Neither carry forth a burden out of your houses on the sabbath day, neither do ye any work, but hallow ye the sabbath day, as I commanded your fathers." (Jer. 17:21-22.)

To the followers of rabbinism this meant: Carry no burden greater than the weight of a fig and no food larger than the size of an olive. Anything, however trifling, that could be put to practical use was a burden. "Thus, two horse's hairs might be made into a birdtrap; a scrap of clean paper into a custom-house notice; a small piece of paper written upon might be converted into a wrapper for a small flagon. In all these cases, therefore, transport would involve sin. Similarly, ink sufficient to write two letters, wax enough to fill up a small hole, even a pebble with which you might aim at a little bird, or a small piece of broken earthenware with which you might stir the coals, would be 'burdens!' " (Edersheim 2:784.)

"It was forbidden to write two letters, either with the right hand or the left, whether of the same size or of different sizes, or with different inks, or in different languages, or with any pigment; with ruddle, gum, vitriol, or anything that can make marks; or even to write two letters, one on each side of a corner of two walls, or on two leaves of a writing-tablet, if they could be read together, or to write them on the body. But they might be written on any dark fluid, on the sap of a fruit-tree, on road-dust, on sand, or on anything in which the writing did not remain. If they were written with the hand turned upside down, or with the foot, or the mouth, or the elbow, or if one letter were added to another previously made, or other letters traced over, or if a person designed to write the letter and only wrote two, or if he wrote one letter on the ground and one on the wall, or on two walls, or on two pages of a book, so that they could not be read together, it was not illegal. If a person, through forgetfulness, wrote two characters at different times, one in the morning, the other, perhaps towards evening, it was a question among the Rabbis whether he had or had not broken the Sabbath." (Geikie, pp. 448-49.)

What if a house or its contents caught fire on the Sabbath? To put out a fire and save a building or its contents was clearly work. However, one might rescue from the fire the scriptures and the phylacteries and the cases that contained them, but liturgical pieces, though they contained the name of Deity, were to be left to the flames. Only the food and drink needed for the Sabbath might be rescued, except that "if the food were in a cupboard or basket the whole might be carried out. Similarly, all utensils needed for the Sabbath meal, but of dress only what was absolutely necessary, might be saved, it being, however, provided, that a person might put on a dress, save it, go back and put on another, and so on." (Edersheim 2:784-85.)

How far might one carry a burden on the Sabbath day? The set distance was an ordinary Sabbath day's journey, which extended two thousand cubits from one's dwelling. But out of practical necessity and by the use of legal fictions this distance might be extended. For instance, if groups of houses could be somehow defined as one dwelling, then burdens could be carried between them. Each house opening onto a private court was, of course, a private dwelling, and so it was unlawful to carry things from one to another on the Sabbath. If, however, all of the families would deposit, before the Sabbath, some food in the common court, a connection would thus be established among them all so that they could be considered one dwelling, and all difficulties about carrying burdens from one to the other would be removed. Or if a man deposited, on Friday, food for two meals, at a distance of two thousand cubits from his dwelling, he thereby constituted that place his dwelling, and on the Sabbath he could carry burdens an extra two thousand cubits. Or if a beam, a wire, or a rope were placed across a blind alley or a narrow street, this made all the houses thereon one dwelling "so that everything was lawful there which a man might do on the Sabbath in his own house." (Edersheim 2:777.)

Practice of the healing arts was work and therefore could not be done on the Sabbath. Broken bones could not be set; surgical operations were not allowed; emetics could not be given. "A plaster might be worn, provided its object was to prevent the wound from getting worse, not to heal it, for that would have been a work. Ornaments which could not easily be taken off might be worn in one's courtyard. Similarly, a person might go about with wadding in his ear, but not with false teeth nor with a gold plug in the tooth. If the wadding fell out of the ear, it could not be replaced. Some, indeed, thought that its healing virtues lay in the oil in which it had been soaked, and which had dried up, but others ascribed them to the warmth of the wadding itself. In either case there was danger of healing—of doing anything for the purpose of a cure—and hence wadding might not be put into the ear on the Sabbath, although if worn before it might be continued. Again, as regarded false teeth: they might fall out, and the wearer might then lift and carry them, which would be sinful on the Sabbath. But anything which formed part of the ordinary dress of a person might be worn also on the Sabbath, and children whose ears were being bored might have a plug put into the hole. It was also allowed to go about on crutches, or with a wooden leg, and children might have bells on their dresses; but it was prohibited to walk on stilts, or to carry any heathen amulet." (Edersheim 2:782.)

Although remedies could not be used for the curing of the sick, certain acts could be performed if there was "actual danger to life." Thus: "If on the Sabbath a wall had fallen on a person, and it were doubtful whether he was under the ruins or not, whether he was alive or dead, a Jew or Gentile, it would be duty to clear away the rubbish sufficiently to find the body. If life were not extinct, the labour would have to be continued; but if the person were dead nothing further should be done to extricate the body." (Edersheim 2:787.)

To kindle a fire on the Sabbath day was forbidden. Food must be prepared, lights kindled, and vessels washed before sunset on Friday. Ovens could not be kept warm for Sabbath use, and there were scores of regulations relative to food that might be eaten. For instance: "If a hen had laid on the Sabbath, the egg was forbidden, because, evidently, it could not have been destined on a weekday for eating, since it was not yet laid, and did not exist; while if the hen had been kept, not for laying but for fattening, the egg might be eaten as forming part of the hen that had fallen off!" (Edersheim 2:787.)

If an object was thrown into the air and caught again with the same hand, it was sin; if caught with the other hand, there was a division of opinion; if caught in the mouth and eaten, there was no guilt because the object no longer existed. "If it rained, and the water which fell from the sky were carried, there was no sin in it; but if the rain had run down from a wall it would involve sin. If a person were in one place, and his hand filled with fruit stretched into another, and the Sabbath overtook him in this attitude, he would have to drop the fruit, since if he withdrew his full hand from one locality into another, he would be carrying a burden on the Sabbath." (Edersheim 2:779.)

We need not go further in our analysis of the degenerate system of Sabbath observance imposed by the Rabbis upon Jesus, Joseph, Mary, Peter, James, John, and all the Jews of their day. We must state pointedly, however, that what is here recited is only a sample, a small sample—not so much as a thousandth part—of what then existed.[1] Obviously the mere recitation of such regulations as these should suffice to show the apostate nature of that Jewish system of worship which was so caustically condemned by Him who said: "Ye made the commandment of God of none effect by your tradition." (Matt. 15:6.)

We must also state that however absurd and lacking in spirituality these Jewish Sabbath regulations seem to us, they were of deep and sincere concern to those who had submitted themselves to that rule of priestcraft out of which they grew. In this connection, there were even times in their long history when they submitted to slavery and death rather than wage war on the Sabbath, although in the days of the Second Commonwealth it had been established that defensive military acts were permissible.[2]

In the light of all this it will come as no surprise—as we hereafter set forth how the Rabbis and those who sat in Aaron's seat opposed the great High Priest who ministered among them—to find religious bigots thirsting for Innocent Blood because the Son of Man defies their traditions and claims Lordship over the Sabbath itself.

NOTES

1. These comments about Jewish Sabbath observance and the illustrations set forth are digested from Edersheim, pages 775-87, and from Geikie, pages 448-50, both of which authors, in turn, digested their material from the Mishnah. The English version of the Mishnah, used in this work by the present author, takes thirty-seven solid pages of fine print to set forth the detailed policies and illustrations that governed Sabbath observance in ancient Jewry (Mishnah, pp. 100-136), plus special Sabbath regulations recited in connection with the feasts and other matters.

2. Josephus gives us an account of how the Jews were persuaded to wage defensive war on the Sabbath. It happened in the day of Mattathias, father of the great Judas Maccabeus. At that time the Syrian king, Antiochus IV (Epiphanes), had forbidden the Jewish religion. Mattathias led a revolt and with some insurgents fled from Jerusalem into the nearby deserts. The pursuing and attacking Syrians "fought against them on the Sabbath-day, and they burnt them as they were in the caves, without resistance, and without so much as stopping up the entrances of the caves. And they avoided to defend themselves on that day, because they were not willing to break in upon the honour they owed the Sabbath, even in such distresses; for our law requires that we rest upon that day. There were about a thousand, with their wives and children, who were smothered and died in these caves: but many of those that escaped joined themselves to Mattathias, and appointed him to be their ruler, who taught them to fight even on the Sabbath-day; and told them that unless they would do so, they would become their own enemies, by observing the law [so rigorously,] while their adversaries would still assault them on this day, and they would not then defend themselves; and that nothing could then hinder but they must all perish without fighting. This speech persuaded them; and this rule continues among us to this day, that if there be a necessity, we may fight on Sabbath-days." (Josephus, *Antiquities*, Book 12, chapter 6.)

212

Chapter 12

JEWISH FAMILY LIFE IN JESUS' DAY

Our fathers have told us [the things of
God]. We will not hide them from their
children, shewing to the generation
to come the praises of the Lord, and his
strength, and his wonderful works
that he hath done.

For he established a testimony in Jacob,
and appointed a law in Israel, which he
commanded our fathers, that they
should make them known
to their children:

That the generation to come might
know them, even the children
which should be born; who should arise
and declare them to their children:

That they might set their hope in God,
and not forget the works of God,
but keep his commandments. (Ps. 78:3-7.)

The Law of Family Worship

All things center in the family, and the family is the center of all things. Salvation itself is a family affair and consists of the continuation of the family unit in eternity. God himself is exalted and omnipotent because he is a Father, and his kingdoms and dominions are composed of his children over whom he rules in equity and justice forever. The whole system of salvation, of revelation, of religion, of worship—all that comes from Deity for the benefit of man—is tied into a divine patriarchal system. If any of us gain the fulness of reward in our Father's kingdom, it will be because we enter into family relationships that are eternal in nature; it will be because we have perfected our own patriarchal family units. These concepts are part of the very foundation upon which true religion rests.

True worship is a family affair. God deals with and through families, righteous families, faithful families, families who will believe and obey. The whole object and end of true religion is to enable a man to become—through celestial marriage—an eternal father in his own right, and to enable a woman to become an eternal mother. It is thus inevitable—it could not be otherwise—that God, who is our Father, deals with chosen and favored families in making his mind and will and purposes known to mortals.

Adam, our first father, received the gospel, became the presiding patriarch over all the earth for all ages, and presided over all of the Lord's earthly affairs during his mortal probation. The congregation of saints in his and succeeding days—or in other words, the Church—was organized on a family or patriarchal basis. From his day to the time of the flood, the Church was a family organization; the priesthood went from father to son; the gospel was taught by parents to their children, and then by children to their children and their children's children.

After our first parents had received the gospel; after they had learned by revelation of the future atonement of the

Only Begotten; after they knew about the redemption, with its immortality for all men, and its eternal life for the obedient, the record says: "And Adam and Eve blessed the name of God, and they made all things known unto their sons and their daughters." (Moses 5:6-12.)

After they knew that to gain salvation men must believe in Christ, repent of their sins, be baptized, receive the gift of the Holy Ghost, and thereafter keep the commandments of God; after they knew that "the Son of God hath atoned for original guilt, wherein the sins of the parents cannot be answered upon the heads of the children"; after they knew that as children "begin to grow up, sin conceiveth in their hearts, and they taste the bitter, that they may know to prize the good"; after they had received the divine commandments relative to this whole system of salvation, then the Lord commanded: "Teach it unto your children." Also: "I give unto you a commandment, to teach these things freely unto your children." That is to say: The fathers were to teach the doctrines of salvation to their children, that all members of the family unit—knowing the truth—might, through obedience, become heirs of salvation. It was imperative that children learn that "no unclean thing can dwell" in the presence of God, and that all men "must be born again" if they are to enter "the kingdom of heaven." (Moses 6:51-62.)

After the flood it was the same. The Church was a family organization and the gospel was taught by fathers to their children. The great Abrahamic covenant—renewed first with Isaac, then with Jacob, and then extended to all the seed of Abraham—was a family covenant, a covenant of eternal increase, through celestial marriage. "Abraham received promises concerning his seed, and of the fruit of his loins," our revelation recites, "which were to continue so long as they were in the world: and as touching Abraham and his seed, out of the world they should continue; both in the world and out of the world should they continue as innumerable as the stars; or, if ye were to count the sand upon the seashore ye could not number them." (D&C 132:30.) Of

Abraham the Lord said: "I know him, that he will command his children and his household after him, and they shall keep the way of the Lord, to do justice and judgment." (Gen. 18:19.)

The house or family of Israel, who are the descendants of the sons of Jacob, was the Lord's chosen family throughout their long history. That his mind and his purposes might be known among them, parents were commanded to teach his law to their children, generation upon generation. "These words, which I command thee this day," Moses said, as he summarized the law to Israel, "shall be in thine heart: And thou shalt teach them diligently unto thy children, and shalt talk of them when thou sittest in thine house, and when thou walkest by the way, and when thou liest down, and when thou risest up."[1]

In principle the Nephites did the same thing, as we see from these words of King Benjamin: "And ye will not suffer your children that they go hungry, or naked; neither will ye suffer that they transgress the laws of God, and fight and quarrel one with another, and serve the devil, who is the master of sin, or who is the evil spirit which hath been spoken of by our fathers, he being an enemy to all righteousness. But ye will teach them to walk in the ways of truth and soberness; ye will teach them to love one another, and to serve one another." (Mosiah 4:14-15.)

When our Lord removed the restriction that limited gospel blessings to the house of Israel—"Go not into the way of the Gentiles, and into any city of the Samaritans enter ye not: But go rather to the lost sheep of the house of Israel" (Matt. 10:5-6) was his initial command to the Twelve—and sent the message of salvation to all men, he was simply enlarging the chosen family. He was putting into active operation the promise that he, as Jehovah, had made aforetime to Abraham: "As many as receive this Gospel shall be called after thy name, and shall be accounted thy seed, and shall rise up and bless thee, as their father." (Abr. 2:10.)

Those who receive the gospel take upon themselves the

216

name of Christ; they are adopted as his sons and his daughters; they become members of his family; he is their new Father. Hence, Paul's statement that those who "have been baptized into Christ have put on Christ. There is neither Jew nor Greek, there is neither bond nor free, there is neither male nor female: for ye are all one in Christ Jesus. And if ye be Christ's, then are ye Abraham's seed, and heirs according to the promise." (Gal. 3:27-29.) And the members of the family of Abraham and of Christ have the same obligation that has always rested upon members of the chosen family: "to bring up your children in light and truth." (D&C 93:40.)[2] "And they shall also teach their children to pray, and to walk uprightly before the Lord." (D&C 68:28.)

Jewish and Gentile Families

In his infinite wisdom, having compassion and solicitude for the welfare of his Son, the Father sent the Lord Jesus into a Jewish home, into a Jewish family circle. In such an environment the Infant Messiah would receive tender and loving care and be exposed to the best teaching and training available in any mortal family unit. Even God's own Son—as he stretched and turned in his swaddling clothes; as he waited to be weaned; as he learned to walk and talk and feed himself; as he learned to read and write and memorize; as he partook of the varied experiences that are the common lot of all who undergo a mortal probation—even he would be influenced by his environment and would be preserved from the defilements of paganism because the home in which he dwelt was Jewish.

The law of family worship, the system revealed by the Great Jehovah to enable his people to gain exaltation through the continuation of the family unit in eternity, was known, in part at least, to the Jews of Jesus' day and in the true sense of the word to no other Old World people. Jewish families, therefore, had a religious foundation and a spiritual status totally unknown among the Gentiles. As a result, those families among them which were pious and devout—whose members looked for the Consolation of Israel and who sought to live by the high standards found in the law and in the prophets—such families lived lives of decency and morality. Husbands and wives were faithful to each other, scriptural study and daily prayer were part of the rituals of life, and the family members lived honest, sober, and upright lives. Such was the environment prevailing in the family circle in which God placed his Son.

In contrast, family life among the Gentiles was defiled, corrupt, devoid of decency, and of such a low order as scarcely to be worthy of the name. "Strange as it may sound," Edersheim says, "it is strictly true that, beyond the boundaries of Israel, it would be scarcely possible to speak with any propriety of family life, or even of the family, as we understand these terms. . . . Few of those who have learned to admire classical antiquity have a full conception of any one phase in its social life—whether of the position of woman, the relation of the sexes, slavery, the education of children, their relation to their parents, or the state of public morality. Fewer still have combined all these features into one picture, and that not merely as exhibited by the lower orders, or even among the higher classes, but as fully owned and approved by those whose names have descended in the admiration of ages as the thinkers, the sages, the poets, the historians, and the statesmen of antiquity. Assuredly, St. Paul's description of the ancient world in the first and second chapters of his Epistle to the Romans must have appeared to those who lived in the midst of it as Divine even in its tenderness, delicacy, and charity; the full picture under bright sunlight would have been scarcely susceptible of exhibition. For such a world there was only one alternative—either the judgment of Sodom, or the mercy of the Gospel and the healing of the Cross."[3]

It is evident—self-evident!—that any nation or people having any reasonable degree of understanding relative to the true status and position of the family in the eternal scheme of things would be unique, separate, distinct, peculiar, a people set apart. And so it was with the Jews of Jesus' day. There was no race and no kindred like them among all the peoples of the earth. They were Jews of Abrahamic ancestry, and all others were Gentiles, lesser breeds without the law.

True, their knowledge was incomplete, and the full glory of perfect familial relationships had been lost among them. But they had been born in the family of Israel; the traditions of their fathers still lingered in their homes; and they did have the holy scriptures, wherein the Abrahamic covenant and the chosen status of Israel were extolled. They were, indeed, a unique people, a peculiar people, a people set apart from all others. Their family-centered way of life, their religious traditions, their social customs all combined to separate them, to make them a people without peer. As Edersheim says: "It may be safely asserted, that the grand distinction, which divided all mankind into Jews and Gentiles, was not only religious, but also social. [Albeit, let us here insert, the social grew out of the religious.] However near the cities of the heathen to those of Israel, however frequent and close the intercourse between the two parties, no one could have entered a Jewish town or village without feeling, so to speak, in quite another world. The aspects of the streets, the building and arrangement of the houses, the municipal and religious rule, the manners and customs of the people, their habits and ways—above all, the family life, stood in marked contrast to what would be seen elsewhere. On every side there was evidence that religion here was not merely a creed, nor a set of observances, but that it pervaded every relationship, and dominated every phase of life." (*Sketches*, p. 86.)

As we view Jewish families and Gentile families, is it any wonder that the Son of God came among the Jews? Though they would take his life in due course, because of priestcraft and iniquity, yet divine providence required an environment and a social and religious climate that would enable him to grow to maturity, unstained, preserved physically and spiritually, so that he could do his appointed work before he laid down his life as our Savior and Redeemer.

How Jewish Families Lived

In Jesus' day the Jews had their temple, their synagogues, and their homes, and around them their whole life revolved. Three times each year faithful men appeared before the Lord in his sanctuary—and would not Jesus, who kept his Father's law, have been among them?—there, by sacrifice, to recommit themselves to Jehovah and to receive anew a remission of their sins.

Many people frequented the sacred courts to teach and be taught and to partake of the spirit of worship that centered in the Holy of Holies.

Every Sabbath and on certain feast days, the faithful— and would not Jesus have been among them?—came to the synagogue to pray, to hear the word of the Lord taught, and to receive the exhortations so important even to the most spiritual of men. But the home was something else—day in and day out, week after week, month added to month, and one year following another; the home was the place where true worship was taught and practiced. Every Jewish home was itself a house of worship, a house of prayer, and—shall we not say it—a house of God.

And Jesus our Lord was nursed and suckled in a Jewish home; he played within its walls as a child; he was guided by a Jewish mother and a Jewish foster father as he learned the customs and discipline and way of life of the race of which he was a part. In the real and practical sense it was his first and chief house of worship. It is true that he went up to the temple when twelve years of age and undoubtedly three times each year from then until the time his active ministry began. It is true that he worshipped as a youth and in his maturing years in Jewish synagogues; we know that during his ministry he used them as teaching centers, as the sites for miracles, and as the reverent and sacred houses of worship that they in fact were.

But we cannot see our Lord in proper perspective unless we see him in the home of Joseph and Mary; unless we know what he was taught within those private walls; unless we are aware of the practices and rituals that were there impressed upon his receptive and truth-seeking mind. Jesus was the Son of God and dwelt among men with native endowments without equal, but he was also a product, as we all are, of his environment; and his Father chose to place him in the care and custody, during his formative years, of Jewish Joseph and Jewish Mary and their Jewish home with all its Jewish teachings, practices, and ways of worship.

Joseph and Mary lived in modest circumstances. They offered in sacrifice, when Jesus was presented in the temple, "a pair of turtledoves, or two young pigeons," rather than the more expensive lamb. (Luke 2:21-24.) What happened to the gifts of "gold, and frankincense, and myrrh" that came to the "young child" we do not know. (Matt. 2:11.) Perhaps they sustained the family during their exile in Egypt; perhaps they were divided among relatives and others of modest means. Their home in Nazareth would have been small, without running water and other amenities common in even the poorer homes today. Such furniture as they possessed would have been well made; their clothing would have been of homespun Galilean wool; and as to their food, the principal fare would have been the meat and vegetables and fruits grown and raised so abundantly in the hills of Galilee. Perhaps they had occasional foods and articles of adornment that were imported.

We can scarcely question that as other sons and daughters came, they lived in close and intimate quarters, with limited amounts of this world's goods, the children sharing food and exchanging clothes as their needs required. Certainly the whole family lived in lesser circumstances of opulence than generally prevails in homes located in the developed nations today. There were wealthy people in

Nazareth and other Palestinian communities whose houses were mansions by any standards, but we have no reason to suppose that the home of Joseph and Mary was in any way pretentious. The Father of the Son placed his Eternal Offspring in modest circumstances: the Prince who was to be King was neither born nor reared in a palace. How fitting it was, rather, that the One who was to ascend above all others should be cradled in a manger and reared in a carpenter's home.

But it is the spirit and teachings, the love and harmony, not the wood and mortar and chairs, that make a true home. And in those things that are important, the home provided by the just and faithful husband of Mary excelled. Perhaps there neither was nor has been one like it in all Israel. Family life being what it is, and having the impact that it does upon the children who are reared in the family circle, surely the Father of us all, who also was the Father of One only in mortality, would have chosen that family circle which was preeminent above all others as the environment for his Only Begotten Son.

When we describe Jewish family life in the day of Jesus, our choice of words strays into the field of the superlatives. The plain fact is that there were not then and have not been since—except among the meridian saints and among the Latter-day Saints, both of which peoples enjoyed a home life hallowed by eternal marriage and all that grows out of it— there were not then and have not been since families like the ancient Jewish families. Such were not found among the Gentiles of Jesus' day and are not found among the Christians of modern Christendom, nor among the modern Jews. Those ancient members of Jacob's house still had the priesthood of Almighty God; they still centered their whole social structure in the revealed word that had come from Moses and the prophets; they had in fact preserved their unique and peculiar status among men by preserving the family teachings and customs, all of which raised family life to a state of excellence seldom excelled even by their righteous forebears. True, Rabbinism, which sought to override the spirit of the law with traditionalism and the worship of the letter, often made void some of the highest family principles. But the Lord's system of familial relationships had been revealed and was known to the people, and among the truly pious and devout the true principles were in active operation.

Men married at sixteen or seventeen years of age, almost never later than twenty; and women at a somewhat younger age, often when not older than fourteen. These ages applied to all, Joseph and Mary included.[4] Children were esteemed to be a heritage from the Lord and were devoutly desired. Birth control was unknown among the Jews, and parents rejoiced in large families and numerous progeny. From the days of Moses, if a man died having no child, his brother was obligated to marry "the wife of the dead," and raise up seed unto his deceased brother, "that his name be not put out of Israel." (Deut. 25:5-10.)[5] There were special provisions for avoiding this responsibility so that the widow could marry another, which was the very thing that made possible the marriage of Ruth and Boaz, through whose lineage our Lord was born. (Ruth 4.)

Mothers taught their children almost from the moment of birth; at least the tutorial processes began by the time infant lips began to lisp their first words and phrases. The Psalms and prayers were used as lullabies. At the age of two years children were weaned, with the occasion being celebrated by a feast. When the children reached about three years of age fathers began to assume their Mosaically imposed obligation to teach them, not nursery rhymes, but verses of scripture, benedictions, and wise sayings. Formal schooling began at five or six, with the Bible as the text. This scriptural study began with Leviticus, extended out to the whole of the Pentateuch, went thence to the Prophets, and finally to the Hagiographa, that portion of the Bible not in the law and the prophets. The children learned to read and write and to memorize the chants of the Levites, those

Psalms which were part of festive celebrations, and the historical recitations that were part of family devotions. At sixteen or seventeen boys were sent to academies taught by the Rabbis. It is no wonder that Jewish Paul was able to say to Jewish Timothy: "From a child thou hast known the holy scriptures, which are able to make thee wise unto salvation." (2 Tim. 3:15.)[6] Such was the heritage of all Jewish children of the day.

But the educational system imposed upon Jewish children was more, far more, than formal schooling arrangements. It was part and portion of their way of life. They learned from what was done as well as from what was said. All male children were circumcised at eight days. A spirit of religion and devotion pervaded every home. Private prayers were offered both morning and evening. Before every meal they washed and prayed, and after every repast they gave thanks. There were frequent special family feasts. Every Sabbath was a holy and sanctified day on which they rested from their labors, worshipped at the synagogue, kept a Sabbath light burning in the home, adorned their homes, ate their best food, and bestowed upon each child the blessing of Israel.

Devout fathers wore phylacteries during prayer (the Pharisees wore them all day long), and these contained parchments whereon were written these four passages from the scriptures: Exodus 13:1-10, Exodus 13:11-16, Deuteronomy 6:4-9, and Deuteronomy 11:13-21. On the doorpost of the home of every devout Jew hung the Mezuzah, which contained a parchment whereon was written, in twenty-two lines, Deuteronomy 6:4-9 and 11:13-21, as both of these passages command. The Shema, composed of Deuteronomy 6:4-9, Deuteronomy 11:13-21, and Numbers 15:37-41, was repeated twice each day by every male. Family prayers were the order of the day in all homes.

Israel's deliverance from Egyptian bondage was recited, formally and in a question-and-answer dialogue, as each family ate the paschal lamb during the Feast of the Passover.

The morning and evening sacrifices and all of the special drama and ritual and ceremony that was part of all the great feasts had the effect of dramatically rehearsing the basic doctrines revealed by Jehovah to his people. On every Sabbath and twice during the week Moses and the prophets were read in the synagogues.

Every pious home had either portions or all of the Old Testament; it is difficult to believe that in the home where our Lord was reared there would have been anything less than the whole of that body of revealed writ which was then available to anyone. There were even little parchment rolls for children that contained such scripture as the Shema, the Hallel, the history of the creation and of the flood, and the first eight chapters of Leviticus.

Jewish homes, Jewish family life, the rearing of Jewish children, indeed, the whole Jewish way of life was founded upon Jewish theology. Jehovah's command to children—so basic that it was decree number five in the Decalogue itself—was: "Honour thy father and thy mother: that thy days may be long upon the land which the Lord thy God giveth thee." (Ex. 20:12.) Jehovah's command to parents—so basic that the Jews carried it in their phylacteries, hung it in their Mezuzahs, recited it twice daily in their Shema—was: 'Bring up thy children in light and in truth.' And that which was to be taught was theological; it was the holy scriptures; it was the mind and will and voice of the Lord to his people. And this is what separated the Jews from all other people.

"In the days of Christ," Edersheim says, "the pious Jew had no other knowledge, neither sought nor cared for any other—in fact, denounced it—than that of the law of God. At the outset, let it be remembered that, in heathenism, theology, or rather mythology, had no influence whatever on thinking or life—was literally submerged under their waves. To the pious Jew, on the contrary, the knowledge of God was everything; and to prepare for or impart that knowledge was the sum total, the sole object of his education. This was the life of his soul—the better, and only true life, to which all else as well as the life of the body were merely subservient, as means towards an end. His religion consisted of two things: knowledge of God, which by a series of inferences, one from the other, ultimately resolved itself into theology, as they understood it; and service, which again consisted of the proper observance of all that was prescribed by God, and of works of charity towards men—the latter, indeed, going beyond the bound of what was strictly due (the *Chovoth*) into special merit or 'righteousness' (*Zedakah*). But as service presupposed knowledge, theology was again at the foundation of all, and also the crown of all, which conferred the greatest merit. This is expressed or implied in almost innumerable passages of Jewish writings. Let one suffice, not only because it sounds more rationalistic, but because it is to this day repeated each morning in his prayers by every Jew: 'These are the things of which a man eats the fruit in this world, but their possession continueth for the next world: to honour father and mother, pious works, peacemaking between man and man, and the study of the law, which is equivalent to them all.' " (*Sketches,* pp. 124-25.)

NOTES

1. Deut. 6:4-9. See also Deut. 6:20-25; 4:9-10; 11:19; 31:10-13. Special provision was also made in the law of Moses that parents should teach their children all things appertaining to the Passover and their deliverance from Egyptian bondage. (Ex. 12:26-27; 13:8, 14.)

2. In this connection how comforting is the scriptural assurance: "Train up a child in the way he should go: and when he is old, he will not depart from it." (Prov. 22:6.)

3. *Sketches,* pp. 123-24. Lest we forget, in the passage to which Edersheim refers, Paul is condemning the Jews for their iniquities and for doing the very things they know will damn the Gentiles. Among other things the apostle says that because the Gentiles rejected the true knowledge of God and worshipped idols, "God also gave them up to uncleanness through the lusts of their own hearts, to dishonour their own bodies between themselves." Also that he "gave them up unto vile affections: for even their women did change the natural use [of their bodies] into that which is against nature: And likewise also the men, leaving the natural use of the woman, burned in their lust one toward another; men with men working that which is unseemly, and receiving in themselves that recompence of their error which was meet. And even as they did not like to retain God in their knowledge, God gave them over to a reprobate mind, to do those things which are not convenient; Being filled with all unrighteousness, fornication, wickedness, covetousness, maliciousness; full of envy, murder, debate, deceit, malignity; whisperers, Backbiters, haters of God, despiteful, proud, boasters, inventors of evil things, disobedient to parents, Without understanding, covenantbreakers, without natural affection, implacable, unmerciful: Who knowing the judgment of God, that they which commit such things are worthy of death, not only do the same, but have pleasure in them that do them." (Rom. 1:18-32.) The second chapter of

Romans carries on with the theme. Our purpose in setting it out here is to make it clear beyond question that there is no exaggeration in the sweeping denunciation of the degraded state of morality and family life among the non-Jewish people.

4. The common concept—shown in pictures and dramatized in fictional renditions of what fertile minds assume may have happened in the lives of members of the Holy Family—that Joseph was an old man when he took Mary as his bride is patently false. This traditional notion arises from two things: (1) The fact that Joseph apparently had died by the time of the crucifixion; at least on that occasion our Lord asked the Beloved Disciple to care for Mary, which John thereafter did. (John 19:25-27.) (2) False traditions which maintain that Mary was a virgin forever, had no sexual association with Joseph, and bore him no children. The only logical circumstances under which Joseph could have been substantially older than Mary would have been one in which he was taking her as a second wife after the death of a previous spouse, or one in which he and Mary were entering into a polygamous marriage. As Edersheim says: "Polygamy . . . undoubtedly was in force at the time of our Lord." (*Temple*, p. 142.) There is no reason to believe that either of these conditions prevailed, and we are left to conclude that Joseph was certainly not older than twenty years when he took Mary as his wife, and she was at least fourteen, perhaps fifteen or sixteen.

5. Manifestly this system of marriage discipline, revealed by Jehovah to Moses, could only prevail in a day when plural marriage was a divinely approved order.

6. This rabbinical declaration, taken from the Mishnah, "quaintly maps out," as Edersheim expresses it, the different periods of Jewish life: "At five years of age, reading of the Bible; at ten years, learning the Mishnah; at thirteen years, bound to the commandments; at fifteen years, the study of the Talmud; at eighteen years, marriage; at twenty, the pursuit of trade or business (active life); at thirty years, full vigour; at forty, maturity of reason; at fifty, for counsel; at sixty, commencement of agedness; at seventy, grey age; at eighty advanced old age; at ninety, bowed down; at a hundred, as if he were dead and gone, and taken from the world." (*Sketches*, p. 105.)

Chapter 13

JEWISH APOSTASY IN JESUS' DAY

This is an evil generation. (Luke 11:29.)

Ye are the children of them
which killed the prophets. Fill ye up then
the measure of your fathers. Ye serpents,
ye generation of vipers,
how can ye escape the damnation of hell?
(Matt. 23:31-33.)

Apostasy through the Ages

Adam and Eve—our first parents, our common ancestors, the mother and father of all living—had the fulness of
the everlasting gospel. They received the plan of salvation
from God himself, it being "declared by holy angels sent
forth from the presence of God, and by his own voice, and
by the gift of the Holy Ghost." (Moses 5:58.) They saw God,
knew his laws, entertained angels, received revelations,
beheld visions, and were in tune with the Infinite. They
exercised faith in the Lord Jesus Christ; repented of their
sins; were baptized in similitude of the death, burial, and
resurrection of the Promised Messiah; and received the gift
of the Holy Ghost. They were endowed with power from on
high, were sealed in the new and everlasting covenant of

marriage, and received the fulness of the ordinances of the house of the Lord.

After baptism, and after celestial marriage, they walked in paths of truth and righteousness, kept the commandments, and endured to the end. Having charted for themselves a course leading to eternal life, they pressed forward with a steadfastness in Christ—believing, obeying, conforming, consecrating, sacrificing—until their calling and election was made sure and they were sealed up unto eternal life.

And they taught all these things unto their children. They preached the gospel in plainness and perfection to all their numerous progeny. They made known the laws and ordinances of salvation—all to the end that the sons of men might believe and obey and come to know the joy of their redemption, "and the eternal life which God giveth unto all the obedient." (Moses 5:11.)

But, alas, sorrow rather than salvation lay ahead for many of the seed of mighty Michael and his lovely consort Eve. Many who were the seed of their bodies apostatized; they departed from the truth; they left the faith of their fathers; they turned from light to darkness, from righteousness to wickedness, from God to Satan. Apostasy consists of two things:

1. *Believing false doctrine.* "And all those who preach false doctrines, . . . wo, wo, wo be unto them, saith the Lord God Almighty, for they shall be thrust down to hell!"

2. *Living after the manner of the world.* "And all those who commit whoredoms, and pervert the right way of the Lord, wo, wo, wo be unto them, saith the Lord God Almighty, for they shall be thrust down to hell!" (2 Ne. 28:15.)

And so, from the very beginning, "Satan came among them, . . . and he commanded them, saying: Believe it not; and they believed it not, and they loved Satan more than God. And men began from that time forth to be carnal, sensual, and devilish." (Moses 5:11-13.) Thus apostasy began; men fell away from the truth even in the day of righteous Adam; men turned to carnal and ungodly practices even in the day when there were living witnesses to tell them of Eden's beauty, of the fall and promised redemption, and of angelic ministrations and heavenly revelations of the mind and will of Him whose they and we are.

Cain, a first generation son of the first man, rejected the gospel, refused to hearken to Adam, and loved Satan more than God. In his carnal and fallen state, Cain "rejected the greater counsel which was had from God," coveted the flocks of Abel, made a covenant with Satan, slew his righteous brother, and gloried in his wickedness. Others followed his course, and apostasy, rebellion, and wickedness became the established order of that and all succeeding days. (Moses 5.)

In Enoch's day there were great wars and rebellions; wickedness was so great in Noah's day that a merciful God swept the wicked and ungodly into a watery grave; Abraham's father worshipped idols; the whole city in which Melchizedek dwelt had departed from the truth; and all the Gentile nations in the days of ancient Israel were outside the pale of saving grace.

Apostasy has been and is the prevailing social and religious state of most men in all ages from Adam's to ours. The devil is not dead: Lucifer lives as surely as God does; he slays others but has not himself been slain. His influence covers the earth and has done so since the fall of man. He seeks to damn men, and "wide is the gate, and broad is the way, that leadeth to destruction." (Matt. 7:13.) Of our own day it is written: "Darkness covereth the earth, and gross darkness the minds of the people, and all flesh has become corrupt before my face." (D&C 112:23.) Also: "The whole world lieth in sin, and groaneth under darkness and under the bondage of sin." (D&C 84:49.) The war that began in heaven is continuing here among mortals, and up to this point most of the victories have been won by the enemy of all righteousness.

Apostasy in Ancient Israel

Israel—the Lord's own people, his own peculiar treasure, a people favored above all the nations of the earth—spent her entire history, as a people, wavering between true and false religion. Like a great pendulum the people swung back and forth between the true worship of Jehovah and the paying of devotions to Baal and all the gods of the degenerate nations in whose custody they found their promised land. The righteousness of parents was swallowed up in the wickedness of their children, with the children's children turning back to the standard of their grandparents. Eli served the Lord, and his sons served Baal. One king kept the feasts and commanded obedience to the law of Moses; the next honored the priests of Baal and worshipped the queen of heaven; and yet the next cut down the groves and destroyed the altars of the heathen. And so it went generation after generation.

Knowing the plagues God had poured out upon Egypt; having seen the waters of the Red Sea part to free them from Pharaoh; seeing the pillar of fire that gave protection by night and the cloud that went before them by day; hearing the rolling thunders and seeing the burning fires that rested on Sinai when the Lord came down to talk with Moses; eating daily the bread that miraculously came down from heaven; brandishing swords and staves that put to flight armies of aliens; seeing the earth open and swallow those who opposed Moses; living and walking, as it were, in the light of daily miracles—yet, in the midst of all this, Israel murmured and forsook the Lord. From time to time her people made a golden calf; they longed for the fleshpots of Egypt; their children were sacrificed in the fires of Molech; the daily sacrifices were done away; the Israelite hosts came not up to Jerusalem to keep the Feast of Tabernacles; they worshipped gods of wood and stone; they bowed before idols that neither hear nor see nor speak; and they kept not the law of Moses, the man of God.

231

As Moses' mortal ministry neared its end, he assembled all Israel and "commanded the people, saying, Keep all the commandments which I command you this day." Thereupon he summarized the blessings of obedience and set forth the cursings of apostasy. Among the curses, plagues, diseases, and torments that should come upon them if they chose disobedience was the assurance that the Lord would destroy their nation by bringing upon them fierce and relentless warriors; that in the siege of their cities delicate Hebrew women would eat their own children; and that the chosen people would be scattered "among all people, from the one end of the earth even unto the other," where they would "serve other gods," which neither they nor their fathers had known, and that they would no longer enjoy the light of heaven in which their fathers had basked. (Deut. 27—33.) That these dire calamities befell them—when Benhadad, king of Syria, besieged Samaria (2 Kgs. 6:26-29); and again when Nebuchadnezzar laid Jerusalem low (Lam. 4:10); and yet again when Titus overthrew the Holy City and tore apart the temple stone by stone—is well known.

As a means of impressing upon the people both the blessings of obedience and the cursings of disobedience, Joshua, as Moses had aforetime commanded, assembled all Israel in the valley between Mount Gerizim and Mount Ebal. Six of the tribes were over against Mount Gerizim to bless the people and the other six against Mount Ebal to respond to the cursings. The Levites then read, one by one, the cursings and the blessings, and the respective groups, speaking for all the house of Israel, gave a solemn response of "Amen," thus binding the whole nation to seek righteousness and shun evil. The concluding statement of this solemn rededication to Jehovah was: "Cursed be he that confirmeth not all the words of this law to do them." (Deut. 27:9-26. See also Josh. 8:32-35.)

We need make no attempt in this present work to recite all that befell ancient Israel because of apostasy and rebellion against the Lord. Let it suffice for our purposes—and we are only laying a foundation for a consideration of that apostasy which culminated in the crucifying of a God—let it suffice simply to point to three passages from Holy Writ.

The first of these involves the final overthrow of Jerusalem by Nebuchadnezzar in the day of Zedekiah, who, though a puppet ruler, had rebelled against Babylonia. "Moreover all the chief of the priests, and the people, transgressed very much after all the abominations of the heathen; and polluted the house of the Lord which he had hallowed in Jerusalem. And the Lord God of their fathers sent to them by his messengers, rising up betimes, and sending; because he had compassion on his people, and on his dwelling place: But they mocked the messengers of God, and despised his words, and misused his prophets, until the wrath of the Lord arose against his people, till there was no remedy. Therefore he brought upon them the king of the Chaldees, who slew their young men with the sword in the house of their sanctuary, and had no compassion upon young man or maiden, old man, or him that stooped for age: he gave them all into his hand." This was the day when the house of the Lord was burned, the walls of Jerusalem broken down, and those who escaped the sword were carried captive to Babylon. (2 Chr. 36:9-23.)[1]

Next, without any exposition, for the meaning is clear from the words themselves, we quote this language from the Psalms: "They did not destroy the nations, concerning whom the Lord commanded them: But were mingled among the heathen, and learned their works. And they served their idols: which were a snare unto them. Yea, they sacrificed their sons and their daughters unto devils, And shed innocent blood, even the blood of their sons and of their daughters, whom they sacrificed unto the idols of Canaan: and the land was polluted with blood. Thus were they defiled with their own works, and went a whoring with their own inventions. Therefore was the wrath of the Lord kindled against his people, insomuch that he abhorred his own inheritance. And he gave them into the hand of the heathen;

and they that hated them ruled over them. Their enemies also oppressed them, and they were brought into subjection under their hand. Many times did he deliver them; but they provoked him with their counsel, and were brought low for their iniquity." (Ps. 106:34-43.)

And third, these words of Isaiah deserve thoughtful consideration, for they not only describe the apostate condition of ancient Israel, but also have application to those who lived in the day of Jesus. "Ah sinful nation," Isaiah intones, "a people laden with iniquity, a seed of evildoers, children that are corrupters: they have forsaken the Lord, they have provoked the Holy One of Israel unto anger, they are gone away backward. . . . Except the Lord of hosts had left unto us a very small remnant, we should have been as Sodom, and we should have been like unto Gomorrah." (Isa. 1:4-9.)

Apostasy Among the Jews

Except for "a very small remnant"; except for a few priests and Levites who sat in Aaron's seat and offered sacrifices as required by the law of Moses; except for a rugged Peter, a visionary John, a guileless Nathanael; except for a believing Mary and a testifying Martha, a submissive Elisabeth, and a zealous Zacharias; except for the untutored and unlearned common people, who received Him gladly because they had not been contaminated by the scribes and Rabbis; except for a relatively few people, "a very small remnant," who would believe on Mary's Son—except for such as these, all the Jews of Jesus' day were apostate.

In that day, chosen and hallowed by Him who is holy as the day for his Son to make flesh his tabernacle; in that day when the light and glory of God should shine forth in the Person of his Beloved Son; in that day when the Lord Omnipotent, who was, and is, from all eternity to all eternity, would minister among his people; in that day when the infinite and eternal atonement should be wrought; in that day—above all days from creation's morn to the hour of the crucifixion — apostasy reigned among the sons of Adam.

It was a day not as Isaiah had said of ancient Israel, that "except" for "a very small remnant" they "should have been as Sodom, and . . . like unto Gomorrah" (Isa. 1:9), but a day when even Jerusalem, their capital city, was identified by John as "the great city, which spiritually is called Sodom and Egypt, where also our Lord was crucified." (Rev. 11:8.)[2] Israel of Isaiah's day, who, except for a few righteous among them, would have become "as Sodom," had now, in Jesus' day, degenerated spiritually until in prophetic language, in spite of the few believing souls among them, they had become both "Sodom and Egypt."

Theirs was no ordinary apostasy. It was not the apostasy of the Amorites and the Philistines who were born to darkness and had never known any course except that of astrology and witchcraft and the sodomic vices. Nor was it the apostasy of a Jeroboam or a Jezebel who openly rejected the God of Israel and swore allegiance to Baal, awful and wicked as such a course was. But the Jewish apostasy in the days of Jesus was one in which they had the greatest measure of truth then possessed by any people, and yet they rejected the Stone, the Cornerstone, upon which their whole religious structure was built. It was an apostasy among a people who actually had the Aaronic Priesthood. It was an apostasy among a people who had "the gospel of repentance and of baptism, and the remission of sins, and the law of carnal commandments, which the Lord in his wrath caused to continue with the house of Aaron among the children of Israel until John" who baptized Jesus. (D&C 84:26-27.)

It was an apostasy among a people who searched the scriptures, who memorized the Messianic prophecies, who knew that the hour of his coming was upon them, and who yet rejected him—though he raised the dead and created loaves and fishes out of nothing, as it were. Theirs was a refined, cultured, congenial apostasy, if we may use such terms to identify those who love darkness more than light because their deeds are evil. Theirs was an apostasy that followed truth in name, but not in deed; one in which they worshipped the true God with their lips, while their hearts were full of adultery and lasciviousness; an apostasy in which light and darkness were so intermixed that the resultant twilight kept even devout men and women from turning to the dawning brilliance of the new day.

Why the Jews of Jesus' Day Were Apostate

Why, of all people, were the generality of the Jews of Jesus' day so completely apostate? Why were they so dulled and insensitive spiritually that they failed to see in Jesus the fulfillment of all their Messianic dreams? How came they to be so hardened and cruel, so lacking in common compassion, that they would cry, "Crucify him, crucify him," as they berated the One who they all knew had opened blind eyes, unstopped deaf ears, and even reanimated cold corpses?

Three reasons are germain to the issues here raised:

1. Since Jesus our Lord came into the world for the express purpose of dying upon the cross for the sins of the world, it follows that a Divine Providence placed him among a people, and in a religious and political climate, where the chief object and end of his mortal sojourn could and would be brought to pass. He came to die; he must be slain; his destiny was to be hanged upon a tree; and the cross was prepared for his crucifixion from the foundation of the world, as it were. It follows that he must live and minister among those who would reject him. He must incur the hatred of those whose spiritual depravity would devise and condone his death. Can we reach any conclusion except that a Divine Providence sent to earth in that day, as part of Jewish Israel, the very spirits who would so harden their hearts as to desire and seek his death?

We are not saying they were foreordained to a course of hatred and murder, only that they were the kind of spirits— the kind of mortals—who found it easy to work wickedness and spread darkness. Like Ahaz and Jezebel, like Pilate and Herod, like Laman and Lemuel, like Antiochus Epiphanes who sacrificed swine on the holy altar, like the wicked and ungodly of all races and places, they found it easy to fight the truth because of their native inclinations to walk in a worldly course. Such was their spiritual inheritance, though, as with all men, it was within their power, at any time, to save themselves by repentance and righteousness.

2. These Jews of Jesus' day—through whose instrumentality, and by means of whose social and political pressure, Roman nails were driven through the hands and feet of Him who came to save them—were apostate for exactly and precisely the same reason that men in all ages have fought the truth. That reason is, they loved darkness rather than light, because their deeds were evil; they chose to live after the manner of the world, and to dull their spiritual senses with lust and adultery and greed, because such were the desires of their hearts; like Cain, they loved Satan more than God, meaning they chose to follow the course charted for them by Satan, who is the God of this world. Apostasy is the result of unrighteousness. No one ever forsakes or rejects the truth who is guided by the power of the Holy Ghost, and the Spirit will not dwell in an unclean tabernacle.

3. But there was something unique about Jewish apostasy in the meridian day. It grew out of one of the most resolute attempts ever made by men to live what they assumed was the will of Jehovah. It grew out of what their Nephite kinsmen, long before, had called "looking beyond the mark." "The Jews were a stiffnecked people," Nephi's brother said, "and they despised the words of plainness, and killed the prophets, and sought for things that they could not understand." These words, spoken concerning the Jews of Jacob's day, applied in full measure also to their descendants in Jesus' day. "Wherefore, because of their blindness, which blindness came by looking beyond the mark, they must needs fall; for God hath taken away his plainness from them, and delivered unto them many things which they can-

not understand, because they desired it. And because they desired it God hath done it, that they may stumble."

This matter of a devout and seemingly religious people becoming spiritually blind "by looking beyond the mark" illustrates perfectly how true and saving religion can become a damning burden. For generations that went before, and then in the day of our Lord's ministry, his Israelite brethren, by "looking beyond the mark," turned the truth of heaven into a system that led them to hell. That is to say, they took the plain and simple things of pure religion and added to them a host of their own interpretations; they embellished them with added rites and performances; and they took a happy, joyous way of worship and turned it into a restrictive, curtailing, depressive system of rituals and performances. The living spirit of the Lord's law became in their hands the dead letter of Jewish ritualism.

To the true order of Sabbath worship they added so many restrictions and performances that what should have been a day of rejoicing and rededication become a gloomy burden. To the true concept about their Messiah, they added the idea of a temporal ruler, so that the Deliverer who was sent to redeem them from death, hell, the devil, and endless torment was pictured as an earthly king with a sword like Caesar's in his hand. With their true system of sacrificial offerings they interwove such greedy practices that their conduct made of the Father's house a den of thieves. And so it went—through one doctrine and performance after another, their additions to what the Lord intended turned pure religion into anything but what it was intended to be. And so Jacob, by way of prophecy, was able to say that "by the stumbling of the Jews they will reject the stone upon which they might build and have safe foundation." (Jacob 4:14-15.)

But whatever the causes, the fact is that darkness covered the land of Palestine in that day and gross darkness filled the hearts of the generality of the people. The fires that should have been eternal had burned out, and the light of heaven

238

no longer guided the people. Spiritual darkness shrouded the nation. So degenerate and wicked were the inhabitants of the land that Jacob, speaking prophetically, said: "Christ . . . should come among the Jews, among those who are the more wicked part of the world." Those who had once walked in the light now stumbled in the darkness. "And they"— Jews of Abrahamic descent; Jews who knew the words of Moses; Jews for whom Joshua had stopped the sun; Jews who had slain one Goliath after another through their long history; these Jews, "the more wicked part of the world"!— "they shall crucify him—for thus it behooveth our God, and there is none other nation on earth that would crucify their God. For should the mighty miracles be wrought among other nations they would repent, and know that he be their God." So prophesied Jacob. Then he gave his explanation as to why the Jews had sunk to such a low level. "Because of priestcrafts and iniquities," he said, "they at Jerusalem will stiffen their necks against him, that he be crucified. Wherefore, because of their iniquities, destructions, famines, pestilences, and bloodshed shall come upon them; and they who shall not be destroyed shall be scattered among all nations." (2 Ne. 10:3-6.)

Priestcrafts and iniquities! And the effects that flow from them! What a lesson modern Christendom, those who should be the Lord's people today, can learn from the Jews, those who should have been the Lord's people yesterday!

NOTES

1. This accords with the prophecy of Jeremiah that says: "Because your fathers have forsaken me. saith the Lord. and have walked after other gods. and have served them, and have worshipped them. and have forsaken me. and have not kept my law: And ye have done worse than your fathers: for. behold. ye walk every one after the imagination of his evil heart. that they may not hearken unto me: Therefore will I cast you out of this land into a land that ye know not. neither ye nor your fathers: and there shall ye serve other gods day and night: where I will not shew you favour." (Jer. 16:11-13.)

2. Edersheim speaks of the "painful evidence [which] comes to us of the luxuriousness of Jerusalem at that time. and of the moral corruption to which it led." He points to "the recorded covert lascivious expressions used by the men. which gives a lamentable picture of the state of morals of many in the city. and the notices of the indecent dress worn not only by women. but even by the corrupt High-Priestly youths." He speaks of "the dignity of the Jerusalemites: of the wealth which they lavished on their marriages: of the ceremony

which insisted on repeated invitations to the guests to a banquet, and that men inferior in rank would not be bidden to it; of the dress in which they appeared; the manner in which the dishes were served, the wine in white crystal vases; and the punishment of the cook who had failed in his duty, and which was to be commensurate to the dignity of the party." (Edersheim 1:131-32.) As the weepings and tears of her King attest, the "Holy City" had become in his day a sodomic den.

Chapter 14

JEWISH SECTS AND BELIEFS IN JESUS' DAY

Now I beseech you, brethren, by the
name of our Lord Jesus Christ, that
ye all speak the same thing, and that there
be no divisions among you; but that ye
be perfectly joined together
in the same mind and in the
same judgment. . . . Is Christ divided?
(1 Cor. 1:10-13.)

What did the Ancient Jews Believe?

All of the ancient Jews who were faithful believed either all or part of the gospel—the gospel of Jehovah, the gospel of the Messiah, the gospel of Christ, the gospel that is the plan of salvation, the gospel that Jesus restored and taught in his day, the everlasting gospel (God does not change!), the same gospel restored in our day through Joseph Smith.

Beginning with Abraham, the father of the Jews; going on down through Isaac, and Jacob, and Joseph, and Ephraim; including Moses and the prophets; considering particularly the kingdom of Judah, which was taken into Babylonian captivity, and then permitted to return and rebuild their temple in Jerusalem—all these Jews, who were faithful, believed either the fulness of the gospel or the preparatory gospel, as the case may be, depending on the degree of their faith and allegiance to the Lord.

Whenever there were legal administrators among them who held the Melchizedek Priesthood, the people had the fulness of the gospel, the same as we do, and, be it remembered, all the prophets held this high and holy order of divine authority. Our best illustration of this is the Nephite people, who both kept the law of Moses and rejoiced in the fulness of the gospel.

The mere presence of the higher priesthood, of itself and in its nature, means that the fulness of the gospel is present. The fulness of the gospel consists in the possession of the Melchizedek Priesthood and the enjoyment of the gift of the Holy Ghost, which gift is conferred by the power of this higher priesthood. The fulness of the gospel consists of all the laws, ordinances, doctrines, powers, and truths needed to assure mortals of a fulness of salvation, which is eternal life in the kingdom of God.

Whenever there were legal administrators among them who held only the Aaronic Priesthood, the people had only the preparatory gospel, the lesser law, the Mosaic law, the law of sacrifices and performances and carnal commandments. The presence of the Aaronic Priesthood, without the Melchizedek Priesthood, so that the lesser order holds rule and sway because there is no greater, means that the preparatory gospel only is present. This gospel, which includes faith and repentance and baptism, is to prepare men to receive the gift of the Holy Ghost and the higher ordinances of salvation, and therefore to prepare them for the fulness of the gospel and the fulness of salvation.

In the day when Jesus began his ministry there were no prophets or righteous men who held the Melchizedek Priesthood. Indeed, our Lord came to restore this higher order. John the Baptist held the Aaronic Priesthood, baptized by immersion in Jordan for the remission of sins, and promised that One would come after, the latchet of whose shoes he felt unworthy to unloose, who would baptize with fire and with the Holy Ghost.

Thus, the Jews in Jesus' day had the preparatory gospel—at least some of those among them did who were faithful; and the Jews of that day looked forward to the receipt of the fulness of the gospel with the advent of their Messiah—at least those did who were faithful. As we are aware, the generality of the people were apostate in their feelings, did not understand the purpose of the preparatory gospel that their priests administered, and failed to receive the fulness of the saving power when it came in the person of the One whose gospel it is.

What Did the Jews in Jesus' Day Believe?

There was no united Jewish religion in our Lord's day any more than there is a united Christianity in our day. It does not suffice to speak of what the Jews believed or how they lived or what their social circumstances were any more than it does to utter similar generalities with reference to modern Christendom. There are Christian churches, so-called, that define a Christian as a person who believes the three basic creeds: the Apostles Creed, the Nicene Creed, and the Athanasian Creed. There are those who say that none are Christians except those who believe in the Trinity as set out in these weather-worn documents from an uninspired past, meaning those who believe that the Father, Son, and Holy Ghost are a spirit essence or power that fills the immensity of space and is everywhere and nowhere in particular present. There are Christians, so-called, who suppose that revelation has ceased, that visions are a thing of the past, that miracles are done away, that apostles and prophets are no longer needed.

On the other hand, there are followers of Christ who believe that the creeds of Christendom are an abomination in the sight of the Lord; that the Father and the Son are personal beings having bodies of flesh and bones as tangible as man's, and that the Holy Ghost is a personage of Spirit; and that without revelation, visions, miracles, priesthood, apostles and prophets, and every gift and grace enjoyed and possessed by the ancients, man does not have the pure gospel and cannot be saved in the kingdom of God.

As with us Christians, so with those Jews. There were Jewish cults, Jewish sects, and Jewish doctrinal aberrations in the day of Jesus. There were those who believed in a resurrection and those who did not; those who believed in angels and visions and revelations and those who did not; those who looked for a Messiah who would be a temporal despot and those who saw in the lowly Nazarene the fulfillment of the Messianic prophecies.

And the very fact that these divisions of thought and conduct existed is of itself proof conclusive of the prevailing apostasy. Paul asked, "Is Christ divided?" In Jewish parlance, and fitted to their circumstances, the query would have been: "Is Jehovah divided? Does he say one thing to the Pharisees, another to the Sadducees, and yet another to the Essenes?"

To study our Lord's life in a setting of reality, we must know about the major sects and cults and doctrinal perversities that prevailed in the minds of those to whom he attempted to teach his gospel and proclaim his own divine Sonship.

Jewish Sects, Parties, and Denominations

We shall note those sects, parties, and denominations—and certain officers who served in connection with them—whose beliefs and activities had a direct bearing on the mortal ministry of the Promised Messiah. Those cults and the cultists who comprised them; those Palestinian persons of affluence and influence; those Jewish patriots and Roman rulers, plus their bootlicking sycophants; those teachers and molders of religious and political thinking in the day of the Natural Heir to David's throne—all of them lumped together—formed the social and cultural and religious milieu in which Jesus ministered and from which his converts came. Their influence upon the inhabitants of the Holy Land influenced in turn what he said and did, where he went, and whom he gathered into his fold. Since the words and works of Jesus were not wrought in a vacuum and cannot be understood as an isolated phenomenon, since no happening in the Gospel accounts is perfectly understood apart from its Jewish setting, and since an understanding of the Christian church in the meridian of time presupposes a knowledge of Jewish history and culture, with which it is inseparably joined by innumerable threads, we shall make a necessary but brief comment about the following peoples and groups:

1. *The Jewish High Priest.*

If Aaron, Israel's first high priest, had returned to his beloved Palestine to observe conditions generally; if, with Eleazar and Ithamar, his priestly sons, he had come into Herod's Temple in the day of Jesus to compare its rites and performances with those that he and they administered in the forerunner of that house of worship; if he had stood in the court of the majestic house of the Lord that crowned Jerusalem, and had looked upon the giant altar and compared the proceedings there with what he did in the tabernacle of the congregation; but, more importantly, if he had contrasted the vain and degenerate and wicked lives of those who then sat in his seat, with the righteousness and godly walk of their ancestors, many generations before, we may suppose he would have been sick at heart and would have felt like lamenting over doomed Jerusalem and its twice doomed temple, even as Jesus himself would soon do. The Jewish high priests of Jesus' day were a far cry from their counterparts in the days of Israel's genesis.

Aaron, who held the Melchizedek Priesthood and qualified by purity of heart, along with Nadab and Abihu and seventy of the elders of Israel, to see the God of that chosen people, was called of God to preside over the lesser priesthood, which ever thereafter would bear his name. He was the presiding bishop of the Church, as it were, and the office was ordained of God to be hereditary, to go from father to son, and to be the rightful inheritance of the oldest man in direct descent among the sons of Aaron.[1] And so it was in the early generations. But in the days of the kings of Israel and Judah, high priests were sometimes installed and banished from office by the unrighteousness of the occupant of the throne, and by the days of Jesus such appointments and removals were made by Gentile overlords as a matter of political expediency and without reference to the lineage of the Levite involved. As a consequence, the high priests were of the same low spiritual stature as the Herods and Pilates who appointed them. But what concerns us is that they wielded great political and religious influence, that they molded public sentiment, and that their conduct became a pattern for Jews in general.

It is worthy of note that these, shall we say, illegitimate sons of Aaron were considered nonetheless to be Jehovah's representatives, that they were subject to secular powers and engaged in political connivings that were outside the bounds of their priestly callings, and that they were a symbol or standard around which the people would rally either to worship or to crucify.

It is also worthy of note that they wielded considerable influence; were overly endowed with this world's goods; received their offices, in some instances, by crime and bribery; and were subject to the mandates and murderous designs of the Great Sanhedrin. They were "high priests by investiture" and not "high priests by anointing," as had been their forebears; and though they could still simulate and wear the breastplate, the Urim and Thummim that Aaron and his original successors once carried upon their breasts had long since been taken from their ungodly hands, and with the loss of these holy interpreters had gone also, in large measure, the spirit of prophecy and revelation.

These high priests did, however, still hold the Aaronic

Priesthood; they still performed sacrificial rites with all the similitudes and symbols that had always attended these sacred ordinances; and they still directed appropriate worship at the great feasts and made atonement for the people on that one day each year when they entered the Holy of Holies and pronounced the Ineffable Name ten times.

As to the two despicable priestly rulers who sought the blood of the Guiltless One and who joined in the conspiracy that carried him to the cross, Edersheim says: "St. Luke significantly joins together, as the highest religious authority in the land, the names of Annas and Caiaphas. The former had been appointed by Quirinius. After holding the Pontificate for nine years, he was deposed, and succeeded by others, of whom the fourth was his son-in-law Caiaphas. The character of the High-Priests during the whole of that period is described in the Talmud in terrible language. And although there is no evidence that 'the house of Annas' was guilty of the same gross self-indulgence, violence, luxury, and even public indecency, as some of their successors, they are included in the woes pronounced on the corrupt leaders of the priesthood, whom the Sanctuary is represented as bidding depart from the sacred precincts, which their presence defiled. It deserves notice, that the special sin with which the house of Annas is charged is that of 'whispering'—or hissing like vipers—which seems to refer to private influence on the judges in their administration of justice, whereby 'morals were corrupted, judgment perverted, and the Shekhinah withdrawn from Israel.' " (Edersheim 1:263.)

2. *Priests and Levites.*

We know that the Aaronic Priesthood itself has been the same from its beginning to the present, meaning that we now have what John the Baptist had, and he possessed what Aaron himself held. We know that in the Aaronic Priesthood today there are four offices—deacon, teacher, priest, and bishop. But we cannot determine from the Old and New Testament accounts what offices there were in the lesser priesthood in previous ages. The priesthood itself is power and authority; the offices in the priesthood are appointments to use the priesthood for specified purposes. When the purposes change for which priesthood is needed and used, it may well be that the offices themselves are changed. From the day of Aaron to the building of Solomon's Temple, for instance, the Levites transported the tabernacle of the congregation and had special care for the ark of the covenant. These functions were no longer needed when the House of the Lord became a permanent rather than a portable dwelling place. Functions that once were laid upon the Levites were no longer needed, and it may well be that the offices in their Levitical Order of priesthood also underwent changes.

In Aaron's day, he and his son were priests. Aaron himself—and his firstborn after him, from generation to generation—was the presiding priest; in this capacity he carried the designation of high priest, and served as the equivalent of the presiding bishop. The other members of the tribe of Levi also held the Aaronic Priesthood, or, as it is also called, the Levitical Priesthood, but they did not hold the office of priest. In the scriptural accounts they are simply called Levites. The offices they held are not named, although the duties assigned them are described. These duties were to assist Aaron's sons in transporting and caring for the tabernacle of the congregation and in various performances in the temple. Their services were comparable to those of deacons and teachers today. Our deacons and teachers cannot baptize or administer the sacrament, and the Levites, although they did some menial work connected with sacrifices, such as preparing the altar and gathering the wood, did not perform the sacrifices themselves. We assume they did not baptize and that this ordinance was left for the priests only. We know there were judges anciently and that a bishop is a common judge in Israel, and so we conclude that the present office is comparable to the ancient one.

Under the Mosaic system the Levites were scattered among the other tribes and received no landed inheritances of the sort distributed by lot to their fellow tribes. All the other tribes paid tithes to the Levites, and they in turn tithed their tithes for the support of the priests. Since our deacons—holding the Aaronic or Levitical Priesthood, as they do—are appointed to teach the gospel, and to warn, expound, and exhort, and to invite all to come to Christ; since our teachers are to watch over the Church always and to be with and strengthen the members; since they are to see that there is no iniquity in the Church and that all the members do their duty; since our priests are to visit in the homes of the members and exhort them to pray vocally and in secret and attend to all family duties, we assume their counterparts anciently—indeed, there can be little question on the matter—had similar responsibilities. It is certainly not an exaggeration to say that the priests and Levites were a sanctifying and uplifting influence on the people generally and that they were looked upon as the Lord's servants and were treated accordingly.

In the day of Jesus, the priests and Levites, whose numbers were comparatively great, administered in the sacrificial services, performed the various rituals at the feasts, cared for the temple, and were expected to be learned in the law. If nothing else, they were an ever-present witness and symbol that the Lord's priesthood was on earth and that men should turn to Jehovah for strength and guidance. That they failed to give that guidance which would have led the people to believe in their true Messiah, when as a mortal he ministered among them, shows the depths to which the Jewish social and religious structure had sunk and justifies the assertion that their priesthood had been perverted into priestcraft. The sons of Levi of that day had become impure. But in the providence of Him whose servants they should have been, the promise is that in the last days he will purify them again that once more they may perform those duties assigned to them in the priestly order which has come down from Aaron.

3. *Scribes.*

"In trying to picture to ourselves New Testament scenes,

the figure most prominent, next to those of the chief actors, is that of the *Scribe*. He seems ubiquitous; we meet him in Jerusalem, in Judea, and even in Galilee. Indeed, he is indispensable, not only in Babylon, which may have been the birthplace of his order, but among the 'dispersion' also. Everywhere he appears as the mouthpiece and representative of the people; he pushes to the front, the crowd respectfully giving way, and eagerly hanging on his utterances, as those of a recognised authority. He has been solemnly ordained by the laying on of hands; and is the *Rabbi*, 'my great one,' Master, *amplitudo*. He puts questions; he urges objections; he expects full explanations and respectful demeanour. Indeed, his hyper-ingenuity in questioning has become a proverb. There is not measure of his dignity, nor yet limit to his importance. He is the 'lawyer,' the 'well-plastered pit,' filled with the water of knowledge 'out of which not a drop can escape,' in opposition to the 'weeds of untilled soil' of ignorance. He is the Divine aristocrat, among the vulgar herd of rude and profane 'country people,' who 'know not the Law' and are 'cursed.' More than that, his order constitutes the ultimate authority on all questions of faith and practice; he is 'the Exegete of the Laws,' the 'teacher of the Law,' and along with 'the chief priests' and 'elders' a judge in the ecclesiastical tribunals, whether of the capital or in the provinces. Although generally appearing in company with 'the Pharisees,' he is not necessarily one of them—for they represent a religious party, while he has a status, and holds an office. In short, he is the *Talmid* or learned student, the *Chakham* or sage, whose honour is to be great in the future world. Each Scribe outweighed all the common people, who must accordingly pay him every honour. Nay, they were honoured of God Himself, and their praises proclaimed by the angels; and in heaven also, each of them would hold the same rank and distinction as on earth. Such was to be the respect paid to their sayings, that they were to be absolutely believed, even if they were to declare that to be at the right hand which was at the left, or *vice versa.*" (Edersheim 1:93-94.)

Israel's divine guidance as a nation began with Moses, the man of God. He spoke and the issue was determined. His voice was the voice of Jehovah. Thereafter there were judges and prophets who had scribes to record their sayings and memorialize their doings, but always the divine word was available for the asking and the mind of the Lord was revealed for the seeking. In post-exilic days the prophetic word began to decrease and the position of the scribe, as the one in whose hands the divine word was found, grew in importance. Ezra was both a prophet and a scribe. After his day, through an evolving course, as inspired utterances were less frequent, the understanding and interpretation of the seeric sayings of the past became more important and the position of the scribes took on a new meaning, until finally their influence excelled all others in molding religious thought and practice.

This same course—for Lucifer has no new ideas, but merely applies what he already knows to new situations—has been followed in apostate Christendom. When there were no longer apostles and inspired men to give the Lord's message and word to living men, the world turned to interpreters— to scholars, to doctors of divinity, to theologians, to professors of religion—to set forth what they thought or imagined the divine word of former days meant. In the opening of our dispensation the Lord, after saying that the creeds of Christendom were "an abomination in his sight" (and these creeds were the interpretations and conclusions of the scribes, as it were), then said that "those professors" (meaning all who, like the scribes, had by their interpretations and teachings perverted the truth and made it of none effect) "were all corrupt." Then he said, paraphrasing Isaiah, "they draw near to me with their lips, but their hearts are far from me, they teach for doctrines the commandments of men, having a form of godliness, but they deny the power thereof." (JS-H 1:19.) This same charge—shall we say curse? yes, for so it is—was the one hurled by the Lord Jesus against the "scribes and Pharisees" of his day, quoting also the same root text from Isaiah. (Matt. 15:1-9; Mark 7:1-9; Isa. 29:13.)

By the time of Jesus, the Jewish scribes, exalted and revered by the people, had become the chief creators and upholders of priestcraft; they had become the devisers of doctrines that condoned and upheld iniquity—and it should be remembered that, according to the prophetic word, it was "because of priestcrafts and iniquities" that our Lord was "crucified." (2 Ne. 10:5.) The scribes had become and were the enemies of Christ. They were the ones who added to the law of Moses those detailed performances and perversions which made the law of no effect. They were the ones approved to explain and teach the law and to make decisions under it. There was a tradition that they alone understood the whole law, and their words came to have more impact and import than the law itself. It is as though they were the law. They were required to learn by heart the oral law, and they spent their time teaching others and disputing among themselves. They were, in effect, false ministers, false teachers, and false prophets, all of which gives great meaning to the scriptural comment that Jesus "taught . . . as one having authority, and not as the scribes." (Matt. 7:29.)

No group had greater influence over the people than they did. Nearly all the judges came from their ranks; they made up almost the whole teaching force of the nation, and they were well represented on the Sanhedrin. No priest could attain a position of prominence and influence unless he was also a scribe. They are the ones spoken of as the lawyers and teachers of the law. In New Testament times, the terms *lawyer* and *scribe* were synonymous. Most of the scribes were also Pharisees, but as a body they were distinct from them. Of them Jesus said: "All their works they do for to be seen of men: they make broad their phylacteries, and enlarge the borders of their garments, And love the uppermost rooms at feasts, and the chief seats in the synagogues, And greetings in the markets, and to be called of men, Rabbi, Rabbi." They are the ones upon whom he heaped perhaps the severest woes ever uttered by him, including the excoriating declaration, "Ye serpents, ye generation of vipers, how can ye escape the damnation of hell?" (Matt. 23.) They were a class who could have been a blessing to the people, for they were privileged to be teachers; but, in fact, they became a cursing, for they taught not the truth. "And all those who preach false doctrines, . . . and pervert the right way of the Lord, wo, wo, wo be unto them, saith the Lord God Almighty, for they shall be thrust down to hell!" (2 Ne. 28:15.)

4. *Rabbis.*

Jesus' counsel to his disciples that they should not be called Rabbi—"for one is your Master, even Christ; and all ye are brethren" (Matt. 23:8)—was itself a condemnation both of the false adulation heaped on the uninspired teachers of the day and a denunciation of Rabbinism itself, that is, of the great body of theological absurdities that had come into being through the warped interpretations of those who were looked upon as lights to the people. As occasion requires, and as we deal with the various vagaries of Jewish theology, we shall see the revolting absurdities imposed by Rabbinism upon a religion that once had divine approval. For the present we need only note that in Jesus' day all scribes were considered to be Rabbis, for the title was merely one of respect that was given by the Jews to all of their doctors and teachers. But the title was not limited to those self-appointed embodiments of all wisdom. Christ and John the Baptist, for instance, were both addressed by respectful persons by rabbinical titles. Different degrees of honor were intended as people used the term *Rab,* meaning master; *Rabbi,* my master; and *Rabboni,* my lord and master, this last and most exalted of all the titles being the one used by Mary outside the open tomb as she bowed before the risen Master. It will suffice for our present purposes merely to be aware that all that was said of the scribes applies in part at least to the Rabbis, and that this latter group must bear much of the responsibility for creating the climate and preparing the way for the crucifixion of a God. What an awesome responsibility one assumes when he chooses to teach false doctrine![2]

5. *Pharisees, Sadducees, Essenes, and Nazarites.*

These all, in effect, were politico-religious sects or parties. Theoretically their bases were religious and their differences doctrinal; in fact, they were also political and social and cultural. They came into being in post-exilic historical settings of anguish and political oppression, and each of them exercised a leavening and sometimes controlling influence in Jewish Israel.

The Pharisees, of whom there were only between six thousand and seven thousand in the day of Jesus, had by all odds the greatest influence over Jewish thought and practice. The bulk of the common people believed as they did and conformed to some extent to their practices. Their number included the scribes, whose self-appointed mission was to tempt, berate, and deride the Son of God; and their doctrine was Rabbinism, that maze of Jewish absurdity which turned living truth into dead letter and imposed such burdens upon men that none but deluded fanatics could bear them in full. Paul was a Pharisee; so also were Gamaliel, Nicodemus, and the Arimathean called Joseph, in whose tomb our Lord was laid.

As best we can determine, from those educated guesses which historians are pleased to call historical facts, the Pharisees were those who continued the work of Ezra in collating, memorizing, and interpreting the law and all the commandments therein recorded. Apparently they began as a distinct group with political influence as the Hasidaeans back in the days of the high priest Onanias III, who was deposed by Antiochus Epiphanes in the second century B.C. Their name signifies "God's loyal ones," and they were traditionally known as "the separated ones." Under John

Hyrcanus (134-104 B.C.) they had great political power, and from that time onward they maintained a dominating position in the Sanhedrin. Such was true in the day when that body condemned our Lord.

Our special interest in the Pharisees centers in what they believed and taught and practiced in that day when the Lord Jesus had one confrontation after another with them. A knowledge of their opinions and practices in that day when our Lord was restoring the gospel again is almost essential to an understanding of the Christianity that then came into being. In that day their interest was not, as it had once been, in keeping or interpreting the law of Moses, in the true sense of the word. Rather, they then had created a new law, an oral law—the portion of the Talmud called the Mishna or "second law"; it is a law founded on tradition instead of revelation, a law that they esteemed to be of greater worth than the Torah, or law of Moses itself. A digest of Jewish traditions as well as a compendium of the ritualistic performances of the law, it was made up of formalistic minutae; of the need for washings before they could eat bread; of the requirement to bathe following a trip to the market; and of the practice of washing cups, pots, and brazen vessels. It included fasting twice a week (on Mondays and Thursdays) between the Paschal week and Pentecost, and between the Feast of Tabernacles and that of the Dedication of the Temple. Their observance of the law of tithing was punctilious beyond belief, even going to the point of refusing to buy food from or to eat food in the homes of non-Pharisees, lest the food should not have been tithed; and so on and so on and so on. And out of these beliefs and practices there grew up among them a feeling of proud self-righteousness, which dulled their spirits and closed their minds against the truths Jesus offered them.

Theologically speaking, the Pharisees believed in the unity and holiness of God, the election of Israel, life after death, the resurrection from the dead, the ministering of angels, and some among them at least in the continuation of the family unit in eternity. They were extreme advocates of the doctrine of observing the Sabbath day, to which doctrine they had appended thirty-nine principal species of prohibited acts on that day. Most of their religious emphasis, however, was on ethical principles rather than doctrinal concepts.

It was not easy to be a Pharisee, but perhaps that was part of the Pharisees' appeal to a people who believed that life never was intended to be easy. In any event they wielded the greatest religious power of any group in our Lord's day.

The Sadducees, fewer in number than their Pharisaic opponents, claimed only four thousand adherents in the day Jesus walked among men. But they were the aristocracy of the nation—the priests and rulers, the wealthy and influential, the consorters with Herod and the friends of Caesar.

Jewish legend places their beginning with Zadok, whose family ministered at the altar in the Lord's house; and among their number was found the presiding high priest, the one who, alone among all his kindred priests, went annually to commune with the Most High in the most holy place. After Cyrus opened the prison that was Babylon and sent Zerubbabel and the others back to the once Holy City to build Jehovah's house again, the remnant of Zadok stood foremost among the priestly families, ministering again, as was their right by lineage, in the sacred sacrificial offerings.

They grew into a reactionary politico-religious organization as part of an insurgent movement against the Maccabean party in the second century B.C. In their veins, at the time of John and Jesus and their apostolic colleagues, flowed the purest Jewish blood of the nation. The whole thrust of their not-too-popular party was one of opposition to the Pharisees and the oral law with all its ritualistic formalities. For them, the temple—not the synagogues, which were dominated by the Pharisees, the Rabbis, and the scribes— was the center of a religious system whose true significance they no longer understood. Being satisfied with life as it then

was, they had little interest in the coming of a Messianic Deliverer, though the Sadducean sacrifices they offered on the
great altar were in similitude of his promised atoning
sacrifice. When Titus set the Roman torch to the temple in
A.D. 70, wrenching each separate stone from the ancient
foundation, the Sadducees died as a party; from then on Judaism centered in the synagogue and not the temple.

"But this priestly aristocracy were by no means the most
zealous for the sanctuary from which they drew their
honours and wealth. They . . . had even sought to turn parts
of the Temple into a splendid family mansion. They had co-
quetted and debased their offices to win favour with the
Ptolemies and the Syrian kings; they had held back, in half
Greek irreligiousness, from taking a vigorous part in the glorious Maccabean struggle, and now [in the day of Jesus]
truckled to heathen procurators, or with a half heathen king,
to preserve their honours and vested interests. To please
Herod, they had admitted Simon Boethus, the Alexandrian,
the father of the king's young wife, to the high priesthood,
from which a strict Jew, Jesus the son of Phabi, had been ex-
pelled to make room for him. They had even shown frank
and hearty submission and loyalty to Rome.

"The nation, with its chosen religious leaders, the
Pharisees—the representatives of the 'Saints' who had conquered in the great war of religious independence—never
forgot the faint-heartedness and treachery of the priestly no-
bility in that magnificent struggle. Their descent might
secure its members hereditary possession of the dignified
offices of the Church, and there might still be a charm in
their historical names; but they were regarded with open dis-
trust and dislike by the nation and the Pharisees alike, and
had to make many concessions to Pharisaic rules to protect
themselves from actual violence.

"The strict fanatical heads of the Synagogue and leaders
of the people, and the cold and polished Temple aristocracy,
were thus bitterly opposed, and it added to the keenest of the
dislike that the dreams by the Rabbinical, or Pharisaic party,

of a restored theocracy, could only be realized through the existing organization of the priesthood, of which the indifferent Sadducees had the control." (Geikie, pp. 538-39.)

Theologically, the Sadducees found little to please them in the beliefs of the Pharisaically inclined masses. Strange as it may seem among a people who praised Jehovah with their lips and had his law written on scrolls of papyrus that were everywhere available for study and scholastic analysis, the Sadducees did not believe in a resurrection. They denied the reality of a future state in which rewards and punishments would be meted out as a result of good or evil acts performed by mortal men. They scoffed at the Pharisaic concepts of the immortality of the soul, and believed neither in preexistence nor the ministering of angels nor the existence of spirits. They did not believe in foreordination or that Divine Providence ruled in the lives of men, but did lay stress on the fact that men had freedom of choice as to good and evil, and concluded that whatever happened in one's life was the direct result of the exercise of such agency.[3]

But in nothing was the difference between Pharisees and Sadducees more marked than in the contrast between the Pharisaic Messianic hope and the Sadducean rejection of or at least indifference to this nationalistic concept. "The Pharisees, as the hereditary representatives of puritans who had delivered the nation in the great struggle against Syria, looked forward with touching though fanatical yearning, to the realization of the prophecies of Daniel, which, as they understood them, promised that Israel, under the Messiah, and with it, themselves, should be raised 'to dominion, and glory, and a kingdom; that all peoples, nations, and languages should serve Him, and that His kingdom should be everlasting.'[4] They believed that this national triumph would be inaugurated so soon as Israel, on its part, carried out to the full the requirements of the ceremonial laws, as expounded in their traditions. It was a matter of formal covenant, in which the truth and righteousness—that is, the justice, of Jehovah were involved. . .

"To this dream of the future, the Sadducees opposed a stolid and contemptuous indifference. Enjoying the honours and good things of the world, they had no taste for a revolution which should introduce, they knew not what, in place of a state of things with which they were quite contented. Their fathers had had no such ideas, and the sons ridiculed them. They not only laughed aside the Pharisaic idea of righteousness, as identified with a life of minute and endless observance, but fell back on the Mosaic Law, and mocked at the Messianic hope from which the zeal of their rivals had sprung. . . .

"The nation zealously supported the Pharisees. The spirit of the age was against the Sadducees. The multitude disliked to hear that what the Maccabeans had defended with their blood was uncanonical. They yielded cheerfully to the heavy yoke of the Pharisaic Rabbis, for, the more burdensome the duties required, the greater the future reward for performance. The Pharisees, moreover, were part of the people, mingled habitually with them as their spiritual guides, and were the examples of exact obedience to their own precepts. Their Messianic dreams were of national glory, and thus the crowd saw in them the representatives of their own fondest aspirations. The Sadducees—isolated, haughty, harsh, and unnational—were hated: their rivals honoured and followed. The extravagances and the hypocrisy of some might be ridiculed, but they were the accepted popular leaders.

"Indeed, apart from all other considerations, the fact that the Sadducees supported zealously every government in turn, was enough to set the people against them. Instead of this, the Pharisees shared and fostered the patriotic and religious abhorrence of the Roman supremacy, and were sworn enemies of the hated Herodian family. The result was that, in the words of Josephus, 'the Pharisees had such an influence with the people, that nothing could be done about divine worship, prayers, or sacrifices, except according to their wishes and rules, for the community believed they sought only the loftiest and worthiest aims alike in word and deed. The Sadducees were few in number; and though they belonged to the highest ranks, had so little influence, that when elected to office, they were forced to comply with the ritual of the Pharisees from fear of the people.' " (Geikie, pp. 541-42.)

If the Pharisees were a "generation of vipers" who could not "escape the damnation of hell" (Matt. 23:33), as Jesus said (and they were), and if the Sadducees used their political influence to bring about our Lord's crucifixion, thus consigning themselves to the same depths of damnation (and so it was), they both had a bedfellow whose departure from the truth and whose apostate practices equaled and even surpassed those of these two more influential sects. We speak of the *Essenes*. In number—there were some four thousand of them in Jesus' day—they were as numerous as the Sadducees. Their influence among the people, however, was slight, and they are not so much as mentioned by name in the New Testament. It was to the Pharisees that the masses turned for religious guidance, and it was to the Sadducees that the people bowed where their sacrificial system was concerned and where their relationships to the Caesars and the Herods were involved.

The Essenes drew into their fold the utter and complete fanatics of the nation. Many of them lived in colonies apart from their fellow Jews, held their property under a communal system, ate at a common table, and lived a rigid agrarian type life, full of ceremonialism. Some were celibates, "the precursors of the Christian monks," Geikie says.

Their doctrine was as far afield from reality as is common in the more freakish cults of Christendom. Their aim in life was to keep the law of Moses, which they studied day and night every day. "To blaspheme the name of Moses was the highest crime, punishable with death, and to give up his Books was a treachery which no Essene would commit, even under the agonies of torture or death." The Dead Sea Scrolls, of relatively modern discovery, were apparently kept by ancient colonies of these super-separatists from the mainstream of Jewish life.

They had their own synagogues, were pacifists, ate no animal food (since the law said, "Thou shalt not kill"), bathed their whole bodies before each meal, and took terrible oaths of secrecy to conceal their doctrines and "the secret names of the angels, which were known to the brotherhood, and gave him who learned them power, by pronouncing them, to draw down these awful beings from heaven."

"They were rigid Predestinarians, believing that all things, in the course of nature and in the life of man, are fixed by fate. When there was no moral freedom, it was idle either to preach or teach, and so they did neither." They did, however, profess to have the gift of prophecy, and were called in, from time to time, by the Herods and others to interpret dreams and give meaning to various superstitions. "The Essenes came in contact with the people," Geikie says, "as healers, prophets, dream-interpreters, and exorcists, not as teachers or preachers." (Geikie, pp. 252-57.) They were, it would seem, not far removed from the sorcerers, astrologers, and magicians of the ancient courts of Babylon and Egypt.

Historians have been wont to ascribe to the Essenes an influence and status wholly disproportionate to that which, in fact, was theirs. Since there are some high moral and ethical principles in their writings, they have been referred to as heralds of that Christianity which was to be. In this connection there has been some intellectual consternation in some quarters to discover in the documents of the Essenes some of the very concepts Jesus gave forth in his teachings, all of which simply means that gospel truths have been revealed in dispensations past and preserved in garbled form among those who have forsaken the full truth.[5]

At least from the days of Moses, both men and women in Israel were privileged to take vows setting themselves apart to serve the Lord in some special way for an appointed period. Such persons, while subject to their vows, were called *Nazarites*. Frequently the period of penance and pondering and worship and devotion was for thirty days. In the case of Samson it was for life, and John the Baptist is considered by some to have had the same lifetime obligation. As set out in Numbers 6:1-21, those so separating themselves unto the Lord, for whatever period was involved, must abstain from wine and strong drink and the eating of grapes or anything coming from the vine tree. They must let their hair grow and avoid any Levitical uncleanness. At the end of their period of separation, they shaved their heads and offered burnt offerings, sin offerings, peace offerings, and meat and drink offerings, with all their attendant formalities. Even Paul, as a temporizing gesture to the partially converted Jewish-Christians in Jerusalem—and after the law of Moses, including the law of sacrifice and the law of the Nazarite, had been done away—participated in these vows and the offerings made incident thereto. (Acts 21:23-26.)

In the days of Jesus, before he fulfilled the law of Moses and ended the offering of sacrifices, Nazarites were present in his congregations and were exerting an influence for good among the people. Their vows were personal matters and their worship a personal attempt to draw near to the Lord, as distinguished from the ascetic brotherhood found in the false worship of the Essenes.

NOTES

1. The office of presiding bishop in the Church today is a hereditary office, designed and intended to go from father to son in the appointed lineage. The Lord, however, up to this point has not revealed the lineage, but undoubtedly will do so at some time in the future, perhaps when the millennial era is ushered in. Speaking of the presiding bishop of the Church, the Lord says: "And if they be literal descendants of Aaron they have a legal right to the bishopric, if they are the firstborn among the sons of Aaron; For the firstborn holds the right of the presidency over this priesthood, and the keys or authority of the same. No man has a legal right to this office, to hold the keys of this priesthood, except he be a literal descendant and the firstborn of Aaron." (D&C 68:16-18.)

2. All scribes were Rabbis, but not all Rabbis were scribes. Jesus and other teachers were Rabbis, but most assuredly they were not scribes. In chapter 6, "The Rabbis at the Time of Christ, and Their Ideas Respecting the Messiah," in *The Life of Christ* by Cunningham Geikie, we find this analysis of the station, influence, and ministry of those Rabbis who also were scribes: "If the most important figures in the society of Christ's day were the Pharisees, it was because they were [that is, among them were most of] the Rabbis, or teachers of the Law. As such they received superstitious honour, which was, indeed, the great motive, with many, to court the title, or join the party.

262

"The Rabbis were classed with Moses, the patriarchs, and the prophets, and claimed equal reverence. Jacob and Joseph were both said to have been Rabbis. The Targum of Jonathan substitutes Rabbis, or Scribes, for the word 'prophets,' where it occurs. Josephus speaks of the prophets of Saul's day as Rabbis. In the Jerusalem Targum all the patriarchs are learned Rabbis. . . . They were to be dearer to Israel than father or mother, because parents [as they falsely supposed] avail only in this world, but the Rabbi for ever. They were set above kings, for is it not written, 'Through me kings reign?' Their entrance into a house brought a blessing; to live or to eat with them was the highest good fortune. To dine with a Rabbi was as if to enjoy the splendour of heavenly majesty. . . .

"To learn a single verse, or even a single letter, from a Rabbi could be repaid only by the profoundest respect. . . . The table of the Rabbi was nobler than that of kings; and his crown more glorious than theirs.

". . . The Mishna declares that it is a greater crime to speak anything to their discredit than to speak against the words of the Law. The words of the Rabbis are to be held as worth more than the words of the prophets. . . .

"Heresy, which would be fatal to the blind unanimity which was their political strength, could only be excluded by rigidly denouncing the least departure from their precepts. The Law and the Prophets must, therefore, be understood only in the sense of their traditions. . . .

"Yet, in form, the Law received boundless honour. Every saying of the Rabbis had to be based on some words of it, which were, however, explained in their own way. The spirit of the times, the wild fanaticism of the people, and their own bias, tended, alike, to make them set value only on ceremonies and worthless externalisms, to the utter neglect of the spirit of the sacred writings. Still, it was owned that the Law needed no confirmation, while the words of the Rabbis did.

"So far as the Roman authority under which they lived left them free, the Jews willingly put all power in the hands of the Rabbis. They or their nominees filled every office, from the highest in the priesthood to the lowest in the community. They were the casuists, the teachers, the priests, the judges, the magistrates, and the physicians of the nation. But their authority went still further, for, by the Rabbinical laws, nearly everything in daily life needed their counsel and aid. No one could be born, circumcised, brought up, educated, betrothed, married, or buried—no one could celebrate the Sabbath or other feasts, or begin a business, or make a contract, or kill a beast for food, or even bake bread, without the advice or presence of a Rabbi. The words of Christ respecting binding and loosing, were a Rabbinical proverb: they bound and they loosed as they thought fit. What they loosed was permitted—what they bound was forbidden. They were the brain, the eyes, the ears, the nerves, the muscles of the people, who were mere children apart from them. . . .

"They were Pharisees as to their party, and Rabbis in their relations to the Law. That one who came, not indeed, to destroy the Law and the Prophets, but to free them from the perversions of Rabbinical theology, should have been met by the bitterest hatred and a cruel death, was only an illustration of the sad truth, to which every age was borne witness, that ecclesiastical bodies who have the power to persecute, identify even the abuses of their system with the defense of religion, and are capable of any crime in their blind intolerance." (Geikie, pp. 52-55.)

3. "The Sadducees uniformly fell back on the letter of the Law, the prescriptive rights of the Temple, and the glory of the priesthood; the Pharisees, on the other hand, took their stand on the authority of the Rabbinical traditions, the value of sacred acts apart from the interposition of the priest, and advocated popular interests generally.

"The contrast between the spirit of the two parties showed itself prominently in the harsh tenacity with which the Temple aristocracy held to the letter of the Mosaic Law in its penalties, as opposed to the milder spirit in which the Pharisees interpreted them, in accordance with the spirit of the times. The Pharisees, for example, explained the Mosaic demand—an eye for an eye and a tooth for a tooth—metaphorically, and allowed recompense to be made in money, but the Sadducees required exact compliance. The Sadducees required that the widow should literally spit in the face of the brother-in-law who refused her the levirate marriage rights, but it was enough for the Pharisees that she spat on the ground before him. The Pharisees permitted the carcass of a beast that had died to be used for any other purpose than food, to save loss to the owner, but the Sadducees denounced the penalties of uncleanness on so lax a practice. They sternly required that a false witness be put to death, according to the letter of the Law, even if his testimony had done the accused no injury, and many did not even shrink from carrying out the reasoning of the Rabbis, that, as two witnesses were always required to condemn the accused, both witnesses should always be executed when any perjury had been committed in the case." (Geikie, p. 540.)

4. Geikie here paraphrased Daniel 7:14, a passage which in fact refers to the Second Coming of the Messiah and his receipt back from the Ancient of Days, who is Adam, of the keys of the earthly kingdom, preparatory to the millennial reign of peace and righteousness.

5. Of those who suppose, in all sincerity, that they are following the course prescribed by Moses or any of the spiritual giants who went before, our revelation, identifying those who shall inherit a telestial kingdom, says: "These are they who are of Paul, and of Apollos, and of Cephas. These are they who say they are some of one and some of another—some of Christ and some of John, and some of Moses, and some of Elias, and some of Esaias, and some of Isaiah, and some of Enoch; But received not the gospel, neither the testimony of Jesus, neither the prophets, neither the everlasting covenant." (D&C 76:99-101.) It is not enough, Essene-like, to die for Moses and his law; it is living and obeying, not defending and dying, that leads to salvation.

Chapter 15

JEWISH SCRIPTURE IN JESUS' DAY

Search the scriptures; for in them ye think ye have eternal life: and they are they which testify of me. (John 5:39.)

All things must be fulfilled, which were written in the law of Moses, and in the prophets, and in the psalms, concerning me. Then opened he their understanding, that they might understand the scriptures.
(Luke 24:44-45.)

Scriptures Guide Men to Salvation

We have in the Holy Scriptures—those inspired and canonized utterances of the holy prophets; those heaven-sent fragments from the records of eternity; those words and phrases spoken by the power of the Holy Ghost—we have in these sacred writings the plan and the pattern, the laws and the requirements, the gospel recitations, that will guide us to eternal life in our Father's kingdom. They chart the course we must pursue to gain peace in this life and glory and honor in the life to come.

We are not saved by the scriptures as such. In the beginning the plan of salvation was "declared by holy angels sent forth from the presence of God, and by his own voice, and by the gift of the Holy Ghost." (Moses 5:58.) The laws and truths so declared were recorded, and such of them as we now have are called the Holy Scriptures. They tell how all men—not the ancients only—may hear the voice of God, entertain angelic messengers, and enjoy the outpourings of the Holy Spirit. The Holy Scriptures are given to guide men to that state of spiritual enlightenment and perfection attained by those of old who worked out their salvation.

"The holy scriptures," Paul told his beloved Timothy, "are able to make thee wise unto salvation through faith which is in Christ Jesus." The scriptures open the door; they mark the course we must pursue; they identify the strait and narrow path; they testify of Christ and his laws; they engender faith; their worth cannot be overstated. But once the path is revealed, men must walk therein to gain the desired eternal reward. Thus, "All scripture," Paul continues, "is given by inspiration of God, and is profitable for doctrine, for reproof, for correction, for instruction in righteousness: That the man of God may be perfect, throughly furnished unto all good works." (2 Tim. 3:15-17.)

The law of the Lord is perfect,
　　Converting the soul:
The testimony of the Lord is sure,
　　Making wise the simple.

The statutes of the Lord are right,
　　Rejoicing the heart:
The commandment of the Lord is pure,
　　Enlightening the eyes.

The fear of the Lord is clean,
　　Enduring for ever:

The judgments of the Lord
Are true and righteous altogether.

More to be desired are they than gold,
Yea, than much fine gold:
Sweeter also than honey and the honeycomb.

Moreover by them is thy servant warned:
And in keeping of them There is great reward.
—Psalm 19:7-11

In the full and complete sense, every word spoken by the power of the Holy Ghost is scripture. It is "the will of the Lord, . . . the mind of the Lord, . . . the word of the Lord, . . . the voice of the Lord, and the power of God unto salvation." (D&C 68:4.) It could not be otherwise, for the Holy Ghost is God, is one with the Father and the Son, and is their witness and revelator. His words are their words whether he speaks them personally or impresses the thoughts upon the minds of men so they find utterance by mortal tongues.

But the scriptures of which we now speak consist of those inspired statements of holy men which have been preserved for the guidance of all men and which find general acceptance by faithful people. This canonical reservoir of revealed writ varies in size and dimensions from one time to another and as between one people and another. One nation in one age has a small library of sacred writings, another in a more blessed day has many shelves stacked high with what the Lord has said to many prophets. As a general rule, the more sacred parts of Holy Writ, such as the sealed portion of the Book of Mormon, are withheld from those of lesser spiritual stature. And oftimes that which is available has been muddied by the carelessness or unbelief or defiant rebellion of those in whose custody the sacred records have rested at any given time, as witness the plain and precious parts of Genesis not found in modern Bibles but restored by revelation in the Pearl of Great Price.

Further, there is the practical matter of interpretation

and of equating and of comparing the written word with the continuing stream of oral utterances that, because the speaking voice has been inspired from on high, are themselves also scripture. Principles revealed in one day must be applied to new situations in another time; the ancient scriptures must live again in the lives of those into whose hands they fall; someone must tell what the word of God, given anciently, means today.

It takes an inspired man to understand and interpret an inspired utterance. No one but a prophet can envision the true and full meaning of prophetic words. Any person of normal mentality can absorb some of the intended meaning from the scriptures, but no one can plumb the depths unless enlightened by the same power that gave the revealed truths in the first instance. Hence, "no prophecy of the scripture is of any private interpretation," as Peter said. Why? Because "the prophecy came not in old time by the will of man: but holy men of God spake as they were moved by the Holy Ghost." (2 Pet. 1:20-21.) Similarly, holy men of God, as moved upon by the Holy Ghost, are the only ones who can make authoritative and complete statements as to the meaning and application of revealed truth.

And therein lies the problem. Such scriptures as were available to our Jewish brethren in the day of our Lord were completely buried under the private interpretations of the Rabbis.

Inspired men were few and far between in that day. Men did not look to living prophets to tell what dead prophets meant by their prophetic words. It was a day when the school of Hillel debated with the school of Shammai, and neither of them came anywhere near the truth. When our Lord and his associates came, speaking with authority, "and not as the scribes" (Matt. 7:29), it was more than a shock: it was the ax of revealed truth and of inspired interpretation chopping down the vines of tradition that encumbered the vineyard of scriptural learning.

Ancient Jewish Scriptures

When Jesus said, "Search the scriptures" (John 5:39); when "the voices of the prophets" (Acts 13:27) were heard, as it were, and the writings of Moses were "read in the synagogues every sabbath day" (Acts 15:21); when Paul spoke of "the holy scriptures, which are able to make thee wise unto salvation" (2 Tim. 3:15), to what books of Holy Writ did they have reference?

Adam and his posterity kept a book of remembrance in which sacred things were recorded. Seth, Enos, Cainan, Mahalaleel, Jared, Enoch, Methuselah, Lamech, and Noah, and all the holy men who lived before the flood wrote down what the Lord said to each of them. Shem and Melchizedek, Abraham and his descendants, and the mighty men of old— who saw God, heard his voice, entertained his messengers, saw within the veil, and knew the mysteries of the kingdom by revelation—all these were the proud possessors of authoritative writings long since lost among the children of men. In due course, as part of the restoration of all things— which Peter promises shall include all things "which God hath spoken by the mouth of all his holy prophets since the world began" (Acts 3:21)—we shall receive again the Book of Enoch, the Book of Joseph, the remainder of the Book of Abraham, plus unnumbered and unknown volumes. No revealed truth, no sacred scripture, no recorded revelation is ever permanently lost; what God has said to one person, he will say to another, and what was known in one age shall come forth again. The more truth a gracious God can give to his people, the better he and they like it.

But the Jews of Jesus' day, even as the sectarians in our day, were denied the blessing of having the fulness of revealed truth to read in their homes and preach in their synagogues. They did have enough to teach them of their Messiah and to direct their feet in the path leading to greater light and added revelation, but the inspiration rained from

269

heaven no longer filled the reservoirs of revelation as had been the case among their fathers. They had the Old Testament, probably more of it than is found in our modern versions, but certainly only a fraction of what should have been compiled upon its pages.

We have every reason to believe that the full and pure accounts that tell of the revelation of the gospel to Adam and Noah, of their baptism and the priesthood they held, and of the Lord's extended dealings with them, as such accounts have been revealed anew through Joseph Smith, were not extant among the Jews in Jesus' day. At least there is no intimation in the teachings of Jesus or in the New Testament writings that the knowledge in these original accounts was then available to the people. It does seem clear, however, that the book of Genesis, as they had it, contained more than does the same record in the King James Version of the Bible. For instance, Jesus, in teaching that he, as Jehovah, was "before Abraham," said: "Your father Abraham rejoiced to see my day: and he saw it, and was glad" (John 8:56-58), no record of which ancient vision is found in Genesis. That Abraham did have such a vision was revealed to Joseph Smith, and he inserted the account in the Inspired Version.[1] It was the unvarying practice of Jesus, when quoting scripture, to take his words from those accounts with which his hearers were or should have been familiar. We must suppose he followed this course in this instance.

An even more conclusive reason to believe that the Jewish Genesis excelled the Christian Genesis is seen in the writings of Paul. He quoted and paraphrased a number of scriptures and referred to some historical facts, which are not in the Bible of Christendom, but which original sources have been restored by the great prophet of latter days. The clearest of these is his reference in Hebrews to ancient worthies "who through faith subdued kingdoms, wrought righteousness, obtained promises, stopped the mouths of lions, Quenched the violence of fire, escaped the edge of the sword, out of weakness were made strong, waxed valiant in fight, [and] turned to flight the armies of the aliens." (Heb. 11:33-34.) This language is, of course, a paraphrase, a quotation, and a summary of what Genesis once contained relative to Melchizedek, which makes it perfectly clear that the Melchizedek material was still in Genesis when Paul wrote to his Hebrew brethren.[2] Paul's statements about "God" preaching "before the gospel unto Abraham" (Gal. 3:8) and his explanations as to how and in what manner Moses was the mediator of the old covenant also show a more extended biblical background than is available to modern writers.[3] There seems, thus, to be little doubt that although the Jews did not have a full and perfect book of Genesis, they did have a better and more accurate one than modern Christendom possesses.

As far as we know, the other prophetic writings and Psalms, had among the Jews in the meridian of time, were substantially the same as those we now have, although, yet again, what is now extant is far less than what once was. The Hebrews on the American continent found on the brass plates of Laban sayings and writings of Joseph who was sold into Egypt, of Moses and Isaiah, of Zenos, Zenock, and Neum, and possibly of Abraham, and perhaps of many unnamed prophets, none of which seem to have been preserved through the Babylonian exile and down to our Lord's day.[4] At least there are no allusions or intimations in the New Testament accounts or the writings of contemporary historians that the Jews then had these precious gems of celestial truth, which would have been theirs had they been in complete harmony with the divine will.

The Old Testament of Jesus' Day

We have come to call the Jewish scriptures the Old Testament, meaning, as men have falsely supposed, that it is a record of Deity's dealings with a people subject to an old testament, an old covenant, a lesser law, which antedated and was less than that Christianity revealed by the Son of

God. The New Testament is supposed to contain the accounts relative to the new covenant, which superseded, fulfilled, and to some degree at least abolished what went before. In fact, both testaments or covenants deal with the eternal principles and truths that make up the everlasting gospel, the gospel of salvation, which is both an old, a present, a new, and a future covenant; it is the new and everlasting covenant. More than a third of the time period covered by the Old Testament was one in which the lesser law was "added" to the higher principles of revealed religion. Many of the ancients, though subject to the law of Moses, continued to live the higher law that had, in fact, antedated everything revealed to Moses and Aaron and their successors. The Old Testament scriptural accounts deal with both the higher gospel truths and the formalities and rigid requirements of the lesser law of Moses.

In the day of Jesus, though there were Hebrew or Aramaic copies of the scripture in usage, the Old Testament of the people, the one used generally, the one quoted by Jesus and Paul and the New Testament authors, was the Septuagint. This Greek version of Holy Writ—commonly referred to as the LXX, because according to tradition it had been translated from Hebrew into Greek by about seventy scholars—was by no means a perfect reflection of the mind and will of Him from whom scripture comes. It contained all of our present Old Testament, plus many apocryphal books, and much license had been taken by the translators. It was completed more than two hundred years before the Christian era, and many of its passages contained gross mistakes, while others presented clarifications of the Hebrew originals. Edersheim says that the "free handling of the text" by Hellenistic translators resulted in "a strenuous effort . . . to banish all anthropomorphisms, as inconsistent with their ideas of Deity." (Edersheim 1:28.)

It was of these ancient scriptures, in their original form and before they fell into evil hands, that an angel said to Nephi: "The book that thou beholdest is a record of the

Jews, which contains the covenants of the Lord, which he hath made unto the house of Israel." Then the angel, speaking more particularly of the New Testament, continued: "Thou hast beheld that the book proceeded forth from the mouth of a Jew; and when it proceeded forth from the mouth of a Jew it contained the plainness of the gospel of the Lord, of whom the twelve apostles bear record." After these scriptures went forth "in purity," they came into the hands of "a great and abominable church, which is most abominable above all other churches." Of this ill-spawned and devil-built perverter of true religion, the angel said: "They have taken away from the gospel of the Lamb many parts which are plain and most precious; and also many covenants of the Lord have they taken away." (1 Ne. 13:23-26.) That is to say, both the Old and the New Testaments found among men in our day have been subject to the deletions, perversions, and alterations of persons whose interests were not compatible with those of the prophets and apostles whose words they dared to twist.

But in addition to LXX—which includes many apocryphal writings—and to the scriptural versions in their own language, the Jews had studied the pseudepigraphic books. As to the Apocrypha, as it is now constituted—and there have been many different selections of apocryphal books over the years—we have these revealed words: "There are many things contained therein that are true, and it is mostly translated correctly." And also: "There are many things contained therein that are not true, which are interpolations by the hands of men." Those who are "enlightened by the Spirit shall obtain benefit" from studying it. (D&C 91:1-6.) Those not so gifted will do better devoting their attention to the scriptures that have greater worth. Apocryphal writings are quoted in the Jewish Talmud.

Other Jewish writings, purporting to be scripture but which never attained either canonical or apocryphal authenticity, because their authors are assumed to be unknown, are called, collectively, the pseudepigrapha. These pseudepigraphic writings contain a remarkable intermixture of truth and error. They do talk about many things found in latter-day revelation that are not otherwise recorded in either the Bible or Apocrypha. Two of these pseudepigraphic books purport to be the writings of Enoch, of whom the world knows almost nothing. Because Jude in his New Testament book quotes from the writings of Enoch the prophecy that "the Lord cometh with ten thousands of his saints, To execute judgment upon" the ungodly (Jude 1:14-15),[5] let us here refer to some of the doctrines found in this so-called Book of Enoch, writings that were known and studied by the Jews in the day Jesus ministered among them.

In the pseudepigraphic writings of Enoch we find visions, prophecies, exhortations, and doctrinal expositions relative to the Second Coming and the Millennium; the names and functions of the seven angels (including Raphael, Michael, and Gabriel); the separation of the spirits of righteous and wicked men as they await the day of judgment; the coming judgment of the wicked; the attainment of salvation by the righteous and elect; the bringing of the Son of Man before "the head of days" (meaning, obviously, the Ancient of Days); the resurrection of the dead and the separation by the Judge of the righteous and the wicked; the translation of Enoch; preexistence and the creation of the souls of all men before the foundation of the world; the war in heaven and the casting out of Satan; the dividing of the eight-thousand-year history of the earth into the first six thousand years, to be followed by one thousand years of rest, after which would come another one thousand years, and then the end; a list of beatitudes, not far removed in wisdom from those of Jesus himself; personal responsibility for sin; the salvation of animals; the state of eternal life for those who keep the commandments; and much, much more.[6]

It will be observed that the matters here recited, though taught in part and by inference in the canonical scriptures of that and our day, are in fact known only in plainness and purity by latter-day revelation. It is far more than coincidence that doctrines attributed to Enoch in the pseudepigraphic writings are the very ones the Lord saw fit to restore in plainness in our dispensation. Unfortunately, the whole of these ancient writings cannot be accepted as the mind and will and voice of Him from whom revelation comes. As with the study of the apocryphal books, so it is with the study of the pseudepigraphic writings: the seeker after revealed wisdom must be guided by the power of the Holy Spirit.

The Old Testament vs. the Talmud

Our Jewish brethren in Jesus' day were blessed with an ample library of inspired writing. They had the Old Testament in a better and more complete form than is now had in Christendom. As we have set forth, after that volume of sacred writing left their hands—during the Dark Ages, when darkness covered the earth and gross darkness the minds of the people—many of the covenants of the Lord were taken from it by evil men who worked for another Master.

Our Jewish brethren in that day had also the numerous apocryphal and pseudepigraphic books, which they believed and accepted on more or less the same basis as those Old Testament writings to which we now attach canonical authenticity. It must be remembered that much found in these latter works was the interpolation of men, was not true scripture, and could and did lead men astray.

But what our Jewish brethren did not have was communion with the heavens; they did not have a prophet to interpret the prophecies; they no longer received revelations; for them the canon of scripture was full. And be it known that whenever a people believe the canon of scripture is complete; whenever they try to feed themselves spiritually upon the prophetic word of the past alone; whenever they are without prophets and apostles to give them the living word; whenever they cease to receive new revelations—then they are no longer capable of interpreting and understanding past revelations. The prophecies of the past can only be understood by living prophets who are endowed with power from on high and whose minds are enlightened by the same Holy Spirit who authored the ancient word. People without revelation take the only course open to them: they turn to interpreters, to scribes, to ministers, to theologians, who tell them what the ancient word meant, making their determination on the basis of intellectuality rather than spirituality.

When the prophets and apostles of the Christian era no longer ministered among men, religionists turned to uninspired men for guidance; they wrote creeds and devised doctrines; they created new ordinances and changed old ones; and they came up with a new religion called by the old name, which had little resemblance to the primitive pattern. And when, after their return from Babylonian exile, the Jews ran out of prophets and no longer had living oracles to reveal and interpret the mind of Jehovah, they turned to scribes and teachers, to Rabbis and politically appointed high priests to tell them what the Lord meant when he said thus and so to Moses and the prophets.

And thus came the Midrash, the Mishnah, the Gemara, and the Talmud, which had the effect of nullifying true religion and sending a whole nation to spiritual destruction and to temporal banishment in a new Babylon, composed of all the nations of the earth, from which bondage they will not be freed until they hear again the voice of their Messiah, as he calls scattered Israel to return to his fold.

After the Jews came back to Jerusalem and their ancient land holdings in Palestine, through the good offices of Cyrus the Persian; after they no longer walked in that heavenly light which rests only upon those who listen to a prophet's voice and hear the word of God; and feeling the need to apply their ancient law to new conditions—they developed gradually, over the centuries, a whole new (and apostate!) system of religious government. Scribes, who once had been keepers of the records and copiers of the scrolls, became interpreters of the law and teachers of the people. And as uninspired men almost never agree on the meaning of scriptural passages, there soon grew up schools and sects and cults, one Rabbi or teacher vying with another, and one voice saying, as it were, Lo here is Christ, and another, Lo there. In the days of Herod the Great, the two most influential rabbinical schools were those of Hillel and Shammai, who agreed or disagreed on points both great and small as suited their fancies, their prejudices, and their nationalistic leanings. To illustrate how devoid they were of the Spirit of the Lord, we need only note that in one deliberative assembly, in order to gain approval of eighteen decrees designed to prevent all intercourse with the Gentiles, the Shammaites first murdered a number of the Hillelites.

For their own purposes of study and usage, the Jews divided the Old Testament into three parts: (1) *the law,* which consists of the Pentateuch, or five books of Moses— Genesis, Exodus, Leviticus, Numbers, and Deuteronomy; (2) *the prophets,* including the former prophets (Joshua, Judges, Samuel, and Kings), and the latter prophets (Isaiah, Jeremiah, Ezekiel, and the twelve so-called minor prophets); and (3) *the writings,* which includes Psalms, Proverbs, Job, and the rest of the book. In the very nature of things, the law was deemed the most important part of the scriptures; therein were the laws and formalities governing their whole system of worship.

Having need to interpret and apply the law to changing conditions, the scribes, no longer guided by revelation, turned to these words in Exodus: "And the Lord said unto Moses, Write thou these words: for after the tenor of these words I have made a covenant with thee and with Israel." (Ex. 34:27.) From them and some related passages, they posited the proposition that there was both a written law, which was found in the Books of Moses, and an oral law, which had been handed down from mouth to mouth. These originally were assumed to be of equal import, but since changes can be supported more easily by tradition that comes down by word of mouth than by the fixed language of divine decrees written by the finger of Jehovah on tablets of stone, the oral law gradually began to take precedence. In other words, tradition triumphed over the scriptures, leading Jesus to make the caustic comment: "Ye made the commandment of God of none effect by your tradition." (Matt. 15:6.)

The oral law was set forth in preaching and by way of oral commentaries that told what the written law was supposed to mean. These spoken interpretations—themselves the traditions of the fathers—were called the Midrash. When they in turn were written down, they became the Mishnah, or Second Law, which took precedence over the scriptures because they explained and applied them. The Midrash was the study and investigation that created the traditions and enabled the Jews to depart from their Mosaic moorings. The Mishnah was the formal, authoritative compilation of these traditions.

By adding the New Testament to their canon of scripture, the Christians changed and altered their whole course of conduct and way of life after our Lord's mortal ministry. By adding the Mishnah to their Old Testament, the Jews—as they prepared the dry ground out of which the Living Root would grow—also changed their whole course of conduct and way of life, becoming thereby the priest-ridden people who would reject and slay their Savior.

What does the Mishnah contain? In size it is almost three times as large as the New Testament; in literary style and craftsmanship it is as far removed from the New Testament as are the mediocre scribblings of untutored students from Shakespeare; and as to subject matter, it deals with rituals and traditions and with all of those priestly procedures which turned a once joyous religion into a millstone of despair. It is, for instance, the source of the Sabbath laws and restrictions set forth in chapter 11 herein.

The Torah (the Law) embraced both the written law and the oral law, the latter itself being also written in the Mishnah, thus making the Mishnah the repository of the culture, religion, and traditions of the people. It is a deposit of four centuries of religious and cultural development in Palestine. In its present form it came into being during the two hundred years before and the two hundred years following our Lord's mortal life, and without question it held a tighter grip on the minds of men when Jesus was here than it has at any other time.

As now published, the Mishnah is divided into six main sections, which are further divided into sixty-three tractates or subsections, which in turn are divided into verses. The subjects covered embrace the whole range of pentateuchal legislation, and the approach is to present the opinions of various sages and Rabbis, many of which are contradictory, and all of which are devoid of inspiration.

But the Mishnah contains only a portion of the traditions of the elders. The balance is contained in the two Talmuds or Gemaras—the Jerusalem Talmud and the Babylon Talmud. These Talmuds are commentaries on the Mishnah; phrase by phrase and thought by thought, they analyze and interpret the Mishnic recordings. Authoritatively collected and edited, they contain discussions, illustrations, explanations, and additions to the Mishnah. "If we imagine," Edersheim says, "something combining law reports, a Rabbinical 'Hansard,' and notes of a theological debating club— all thoroughly Oriental, full of digressions, anecdotes, quaint sayings, fancies, legends, and too often of what, from its profanity, superstition, and even obscenity, could scarcely be quoted, we may form some general idea of what the Talmud is." (Edersheim 1:103.)

This, then, was the state of religious understanding and scholarship among our Jewish brethren in Jesus' day. They had the scriptures, which was all well and good, but for want of inspiration they could not understand them and did not apply them to their lives. They had the apocryphal and pseudepigraphic writings, which in large measure led them astray. They had lost the theology of the past and were reveling instead in the traditions of the elders. Edersheim summarizes their religious and cultural state in these words:

"In truth, Rabbinism, as such, had no system of theology: only what ideas, conjectures, or fancies the Haggadah [that which was said by the elders] yielded concerning God, Angels, demons, man, his future destiny and present position, and Israel, with its past history and coming glory. Accordingly, by the side of what is noble and pure, what a terrible mass of utter incongruities, of conflicting statements and too often debasing superstitions, the outcome of ignorance and narrow nationalism; of legendary colouring of Biblical narratives and scenes, profane, coarse, and degrading to them; the Almighty Himself and His Angels taking part in the conversations of Rabbis, and the discussions of Academies; nay, forming a kind of heavenly Sanhedrin, which occasionally requires the aid of an earthly Rabbi. The miraculous merges into the ridiculous, and even the revolting. Miraculous cures, miraculous supplies, miraculous help, all for the glory of great Rabbis, who by a look or word can kill, and restore to life. At their bidding the eyes of a rival fall out, and are again inserted. Nay, such was the veneration due to Rabbis, that R. Joshua used to kiss the stone on which R. Eliezer had sat and lectured, saying: 'This stone is like Mount Sinai, and he who sat on it like the Ark.' Modern ingenuity has, indeed, striven to suggest deeper symbolical meanings for such stories. It should [however] own the terrible contrast existing side by side: Hebrewism and Judaism, the Old Testament and traditionalism; and it should recognise its deeper cause in the absence of that element of spiritual and inner life which Christ has brought. Thus as between the two—the old and the new—it may be fearlessly asserted that, as regards their substance and spirit, there is not a difference, but a total divergence, of fundamental principle between Rabbinism and the New Testament, so that comparison between them is not possible. Here there is absolute contrariety." (Edersheim 1:106-7.)

Truly, the time was upon them when it would take God's own Son—if they would heed his voice—to save them from the religious and cultural degeneracy into which their whole nation had sunk! What a fearful thing it is to depart from the living God, from the scriptures that flow from the pens of his prophets, and from the living oracles whom the Lord seeks to send to all who will heed their words, and to turn instead to the traditions of men!

NOTES

1. After Abraham, who then had no seed and whose wife Sarah was past the childbearing age, was told that his seed should be as the stars of heaven in number and should possess the land of Canaan, the restored scriptural account says: "Abram [for his name had not yet been changed] said, Lord God, how wilt thou give me this land for an everlasting inheritance? And the Lord said, Though thou wast dead, yet am I not able to give it thee? And if thou shalt die, yet thou shalt possess it, for the day cometh, that the Son of Man shall live, but how can he live if he be not dead? he must first be quickened. And it came to pass, that Abram looked forth and saw the days of the Son of Man, and was glad, and his soul found rest, and he believed in the Lord; and the Lord counted it unto him for righteousness." (JST, Gen. 15:1-12.)

2. We have no greater passage on the power and authority of the holy priesthood, nor one that shows better the great spiritual insight of the Prophet Joseph Smith, than the one here involved. It not only contains words and phrases reciting that "Melchizedek was a man of faith, who wrought righteousness; and when a child he feared God, and stopped the mouths of lions, and quenched the violence of fire," and says that in the priesthood is the power "to put at defiance the armies of nations" and tells how Melchizedek's people "wrought righteousness, and obtained heaven," but also tells of Enoch and his city, of the laws governing the translation of the righteous, and of the return of Zion in "the latter days, or the end of the world." (JST, Gen. 14:25-40.)

3. "Moses," Paul says, as he tells things that are not recorded in our present Old Testament, "was ordained by the hand of angels to be a mediator of this first covenant, (the law.) Now this mediator was not a mediator of the new covenant; but there is one mediator of the new covenant, who is Christ." (JST, Gal. 3:19-20.)

4. The beginning point for those desiring to research this matter is found in the Book of Mormon references to the named individuals.

5. Jude also, in the brief twenty-five verses of his one-chapter New Testament book, speaks of Michael contending for the body of Moses (verse 9), which is an allusion to the pseudepigraphic book The Assumption of Moses. This book tells of Moses' translation and his ascent as a fiery angel into heaven. (R. H. Charles, *The Apocrypha and Pseudepigrapha of the Old Testament in English* 2:407-24.) From the Book of Mormon and other sources we are led to believe that Moses was translated so he could return, in his body, before the day of resurrection, along with translated Elijah, to give the keys of the priesthood to our Lord on the mount of transfiguration. See *Mormon Doctrine*, 2nd ed., pp. 515-16.

6. Charles, *op cit.*, 2:163-281, 425-69.

Chapter 16

THE SOIL IN WHICH THE ROOT WAS PLANTED

He shall grow up before him as a tender plant, and as a root out of a dry ground. (Isa. 53:2.)

Omnipotence Prepares the Way

A God is coming to earth to dwell as a mortal among men. His mission: to do that which he alone can do; to work out the infinite and eternal atonement and bring to pass the immortality and eternal life of the offspring of the Father on worlds without number; to do that which never again, in an eternity of time, shall ever occur among the mortals who dwell on this or any of the numberless earths of their creating.

A God is coming to earth, and all things incident to this birth and life and ministry and death and resurrection and ascension to eternal glory are foreknown and foreprepared. He is to be sired by an Immortal Father, to be conceived in a mortal womb, to be born in Bethlehem, to be cradled in a manger, to be the natural heir of David, upon whose throne he shall reign. A new star is to arise in the firmament to signal his birth, and heavenly choirs, composed of the harmonious voices of angels, are to herald his coming. His mother is to be a virgin, a holy and pure vessel of the house and lineage of Solomon and David and Jesse and Boaz. She is to live in Nazareth of Galilee, to travel to Jerusalem's environs for the birth, to go into Egypt with the young child, to return to her home village, and to have other sons and daughters from her carpenter husband.

A God is coming to earth. He is to be visited by the wise men from the East and to be preserved from Herod's sword, though all those two years of age and under in all the coasts of Bethlehem are to have their innocent blood poured out upon the arid soil of Caanan. He is to grow up in subjection to his earthly parents; to know, when twelve years of age, of his divine Sonship; to minister for three and a half years among his Jewish kinsmen; and then to die upon the cross for the sins of the world.

A God is coming to earth. He is to be baptized in Jordan at Bethabara by John, and the Holy Ghost is to descend upon him, as his Father acclaims that he is God's Son. He is to preach the gospel, heal the sick, raise the dead, and call apostles and seventies to carry his message to the world and to testify of his divinity. He is to be rejected, reviled, spit upon, scourged, and crucified. He is to stand dumb before his accusers, but to bear testimony of his own divine Sonship before the faithful. He is to give up his life voluntarily, to lie three days in a borrowed tomb, to preach to the spirits in prison, to come forth in glorious immortality, to perfect his work, and to ascend up on high.

A God is coming to earth and we can scarce record a thousandth or a ten thousandth of the things he was destined to do, the words he was destined to speak, the people he was destined to heal—all of which things were known in advance and were foretold by one prophet or another on one continent or on another. Zechariah said he would ride upon the colt of an ass into Jerusalem while being acclaimed by the multitudes; that he would be betrayed for thirty pieces of silver, which would be used to purchase a potter's field; that his hands and feet and side would be wounded; and that the Jews would look upon him whom they had pierced, while Isaiah said he would pour out his soul unto death and make his grave with the rich, and so on and so on, through literally hundreds and thousands of detailed prophecies that these and hosts of prophets foreknew and foretold—all of which must be fulfilled at the appointed time. *The Promised Messiah: The First Coming of Christ* is a more than six-hundred-page analysis of the Messianic prophecies and their fulfillment.

But what more particularly concerns us here is that a God is coming to earth to fulfill all that was promised by all of the prophets during four thousand years of prophetic utterances. All must be in readiness for his Advent. Nothing must be left to chance. There must be no failure, not so much as one jot or one tittle of the inspired accounts. No "T" must be left uncrossed; no "I" must be left undotted; every comma and period must be where it is designed to be. The divine life must conform to the divine and foreordained pattern.

A God is coming to earth and everything connected with his birth and life and ministry and resurrection and ascension to eternal glory—everything!—must be perfect. It must conform to what the prophets have foreseen, foreknown, and foretold.

Mortal Mary must be living in her Galilean home. Joseph must have his carpenter shop in Nazareth. Augustus Caesar must command the Jews to go to their homelands to be taxed. Mary and Joseph must go to Bethlehem; there must be no room in the inns; the angelic choirs must be trained and be in readiness; the whole sidereal heavens must be awaiting the rise of a blazing new star. And we speak not alone of the spiritual preparations, but of the bringing to pass of *all* the temporal circumstances that were needed. The Jewish culture must be at a low ebb, and the Jewish religion but a space away from the gates of hell. Palestine must wear a Roman yoke and the sword of Caesar must be in the hands of Herod and Pilate.

Can we suppose anything was left to chance? Were not

the shepherds on the Judean hills chosen and prepared in advance so that their spiritually attuned ears could hear the angelic choirs? Did not the Spirit guide the wise men to travel from their eastern home with the gold and myrrh and frankincense? And what of Herod—was he not destined to reign as king of the Jews? Did not the Lord know in advance that this Idumean despot would have already shed so much blood, including that of wives and children, that the slaughter of all the babies near Bethlehem would scarce add more blood to his red hands or blacken any further the evil heart that kept his then degenerating body a step from its own grave?

Can we do aught but conclude that the people, the land, the government, the religious hierarchy, the evil rulers, the adulterous sign seekers, the priests and Pharisees and Rabbis, the Sadducees and Herodians—yes, and the sprinkling of truly spiritual people among that degenerate generation of Jews—can we do aught but conclude that all this was prepared in advance?

Mary and Martha and Lazarus were sent to earth at that time to be his friends, in whose house he could escape the barbs and revilings of his enemies. Peter and James and John were prepared from before the foundations of the world to be his chief apostles. Judas was where the betrayer must be. Caiaphas and Pilate and Herod and the Roman soldiers were all in their appointed places. The Caesars in Rome, the Rabbis in Jerusalem, the scribes in their schools, the priests before the altar, the Hellenists with their intellectual approaches, the common people, some of whom heard him gladly—all were in their appointed places. John, now conceived in Elisabeth's womb, would soon stand on the banks of Jordan crying repentance and baptizing the contrite.

Truly Omnipotent Wisdom had left nothing to chance. A God was coming into the world, and the world must be ready for his Advent.

From Cyrus to Herod

Brief mention must be made of the centuries of Jewish life in which the culture and religion of Jesus' day were molded and formed. From Abraham to the going down into Egypt, the Hebrew people had the light of the gospel. How dim that light became under the Pharaohs who knew not Joseph is seen by the spiritually sick state of the people who four hundred years later followed Moses out of Egypt, through the Red Sea, and who were then led by Joshua into the land of the Canaanites, Hittites, Amorites, Perizzites, Hivites, and Jebusites. Under the judges and kings, periods of rebellion and of righteousness followed each other as a pendulum swings from one extreme to the other. With the destruction of Jerusalem by Nebuchadnezzar, shortly after Lehi left that City of David, and with the taking of the Jews into Babylon, the Hebrew way of life that had prevailed for more than a thousand years came to an abrupt and final end.

The first group of exiles, some fifty thousand in number, returned in 536 B.C. under Zerubbabel, who built again the House of the Lord. This was a day when there were still prophets in Israel; Daniel was yet alive; Haggai and Zechariah were there to encourage completion of the temple. Nehemiah, Ezra, and Malachi would yet stand in the prophetic office. But with it all, the ex-exiles were no longer what they had once been as a people; they had brought back from Babylon much that was foreign and idolatrous. Worldly customs and dogmas would never again be thrown off in their entirety by the succeeding generations of the chosen people, and, with Malachi, prophetic guidance—at least of the kind and quality known among their fathers—would cease.

After Nehemiah's day, the Jewish nation became a province of Syria, although the people maintained a certain allegiance to Persia until that empire was overthrown by Alexander the Great in 332 B.C. The Syrian governors adopted the practice of ruling the nation by high priests whom they appointed. This placed both civil and ecclesiastical rule in the hands of priests who were chosen, not by the Lord, not because they were the sons of Aaron, but by foreign and worldly overlords whose interests were not spiritual but temporal. That the Levites as a priestly class continued to serve by right of lineage and to administer in sacrificial and other matters is clear, but the overlordship and civil rule of the nation was now vested in unclean hands; and it never again would escape from the clutches of those who served a different master than had the high priests of old. This means that the office of high priest was bought and sold; that one man murdered another to gain the coveted seat; and that it was gained and dispensed like any overlordship among the Gentiles, without any divine guidance or approval.

When Persia fell at the hands of Alexander, the Macedonians imposed their rule upon the Jews. After the death of Alexander, Palestine became subject to Egypt, then to Syria, and again to Egypt. These were days of sorrow and war and intrigue. Ungodly murderers ministered in priestly offices. They are important to our present purposes simply to show that for centuries the world and all that is wicked and evil had been imposed upon the Jewish people, and that those of Jesus' day were walking in the paths charted for them by generations of their fathers.

In the beginning of the second century B.C., the Syrian Antiochus IV (Epiphanes) became master of Palestine. If ever there were dark days for the Jews, this was the time. Jerusalem was twice overrun, and thousands were slaughtered and sold into slavery each time. The religion of the Jews was forbidden, a great swine was offered in sacrifice on the altar in the temple, the daily sacrifice was discontinued, the temple was dedicated to Jupiter Olympus, and pagan images and offerings defiled its courts. Antiochus forbade the reading of the law, and tortured and slew those who persisted in their form of worship, and by 168 B.C. Jerusalem was left nearly desolate.

At this dark hour, in the providences of the Lord, the

house of Mattathias, called the Maccabees, began to rally their Jewish compatriots against the Syrian armies. One of the sons, Judas Maccabeus, routed the Syrians in one engagement after another, became a national hero, restored the daily sacrifice and the service of the temple, and became governor of Judea, thus starting a dynasty, the Asmonean, which ruled for 126 years.

The Feast of Dedication—attended by Jesus when he announced himself as the Good Shepherd, and said: "I and my Father are one. . . . I am the Son of God" (John 10)—was instituted in the days of Judas Maccabeus as the temple was rededicated after its vile desecration by Antiochus Epiphanes. And it was into the mouth of the Maccabean hero— "truly God's Hammer," Edersheim says of him—that Longfellow put these words:

> Antiochus,
> At every step thou takest there is left
> A bloody footprint in the street, by which
> The avenging wrath of God will track thee out!
> It is enough. Go to the sutler's tents:
> Those of you who are men, put on such armor
> As ye may find; those of you who are women,
> Buckle that armor on; and for the watchword
> Whisper, or cry aloud, "The Help of God."

This Asmonean rule continued until Jerusalem was taken by Pompey and the Jews were made tributary to Rome. Then it was that Antipater of Idumea was appointed by Julius Caesar to be procurator of Judea, thus starting the new dynasty that was to lay its heavy hand upon Jesus and those who followed the new revelation that he brought from his Father. Herod the Great, the son of Antipater, through the influence of Mark Antony and his own hefty sword, which was wielded with zeal in many battles, acquired the Jewish throne upon which he sat, bathed in blood, until John was born to fulfill the old dispensation and Jesus came to give life to the new one. These two prophets were born shortly before Herod's death, and one of the last acts of madness of this then-demented ruler was the slaughter of the innocents in Bethlehem in a vain attempt to destroy the true King.

The World That Awaited Our Lord

God sent his Son to overcome the world—the world of carnality and evil; the world of lust and lewdness and license; the world of hate and sin, of war and murder, of wickedness and ungodliness. The Son of Righteousness came to bring righteousness and peace. And when he came, the world had sunk into a lower abyss than at any time since all flesh, being corrupt and evil, save eight souls only, had been drowned in the waters of Noah.

There had been pockets of wickedness and kingdoms of evil-doers in many places after Noah's day. Upon the cities of the plains—Sodom, Gomorrah, Admah, and Zeboim—in order that their wicked practices should cease, the Lord rained fire and brimstone and salt and burning, so that all the people were slain and their lands left utterly desolate. The Amorites and their ilk—whose ways were ways of wickedness, of astrology, witchcraft, necromancy, and sexual debauchery—were destroyed to make way for the chosen seed. Egypt, Assyria, Babylon, Persia, Greece, and all the kingdoms of the world had ruled by blood and the sword, by torture and death. But always there had been a leaven of righteousness, a kingdom devoted to goodness, a few people who loved the Lord and sought his face. Abraham and his seed had been a leavening and preserving influence among the nations. As few as ten righteous souls in Sodom would have saved the city from the brimstone of death.

But now, in the time set apart for our Lord's coming, corruptions and evils were everywhere. A few righteous souls—a Zacharias here, an Elisabeth there—stayed, as it were, the plagues of destruction, but the wickedness of the world was everywhere and the stench of sin covered the earth. Even the

289

covenant people, in the main, had gone astray. No longer were they a leaven to the worldly lump; subject to their priestcrafts, they would soon be in a state where they would crucify a God. Naught but a new day of righteousness and light, ushered in by one greater than the prophets, could bring hope again to men.

Such moral and ethical standards as are found among heathen people can only come from two sources: either they are remnants of gospel truths that have been handed down from those who possessed the light of heaven, or they come by the promptings of that Spirit, the light of Christ, which enlighteneth every man born into the world. Such intuitive guidance is called conscience. In the meridian of time the heathen nations were far removed timewise from ancestors who had the true standards of decency and morality, and the consciences of the people generally were so seared with the hot iron of wickedness that there were few, if any, moral standards among them.

As a summary of "the degraded morality taught by heathen sages, and legalized by the most enlightened heathen states" of ancient times, we quote these words of Edward Usher: "Socrates taught that Greeks should regard all mankind, except their own countrymen, as natural enemies; Aristotle and Cicero taught that the forgiveness of injuries is cowardly and mean; Zeno and Cato taught that there is no distinction of degree, aggravation, or heinousness in crimes; Plato taught that excessive drinking was allowable during the festival of Bacchus; Aristotle taught that deformed or infirm children ought to be destroyed; Cicero taught that fornication is in no instance wrong; Plato taught that a community of women would conduce to good, and that soldiers ought not to be restrained from even the grossest indulgence; Menander taught that a lie was better than a hurtful truth; and Zeno and Cato recommended suicide by their example, while other philosophers inculcated it in precept. And Solon enacted that sensuality was irreproachable, except when practised by a slave; several states of Greece legalized unnatural lust, and encouraged it by public statutes; philosophers and legislators sanctioned the grossest indecency, drunkenness, and lewdness during the festivals of Bacchus, Cybele, and Ceres; and Rome was distinguished by licentious divorces, and procuring of abortions, the exposing of infants, the nuisance of public stews, the sports of gladiators, the maltreatment of slaves, etc., all of which were sanctioned or connived at by both sages and legislators. Such was the state of morals among the ancient heathen." (John Fleetwood, *The Life of Our Saviour Jesus Christ*, 1862, p. 20.)

Writing of this same period, and viewing the same irreligious—even depraved—beliefs and practices, Geikie says: "The religions of antiquity had lost their vitality, and become effete forms, without influence on the heart. Philosophy was the consolation of a few—the amusement or fashion of others; but of no weight as a moral force among men at large. On its best side, that of Stoicism, it had much that was lofty, but its highest teaching was resignation to fate, and it offered only the hurtful consolation of pride in virtue, without an idea of humiliation for vice. On its worst side—that of Epicureanism—it exalted self-indulgence as the highest end. Faith in the great truths of natural religion was well-nigh extinct. Sixty-three years before the birth of Christ, Julius Caesar, at that time the Chief Pontiff of Rome, and, as such, the highest functionary of the state religion, and the official authority in religious questions, openly proclaimed, in his speech in the Senate, in reference to Catiline and his fellow-conspirators—that there was no such thing as a future life; no immortality of the soul. He opposed the execution of the accused on the ground that their crimes deserved the severest punishments, and that, therefore, they should be kept alive to endure them, since death was in reality an escape from suffering, not an evil. 'Death,' said he, 'is a rest from troubles to those in grief and misery, not a punishment; it ends all the evils of life; for there is neither care nor joy beyond it.'

"Neither was there any one to condemn such a sentiment even from such lips. Cato, the ideal Roman, a man whose aim it was to 'fulfil all righteousness,' in the sense in which he understood it, passed it over with a few words of light banter; and Cicero, who was also present, did not care to give either assent or dissent, but left the question open, as one which might be decided either way, at pleasure.

"Morality was entirely divorced from religion, as may be readily judged by the fact, that the most licentious rites had their temples, and male and female ministrants. In Juvenal's words, 'the Syrian Orontes had flowed into the Tiber,' and it brought with it the appalling immorality of the East. Doubtless, here and there, throughout the empire, the light of holy tradition still burned on the altars of many a household; but it availed nothing against the thick moral night that had settled over the earth at large. The advent of Christ was the breaking of the 'dayspring from on high' through a gloom that had been gathering for ages; a great light dawning on a world which lay in darkness, and in the shadow of death." (Geikie, p. 20.)

The Roman Yoke on Jewish Religion

The Jewish religion, with its worship of one God; the faith of their fathers, as handed down to them from Moses and the prophets; the whole way of life of the chosen people—all these, in a dark day in 63 B.C., were placed forever under the yoke of Rome. No law in Israel was more strictly enforced than the one that closed the Holy of Holies to all but one man, the high priest, who could pass through the veil into that hallowed spot on one day only each year.

Then came Pompey and the conquering legions of Rome. He and his staff, defying the strictest decree of Jehovah, entered the Holy of Holies. These Godless Gentiles, who lived and died by the sword, desecrated the House of the Lord, profaned its most holy sanctuary, and let it be known thereby that from that hour Jewish worship was subject to Roman rule. And that rule, written in blood and enforced by one emperor and king after another, continued until Titus took the temple apart stone by stone and the whole Jewish nation was scattered in all the nations of the earth. Indeed, in the just over one hundred years from the accession of Herod the Great to the destruction of Jerusalem by Titus, the Roman rulers appointed twenty-seven successive high priests to sit in Aaron's seat, in a priestly office that should have been hereditary and should have lasted in each instance for the whole lifetime of its occupant.

Herod was a Gentile who pretended to be a Jew. His ancestry stemmed back to Abraham through Esau, who is Edom, but his religious beliefs were Jewish, and his way of life worldly, even Satanic. His half-Jew, half-Gentile stance was a convenient one for him to take in controlling his kingdom. He built again the temple in Jerusalem, constructing it with a magnificence beyond that of either Solomon or Zerubbabel. But he also built a temple to Augustus in Caesarea, wherein was placed a statue of the emperor as Olympian Zeus. He placed over the great gate of the temple in Jerusalem a massive golden eagle as a symbol of Roman dominion. He built a number of towns, inhabited by Gentiles, as a means of tempering Jewish nationalism. At a later time Pilate introduced images of the emperor into Jerusalem, and even a statue of Caligula was placed in the temple itself.

It is true that under the Roman rule the Jews were granted numerous concessions, such as the right to observe the Sabbath as they chose, except that they could not (legally, that is) impose the death penalties for violations as Moses had once done. And it was to the Romans that they turned to have a Man crucified who, they said, according to their law, was worthy of death.

We shall not here particularize further as to the supremacy of the Roman world over the Jewish world. It suffices for the present to know that Caesar took precedence over Christ, through all Canaan and the civilized world, in all things both temporal and spiritual. Roman tolerance with all religions, however, was proverbial. The rulers from the land of the Tiber accepted and revered—nay, oftimes worshipped—the gods of all the conquered lands. Caesar felt no compunction in granting freedom of religion to Christ so long as it did not hinder or deter the purposes of absolute autocracy as found in the hands of the emperor. The forces against free religion that led a Jew to Calvary were not of Roman origin, though it took the iron hand of Roman authority to drive the nails and raise the cross.

As occasion requires, we shall hereafter weave into our account of the life of a Jew who was born into both a Roman and a Jewish world—and who came to save them both—such commentary about social patterns, education, trade, agriculture, fishing, business and enterprises, and local customs and life as seems appropriate. We shall speak of Palestinian roads, of the Jewish Sanhedrin, of the levirate laws of marriage, and of the Mosaic manner of divorce. We shall concern ourselves with the Herodians, Hellenists, and Publicans; with the Galileans, Pereans, and Judeans; with the various Herods and their evil ways—all as the unfolding needs of the greatest story ever told seem to warrant. As we begin this story it suffices to know that Rome ruled Jerusalem and that worldly influence abounded in Judaism itself. It was the type of a world, the kind of a social structure, the very governmental arrangement, the level of decency among the people—and all else—that Omnipotent Wisdom chose as proper for the birth and ministry and death of his Son. It could not have been otherwise; all things were to be done in the wisdom of him who knoweth all things.

The Signs of the Times

The signs of the times: what are they? It depends on what signs we are talking about and what times we are considering; it depends on what period of time is involved and what great event is being ushered in. When the signs of the times, for our day, are fulfilled and all things are come to pass which were of old foretold, the Son of Man will come in power and great glory to usher in millennial peace. When Jesus asked the Pharisees and Sadducees, "Can ye not discern the signs of the times," he referred to the signs and wonders attesting his divine Sonship, signs that were everywhere manifest before them. (Matt. 16:1-4.) In like manner we might say that the signs of the times, as pertaining to the birth of the Savior, were poured out upon the people to whom he was destined to come. Deity never sends a portentous or wondrous happening without heralding its coming and preparing the way for its occurrence. That the Jews of our Lord's day were to some extent reading the signs presaging his coming and ministry is clear from the universal ferment of Messianic expectancy to be found on every hand.

Not the least of the signs of Messiah's first coming were the religious, social, cultural, and governmental conditions existing in Palestine and elsewhere in the latter years of Herod's reign. The Messiah was to come as the Son of David, a Jew of the Jews, in a dark and dreary day; and his mission was to deliver his people, redeem the nation, triumph over the world, and reign as King of kings.

He was to be planted in arid soil; to grow up as a tender plant, as a root out of dry ground. Babylonia, Persia, Egypt, Syria, Greece, and Rome—each in turn—had ploughed in the fields of Palestine. Each had reaped harvests without dunging the land. The early rains of revelation and the latter rains of prophetic guidance had not watered the soil for centuries. The thistles and weeds and briers of sin encumbered the vineyards. There was a famine of hearing the word of the Lord.

The first Adam brought his own environment and was born into a garden of beauty and peace; the second Adam was born into an apostate world and a degenerate social order. He came to dwell among a people who drew near to the Lord with their lips, but whose hearts were far from him.

He came to be a Jew in a day when the Jewish society could provide no nutrient for his soul.

Jesus was a Jew; he was of the tribe of Judah. David, the Jew, was his father, and Mary, the Jewess, his mother. He grew up in a Jewish home, spoke the Jewish Aramaic of his day, learned Jewish customs and traditions, studied in Jewish schools, read Jewish scripture, attended Jewish synagogues, and participated in Jewish worship. From Bethlehem to Calvary, he was a Jew of the Jews.

He ministered among the Jews, called Jews to repentance, baptized Jews, ordained Jews to priesthood offices, and left twelve Jews to carry on his work among men. From a mortal standpoint he was the product of the Jewish system, which in turn was the product, in large measure, of everything that had happened to that people from Nebuchadnezzar to Herod. As Jesus ministered and taught among his Jewish kinsmen, he did so with their background, using the colloquialisms with which they were familiar and the illustrations they understood.

How well he did we shall now see as we meet him in Bethlehem, as we stay at his side till he climbs the hill of Calvary, as we see him, on Olivet, ascend to his Father, there to reign with everlasting power until that great day—the year of his redeemed—when he shall come again in all the glory of his Father's kingdom.

Blessed be his holy name!

SECTION II

JESUS' YEARS OF
PREPARATION

JESUS' YEARS OF PREPARATION

The Only Begotten of the Father ...
came and dwelt in the flesh. . . . he
received not of the fulness at the first,
but received grace for grace.
(D&C 93:11-12.)

Even a God—when clothed in mortal flesh; when as Adam's Son he dwells among his fellowmen; when here on earth to work out his own salvation—even a God receives not of the fulness of the Father at the first. Even he must be subject to the vicissitudes and trials of mortality; even he must be tried and tested to the full; even he must overcome the world.

And so we see him—during his years of preparation—as he makes himself ready for the work that he only can do.

We see Gabriel come to Zacharias, to Mary, and to Joseph, proclaiming to each in turn a portion of the glad tidings of His birth. We learn who shall declare his generation and whose Son he shall be.

Then, lo, he is born of Mary; heavenly manifestations attend. He is circumcised, named, and taken into Egypt to escape the vengeance of Herod.

We see him called out of Egypt and grow up in Nazareth; we hear him testify, when but twelve years of age, of his own divine Sonship. He continues to grow in stature and wisdom, and in favor with God and man.

Then John comes, preaching in power and preparing a people to receive Him. He is baptized in Jordan; the Holy Ghost descends upon him; he is led by the Spirit into the wilderness to be with God for forty days. Thereafter Lucifer comes, tempting, testing, fighting against God.

Our Lord triumphs. He has made flesh his tabernacle; he has attained physical and spiritual maturity. The years of his preparation are fulfilled, and the hour of his ministry has arrived.

"Hear ye him!"

Chapter 17

GABRIEL COMES TO ZACHARIAS

Gabriel, make this man to understand
the vision. . . .

Whiles I was speaking in prayer, even
the man Gabriel, whom I had seen in
the vision at the beginning, being
caused to fly swiftly, touched me about
the time of the evening oblation.

And he informed me, and talked with
me, and said, . . . I am now come forth
to give thee skill and understanding.
(Dan. 8:16, 9:21-22.)

"He Shall Prepare the Way Before Me"
(Malachi 3:1)[1]

One such as he must not come unannounced!

When God's own Son leaves his eternal throne and
makes flesh his tabernacle, all the legates of the skies must
herald his coming!

When the Promised Messiah takes upon himself the form
of a man, so that he may abolish death, and bring life and

immortality to light through his gospel,[2] mortal men are entitled to receive the word from the lips of an authorized witness.

The Mortal Messiah must be identified to his fellow mortals. His servants must prepare the way before him— make ready the manger, prepare the bridal chamber, sweep clean the temple courts, frame the cross, prepare the tomb, and, above all, testify to the people of the divinity of the One sent among them by his Father.

The providences of the Lord do not call for the heavens to rend, or the mountains to melt, or the earth to shake. His way is to send living witnesses to testify: 'Behold, the Lamb of God, who taketh away the sins of the world. This is he of whom all the prophets have testified. Believe in him; hear his word; walk in his paths and be saved.'

His kinsman, John, must be in the appointed place, at the proper time, to bear the witness he was sent to bear. Faithful Anna and saintly Simeon must be in the court of the Holy House when the Consolation of Israel is presented before the Lord as Moses commanded. The voices of the forerunners and the witnesses, of the Eliases and those who prepare the way, must be heard. His word, given through Malachi, must be fulfilled: "Behold, I will send my messenger, and he shall prepare the way before me: and the Lord, whom ye seek, shall suddenly come." (Mal. 3:1.)

And how fitting that his chief forerunner—than whom there has been no greater prophet born of woman—should precede him in birth, precede him in his ministry, precede him in death, and precede him in his future Second Advent. As the voice of one crying in the wilderness of unbelief, John came to prepare the way before his Lord in this life; and then, laying down his life for the testimony of Jesus that was his, he went as a forerunner into the paradise of God to announce that He whose mission it was to free the captives would soon be there to open the prison doors. And with a divine fitness and propriety, the resurrected John has raised his voice again to mortals in our day, preparing the way for the coming of Him who shall this time rend the heavens, and melt the mountains, and shake the earth when his presence is again revealed.

And how fitting that the same angelic ministrant who came to the mother of our Lord came also to the father of John—in each instance proclaiming a miraculous conception and the birth of a foreordained prophet.

Zacharias—His Ministry and Mission

There were many widows in Israel when Elijah sealed the heavens for "three years and six months, when great famine was throughout all the land," but only to one—the widow of Zarephath—was Elijah sent, that he might command her "barrel of meal" to "not waste," and her "cruse of oil" to not fail, "until the day that the Lord sendeth rain upon the earth." And there were, no doubt, many widows whose children died, but she alone had her son raised from death by the man of God. (Luke 4:25-26; 1 Kgs. 17.)

There were also many lepers in Israel in the day of Elisha the prophet, "and none of them was cleansed, saving Naaman the Syrian," who swallowed his pride, believed the promise given him, and washed seven times in the dirty waters of Jordan, as Elisha commanded. (Luke 4:27; 2 Kgs. 5.)

So also was it with Zacharias, who fathered the forerunner of the Messiah. There were many priests in Israel in his day, many lineal descendants of Aaron—between twenty thousand and twenty-four thousand of them—whose right it was to offer temporal sacrifices in similitude of the eternal sacrifice of their expected Deliverer. But none of these saw the angelic face and none received the heaven-sent message of comfort and hope save only Zacharias of Hebron, who, with his wife, Elisabeth, walked blamelessly before the Lord.

It was a day when the priestly office, once held by Aaron's worthy sons, was now held by their unworthy descendants. Pride, disbelief, dishonesty, violence, immorality, and even the shedding of innocent blood—all these prevailed and were more common than not among those who should have been lights to the people. Few of the priests envisioned to any real degree the true significance of the sacred ordinances it was their privilege to perform.

David, a thousand years before, had divided the priests into twenty-four courses, or houses, or families. Only four of these had returned from Babylon, but the balance had been reconstituted, and they lived in thirteen towns, mostly near Jerusalem. Those of each course went up to that city twice a year, in rotation, for six days and two Sabbaths each time, to serve in the temple. While there they lived in the temple, their wives and families remaining in their home villages.

Priestly duties were many and varied. They were teachers of the law, instructors of the people, and the judges and magistrates of their communities. They examined all cases of ceremonial uncleanness and watched over all of the affairs of the temple. "It was their awful and peculiar honour to 'come near the Lord.' None but they could minister before Him, in the Holy Place where He manifested His presence: none others could 'come nigh the vessels of the sanctuary or the altar.' It was death for any one not a priest to usurp these sacred prerogatives. They offered the morning and evening incense; trimmed the lamps of the golden candlestick, and filled them with oil; set out the shewbread weekly; kept up the fire on the great altar in front of the Temple; removed the ashes of the sacrifices; took part in the slaying and cutting up of victims, and especially in the sprinkling of their blood; and laid the offerings of all kinds on the altar." (Geikie, p. 65.)

These duties, with all that they include and imply, plus the host of other normal functions applicable to all priests, were part of the ministry of Zacharias, and indeed it was in the performance of some of them that the Lord manifested to this son of Aaron his higher and more noble mission. Zacharias, like the son he was to sire, was foreordained to bring the Lord's forerunner into mortality. And Zacharias, in this life, walked uprightly before the Lord and manifested a faith in Jehovah not found among his fellow priests. As with the widow of Zarephath and as with Naaman of Syria, John's father was singled out from the thousand score and more priests for the work that was his. Angels do not minister unto carnal and godless souls; it is those who seek, by righteousness, the blessings of heaven who are permitted to see within the veil.

Zacharias's mission was to bear an even greater son and to endow that offspring with the talents and abilities that would enable him to prepare the way before the Lord. How well he did this is now written in the records of eternity. As it happens, both Zacharias and his son were called upon, in the providences of the Lord, to lay down their lives as part of the missions assigned them from on high; both died because of the mad anxieties of demented kings. "When Herod's edict went forth to destroy the young children," as the Prophet Joseph Smith taught, "John was about six months older than Jesus, and came under this hellish edict, and Zacharias caused his mother to take him into the mountains, where he was raised on locusts and wild honey. When his father refused to disclose his hiding place, and being the officiating high priest at the Temple that year, [he] was slain by Herod's order, between the porch and the altar, as Jesus said." (*Teachings*, p. 261; Matt. 23:35.)

Zacharias Ministers in the Temple
(*Luke 1:5-10; JST, Luke 1:8-9*)

Twice each year, in April and October, the priests of the course of Abia, named for Abijah, traveled from their village homes to the House of the Lord in Jerusalem, there to take their week-long turns at performing those sacred rites and ordinances which for fifteen hundred years had been the center of Israel's worship. One of these priests, Zacharias, whose wife, Elisabeth, was both barren and past the childbearing age, dwelt in a village in the hill country of

Judea, believed to be Hebron. It was the very locale where Abraham had lived with Sarah, who also was both barren and past the childbearing age when the Lord himself saw fit to tell the Father of the Faithful that his beloved Sarah would conceive and bear Isaac, through whom the blessings of the Abrahamic covenant would continue.

It was October, the autumn of the year, when Zacharias left his beloved Elisabeth—both of them being in the autumn of their lives—to travel the some twenty lonely miles to Jerusalem. At least it was the custom to leave family members at home, for the priests dwelt in the temple itself during their week-long ministry. But perhaps he went with other priests of his course, and if so, as was common among them in that era of great expectation, they would have discussed the Consolation of Israel who was to come and deliver his people.

As nearly as we can determine, the month was October and the year was 6 B.C.[3] Herod the Great, who died in 4 B.C., was winding up his long and evil and bloody reign. Gentile by birth, Jewish by belief, and ruling with Roman authorization, Herod lived in the day in which the scepter was departing from Judah to make way for the coming of Shiloh. And what would have been more natural than for the priests traveling to the temple to perform sacrifices in similitude of that Shiloh whom they expected, and longing for release from Roman rule, to discuss their long-expected Deliverer.

In any event, Zacharias arrived at the temple and walked worthily through its sacred portals, for both he and the daughter of Aaron who stood as his wife were "righteous before God, walking in all the commandments and ordinances of the Lord blameless." With his fellow priests, he then drew lots, as was the custom, so that each of the sons of Aaron serving that week might be assigned his duties. There was one service, favored above all others, that a priest to whose lot it fell might perform but once in a lifetime. It was the burning of incense on the altar of incense in the Holy Place, near the Holy of Holies where the very presence of Jehovah came on occasion. And, lo, this time the lot fell to Zacharias; he was chosen of the Lord to perform the great mediatorial service in which the smoke of the incense, ascending to heaven, would symbolize the prayers of all Israel ascending to the divine throne. That Zacharias was to be the central figure in the temple, through this service, all the assembled worshippers knew; and that heaven itself was to respond with divine approval shining forth, they would soon learn.

In the court of the priests stood the great altar of unhewn stones whereon the sacred sacrifices were offered; this was open to the view of the people. Entrance was gained to the Holy Place through two great gold-plated doors. In this sanctuary were the two tables—one of marble, one of gold— on which the priests laid the candlestick with its seven lamps and, most importantly, the altar of incense.

It was into this sacred sanctuary that Zacharias went, accompanied by another priest who bore burning coals taken from the altar of sacrifice; these he spread upon the altar of incense and then withdrew. It then became the privilege of Elisabeth's husband to sprinkle the incense on the burning coals, that the ascending smoke and the odor might typify the ascending prayers of all Israel. This performance is also but a type of what John saw in heavenly vision and recorded in these words: "And another angel came and stood at the altar, having a golden censer; and there was given unto him much incense, that he should offer it with the prayers of all saints upon the golden altar which was before the throne. And the smoke of the incense, which came with the prayers of the saints, ascended up before God out of the angel's hand." (Rev. 8:3-4.)[4]

What prayers did Zacharias make on this occasion? Certainly not, as so many have assumed, prayers that Elisabeth should bear a son, though such in days past had been the subject of the priest's faith-filled importunings. This was not the occasion for private, but for public prayers. He was acting for and on behalf of all Israel, not for himself and

Elisabeth alone. And Israel's prayer was for redemption, for deliverance from the Gentile yoke, for the coming of their Messiah, for freedom from sin. The prayers of the one who burned the incense were the prelude to the sacrificial offering itself, which was made to bring the people in tune with the Infinite, through the forgiveness of sins and the cleansing of their lives. "And the whole multitude of the people were praying without at the time of incense"—all praying, with one heart and one mind, the same things that were being expressed formally, and officially, by the one whose lot it was to sprinkle the incense in the Holy Place. The scene was thus set for the miraculous event that was to be.

"Thou Shalt Call His Name John"
(*Luke 1:11-13*)

As the clouds of sweet incense ascend heavenward, and as the prayers of Zacharias come up into the ears of the Lord of the whole earth—and we cannot but feel that his prayers on this occasion were guided by the Spirit and uttered with a reverence, in an awe, and with a deep feeling of spirituality that is seldom equaled—as his expressions of thanksgiving and his petitions for blessings and good things reach their climax, just at this moment the veil is rent. Gabriel stands before him.[5]

At the right of the altar, near the Holy of Holies, where Jehovah himself would stand if he came personally, there stands Gabriel, the archangel next in authority to mighty Michael.

After so many years, as a herald of things to come, an angel's voice is heard again. Once more in Israel, as it had been almost always in olden times, the angelic visage is clearly seen in vision. Soon angels will be coming to others, many others, and the long night of darkness will pass. And soon God's own Son will minister among men and have his person identified by a heavenly voice. Revelation is commencing anew in Israel; the prospects are bright for a great

308

outpouring of gospel truth, and a humble priest, who has even been denied seed to bear his priesthood after him, is the recipient of the heaven-sent message. A new day is dawning in Israel.

Zacharias is troubled, fearful, but such is a normal reaction; so also were those of old in like circumstances. His reaction is simply that of Father Jacob, who, seeing the vision of the ladder reaching up into heaven, with angels ascending and descending, exclaimed: "How dreadful is this place! this is none other but the house of God, and this is the gate of heaven." (Gen. 28:10-22.) To calm his troubled mind, the angel speaks: "Fear not, Zacharias: for thy prayer is heard." 'And the Lord shall grant thy petition: The Consolation of Israel truly shall come; he shall deliver and redeem his people; and, lo, the time is at hand, for thou hast been chosen to be the father of the one who shall prepare the way before him.' "And thy wife Elisabeth shall bear thee a son, and thou shalt call his name John."

Gabriel Announces the Mission of John
(Luke 1:14-25)

Gabriel continues to speak: 'Thou shalt have joy and rejoicing in thy son; and many shall rejoice at his birth, for what is done this day shall be in their hearts, and they shall remember it with gladness and tell it to others. And John shall be great in the sight of the Lord, of whom he shall testify; and he shall drink neither wine nor strong drink, for it shall be with him as though he were a Nazarite for life, for he shall be as one who has vowed a vow and been set apart for a special work all the days of his life.

'And he shall be filled with the Holy Ghost, even from within his mother's womb, so that before he is born the Holy Ghost shall come upon him, and he shall leap as it were for joy at the presence of the mother of his Lord.

'And many of the children of Israel shall he turn to the Lord their God, for he shall cry repentance, and baptize for the remission of sins, and cause many to follow the Lamb of God who taketh away the sins of the world. And he shall go before the Lord, who is Christ, in the spirit and power of Elias, preparing the way, making the rough places smooth and the crooked straight. He shall even turn the hearts of those disobedient ones, who are the children of the prophets, back to their just fathers, who foresaw this day and prophesied of it, and the hearts of the fathers shall rejoice that their children on earth believe in that Messiah whose life and labors they foresaw.

'And through all that he does, he shall make ready a people prepared for the Lord, and this people shall then follow their Messiah and be saved.'

Gabriel ceased to speak. Zacharias in wonder and amazement—perhaps overwhelmed that all this could happen to persons as aged as he and Elisabeth, perhaps guided by the Spirit in what he asked—said to the heavenly visitant, as if in a spirit of unbelief: 'How shall I know that these things shall come to pass?'

Why did he need a sign? Does not the word of one who stands in the presence of God suffice? May it not be that the main purpose of his query was to provide an occasion for "the man Gabriel" to do the thing that would cause those then present, and all who heard the account thereafter, to know that the hand of the Lord was in the doings of the day? If Zacharias had come out of the Holy Place, given the usual benediction to the people, and then said that he had seen an angel and that his barren wife, though well stricken in years, should bear a son, and then had she in fact done so, it would have been a dramatic thing. But how much more impressive did it become when Zacharias came out *both deaf and dumb,* so that he could not speak or give the usual benediction to the people there assembled, and—be it noted—so that he could not hear what the others said, even more than nine months later, when the young John was brought on the eighth day in to the temple to be circumcised. On that occasion those who were present had to make signs to the deaf

310

Zacharias before he could signify in writing what his son's name should be.

Immediately after the happenings of this unprecedented day—the day on which angelic ministrants commenced again to commune with their fellow mortals—Elisabeth conceived, and she rejoiced that the Lord had taken away the reproach of barrenness, for, from the day Rachel said "Give me children, or else I die" (Gen. 30:1), so it was considered in Israel.

Then Elisabeth retired from public view until the day that Mary, herself then also with child, visited her in the hill country village of Hebron.

NOTES

1. Under each subheading, where they apply, we shall hereafter place the citations from the Gospels in which the matters under consideration are set forth by Matthew, Mark, Luke, and/or John, as the case may be. When more than one New Testament author speaks of the same event, the citations will be listed in their assumed order of importance. Then, in that subsection, direct quotations, recorded within double quotation marks (". . . ."), will not be identified by a scriptural reference. Single quotation marks ('. . . .') will be used to set off and identify paraphrasing and interpreting quotes that give the meaning and thought content of what the speaker is saying or teaching.

2. Paul says, in Philippians 2:7-8, that Christ "took upon him the form of a servant, and was made in the likeness of men." Also, that he was "found in fashion as a man." The apostle also says, in 2 Timothy 1:10, that Christ "hath abolished death, and hath brought life and immortality to light through the gospel." These two passages are the ones alluded to and paraphrased in the text. Except in cases of special need, we shall not hereafter use quotation marks or give footnotes identifying the source of scriptural or other inspired statements that are paraphrased, summarized, alluded to, or in some instances quoted verbatim. All such will be considered part of the running text. When passages themselves are being analyzed (except those cited under the subsection headings), they will be identified in the usual way.

3. The date, which it is difficult to determine, affects the time of our Lord's birth, which problem is considered in footnote 2 of chapter 20 herein.

4. David spoke of this matter in these words: "Let my prayer be set forth before thee as incense; and the lifting up of my hands as the evening sacrifice." (Ps. 141:2.)

5. Why Gabriel? Why not Michael or Raphael or one of the host of unnamed angels who from time to time have parted the veil to converse with their fellow servants in mortality? Clearly there is an angelic hierarchy—a heavenly hierarchy—as well as an earthly hierarchy. Some angels take precedence over and give direction to others; it is no different in the heavenly church than in the earthly; there are those who give direction and others who go at their behest.

Michael, the archangel, the greatest of all, the one who stands next to Christ, is the one who led Jehovah's hosts when there was war in heaven and the devil and his angels were cast out; and he it is who shall again lead the armies of righteousness in the great battles ahead when all things relative to the salvation of men shall be completed. As commander-in-chief, he will have others, from general to private, serving under him. He came to earth as Adam, and the "angels are under the direction of Michael or Adam, who acts under the direction of the Lord." (*Teachings*, pp. 167-69.)

Adam, who is Michael, holds the keys of the priesthood "from generation to generation," and "Noah, who is Gabriel . . . stands next in authority to Adam in the Priesthood." (*Teachings*, p. 157.) What could be more fitting, then, than for Michael, who presides over the angels and directs their labors, to send Gabriel, his next in command, to announce to the mortals involved those things they needed to know concerning the Promised Messiah and his Elias?

It may even be that, as Michael is in charge of all things (under Christ), so Gabriel is in charge (under Michael) of those angelic ministrations which speak of Messiah's coming, and that either he or those serving under him make the necessary visitations to mortals. In this connection it was "the man Gabriel" himself who came to Daniel to tell that worthy one of the coming of "Messiah the Prince" who would "make reconciliation for iniquity" and "bring in everlasting righteousness." (Dan. 9:20-27.) Contrary to the sectarian traditions, it is Michael, not Gabriel, who shall sound the trump of the Lord in the last days as part of the great winding-up scene.

Chapter 18

THE ANNUNCIATION TO MARY

Behold, a virgin shall conceive, and
bear a son, and shall call his name
Immanuel. (Isa. 7:14.)

And I beheld the city of Nazareth;
and in the city of Nazareth I beheld a
virgin, and she was exceedingly fair and
white. . . . [Yea], A virgin, most
beautiful and fair above all other
virgins. (1 Ne. 13-15.)

"Knowest Thou the Condescension of God?"
(*1 Nephi 11:16*)

John is now conceived in Elisabeth's womb; the son of
Zacharias will soon be born; our Lord's forerunner, destined
to be six months his senior, shall soon breathe the breath of
life. The words of Gabriel are coming to pass, and soon the
Son of God must be sired, conceived, born, and laid in a
manger.

But how can a God be born into mortality? How can the
Eternal One take upon himself flesh and blood, and let
himself be fashioned as a Man? A child—any child, includ-

ing the Child—must have progenitors; he must have parents, both a father and a mother. Gabriel will soon tell the Virgin of Galilee that she shall be the mother. As to the father—he is Elohim. The Son of God shall have God as his Father; it is just that simple, and it could not be otherwise. The doctrine of the divine Sonship lies at the foundation of true religion; without it, Christ becomes just another man, a great moral teacher, or what have you, without power to ransom, to redeem, and to save.

Having seen in vision—more than six hundred years before the events themselves transpired—the city of Nazareth and a gracious and beautiful virgin therein, Nephi was asked by an angel: "Knowest thou the condescension of God?" He responded by saying he knew of the Lord's love for his children, but not the full answer to the profound query framed by angelic lips. Then the angel answered his own question by saying: "Behold, the virgin whom thou seest is the mother of the Son of God, after the manner of the flesh." That is to say, the condescension of God lies in the fact that he, an exalted Being, steps down from his eternal throne to become the Father of a mortal Son, a Son born "after the manner of the flesh."

Immediately after hearing these words, Nephi saw that the virgin "was carried away in the Spirit; and after she had been carried away in the Spirit for the space of a time," Nephi saw "the virgin again, bearing a child in her arms." Thereupon the angel said: "Behold the Lamb of God, yea, even the Son of the Eternal Father!" To be "carried away in the Spirit" means to be transported bodily from one location to another, as witness the fact that Nephi, at the very time he beheld these visions, had been "caught away in the Spirit of the Lord" and taken bodily "into an exceeding high mountain," which he never "had before seen," and upon which he "never had before" set his "foot." (1 Ne. 11:1, 13-21.)

Without overstepping the bounds of propriety by saying more than is appropriate, let us say this: God the Almighty; the Maker and Preserver and Upholder of all things; the

Omnipotent One; he by whom the sidereal heavens came into being, who made the universe and all that therein is; he by whose word we are, who is the Author of that life which has been going on in this system for nigh unto 2,555,000,000 years;[1] God the Almighty, who once dwelt on an earth of his own and has now ascended the throne of eternal power to reign in everlasting glory;[2] who has a glorified and exalted body, a body of flesh and bones as tangible as man's; who reigns in equity and justice over the endless billions of his spirit children who inhabit the worlds without number that roll into being at his word—God the Almighty, who is infinite and eternal, elects, in his fathomless wisdom, to beget a Son, an Only Son, the Only Begotten in the flesh.

God, who is infinite and immortal, condescends to step down from his throne, to join with one who is finite and mortal in bringing forth, "after the manner of the flesh," the Mortal Messiah.

"Who Shall Declare His Generation?"
(Matthew 1:1-17; Luke 3:23-38; JST, Luke 3:30-31, 45)

If God, who is eternal, steps down from his high and holy place to beget an Only Begotten Son "after the manner of the flesh," who can know it? How can such wondrous knowledge be given to carnal men? It may be easy to find someone who would claim to be the mother, but how can her selection for such an exalted position of motherhood be known for sure? Who shall declare Messiah's generation?

True, he cometh in the fulness of his own time to fulfill all that has been spoken—concerning that coming and ministry—by the mouths of all the holy prophets since the world began; he cometh to merit all the praise and adoration and thanksgiving and reverence and worship that has foredwelt in the hearts of the righteous of all preceding ages; he cometh to make flesh his tabernacle, to take upon himself the form of men, and to do the will of the Father whose Son he is. But who shall declare his generation? Who knows his genesis? Or who can tell whence and how he came? Who are his parents? When God has a Son, how can this be known among mortal men?

Matthew identifies his Gospel as "The book of the generation of Jesus Christ, the son of David, the son of Abraham." Then he gives a genealogy down to "Joseph the husband of Mary, of whom was born Jesus, who is called Christ." Luke begins with this same Joseph and traces the genealogy back to "Adam, which was the son of God," or, as the Joseph Smith Translation has it, to "Adam, who was formed of God, and [was] the first man upon the earth."

Matthew's and Luke's accounts seemingly do not agree, though, in fact, the two of them taken together give a perfect picture of what is involved. Both purport to give the genealogy of Joseph, whose bloodline is not involved, but who was of the royal lineage. It is generally agreed that Matthew's account gives the royal lineage and therefore records names of those whose right it was to sit on David's throne, and that Luke's record contains the personal pedigree of Mary's husband. Matthew says Joseph was a son of Jacob, and Luke says that he was a son of Heli. It appears, however, that Jacob and Heli were brothers and that Heli was the father of Joseph and Jacob the father of Mary, making Joseph and Mary first cousins with the same ancestral lines. How fitting it is that the New Testament should preserve both a royal and a personal pedigree of these two, so that there could be no question, either by blood or by kingly right, as to the noble and exalted status of the Son of David. "Had Judah been a free and independent nation, ruled by her rightful sovereign, Joseph the carpenter would have been her crowned king; and his lawful successor to the throne would have been Jesus of Nazareth, the King of the Jews." (Talmage, p. 87.)

But our question still remains: "Who shall declare his generation?" (Isa. 53:8.) And the answer is: Since we are dealing with spiritual things, which can only be known by the power of the Holy Spirit, no one can declare the generation of "Jesus, who is called Christ," except by the power of the Holy Ghost. "No man can say [know] that Jesus is the Lord, but by the Holy Ghost." (1 Cor. 12:3.)[3] There is no other way. When the theologians of our day deny the divine Sonship, they are thereby testifying that the Holy Ghost does not speak by their mouths, and that they are, as a consequence, false prophets.

And so it is that Matthew, who, in all the majesty of his apostolic office, took it upon himself to set forth our Lord's ancestry, proceeds to speak of his birth to a virgin, as we shall hereafter recite.

Gabriel Comes to Mary
(Luke 1:26-38; JST, Luke 1:28-29, 34-35)

Angels, Alma says, come to men, women, and children to impart the word of God. (Alma 32:23.) And never was there a case when angelic ministration was more deserved, or served a greater purpose, or was manifest in a sweeter and more tender way, than when Gabriel, who stands in the presence of God, came to Mary to announce her divine call to be the mother of the Son of God. She at the time dwelt in Nazareth, a city of Galilee, located some eighty miles northward from the Holy City and the Holy Temple, where last the angelic form had been seen and the angelic voice heard.

Mary was espoused to Joseph, meaning she had made a formal contract of marriage with him that yet had to be completed in a second ceremony before they would commence living together as husband and wife. She was, however, considered by their law to be his wife; the contract could be broken only by a formal "bill of divorcement," and any infidelity on her part would be classed as adultery, for which Jehovah had of old decreed death as the penalty.

Faithful Jews prayed in their homes three times daily—at the time of the morning offering, at noon, and at the time of the evening sacrifice. Perhaps at such a time (for the veil grows thin when prayers flow from the heart) the man Gabriel "came in" to her humble home. She was alone; her spiritual eyes were open; and she saw the minister from heaven. He spoke: "Hail, thou virgin, who art highly favoured of the Lord. The Lord is with thee, for thou art chosen and blessed among women."[4]

Understandably the humble, perhaps even shy and timid, Maid of Nazareth was troubled by such lavish praise from one sent from the other world and who spoke only the truth. Sensing her feelings, Gabriel continued: "Fear not, Mary: for thou hast found favour with God. And, behold, thou shalt conceive in thy womb, and bring forth a son, and shalt call his name Jesus."

Jesus, blessed name—signifying *Jehovah is salvation*—her Son to be a Savior! Had she ever hoped or thought that the Messiah, expected by her people, would be born as her Son? Had the Spirit, even before Gabriel came, whispered any message of hope or comfort or expectancy to the soul of one so attuned to spiritual things as she was?

But there was more, telling her in plain words the status and mission and dominion of him who was to be her Son: "He shall be great, and shall be called the Son of the Highest: and the Lord God shall give unto him the throne of his father David: And he shall reign over the house of Jacob for ever; and of his kingdom there shall be no end."

"The Son of the Highest"—the Supreme God shall be his Father! "The throne of his father David"—the symbol of all Jewish hope and triumph and glory and freedom and deliverance! An eternal kingdom—the kingdom of our God and of his Christ, and they shall reign forever and ever!

Mary asked, "How shall this be, seeing I know not a man?" Obviously she could, at the proper time, know Joseph, and he could be the father of all her children, not just those who would come after the Firstborn. She knew that. But already the concept was framed in her mind that the promised Son was not to originate from any power on earth. This offspring was to be himself almighty—God's Almighty

Son. How and by what means and through whose instrumentality does such a conception come?

Gabriel explains: "The Holy Ghost shall come upon thee, and the power of the Highest shall overshadow thee: therefore also that holy thing [better, that holy child] which shall be born of thee shall be called the Son of God."

Again the answer is perfect. There is a power beyond man's. When God is involved, he uses his minister, the Holy Ghost, to overshadow the future mother and to carry her away in the Spirit. She shall conceive by the power of the Holy Ghost, and God himself shall be the sire. It is his Son of whom Gabriel is speaking. A son is begotten by a father: whether on earth or in heaven it is the same.

The great message has been spoken. One who stands in the Divine Presence has brought the great announcement to the one who will hold the Divine Presence in her bosom. Now Gabriel speaks to Mary of personal things: "And, behold, thy cousin Elisabeth, she hath also conceived a son in her old age: and this is the sixth month with her, who was called barren. For with God nothing shall be impossible."

This news was to be a sign to Mary of the truth of the greater message that had preceded it. Elisabeth, stricken in years and past the childbearing age, was to have a child, because with God nothing is impossible, even as Sarah, also stricken in years and past the childbearing age, was promised a son by the Lord, who said: "Is any thing too hard for the Lord?" (Gen. 18:14.) Gabriel's announcement about Elisabeth was unspoken counsel to Mary to go and receive comfort and help from her cousin, whom she no doubt loved and revered—the inference is that Mary's mother was dead—and who, being herself with child in a miraculous manner, could speak peace to the young virgin's heart as no other mortal could.

Then Mary gave the answer that ranks, in submissive obedience and divine conformity, along with the one given by the Beloved and Chosen One in the councils of eternity. When he was chosen to be the Redeemer and to put into operation the terms and conditions of his Father's plan, he said: "Father, thy will be done, and the glory be thine forever." (Moses 4:2.) Mary said simply: "Behold the handmaid of the Lord; be it unto me according to thy word." Gabriel then departed.

Having so spoken, Mary contented herself until the divine conception had come to pass, and then she arose and went in haste to her cousin Elisabeth, a hundred and more miles hence in Hebron of Judea.

Mary Visits Elisabeth
(Luke 1:39-45; JST, Luke 1:43-44)

There is high drama here. We can scarce conceive how deep the emotions were, or what anxieties and fears bore in upon the tender feelings of Mary and Elisabeth. Nor can we envision how Joseph felt as he learned his betrothed was with child by another, or how subdued and chastened, yet how exalted and exulting, Zacharias was as he pondered what had happened to him in the Holy Place.

Zacharias could no longer speak or hear. He had doubted for a moment the angelic voice, and the penalty of his disbelief rested heavily upon him. For more than nine months he was shut out completely from the normal communion and the usual intercourse with his Judean friends. We suppose he went about his priestly duties as best he could, even journeying back to the temple after a six-month interval, for his assigned week of ceremonial service. No doubt he wrote, for Elisabeth to read, the account of the angel who stood between the golden altar of incense and the seven-branched candlesticks, and proclaimed that she and he would bring forth the one to prepare the way for the great Messiah. And now Elisabeth, with child in her advanced years, needed special care and attention. The trials of life and the testing and anxieties of mortality surely were increasing in the life of this pious priest who yet continued as theretofore to walk blamelessly before the Lord.

320

Elisabeth—a daughter of Aaron, highly endowed spiritually, rich in faith—she too was being tested and tried and purified. With child in her advanced years, facing problems foreign to younger women who bear children, emotionally troubled, fearing to face her friends of years, she "hid herself five months," to return to normal associations just before Mary's visit. That she was overwhelmed at the honor that was hers to bear the soul of him who would prepare the way for Israel's King, we can well imagine. That the fruit of her womb was so important in the Lord's plan, and that Gabriel himself came to announce the conception, was almost beyond human comprehension. Faithful Elisabeth was being tested and rewarded.

Joseph—a just man, one who loved the Lord and waited for the Consolation of Israel—what a refiner's fire he must have gone through during the weeks and months before Gabriel spoke peace to his soul! Mary—his beloved, the one to whom he had given a writing of espousement, the fairest and most spiritually endowed of all the virgins of the land—his espoused wife, she was with child by another! Joy and gladness, thanksgiving and the sound of melody—once these had filled his soul. Now there was despondency and despair. What should he do? Surely he could not make her a public example. She must not bear the onus of adultery. Yes, instead, he would put her away privily; he would ease her burden as best he could.

And Mary—what of her? Should her testing be any easier, her mortal trials lessened, because she carried in her womb the Son of the Highest? Should she be free from the burdens borne by Sarah and Miriam—whose very name in Hebrew she bore—and by the other great women of Abrahamic lineage? Nay, rather, should not her burdens be greater? Whenever was there a great prophet—Moses, Elijah, Isaiah, Nephi, Joseph Smith—who was not tested to the full? Whenever were the women who stood by their sides freed from the tests and trials of mortality? The greater the prophet, the more severe the test! The nobler the woman, the more she is called to bear! It was the Son of God who descended below all things that he might rise to heights unknown. It was his mother who was subjected to the most trying of all circumstances that she too might ascend the throne of eternal power, as had Rebecca and Rachel and her ancestors of old.

And so we find Mary, about fifteen years of age and inexperienced in meeting the trials of life, under contract to marry one she loved, but with child by the power of the Holy Ghost. We find her in a city of Galilee—rough, rugged, untempered Galilee—where a self-righteous people were quick to condemn, ever ready to punish; where the tongue of gossip would cut her tender feelings to the bone; where she would become a hiss and a byword among her friends and relatives, for she had (as they would view it) committed the sin next only in wickedness to murder. Those among whom she dwelt would no more believe her strange tale that an angel had come to her—angels no longer came to mortals, everyone knew that!—or that the Almighty himself was the Father of that which was in her womb; they would no more believe these claims than they would believe the testimony of the fruit of her womb when he testified in their own city that he was the Messiah of whom Isaiah had spoken.[5]

What course, then, was open to the young virgin? Where could she go for the help and comfort and guidance she so much needed? Had not Gabriel pointed the way? 'Go to thy cousin Elisabeth,' he said. 'She will comfort and sustain thee. She also is with child in a miraculous way—she will understand. She is wise and experienced. She will counsel and help you, and the Lord will give you power to overcome.'

Thus we find Mary facing the trials of life—there would be others, as her Son ministered among men; as he hung on the cross; as he lay in a borrowed tomb; yes, there would be others, and her present troubles were but the beginning of sorrows—but we find her facing her problems and, of her own choice, fleeing to the side of Elisabeth. The distance was more than one hundred miles. No doubt she walked; at least she was in poor circumstances and could have ill afforded other means of travel. Certainly she was accompanied—a sister and brother and other family members or relatives, perhaps; she would not, in wisdom, have gone alone, camping out, and facing the ever-present threat of thieves and robbers. But whatever the arrangements may have been, the journey was completed. Elisabeth was no longer in seclusion, and Mary "entered into the house of Zacharias, and saluted Elisabeth."

Then came the miracle. When the trials are past and the humble suppliant has remained true to every covenant and trust, the Lord speaks. Thus, "it came to pass, that, when Elisabeth heard the salution of Mary, the babe leaped in her womb; and Elisabeth was filled with the Holy Ghost."

Elisabeth was filled with the Holy Ghost—the same Holy Spirit who spake by the mouth of all the holy prophets; the same power from on high that fell on Peter in the coasts of Caesarea Philippi, when he said: "Thou art the Christ, the Son of the living God" (Matt. 16:13-16); the same Comforter whose companionship would be offered to all the saints on the day of Pentecost—the Holy Ghost came upon Elisabeth! She became a living witness, by revelation, of what Gabriel had said to Mary.

And the Holy Ghost fell also upon the unborn baby, for Elisabeth's whole being was filled with that divine power. It is always a miracle when the Holy Ghost rests upon a mortal person, and that very fact makes the recipient a prophet. But it is more than a miracle when the Spirit enlightens the mind and quickens the intellect of a human soul who is yet in his mother's womb; and shall we not conclude that such a recipient of divine truth is more than a prophet? So the Baptist would be designated by our Lord in due course.

It was, on this sacred occasion, as though the unborn John—who in life would say: "Behold the Lamb of God, which taketh away the sin of the world" (John 1:29)—was bearing testimony before birth, by the mouth of his mother, the only mouth that could then frame his words.

323

Then Elisabeth—speaking for herself and for her unborn infant, and echoing the sentiments in Zacharias's heart, for he too believed—repeated to Mary what she had already heard from the lips of Gabriel: "Blessed art thou among women, and blessed is the fruit of thy womb." Then she asked, and the question itself was a testimony: "And why is it, that this blessing is upon me, that the mother of my Lord should come to me?" By way of explanation, Elisabeth continued her prophetic words: "For, lo, as soon as the voice of thy salutation sounded in mine ears, the babe leaped in my womb for joy.[6] And blessed art thou who believed, for those things which were told thee by the angel of the Lord, shall be fulfilled." Mary had believed Gabriel and all that he had told her concerning the divine conception of her Son, and relative to his birth, life, ministry, and mission.

Would it be amiss to here interject a pleasing historical fact: There were here assembled, as it were, the first Christians of Jesus' day, and they were holding their first meeting. Mary and Elisabeth, both true believers, were present, and they preached the sermons. John, in the flesh in his mother's womb, also a believer, let his witness be heard. We suppose Zacharias was there and that he could feel the spirit of the meeting, though for the moment and until John was born, his lips were sealed and his ears were stopped. Those who traveled with Mary—probably unbelievers and non-Christians, as it were—may also have witnessed the scene and felt the spirit of the participants. Needless to say, the account preserved for us by Luke—and his source must have been the blessed Virgin herself—is abbreviated and does not tell all that was spoken between the two cousins, whose sons were to change the history of the world.

Mary, however, was now in good hands. Elisabeth was wise and she could help, and what was more important, the Lord had now revealed to Elisabeth—and how often revelation comes to the woman Rebecca as well as to the man Isaac—that Mary was the one who should bear the Son of

God. There was another witness; Mary no longer had to bear the burden alone. Now if only Joseph could also know—and that too was soon to be.

The Magnificat
(*Luke 1:46-56; JST, Luke 1:46, 48-49*)

Elisabeth, as moved upon by the Holy Ghost, pays homage to Mary as the mother of the Son of God, an homage that was deserved and true and continues to this day as the perfect testimony of the goodness and grace of her who was foreordained to bear God's Son.

Then Mary responds. Her words are inspired from the same source; she also is filled with the Holy Ghost, and the utterance she makes, like that of her cousin before her, is the voice of the Lord heard through her lips. Mary's words—appropriately—pay homage to the Father, for it was by and through him that the conception of her Son had taken place, and that she, a virgin, should bear a Son.[7]

Psalmic utterances of praise and thanksgiving had always been in the highest tradition of the Israelite people. The Psalms of David and Solomon and Moses and others, preserved in the Old Testament, are still read and sung in the churches of Christendom. Great psalmic utterances of Nephi are found in the Book of Mormon. Miriam, a prophetess, the sister of Aaron, led the women of Israel in a psalm of rejoicing after they had passed through the Red Sea. Deborah, a prophetess, who judged Israel in her day, sang a great hymn of praise when the Lord, through her instrumentality, slew Sisera and saved Israel from the king of Canaan. Hannah, the mother of Samuel, burst forth in a great accolade of praise when she delivered her son to Eli. And now Mary, filled with the same Spirit and exhibiting a profound knowledge of Old Testament history and Hebrew idiom and concepts, gives forth one of the great psalms of praise of all time.

My soul doth magnify the Lord,
And my spirit rejoiceth in God my Savior.
For he hath regarded the low estate of his handmaiden:
For, behold, from henceforth all generations shall call me
   blessed.

For he who is mighty hath done to me great things;
And I will magnify his holy name,
For his mercy on those who fear him
From generation to generation.

He hath shewed strength with his arm;
He hath scattered the proud in the imagination of their
   hearts.
He hath put down the mighty from their high seats;
And exalted them of low degree.

He hath filled the hungry with good things;
And the rich he hath sent empty away.
He hath holpen his servant Israel,
In remembrance of his mercy,
And he spake to our fathers,
To Abraham, and to his seed for ever.

The condescension of God has been manifest; our Lord's generation is declared. Gabriel has counseled Mary, and Elisabeth has comforted her. The Holy Ghost has fallen upon two great women and one unborn child. Wondrous things have been spoken, and now it remains but for Joseph, the carpenter of Galilee, to hear from heaven the divine message, and the heart of Mary will then be at peace.

NOTES

1. See footnote 7 of chapter 2.
2. See footnote 3 of chapter 2.
3. It was the Prophet Joseph Smith who changed the word *say* to *know* in this verse. (*Teachings*, p. 223.)
4. Can we speak too highly of her whom the Lord has blessed above all women? There

was only one Christ, and there is only one Mary. Each was noble and great in preexistence, and each was foreordained to the ministry he or she performed. We cannot but think that the Father would choose the greatest female spirit to be the mother of his Son, even as he chose the male spirit like unto him to be the Savior. This is not to say that we should give any heed or credence to the false doctrines that say that Mary has been assumed bodily into heaven; that she is an intercessor who hears prayers and pleads with her Son on behalf of those who pray to her; or that she should be esteemed as co-redemptrix with the Redeemer—all of which are part of a great system of worship that did not originate in the courts on high. As our spirits recoil from these perversions of true religion, we should nonetheless maintain a balanced view and hold up Mary with that proper high esteem which is hers.

5. Nor would Mary's story have been believed any more than was Joseph Smith's when he—about the same age as Mary was at the time—announced that the Father and the Son had visited him to usher in a new gospel dispensation. Visions and revelations (to the carnally minded) were things of the past; everyone knew that!

6. Our revelation, hearkening back to the sacred events here recited, describes Elisabeth's son as "John, whom God raised up, being filled with the Holy Ghost from his mother's womb." (D&C 84:27.) From the scriptural accounts it is clear that this means, not alone from the time he came forth out of the womb, but from the time that he as a conscious identity, the spirit having entered the body, was yet encased therein.

7. The virgin birth must not be confused with the so-called immaculate conception. "From the moment of her conception, Mary, the mother of our Lord, in the false Catholic view of things, is deemed to have been free from the stain of original sin. This supposed miraculous event is called the doctrine of the *immaculate conception.* After reciting the universal prevalence of so-called original sin, Cardinal Gibbons says: 'The Church, however, declares that the Blessed Virgin Mary was exempted from the stain of original sin by the merits of our Savior Jesus Christ; and that, consequently, she was never for an instant subject to the dominion of Satan. This is what is meant by the doctrine of the Immaculate Conception.' (James Cardinal Gibbons, *The Faith of Our Fathers*, p. 220.) The virgin birth has reference to the birth of Christ and is a true doctrine; the immaculate conception has reference to the birth of Mary and is a false doctrine." (*Mormon Doctrine*, 2nd ed., pp. 375-76.)

Chapter 19

THE ANNUNCIATION TO JOSEPH

And he shall be called
Jesus Christ, the Son of God,
The Father of heaven and earth,
The Creator of all things from the beginning;
And his mother shall be called Mary.
                                    (Mosiah 3:8.)

"Whose Son Is He?"
(*Matthew 1:18*)

We have spoken of the condescension of God in begetting a Mortal Son; we have identified those Spirit-guided persons who have power to declare the generation of a Divine Being, one of whom is Matthew; and we now take up his witness as to whence and by what means our Lord obtained mortality. Having recited the generations of mortals from Abraham down to "Joseph the husband of Mary, of whom was born Jesus, who is called Christ," a recitation that appears to be the royal line of Mary's husband, Matthew comes to the heart of the matter by saying: "Now the birth of Jesus Christ was on this wise: When as his mother Mary was espoused to Joseph, before they came together, she was found with child of the Holy Ghost."

The issue is thus squarely set. Mary is the mother, a fact

328

no one questions. But what does it mean to be "with child of the Holy Ghost"? Who is the Father of Mary's Son?

We suppose those in Christendom who believe the creeds are here faced with an insurmountable obstacle. Those creeds clearly recite—if such a word may be used to describe the maze of conflicting language found in them—and the doctrines based on those creeds clearly recite, that God is a spirit essence who or which fills the immensity of space, and who or which is everywhere and nowhere in particular present. They speak of an immanent, indwelling presence in all immensity; of three Gods in one, who are without body, parts, or passions; of a spirit being (if he may so be called), in whom we live and move and have our being; and, in saying that God is a spirit, the creeds intertwine the Father, Son, and Holy Ghost into one being, essence, or power, in which none of the three can be separated from the others. Each designation is said to be a variant manifestation of the same force or law or power or whatever. Those so asserting, and we suppose so believing, are at great pains to specify that there is nothing personal, in an anthropomorphic sense, about the God or Gods they worship; that all scriptural statements to the contrary are simply accounts that were so written for teaching purposes; and that their clear meanings must be spiritualized away in this more enlightened day.

We suppose, therefore, that those so believing have difficulty in determining the paternity of the Man of Galilee. We do know that they sometimes interpret the expression "with child of the Holy Ghost" to mean that the Holy Ghost was the Father of Christ, which from their standpoint presents no particular problem because they envision no difference between or among the Father, Son, and Holy Ghost anyway.

To those, however, who know that the Godhead is composed of three separate and distinct personages, who are one in spirit and power, the issue takes on quite a different aspect. The Father is a personage of tabernacle; he has a body of flesh and bones as tangible as man's; he is in one place at one time; he lives and moves and has a being; his influence is spread through all immensity, but he is a personal Being in whose image man is created, and he is the Father of the spirits of all men. The Son was a personage of spirit, the firstborn of the Father, for that infinitely long period before he was born into mortality; since his resurrection he has been and will continue to be an exalted and perfected Holy Man, in form, appearance, and image like his Father, who also is a resurrected personage. The Holy Ghost is a personage of spirit, a spirit man, an individual, whose power and influence, however, is felt throughout all immensity, as is the power and influence of the Father and the Son. The Father, Son, and Holy Ghost are all male personages.

The Son, existing first as a spirit man, was born into mortality as a mortal man; and he has now risen in the resurrection as an immortal man. As far as this life is concerned, he was born of Mary and of Elohim; he came here as the offspring of that Holy Man who is literally our Father in heaven. He was born in mortality in the literal and full sense as the Son of God. He is the Son of his Father in the same sense that all mortals are the sons and daughters of their fathers.

Matthew's statement "with child of the Holy Ghost" means Mary was with child by the power of the Holy Ghost, not that the Holy Ghost was the parent of the fruit of her womb. Matthew's words have the same meaning as those used by Gabriel to Mary: "The Holy Ghost shall come upon thee, and the power of the Highest shall overshadow thee." (Luke 1:35.) They have the same meaning as those used by Alma in one of his great Messianic prophecies: "The Son of God cometh upon the face of the earth," he said. "And behold, he shall be born of Mary, . . . she being a virgin, a precious and chosen vessel, who shall be overshadowed and conceive by the power of the Holy Ghost, and bring forth a son, yea, even the Son of God." (Alma 7:9-10.)

As far as those who understand the scriptures and the plan of salvation are concerned, the issue is not "Whose Son

330

is he?"—for that is well established: he is the Son of God, born in the manner we have set forth. The issue is, Was the child in Mary's womb the Son who had been sired by the Father? Had Elohim and Mary joined together to bring into mortality the One who would abolish death and bring life and immortality to light through the gospel? Was this child to be the Savior, the Redeemer, the Deliverer, the King of Israel?

This was the problem that confronted Joseph, the carpenter of Galilee. To it he must find the answer—for his own sake, for Mary's, and for the sake of all who would thereafter hear his witness.

Gabriel Comes to Joseph in a Dream
(Matthew 1:19-25)

When Mary told Joseph that she was with child by the power of the Holy Ghost, his reaction was one not only of shock, of sorrow, and of dismay, but also of disbelief. His soul had yet to feel the flames of the refiner's fire before so great a spiritual truth could rest easily in his heart; as with all men, his faith and his willingness to submit to the divine will in all things must be tested.

For Mary it was no easy thing to tell the man she loved that their relationship was different from that of other faithful couples. And yet Gabriel himself had brought the word! When she recited to Joseph what the aerial ambassador had told her, great and wondrous as the promises were, it must yet have been as a sword piercing her soul, a sword that would wound her feelings time and again, until that day when she, at the foot of a cross, would weep for the Son whom she had brought into the world.

For Joseph it was the beginning of a period of agony and uncertainty. That he wanted to believe Mary, but did not, is shown by his determination "to put her away privily" with as little embarrassment as possible. He planned to give her a letter of divorce in the presence of two witnesses only, as the

331

law permitted, rather than to make the dissolution of their contract to marry a matter of public knowledge and possible gossip. It must have been at this point that Mary sped hastily to Hebron to find comfort in the arms of Elisabeth.

Joseph pondered and prayed. Was Mary with child by the power of the Holy Ghost or in some other way? As to the true father of the unborn child, Mary knew; Elisabeth knew; Zacharias knew. They all gained their testimonies by revelation, and Joseph must now learn for himself in the same way. As we have seen, there is no way for anyone—neither Joseph, nor Mary, nor any living soul—to know and declare the generation of the Son of God, except by the whisperings of the Holy Spirit. Joseph must learn by powers beyond those exercised by mortal men that Mary's child was God's Son. Until this happened, their marriage could not be completed and their union consummated; until this occurred the Holy Family could not be perfected according to the divine plan. This knowledge must come to Joseph to prepare him to provide proper paternal influence in Mary's home during the infant and maturing years of the Son whose Father is above.

It was at this point of hope and faith that Joseph prevailed with the Lord. His prayers were answered. "The angel of the Lord appeared unto him in a dream."[1] His message: "Joseph, thou son of David"—for Joseph, like Mary, was of the house and lineage of Israel's greatest king—"Fear not to take unto thee Mary thy wife: for that which is conceived in her is [by the power] of the Holy Ghost. And she shall bring forth a son, and thou shalt call his name Jesus: for he shall save his people from their sins."

Joseph now knew! Doubt fled. The circle of true believers was growing. He had the same testimony, from the same source, as did Mary and Elisabeth and Zacharias; and, according to their law, in the mouths of two or three witnesses shall every word be established. The Lord was providing his witnesses, and soon the whole nation and the whole world would be bound to believe, and that at the peril of their salvation. How often Joseph bore the special witness that was his we do not know, but that he remained true to every trust and that he performed the mission assigned him by the Lord, there can be no doubt.

At this point Matthew—whose habit it was to note the fulfillment of the Messianic prophecies—says that all these things were done to fulfill Isaiah's promise that a virgin would bring forth a son named Emmanuel, which means "God with us," or in other words that the Son would be God in mortal flesh. "Then Joseph being raised from sleep did as the angel of the Lord had bidden him, and took unto him his wife: And knew her not till she had brought forth her firstborn son: and he called his name Jesus."

We may well suppose that Mary told Joseph of her condition; that she then went to Elisabeth; that Joseph struggled with his problem for nearly three months, being fully tested; that Gabriel brought the word; that Joseph sent word to Mary of his conversion; that she returned again in haste and joy; that immediately the second part of the marriage ceremony was performed; and that Joseph, to preserve the virginity of the one who bore God's Child, refrained from sexual association with her until after Jesus came forth as her child.

John Is Born
(Luke 1:57-63)

Zacharias is tiring of the curse he bears; Elisabeth's time has come; Mary, in her condition, to avoid the spotlight that would attend John's birth—because of his miraculous conception in Elisabeth's old age—and to be again with her beloved Joseph, has returned to Nazareth, and so now John the Baptist is born. Elisabeth's cousins and neighbors, knowing of the heavenly visitant who announced the coming of the Lord's Elias, and knowing of the great mercy the Lord had poured out upon Zacharias's wife, rejoiced with her at the blessed birth. The man child who would join Moses and the prophets, among earth's greatest souls, was now on earth. It but remained for his Lord to come, and soon the glory of the new dispensation would begin to shine forth in Israel and in all the world.

> John, than which man a sadder or a greater
>   Not till this day, has been of woman born,
> John, like some iron peak by the Creator
>   Fired with the red glow of the rushing morn—
>
> This when the sun shall rise and overcome it
>   Stands in his shining desolate and bare,
> Yet not the less the inexorable summit
>   Flamed him his signal to the happier air.[2]

Now the man child must be circumcised; it is God's law, in force since Abraham, a token, written in the flesh, of his people. "And I will establish a covenant of circumcision with thee," he had said to Abraham, "and it shall be my covenant between me and thee, and thy seed after thee, in their generations; that thou mayest know for ever that children are not accountable before me until they are eight years old." (JST, Gen. 17:11.) Little children are not accountable, but they must be brought up in the nurture and admonition of the Lord, so that when they become accountable, they will continue to walk in his paths and be saved. Circumcision is the token, cut into the flesh so that it can never be removed or forgotten, that their parents have subjected them, in advance and by proxy as it were, to the Abrahamic covenant, the covenant that assures the faithful of eternal increase, of a progeny as numerous as the sands upon the seashore or as the stars in heaven for multitude.

"By circumcision," Edersheim says, "the child had, as it were, laid upon it the yoke of the Law, with all of duty and privilege which this implied. . . . It was, so tradition has it, as if the father had acted sacrificially as High-Priest, offering his child to God in gratitude and love; and it symbolised this deeper moral truth, that man must by his own act complete what God had first instituted." The rite itself probably commenced with "a benediction," and after it had been performed "the child received his name in a prayer," offered along these lines: "Our God, and the God of our fathers, raise up this child to his father and mother, and let his name be called in Israel Zacharias, the son of Zacharias. Let his father rejoice in the issue of his loins, and his mother in the fruit of her womb," all in harmony with the various scriptures, such as: "Thy father and thy mother shall be glad, and she that bare thee shall rejoice," which scriptures were recited, along with other petitions and expressions of thanks, as part of the prayer. (Edersheim 1:157-58; Prov. 23:25.)

It was a common practice to name a firstborn son after the father. When the officiators attempted to do so in this case, Elisabeth said: "Not so; but he shall be called John." They remonstrated with her: surely she wanted to follow the custom and pattern of their fathers; surely she wanted to honor the name of the sire. "There is none of thy kindred that is called by this name," they said. "And they made signs to his father"—indicating he was deaf as well as dumb—"how he would have him called." The child's father then wrote on a tablet: "His name is John," *Jochanan,* meaning "the grace or mercy of Jehovah," in John's case the one who would go forth to proclaim the goodness and grace of the Lord and the great plan of mercy that made salvation available to the penitent.

The Benedictus
(*Luke 1:64-80; JST, Luke 1:67-78*)

Struck dumb at Gabriel's word, Zacharias was unable to give the blessing and benediction to the waiting worshippers on that fateful day in the temple in Jerusalem. Now, with the naming of John, probably in his own home in Hebron, the tongue of the dumb is loosed, and his first words are cries of praise and exultation and benediction. He picks up where he

left off more than nine months before, only this time the
Holy Spirit rests mightily upon him, and his hymn of praise
rises to glorious heights of grandeur. Zacharias's old-words
were expressions of doubt and unbelief; his new-words come
forth in tones of rapture and faith. In the interval, he has
mellowed; he has confessed his sin of unbelief; he has communed with the Lord; and he is now pliantly submissive.

Filled with the Holy Ghost, speaking as with the tongue
of angels, using language and thoughts found in the numerous Jewish benedictions that he had learned as a priest—
thus showing how one dispensation slips easily into the
next—the ancient priest burst forth with these words:

Blessed be the Lord God of Israel;
 For he hath visited and redeemed his people,
And hath raised up an horn of salvation for us,
 In the house of his servant David,
As he spake by the mouth of his holy prophets,
 Ever since the world began,
That we should be saved from our enemies,
 And from the hand of all who hate us;
To perform the mercy promised to our fathers,
 And to remember his holy covenant;
The oath which he sware to our father Abraham,
 That he would grant unto us,
That we, being delivered out of the hand of our enemies,
 Might serve him without fear,
In holiness and righteousness before him,
 All the days of our lives.

And thou, child, shalt be called the prophet of the Highest,
 For thou shalt go before the face of the Lord
To prepare his ways,
 To give knowledge of salvation unto his people,
By baptism for the remission of their sins,
 Through the tender mercy of our God;
Whereby the day-spring from on high hath visited us,
 To give light to them who sit in darkness

And the shadow of death;
To guide our feet into the way of peace.

And so, even before the old dispensation died, the first dawning rays of the new day were beginning to pierce the darkness of the past. Miracles had come again: the wondrous miracle of angelic visitation; of miraculous births; of the gift of prophecy; of God's Holy Spirit dwelling again in the hearts of men; of the Shekinah seeking entrance, as it were, to the Holy of Holies.

Gabriel had come to Zacharias, and he knew it and Elisabeth knew it and the worshippers in the temple knew it. Gabriel had come to Mary and been seen by Joseph, and they knew it. One child was born and another was already in a virgin's womb.

He was coming! The way was being prepared even before the forerunner—who must still grow and wax strong in the Spirit and wait in the deserts of Hebron for his showing to Israel—before he should cry out in Bethabara, before he should introduce the Lamb of God.

The glad tidings so far received were being heralded forth; fear was falling on those who heard the accounts, and the whole hill country of Judea, to say nothing of the mountains and valleys of Galilee—all were ablaze with the new knowledge, at the doings of the Almighty among his people.

Men were laying up the happenings of the hour in their hearts. As to John they were saying: "What manner of child shall this be!" As to the Promised Messiah, they were asking: 'When will he come?' There was an aura of expectancy. Things were building up to a climax. The forerunner had come; when would the Messiah show himself? When would the Dayspring from on high visit his people, to give light to them that sit in darkness and in the shadow of death, and to guide their feet in the way of peace?

"Surely I come quickly."
"Even so, come, Lord Jesus." (Rev. 22:20.)

NOTES

1. It was a dream and yet the angel was there. The line between dreams and visions is not clearly drawn. Lehi said: "Behold, I have dreamed a dream, or, in other words, I have seen a vision." (1 Ne. 8:2.) In general, a vision comes when one is awake, a dream while one sleeps. They may be the same, or they may differ, as the case may be. In this instance the clear inference is that the angel was there in person, as he had been when he conversed, first with Zacharias and then with Mary. It is, of course, implicit in the whole account that the angel involved was Gabriel, he having the assignment, as we suppose, to transmit the knowledge of the Savior to those immediately involved.

2. Frank W. Gunsaulus, *The Man of Galilee,* p. 27.

Chapter 20

JESUS IS BORN

Upon Judea's Plains

I stood upon Judea's plains
And heard celestial sounds and strains;
I heard an angel, free from sin,
Announce the birth of David's kin.

On shepherds watching sheep by night
There came a shining, glorious light,
As holy choirs from heaven's dome
Saw God's own Son make clay his home.

And voices sweet sang this reprise:
"To God on high, let praise arise;
And peace, good will to men on earth;
This is the day of Jesus' birth."

To me there came this witness sure:
He is God's Son, supreme and pure,
To earth he came, my soul to save,
From sin and death and from the grave.
—Bruce R. McConkie

Joseph and Mary Go to Bethlehem
(*Luke 2:1-5; JST, Luke 2:1*)

Mary—in whose womb the Child was growing, within whose flesh the Eternal One was in process of making flesh his tabernacle—dwelt in love and peace in Nazareth of Galilee. She was sheltered and steadied by the kind arm of Joseph, her husband, for the marriage was now completed; Joseph had obeyed the command of Gabriel and taken the young virgin as his wife. His name and his influence now gave comfort to the one who would soon be a mother, to the one who would bear a Son, conceived under the most unusual circumstances ever known on earth. With Joseph's name and comforting assurances she no longer feared the gossip and shame that otherwise might have attended her forthcoming ordeal.

But Bethlehem, more than eighty dusty, dreary miles away, was the destined place for the birth of the great Deliverer. So it was written by the prophets; so it must be. Out of this small place, insignificant among the villages of Judea, must come Him whose goings forth have been from of old, from everlasting. Mary knew this and Joseph knew it; both had seen an angel; both knew, by means beyond mortal comprehension, that the Holy Thing that was in her was to "be called the Son of the Highest," who should rule on the throne of David his father forever. They must go to Bethlehem and there attend to the coming forth of a Son, lest any of the Messianic prophecies, by so much as a hair's breadth, should fail.

And so to Bethlehem they went. Was it to be taxed? Yes, for Octavian—the great Caesar Augustus—had so decreed All the world must be taxed; Rome is supreme; even the chosen people must bow to the rod of Rome, silence their hatred, swallow their pride, and obey the imperial will. Caesar speaks and the world trembles. For the Palestinian part of the world, Herod will attend to the details. He is the sycophant who licks Caesar's boots for that part of the earth;

he will humor the Jews in their traditions and let them be counted and enrolled on the taxing lists in their own cities; he will decree that they return for this purpose to the tribal areas of their ancestors. Joseph and Mary—both descendants of David, both of the tribe of Judah—must enroll in the land of Judah and in the City of David, in Bethlehem.

They went to Bethlehem because they had no choice: Caesar had spoken, and Herod was echoing the word. But this was only the occasion, the vehicle, the excuse, as it were. They would have moved heaven and earth, if need be, to place themselves in the City of David when the hour arrived for the coming of the Son of David. We cannot suppose that a considerate and loving husband, having a wife big with child, would cause her to walk, or ride a slow stepping donkey, or traverse in any manner the dusty roads of Palestine, camping out overnight as they traveled—all as the hour of her confinement approached—unless there was a reason. Joseph and Mary were going to Bethlehem for a purpose. It was the one and only place where the Messiah could be born, and we cannot but suppose that they knew it and acted wittingly.

As to why they did not reside in this city of Judah in the first instance, we can only say that the providences of the Lord called for them to live in Nazareth where Joseph carpentered for a living. Jesus was to be a Nazarene; so also was it written. And as to why they did not leave Nazareth earlier, we are left to assume that Divine Providence planned a late arrival, an arrival when there would be no room in the inns, when the new baby would be brought forth under the most humble circumstances.

Jesus Is Born in a Stable
(3 Nephi 1:4-14; Luke 2:6-7; JST, Luke 2:7)

As Caesar was shuffling souls around in the Old World, and as Herod was carrying out the whims and fiats of the Roman tyrant—both unwittingly preparing the way for the birth of a King whose kingdom would break in pieces all other kingdoms and bring the whole world under righteous rule—as these things went forward in the lands of which we speak, other like commotions were in progress in the New World.

Among the Nephites in the Americas the same anxieties and expectancies prevailed as to the coming of the Son of God in the flesh as were found in the home country of the Jews. The Nephite prophets had told them plainly that the Messiah would come in six hundred years from the time that Lehi left Jerusalem. According to their calculations, the time was at hand; but among them, as among their Old World kindred, there were unbelievers who opposed and fought the truth. It is the way of the wicked to shut out light and truth and to reject the Author of them.

Unbelieving Nephites were saying that the time of the Messiah's coming was past, that the signs promised by the prophets had failed, and that the beliefs of the members of the church were pious nonsense. These rebellious and spiritually illiterate persons made "a great uproar throughout the land; and the people who believed began to be very sorrowful, lest by any means those things which had been spoken might not come to pass." The saints fasted and prayed and watched; the unbelievers set a day apart on which they would slay the saints unless the signs were manifest; and Nephi prayed mightily all the day long for the safety and deliverance of his people.

Then, in wondrous glory, the voice of the Lord came unto him, speaking these words: "Lift up your head and be of good cheer; for behold, the time is at hand, and on this night shall the sign be given, and on the morrow come I into the world, to show unto the world that I will fulfill all that which I have caused to be spoken by the mouth of my holy prophets. Behold, I come unto my own, to fulfill all things which I have made known unto the children of men from the foundation of the world, and to do the will, both of the Father and of the Son—of the Father because of me, and of the Son because of my flesh. And behold, the time is at hand, and this night shall the sign be given."[1]

And that night the sign was given, as we shall hereafter note; and that night the Son of God came into the world in Bethlehem of Judea. Of this most important of all births, Luke says simply: "And she brought forth her firstborn son, and wrapped him in swaddling clothes, and laid him in a manger, because there was none to give room for them in the inns."[2]

No room in the inns! Hospitality was universal, freely extended, and everywhere to be found. People in all walks of life took strangers into their homes, fed them, washed their feet, and cared for their beasts of burden. It was a way of life. No one can fault the Jewish practice of caring for travelers, whether they were kinfolk or strangers. Had Joseph and Mary come days earlier, they might have found lodgment in the home of a relative, a friend, or a hospitable stranger, any one of whom would have summoned a midwife and prepared a cradle for the Coming One. Had they even arrived earlier in the day, there would have been a place in the rooms or inns rather than in the court, where those beasts were tethered among whom the Coming One came.

No room in the inn—not an inn of western or modern make, but a *kahn* or place of lodgment for strangers, a *caravanserai* or place where caravans or companies of travelers bedded down for the night. It may have been a large, bare building, built of rough stones, surrounding an open court in which animals could be tied up for the night. A foot or two above this courtyard were the small recesses or "low small rooms with no front wall" where the humans tethered themselves.[3]

Of these rooms Farrar says: "They are, of course, perfectly public; everything that takes place in them is visible to every person in the kahn. They are also totally devoid of even the most ordinary furniture. The traveller may bring his own carpet if he likes, may sit cross-legged upon it for his meals, and may lie upon it at night. As a rule, too, he must bring his own food, attend to his own cattle, and draw his own water from the neighbouring spring. He would neither expect nor require attendance, and would pay only the merest trifle for the advantage of shelter, safety, and a floor on which to lie. But if he chanced to arrive late, and the *leewans* [rooms] were all occupied by earlier guests, he would have no choice but to be content with such accommodation as he could find in the court-yard below, and secure for himself and his family such small amount of cleanliness and decency as are compatible with an unoccupied corner on the filthy area, which he would be obliged to share with horses, mules, and camels. The litter, the closeness, the unpleasant smell of the crowded animals, the unwelcome intrusion of the pariah dogs, the necessary society of the very lowest hangers-on of the caravanserai, are adjuncts to such a position which can only be realised by any traveller in the East who happens to have been placed in similar circumstances." (Farrar, p. 4.)

In the area of Bethlehem, sometimes the whole kahn, sometimes only the portion where the animals were kept, was located within a large cave, of which there are many in the area. But unless or until some of the saints—and such a thing is by no means improbable or beyond the realm of expectancy—see in a dream or a vision the inn where Joseph and Mary and Jesus spent that awesome night, we can only speculate as to the details.

For the present also, we have no way of knowing how or in what manner the Babe of Bethlehem was delivered. Was there a midwife among the travelers who heard the cries of travail and came to Mary's aid? Did Mary alone wrap the swaddling clothes around her infant Son, or were there other hands to help? How were her needs cared for? Needless to say, the Gospel narratives are silent on these and a lifetime of personal matters relative to the greatest life ever lived. All we can now know—perhaps all we need to know—is that he was born in the lowest conceivable circumstances.

Though heaven was his habitation and earth his footstool, he chose to lie as an infant in a manger, surrounded by horses and camels and mules. Though he laid the foundations of the earth, and worlds without number had rolled into orbit at his word, he chose to come into mortality among the beasts of the field. Though he had worn a kingly crown in the eternal courts on high, he chose to breathe as his first mortal breath the stench of a stable. Though he would one day come forth—born then in glorious immortality—with all power in heaven and on earth, for now, as the helpless child of a peasant girl, he chose to begin the days of his probation as none of Adam's race had ever done before. And there, even in such a birth, he was rejected by his people, symbolically at least, for none in the recesses and rooms of the inn had seen fit to make room for a weary woman, great with child, who needed above all at that hour the kind hands and skill of those who had attended her cousin Elisabeth in more fortuitous circumstances.

But with it all, a God had come into mortality, inheriting from his mother the power of mortality and from his Father the power of immortality. Soon the infinite and eternal atonement—sought and desired by the righteous for four thousand years—would be a living reality. Soon all that had been hoped and promised and foreseen would come to pass. Is it any wonder that angelic choirs, even now, were awaiting the cue to sing forth great anthems of praise, some of which would be heard by shepherd ears on the nearby Judean hills!

Heavenly Manifestations Attend His Birth
(Luke 2:8-20; JST, Luke 2:12; 3 Nephi 1:15-20)

The Messiah has come, not yet to minister among men, but first to grow up as a Tender Plant in the dry ground of Palestine. When he applies to John for baptism, his forerunner will tell all Israel who he is, and apostolic witnesses will shortly thereafter begin to proclaim his divine Sonship in every city and village of that land which shall be called holy because he was born in it. But even now, while he yet lies in a manger in a stable, shall not the word begin to go forth? Is it not requisite that his fellow mortals begin to hear of his birth and to ponder its eternal import in their souls? If the infant's birth is divine, no doubt his ministry three decades later will also measure up to heaven's standards.

And Divine Providence so decreed. The birth in Bethlehem shall be known; the coming of God's Son is no secret; as soon and as often as men can receive the word, it will be given to them. For scattered Israel, separated by half a world from the sacred happenings of that hour, the word will come with sidereal majesty, so that every man among them must believe it or face the loss of his soul. For home-bound Israel, found in the surrounding fields and villages and cities, the word will come—as all gospel truths come—by the mouths of messengers who have first received their errand from the Lord, and have then been sent to tell it to their fellowmen. Those in the land where he is born and shall minister are to hear the message in the normal way because the day in which it comes to them is the day of their salvation. Those who live on the isles of the sea will see the sign of his birth written in the heavens, and they will then be expected to turn to the living oracles among them to hear the message of salvation designed for their ears. But for both the Jews and the Nephites, and for all Israel, and for all men, since he came from heaven, naught but heaven can herald the message. And such, as we shall now see, was the case.

In the Americas, Nephi had heard the voice—" the time is at hand, and on this night shall the sign be given, and on the morrow come I into the world"—and on that night the sign was given, "for behold, at the going down of the sun there was no darkness." The people were astonished. Fear fell upon them, and many fell to the earth "and became as if they were dead. . . . And it came to pass that there was no darkness in all that night, but it was as light as though it was mid-day. And it came to pass that the sun did rise in the morning again, according to its proper order; and they knew that it was the day that the Lord should be born, because of the sign which had been given."

There was no excuse for any of the inhabitants of the New World not to know of the coming of their Messiah. Samuel the Lamanite had prophesied that there would be no darkness during the night of his birth, and the promised sign had now been seen by all. When else was there ever a night when the brightness of noonday prevailed over whole continents from the going down of the sun on one day to its rising on the next?

In the Old World the message came from heaven in a different way. In the fields of Bethlehem, not far from Jerusalem and the Temple of Jehovah, there were shepherds watching their flocks by night. These were not ordinary shepherds nor ordinary flocks. The sheep there being herded—nay, not herded, but watched over, cared for with love and devotion—were destined for sacrifice on the great altar in the Lord's House, in similitude of the eternal sacrifice of Him who that wondrous night lay in a stable, perhaps among sheep of lesser destiny. And the shepherds— for whom the veil was then rent: surely they were in spiritual stature like Simeon and Anna and Zacharias and Elisabeth and Joseph and the growing group of believing souls who were coming to know, by revelation, that the Lord's Christ was now on earth. As there were many widows in Israel, and only to the one in Zarephath was Elijah sent, so there were many shepherds in Palestine, but only to those who watched over the temple flocks did the herald angel come; only they heard the heavenly choir. As Luke's idyllic language has it: "And, lo, the angel of the Lord came upon them, and the glory of the Lord shone round about them: and they were sore afraid."

"The glory of the Lord!"—a part of that ancient glory, the Shekinah, which had of old rested in the Holy of Holies and which soon would shine forth on the Holy Mount where Peter, James, and John, and Jesus would be the only mortals present!

"Sore afraid!"—holy fear; the fear of the Lord; the fear felt by Mary and by Zacharias when Gabriel came to each of them from the presence of God; the fear that leads to spiritual progression; the fear that enlarges the soul, as it is written: "The glory of the Lord is risen upon thee, . . . and thine heart shall fear, and be enlarged." (Isa. 60:1, 5.)

And the angel said unto them, Fear not: for, behold, I bring you good tidings of great joy, which shall be to all people. For unto you is born this day in the city of David a Saviour, which is Christ the Lord. And this shall be a sign unto you; Ye shall find the babe wrapped in swaddling clothes, lying in a manger.

His message delivered, the angel—was it Gabriel again?—ceased to speak; the shepherds must heed the heavenly voice, find the Savior, and then commence the infinitely great and eternally important work of taking the "good tidings of great joy . . . to all people." How they will tell the message to their wives and children! How they will explain it to their neighbors and friends, and even to strangers! How they will gather the people in the courts of the temple, at the time of the morning and evening sacrifice—when the very sheep they had cared for so tenderly are attaining their divine destiny on the holy altar— and tell their fellow Jews what they have heard from heaven! And how Anna and Simeon and other devout souls, who also wait for the Consolation of Israel, will rejoice!

But wait—the heavens are still opened to them. There is now not one angel, but many. The whole heavens resound. The music, written by celestial souls for a celestial choir and sung by celestial voices with celestial fervor, rings from one end of heaven to the other. They praise the Lord; they sing of his goodness and grace; they tell of what his arm hath done; they speak of the tree upon which he shall hang; they exult at the open door of an empty tomb; they tell of prison doors being opened, and of ransomed souls rising to eternal glory. Then in a crescendo of climax comes this glorious benediction:

Glory to God in the highest, and on earth peace, good will toward men.

Then the shepherds find the Child and begin to make known what God has revealed to them. "But Mary kept all these things, and pondered them in her heart," awaiting the day when she too will bear witness of all that she feels and believes and knows concerning the Son of David, who was born in the city of David, and who came to reign on the throne of David forever.

NOTES

1. These words, spoken in the name of the Lord Jesus, are sometimes used, erroneously, as an argument that the Spirit Christ was not in the body being prepared in Mary's womb, and that therefore the spirit does not enter the body until the moment of birth, when the mother's offspring first breathes the breath of life. This is not true.

As amply attested by the writings and teachings of President Brigham Young and others, the spirit enters the body at the time of quickening, whenever that is, and remains in the developing body until the time of birth. In a formal doctrinal statement the First Presidency of the Church (Joseph F. Smith, Anthon H. Lund, and John R. Winder) have said: "The body of man enters upon its career as a tiny germ or embryo, which becomes an infant, quickened at a certain stage by the spirit whose tabernacle it is, and the child, after being born, develops into a man." (Cited, *Mormon Doctrine*, 2nd ed., p. 17.)

With reference to the words here spoken by the Lord Jesus on the night of his birth, we must understand that someone else, speaking by what is called divine investiture of authority, is speaking the words in the first person as though he were the Lord, when in fact he is only speaking in the Lord's name. In many revelations the Son speaks in this same way as though he were the Father. For an extended analysis of this matter, see *The Promised Messiah: The First Coming of Christ*, chapter 4.

2. What is the date of our Lord's birth? This is one of those fascinating problems about which the wise and the learned delight to debate. There are scholars, of repute and renown, who place his natal day in every year from 1 B.C. to 7 B.C., with 4 B.C. being the prevailing view, if we may be permitted to conclude that there is a prevailing view. How much the answer really matters is itself a fair question, since the problem is one, in part at least, of determining whether there have been errors made in the creation of our present dating system.

We do not believe it is possible with the present state of our knowledge—including that which is known both in and out of the Church—to state with finality when the natal day of the Lord Jesus actually occurred. Elder James E. Talmage takes the view that he was born on April 6, 1 B.C., basing his conclusion on Doctrine and Covenants 20:1, which speaks of the day on which the Church was organized, saying it was "one thousand eight hundred and thirty years since the coming of our Lord and Saviour Jesus Christ in the flesh." April 6 is then named as the specific day for the formal organization. Elder Talmage notes the Book of Mormon chronology, which says that the Lord Jesus would be born six hundred years after Lehi left Jerusalem. (Talmage, pp. 102-4.)

Elder Hyrum M. Smith of the Council of the Twelve wrote in the *Doctrine and Covenants Commentary:* "The organization of the Church in the year 1830 is hardly to be regarded as giving divine authority to the commonly accepted calendar. There are reasons for believing that those who, a long time after our Savior's birth, tried to ascertain the correct time, erred in their calculations, and that the Nativity occurred four years before our era, or in the year of Rome 750. All that this Revelation means to say is that the Church was organized in the year commonly accepted as 1830, A.D." Rome 750 is equivalent, as indicated, to 4 B.C.

President J. Reuben Clark, Jr., in *Our Lord of the Gospels,* a scholarly and thoughtful work, says in his preface that many scholars "fix the date of the Savior's birth at the end of 5 B.C., or the beginning or early part of 4 B.C." He then quotes the explanation of Doctrine and Covenants 20:1 as found in the *Commentary,* notes that it has been omitted in a later edition, and says: "I am not proposing any date as the true date. But in order to be as helpful to students as I could, I have taken as the date of the Savior's birth the date now accepted by many scholars,—late 5 B.C., or early 4 B.C., because Bible Commentaries and the writings of scholars are frequently keyed upon that chronology and because I believe that so to do will facilitate and make easier the work of those studying the life and works of the Savior from sources using this accepted chronology." This is the course being followed in this present work, which means, for instance, that Gabriel came to Zacharias in October of 6 B.C.; that he came to Mary in March or April of 5 B.C.; that John was born in June of 5 B.C.; and that Jesus was born in December 5 B.C., or from January to April in 4 B.C.

To illustrate how the scholars go about determining the day of Christ's Nativity, we quote the following from Edersheim: "The first and most certain date is that of the death of Herod the Great. Our Lord was born *before* the death of Herod, and, as we judge from the Gospel-history, very shortly before that event. Now the year of Herod's death has been ascertained with, we may say, absolute certainty, as shortly before the Passover of the year 750 A.U.C., which corresponds to about the 12th of April of the year 4 before Christ, according to our common reckoning. More particularly, shortly before the death of Herod there was a lunar eclipse which, it is astronomically ascertained, occurred on the night from the 12th to the 13th of March of the year 4 before Christ. Thus the death of Herod must have taken place between the 12th of March and the 12th of April—or, say, about the end of March. Again, the Gospel-history necessitates an interval of, at the least, seven or eight weeks before that date for the birth of Christ (we have to insert the purification of the Virgin—at the earliest, six weeks after the Birth—The Visit of the Magi, and the murder of the children at Bethlehem, and, at any rate, some days more before the death of Herod). Thus the birth of Christ could not have possibly occurred after the beginning of February 4 B.C., and most likely several weeks earlier." (Edersheim 2:704.)

We should add that if the slaughter of the Innocents by Herod occurred not weeks but a year or so after our Lord's birth, as some have concluded from the recitation in Matthew 2, then this whole reasoning of Edersheim would be extended an appreciable period, so that Christ could have been born on April 6 of 5 B.C. We repeat, as President Clark repeated, that this is not a settled issue. Perhaps also it does not matter too much as long as we have an accepted framework of time within which to relate the actual events of his life, and one that gives us a reasonably accurate view of when those events took place.

3. For an explanation of the word *katalyma,* which was translated *inn* in the King James Version but was rendered as *inns* in the Joseph Smith Translation, see chapter 95. In the only other place where this word is found in the New Testament, it was translated as *guestchamber.* There is no real English equivalent.

Chapter 21

FROM BETHLEHEM TO EGYPT

For unto us a child is born, unto us a
son is given. (Isa. 9:6.)

He is thy Lord; and worship thou him.
(Ps. 45:11.)

Jesus Is Circumcised and Named
(*Luke 2:21*)

Mary's son was a Jew of the tribe of Judah into whose
flesh the sign of Abraham must be cut. He must be circumcised. When eight days old, neither before nor after, this
sacred rite must be performed. The Seed of Abraham must
have written in his flesh the token of the covenant that he
himself, as Jehovah, had made with Abraham his father. As
the Giver of the covenant he must also be the heir of its obli-
gations and of its blessings; and as we noted at the circumcision of John, the Abrahamic covenant is one of eternal
increase and exaltation for all of the faithful.

Through circumcision the male children in Israel become
subject to the law. And Jesus, one of these children, though
he came to fulfill the law, came also to obey all of its requirements; even he will conform to the law, as each event in his
life requires, until that day when it shall be nailed with him

351

to the cross, there to die, so that a new law can rise with him as he comes forth from the tomb in a newness of life. We might even be permitted to indulge the thought that Christ's blood, first shed at circumcision, was to keep the old Mosaic law, while that same blood, shed in Gethsemane and at Calvary, was to abolish the old law and bring in the new—the new law that would ever thereafter govern all men.

We do not know where or under what circumstances Jesus was circumcised. It could have been in the house in Bethlehem where Joseph and Mary now lived, or, sensing a need to gain the inspiration of a hallowed place, they could have gone the six miles to the temple in Jerusalem. But following the rite our Lord was given his mortal name. "Thou shalt call his name Jesus," were the words of Gabriel to Joseph. 'Thou, Joseph, shall give Mary's son the name Jesus, for thou art the head of the house.'

Why this name? It was a common name among the Jews then, and it has become a sacred and holy name now among all the faithful. It derives from *Hoshea,* which means *salvation;* from *Joshua,* meaning *salvation is Jehovah;* from *Jeshua* (Jesus), meaning *Jehovah is salvation.* Our Lord was so named because, as Gabriel said, "he shall save his people from their sins."

Jesus Is Presented in the Temple
(*Luke 2:22-24, 39*)

Jesus is now at least forty-one days old; the Holy Family are yet living in Bethlehem; and Joseph and Mary and "their" Son go to Jerusalem to the temple. They have two reasons: The child Jesus, as the firstborn son, must be redeemed; and Mary, having born a son, must be purified. Such was the law, to which in all points the Holy Family conformed.

When Jehovah slew the firstborn in all the homes in Egypt, from the firstborn of Pharaoh in his palace to the firstborn of the basest serf in the lowliest hovel in the land,

and when he saved alive the firstborn in every family in Israel, on whose door the saving blood had been sprinkled, he took in payment, that his goodness might be remembered to all generations, the firstborn of all the Israelites. These would be his ministers; when the sacrificial rites and other holy ordinances were performed, it would be the firstborn in every family who would minister before Jehovah. Had this provision remained in force, Jesus would have been, like Zacharias, a priest in the temple.

But later, the Levites, as a reward for special devotion and valiance, were chosen, as a tribe, to serve in the place and stead of the firstborn in all of the families of all of the tribes. These latter were to be redeemed, each individually, from their obligation of a life of priestly service by the payment of five shekels of the sanctuary. This sum Joseph paid to redeem "his" Son, and thus was accomplished the first purpose for their visit to the Holy House.

Now Mary must undergo the rite of purification; she must become ceremonially clean. For this the law requires the offering of a lamb for a burnt offering (that is, a sacrifice of service and devotion, of worship and self-surrender to the Lord) and also the offering of a turtledove or young pigeon as a sin offering (that is, as its name implies, a sacrifice for the remission of personal sins that had been committed through ignorance). Those too poor to pay for a lamb—and such was the case with Mary—could substitute another turtledove or young pigeon.

On this occasion Mary entered the Court of the Women; dropped the price of her sacrifice into one of the thirteen trumpet-shaped chests; heard the sound of the organ, announcing that incense was about to be kindled on the Golden Altar; made her way, as one for whom a special sacrifice was being offered, to a place near the Sanctuary; and there, while the ordinance was performed, offered up the unspoken prayers of praise and thanksgiving of a grateful heart. Thus she became Levitically clean.

And so Luke says: "And when they had performed all

things according to the law of the Lord, they returned into Galilee, to their own city of Nazareth."

Simeon and Anna Testify of Christ
(*Luke 2:25-38; JST, Luke 2:35-36*)

One by one—one of a city and two of a family, as it were—the circle of living witnesses of the Lord's Christ is enlarging. Others besides those involved in the birth of Jesus and of his forerunner are receiving the divine witness and being called to share the burdens always imposed upon those who know truth by the power of the Holy Spirit. Simeon and Anna are now added to the list of true believers. Had they, forty days before in those same temple courts, heard the excited words of the shepherds who saw the angel and heard the heavenly choir? Had they, "waiting for the consolation of Israel," hoped to see him in the flesh, perhaps even when his "parents" came to redeem him from the priests and to purify his mother as the law required?

This much we know: "It was revealed" unto Simeon "by the Holy Ghost, that he should not see death, before he had seen the Lord's Christ. And he came by the Spirit into the temple." This makes Simeon a prophet; he is receiving revelation; he knows what none can know except they gain it from the same Source. Luke says he was "just and devout, . . . and the Holy Ghost was upon him." He took the Child "in his arms, and blessed God, and said, Lord, now lettest thou thy servant depart in peace, according to thy word: For mine eyes have seen thy salvation, Which thou hast prepared before the face of all people; A light to lighten the Gentiles, and the glory of thy people Israel." Even now, as the first recorded testimony borne by mortal lips is heard in the courts of the Lord's Holy House, the announcement is made that salvation comes through Christ for all people; true, he is the glory of his people Israel, but he also came to bring light to the Gentiles and salvation to all people.

Then Simeon blessed Joseph and Mary, and said to

Mary: "Behold, this child is set for the fall and rising again of many in Israel; and for a sign which shall be spoken against; (Yea, a sword shall pierce through thy own soul also,) that the thoughts of many hearts may be revealed." Would that we knew all else that he spoke, including the words of blessing pronounced upon the couple in whose custody the Child was placed. Always—as we shall see throughout this whole work—there was more uttered orally to those who then lived, usually far more, than was recorded and preserved for those who should thereafter hear the accounts. At least we know that Simeon foresaw that Jesus and his message would divide the house of Israel; that men would rise or fall as they accepted or rejected his words; that he was a sign or standard around which the righteous would rally; and that Mary, who now had joy in the growing life of the infant Son, would soon be pierced with the sword of sorrow as she saw him during his waning hours on the cross of Calvary.

At this instant, Anna, a faithful widow of great age, who like the widow of Zarephath had been set apart from all the widows of Israel, came in. She bore a like testimony, for women are not one whit behind men in the receipt of spiritual gifts. She knew that Jesus was the Lord. This knowledge she would take to her grave, and this knowledge would still be with her when she saw his face again, as he ministered among the righteous in the paradise of God; there he would greet her and bless her for the witness she bore when he was yet in Mary's arms. But for now, while she yet dwelt on earth, she gave thanks unto the Lord, "and spake of him to all them that looked for redemption in Jerusalem." The witness of truth was going forth, and the seeds were being planted, from which a crop would yet be harvested, when some thirty years later his voice would call men to the kingdom he was then establishing among men.

"And Joseph and his mother marvelled at those things which were spoken of him." Though they had both seen Gabriel, and though they both knew of the divine Sonship of the Child, yet the magnitude and glory of his mortal ministry and the greatness of the work he would do among men would dawn upon them gradually.

Wise Men from the East Seek Christ
(Matthew 2:1-12; JST, Matthew 3:2-6; 3 Nephi 1:21-22)

We know that Joseph's family stayed in Bethlehem until Jesus, then more than forty days old, was presented in the temple, where Simeon and Anna acclaimed his divine Sonship. Luke, who makes no mention of the coming of the wise men from the East nor of the flight into Egypt, tells us that immediately after the temple appearance the Holy Family went to Nazareth. According to the chronology we are following—and it is the same followed by President J. Reuben Clark, Jr., in *Our Lord of the Gospels*—Jesus was born in December of 5 B.C., he was circumcised in January of 4 B.C., he was presented in the temple in February, 4 B.C., and the family probably returned to Nazareth that same month. The visit of the Magi, the flight into Egypt, and the slaughter of the Innocents, also, are all presumed to have been in February of 4 B.C. The events incident to them, of course, took place in Bethlehem.

No reason is given why Joseph took his family the 180 miles or so—on foot, by donkey, or however—from Bethlehem to Nazareth and back. Perhaps they had decided to live in the land of their ancestors, near the sacred events that already had become so much a part of their very being. Their brief return visit in Nazareth may have been to close the carpentry shop and to take leave of friends and loved ones. We have already noted the view that Zacharias was slain by Herod's order when he refused to reveal the hiding place of the child John. Since we have no reason to believe that Herod's assassins were slaying children as far away as Hebron, this gives rise to the thought that Zacharias and Elisabeth may also have chosen Bethlehem for their home. Perhaps Mary and Elisabeth desired to be near each other. It does appear that when the Holy Family returned from Egypt, Joseph intended to settle again in Bethlehem, but was sent instead by angelic decree to Nazareth.

But whatever their immediate plans were, eternal purposes were at work. There was a planned and programmed course for the newborn Messiah to follow; there was a fore-ordained destiny as to where he lived, and what he did, and how he was received by those among whom he had made flesh his tabernacle. From the eternal perspective, those of whom we speak must be in Bethlehem so that Jesus might be worshipped by the wise men from the East; so that the Innocents of Bethlehem might be slaughtered, at Herod's word; and so that the custodians of the Child might take him into Egypt, at an angel's word—all with a view to fulfilling the Messianic prophecies about the new star that should arise, about Rachel's weeping for her children, and about the Lord calling his Son out of Egypt.

There has been more speculation about, and more legends created concerning, the so-called Magi who visited Joseph and Mary in their house in Bethlehem than about almost any other biblical event. There is an air of mystery here that appeals to the speculative mind, and the fictional accounts—as to who they were, whence they came, and the symbolical meaning of all that they did—fill many volumes.

They are presumed to be kings because of the richness of their gifts; it is said they were Gentiles, showing that all nations bowed before the newborn King; it is thought they were masters of some astrological cult that could divine great happenings from the stars. They are even named, identified, and described; their ages are given, and the color of their skin; and one can, or could in times past, at least, even view their skulls, crowned with jewels, in a cathedral in Cologne. They are thought to have dealt in magic, to be magicians of a sort, and they have become great heroes of the mystical and unknown.

And the type of speculation that surrounds the men themselves applies in a degree to the star they followed. It is supposed to be a comet or a blazing new light coming from a conjunction of Jupiter and Saturn in the constellation of Pisces, or something else. Astronomers, tinged somewhat with astrology, have a field day here. And then all of it is tied back into Balaam's prophecy—"There shall come a Star out of Jacob" (Num. 24:17)—he, Balaam, being assumed to be one of the greatest Magi of them all.

As to the wise men and their stated purpose, all we learn from Matthew—and he alone records the account—is that "there came wise men from the east to Jerusalem." Their question was: "Where is he that is born King of the Jews?" Why did they ask? "We have seen his star in the east," they said, "and are come to worship him."

Who were they? We do not know, nor does anyone. How many were there? Two or more; perhaps three, perhaps twelve, or twenty; maybe a whole congregation. They may have come together; they may have come alone, or in groups.

As to the men themselves, one thing is clear. They had prophetic insight. It was with them as it had been with saintly Simeon: the Lord had revealed to them, as it were, that they should not taste death until they had seen and worshipped the Christ. They knew the King of the Jews had been born, and they knew that a new star was destined to arise and had arisen in connection with that birth. The probability is they were themselves Jews who lived, as millions of Jews then did, in one of the nations to the East. It was the Jews, not the Gentiles, who were acquainted with the scriptures and who were waiting with anxious expectation for the coming of a King. And that King was to come to them first; he was to deliver his message to them before it went to the Gentile world, and his first witnesses were to come from his own kinsmen, from the house of Israel, not from the Gentile nations, not from the nations composed of those who knew not God and who cared nothing for the spirit of prophecy and revelation found among the Lord's people.

As to the star, there is nothing mysterious about it. The Magi, if so they are to be designated, were not reading portents in the skies nor divining the destinies of men by the movement of celestial bodies in the sidereal heavens. The new star was simply a new star of the sort we are familiar with. No doubt it exhibited an unusual brilliance, so as to attract special attention and so as to give guidance to those who walked in its light, but it was, nonetheless, a star. There was among the Jews of that day a prophecy that such a star would arise at the time of Messiah's coming, and these men who came to Jerusalem in search of that Holy Person had seen and identified the star by the spirit of inspiration. Edersheim quotes from the ancient Jewish writings relative to the prophetic knowledge then had as to such a Messianic star. One such writing says: "A star shall come out of Jacob. . . . The star shall shine forth from the East, and this is the Star of the Messiah." Another said that "a Star in the East was to appear two years before the birth of the Messiah." (Edersheim 1:211-12.)

That these traditions were true, we know from the Book of Mormon account. Samuel the Lamanite prophesied that at our Lord's birth "great lights in heaven" should appear; that during a whole night it should remain light, "And behold, there shall a new star arise, such an one as ye never have beheld; and this also shall be a sign unto you." (Hel. 14:2-6.) The fulfillment of this prophecy is stated in these simple words: "And it came to pass also that a new star did appear, according to the word."

The appearance of these wise men, whose credibility was not questioned, sent a tide of concern through all Jerusalem that grew into a flood of paranoiac proportions in the palace itself. "Herod the Great, who, after a life of splendid misery and criminal success, had now sunk into the jealous decrepitude of his savage old age, was residing in his new palace in Zion, when, half maddened as he was already by the crimes of his past career, he was thrown into a fresh paroxysm of alarm and anxiety by the visit of some Eastern Magi, bearing the strange intelligence that they had seen in the East the star of a new-born king of the Jews, and had come to worship him. Herod, a mere Idumæan usurper, a more than suspected apostate, the detested tyrant over an unwilling people, the sacrilegious plunderer of the tomb of David— Herod, a descendant of the despised Ishmael and the hated Esau, heard the tidings with a terror and indignation which it was hard to dissimulate. The grandson of one who, as was believed, had been a mere servitor in a temple at Ascalon, and who in his youth had been carried off by Edomite brigands, he well knew how worthless were his pretensions to an historic throne which he held solely by successful adventure. But his craft equalled his cruelty, and finding that all Jerusalem shared his suspense, he summoned to his palace the leading priests and theologians of the Jews— perhaps the relics of that Sanhedrin which he had long reduced to a despicable shadow—to inquire of them where the Messiah was to be born. He received the ready and confident answer that Bethlehem was the town indicated for that honour by the prophecy of Micah. Concealing, therefore, his desperate intention, he dispatched the wise men to Bethlehem, bidding them to let him know as soon as they had found the child, that he too might come and do him reverence." (Farrar, pp. 19-20.)

Guided by the light of the star, but guided even more surely by the light of that Spirit which had directed their steps from the beginning, the wise men found "the young child with Mary his mother" in the house where the Holy Family then dwelt. There is no indication whether Joseph was present, although it is presumed he was. There they worshipped the Lord Jesus, gave him "gold, and frankincense, and myrrh. And being warned of God in a dream that they should not return to Herod, they departed into their own country another way." They were still receiving revelation and guidance from on high.

And thus ends our sure knowledge of the wise men from the East. The Lord guided them to Jerusalem; they bore a witness before Herod that would not have been heeded had it come from a Simeon or an Anna, or from simple shepherds, claiming to have seen an angel and to have heard angelic choirs; and they returned to their homeland, still guided from beyond the veil and basking in the light of Him in whose presence they had knelt. We can assume they went back to their own people to testify—as Simeon and Anna had gone out among their own people—that the King of Israel, the Light to lighten the Gentiles, now dwelt upon earth. Truly, there is a divine providence attending the witness that is now beginning to go forth of the birth of a King who three short decades hence shall ask, first, Israel, and then all men, to let him reign in their hearts.

Herod Slays the Innocents
(Matthew 2:13-18; JST, Matthew 3:13-14)

We come now to one of the crowning acts of infamy and evil of Herod's infamous and evil reign, and yet the blood he is now to shed will scarce add to the crimson pool that stinks and smells at his palace door. "His whole career was red with the blood of murder. He had massacred priests and nobles; he had decimated the Sanhedrin; he had caused the High Priest, his brother-in-law, the young and noble Aristobulus, to be drowned in pretended sport before his eyes; he had ordered the strangulation of his favorite wife, the beautiful Asmonæan princess Mariamne, though she seems to have been the only human being whom he passionately loved. His sons Alexander, Aristobulus, and Antipater—his uncle Joseph—Antigonus and Alexander, the uncle and father of his wife—his mother-in-law Alexandra—his kinsman Cortobanus—his friends Dositheus and Gadias, were but a few of the multitudes who fell victims to his sanguinary, suspicious, and guilty terrors. His brother Pheroras and his son Archelaus barely and narrowly escaped execution by his orders. Neither the blooming youth of the prince Aristobulus nor the white hairs of the king Hyrcanus had protected them from his fawning and treacherous fury. Deaths by strangulation, deaths by burning, deaths by being cleft asunder, deaths by secret assassination, confessions forced by unutterable torture, acts of insolent and inhuman lust, mark the annals of a reign which was so cruel that, in the energetic language of the Jewish ambassadors to the Emperor Augustus, 'the survivors during his lifetime were even more miserable than the sufferers.' . . . Every dark and brutal instinct of his character seemed to acquire fresh intensity as his life drew towards its close. Haunted by the spectres of his murdered wife and murdered sons, agitated by the conflicting furies of remorse and blood, the pitiless monster, as Josephus calls him, was seized in his last days by a black and bitter ferocity, which broke out against all with whom he came in contact." (Farrar, pp. 32-33.)

Augustus Caesar himself said of Herod: "It is better to be Herod's pig than his son," which in the language spoken was a pun, and meant that since Herod was a Jew, he could not kill and eat his pig and it would therefore be safer than his son. Truly, it is as though the most fiendish and bloody occupant ever to sit on David's throne was its occupant in the very day when He came whose throne it was, and who would in due course reign in righteousness thereon.

And so, in this setting, the angel commanded Joseph: "Arise, and take the young child and his mother, and flee into Egypt, and be thou there until I bring thee word: for Herod will seek the young child to destroy him."

They fled by night. Then Herod in his hate and bitterness, acting as though Satan himself possessed his soul, went forth "and slew all the children that were in Bethlehem, and in all the coasts thereof, from two years old and under, according to the time which he had diligently inquired of the wise men."[1]

How the work of slaughter went forward we do not know. Recognizing Herod's penchant for intrigue and secrecy, and recalling that the soldiers slew Zacharias because he would not reveal the desert hiding place of the infant John, we assume that the children were ferreted out by assassins and informers, who went as Judases in disguise. Both Edersheim and Farrar conclude that the number slain did not exceed twenty. But whatever the number, the cries of weeping parents, relatives, and friends—in fulfillment of Jeremiah's prophecy concerning Rachel and her children—ascended up to the Lord, by whom they will be replayed in Herod's ears when he is brought before the bar of the Great Jehovah to give account of the deeds done in the flesh.

"Out of Egypt Have I Called My Son"
(Matthew 2:15, 19-23; JST, Matthew 3:19, 22)

How wondrous are the similitudes and the shadows used by the Lord to teach the great truths of his eternal plan!

How aptly he has chosen the ordinances and guided the historical happenings that testify and bear record of those things upon which the minds of men should dwell!

Lehi says to Laman: "O that thou mightest be like unto this river, continually running into the fountain of all righteousness!" and to Lemuel: "O that thou mightest be like unto this valley, firm and steadfast, and immovable in keeping the commandments of the Lord!" (1 Nephi 2:9-10)—hoping that his eldest sons, as they drink from the river and dwell in the valley, will remember the eternal truths for which they have been made a symbol.

Jacob gives his son Joseph a coat of many colors; a blood-stained coat remnant is later taken to Jacob with the false tale that its owner has been destroyed by wild beasts; and Jacob, as he handles the part of the garment that "was preserved and had not decayed," prophesies: "Even as this remnant of garment of my son hath been preserved, so shall a remnant of the seed of my son be preserved by the hand of God, and be taken unto himself, while the remainder of the seed of Joseph shall perish, even as the remnant of his garment" (Alma 46:24)—all to the end that whenever the seed of Joseph think upon the coat, upon the sale of their ancestor to the Ishmaelites, and upon the wondrous work he wrought in Egypt, they will rejoice also in the goodness of the Lord to his seed in the latter days.

Moses raises a brazen serpent on a pole before all Israel, even as the Son of God shall be lifted up, so that "as many" of those bitten by the poisonous serpents "as should look upon that serpent should live, even so as many as should look upon the Son of God with faith, having a contrite spirit, might live, even unto that life which is eternal" (Hel. 8:13-15)—all with a purpose of centering the hearts of the people upon the atoning sacrifice of the Son of God.

Abraham takes Isaac, his only begotten son, up upon Mount Moriah, there to sacrifice him at the Lord's command; and Isaac, reputed by Jewish tradition to be thirty-seven years of age at the time, submits willingly to his father's will—all as "a similitude of God and his Only Begotten Son." (Jacob 4:5.)

And now Joseph, as directed by an angel, takes Jesus into Egypt for a short season, "that it might be fulfilled which was spoken of the Lord by the prophet, saying, Out of Egypt have I called my son"—all to the end that whenever Israel remembers how God had delivered them with a mighty hand from the bondage of Egypt, they will think also that the Son of God was called out of Egypt to deliver them from the bondage of sin.

All Israel went down into Egypt to save themselves from death by famine, even as the infant Jesus was taken down into Egypt to save him from an assassin's sword. As the Lord's chosen people came out of Egypt into a land of promise to receive his law and walk in his paths, so his Beloved and Chosen came out of Egypt into that same promised land to dispense the new law and invite the chosen seed to walk in the appointed course.

In the minds of ancient Israel there was no greater miracle than their mighty deliverance from Egypt: a deliverance made possible by an outpouring of plagues upon Pharaoh's people; a deliverance assured by the saving power of a wall of water on the right hand and a wall of water on the left, as Moses led them through the Red Sea; a deliverance made effective because the Lord rained bread from heaven upon them lest they die from famine.

But now, in the minds of all men, there should be the thought of an even greater deliverance: a deliverance from the chains of sin; a deliverance from death, hell, the devil, and endless torment; a deliverance from mortality to immortality; a deliverance from spiritual death to eternal life—all through the great Deliverer, who like Israel of old overcame the Egypt of the world to dwell in the promised land.

And so Joseph, having saved Jesus by taking him into Egypt, now brings him back to Palestine that he might bring salvation to all men. Again it is at angelic direction. Herod the wicked king is dead; that much Joseph learns from the angel. He returns to Palestine, with the apparent purpose of settling in Bethlehem. Then he learns what the angel had not divulged: Archelaus reigns in Judea, "in the room of his father Herod." And so, warned again in a dream—and how providential it was that Joseph was spiritually attuned to the Infinite—"he came and dwelt in a city called Nazareth: that it might be fulfilled which was spoken by the prophets, He shall be called a Nazarene."

Jesus, the Lord of Life, has now taken upon himself mortal life. His conception, his birth, his circumcision, his flight into Egypt, his return to Nazareth—all have followed the foreordained plan. His forerunner is now growing up in the deserts of Judea. His witnesses—Zacharias, Elisabeth, Mary, Joseph, the shepherds, Simeon, Anna, the wise men from the East, and many who have believed on their words—all are letting it be known, "to all them that look for redemption," that the day of the Deliverer is at hand. It now remains but for him to mature and prepare, in Nazareth or elsewhere as his Father intends.

NOTES

1. Children are counted as being two years of age until they attain their third birthday. Apparently the decree of slaughter included all those who were two years of age and younger. Since Matthew expressly states, twice in the account, that the age of slaughter was determined by the time the wise men saw the star, which event coincided with the birth of the King, it appears the young Jesus could have been as old as two years and some months at this time. The usually accepted chronology makes him two or three months old. If his birth were placed a year or more back from December, 5 B.C., it would mean that the Holy Family stayed in Nazareth for the added period before returning to Bethlehem, which of course is a distinct possibility.

Chapter 22

FROM INFANCY TO MANHOOD

Jesus . . . made himself of no
reputation, and took upon him the form
of a servant, and was made in the
likeness of men: And being found in
fashion as a man, he humbled himself,
and became obedient unto death, even
the death of the cross. (Philip. 2:5-8.)

And he received not of the fulness at
first, but continued from grace to grace,
until he received a fulness.
(D&C 93:13.)

Jesus Grows from Infancy to Manhood
(JST, Matthew 3:24-26; Luke 2:40, 51-52.)

Jesus walked the same road from infancy to manhood
that has been trod by every adult mortal, from first to last,
who ever breathed the breath of life. There is only one way
for a mortal to be born, to grow to maturity, to pass into the
great beyond; and we are left to suppose that every law of
mortal life applied to the mortal Son of the mortal Mary.

Our Lord's physical body, conceived in Mary's womb,

partook of Mary's nature; mortal genes, if you will, passed from mother to Son. His features, stature, and general appearance were passed on as much by his mortal mother as by his immortal Father. He was as much the product of the mother who bare him as were her other children. As a babe he began to grow, normally and naturally, and there was nothing supernatural about it. He learned to crawl, to walk, to run. He spoke his first word, cut his first tooth, took his first step—the same as other children do. He learned to speak; he played with toys like those of his brothers and sisters; and he played with them and with the neighbor children. He went to sleep at night and he awoke with the morning light. He took exercise, and his muscles were strong because he used them. During his ministry we see him walk long dusty miles, climb mountains, drive evil men—with force—from his Father's House.

We cannot do other than believe he was subject to disease and illness on the same basis as we all are. We know he was hungry, weary, and sorrowful; that his eyes were keen, his ears alert, and his tongue fluent. We know he seemed to his enemies as but another man, that he had to be singled out and identified with a traitor's kiss, and that he felt the stabbing pain of the Roman nails in his hands and feet the same as any mortal would. We cannot state too plainly that as a man he felt what other men feel, did what other men do, had the same appetites and passions as others have—all because he had been sent into mortality by his Father to be a mortal.

And as with our Lord's physical growth and development, so with his mental and spiritual progression. He learned to speak, to read, to write; he memorized passages of scripture, and he pondered their deep and hidden meanings. He was taught in the home by Mary, then by Joseph, as was the custom of the day. Jewish traditions and the provisions of the Torah were discussed daily in his presence. He learned the Shema, reverenced the Mezuzah, and participated in prayers, morning, noon, and night. Beginning at five or six he went to school, and certainly continued to do so until he came a son of the law at twelve years of age.

On Sabbaths and on week days he attended the synagogue, heard the prayers and sermons, and felt the spirit of the occasion. He participated in the regular worship during the feasts, particularly at Passover time. Indeed, the whole Jewish way of life was itself a teaching system, one that made the Jews a unique and peculiar people, a people set apart from all the nations of the Gentiles. It is also apparent that Jesus learned much from nature—from observing the lilies of the field, the birds of the air, and the foxes that have holes for homes.

It seems perfectly clear that our Lord grew mentally and spiritually on the same basis that he developed physically. In each case he obeyed the laws of experience and of learning, and the rewards flowed to him. The real issue of concern is not that he grew and developed and matured—all in harmony with the established order of things, as is the case with all men—but that he was so highly endowed with talents and abilities, so spiritually sensitive, so in tune with the Infinite, that his learning and wisdom soon excelled that of all his fellows. His knowledge came to him quickly and easily, because he was building—as is the case with all men—upon the foundations laid in preexistence. He brought with him from that eternal world the talents and capacities, the inclinations to conform and obey, and the ability to recognize truth that he had there acquired. Mozart had musical ability at the age of six that only a handful of men have ever gained in a whole lifetime. Jesus, when yet a child, had spiritual talents that no other man in a hundred lifetimes could obtain.

Further: In his study, and in the learning process, he was guided from on high in a way that none other has ever been. Being without sin—being clean and pure and spotless—he was entitled to the constant companionship of the Holy Spirit, the Spirit that will not dwell in an unclean tabernacle, the Spirit that, conversely, always and everlastingly dwells with the righteous. The Holy Ghost is a revelator and a sanctifier. Anyone who receives the Holy Ghost receives revelations; anyone who obtains the companionship of the Holy Spirit is sanctified. Of the Lord Jesus the scripture says: "God giveth not the Spirit by measure unto him" (John 3:34), which is to say that he enjoyed, at all times, the fulness of that light and guidance and power which comes by the power of the Holy Ghost to the faithful.

With reference to Jesus' early years—those before he went to the temple at the age of twelve to discuss the doctrines of salvation with the Rabbis—Luke tells us: "And the child grew, and waxed strong in spirit, filled with wisdom: and the grace of God was upon him." We shall glimpse the wisdom here named when we assay to determine what was in the mind of the young lad as he traveled to Jerusalem, as he participated in the Passover, and as he, remaining behind, conversed with the learned of the land. As our discussion shall then show, we cannot escape the conclusion that the knowledge then manifest in the temple had been gained gradually during the years that went before.

With reference to Jesus' latter years of preparation—those between twelve and thirty—Luke says: "And Jesus increased in wisdom and stature, and in favour with God and man." Of the developing and maturing years of our Lord's life, Matthew tells us:

> And it came to pass that Jesus grew up with his brethren, and waxed strong, and waited upon the Lord for the time of his ministry to come. And he served under his father, and he spake not as other men, neither could he be taught; for he needed not that any man should teach him. And after many years, the hour of his ministry drew nigh.

This wondrous exposition—"he needed not that any man should teach him"—applies to a degree to all of the prophets of all of the ages. They are taught from on high. A single glimpse beyond the veil reveals more of heaven and its laws than all the sermons of uninspired preachers combined. One flash of inspiration is worth more than all the causistry of the

Mishnah. All the traditions of the Talmud sink into darkness before one ray of revealed truth. There is no substitute for the gift of the Holy Ghost.

One day soon, the people of Nazareth, among whom he matured and by whom he was known, will ask: "Whence hath this man this wisdom?" And the answer, though not then given, will be: 'In the same way as all the prophets. He labored and studied and struggled; he treasured up words of light and truth; he pondered the scriptures—all under the influence of the Holy Spirit of God, which came to him without measure and without limit, because he was clean and pure and upright.'

The Passover Journey to Jerusalem
(Luke 2:41-42)

Jesus, now twelve, a son of the law, goes with Joseph and Mary from Nazareth to Jerusalem to keep the Passover. It is April of A.D. 8. His parents went every year, and Jesus may have been with them on some or all of these prior occasions. But this year is different: he is now a son of the law; his voice can legally be heard, and he is about to raise it among the doctors of the law, whose self-assumed wisdom knows no bounds, as they suppose.

This appearance in the temple is the sole New Testament record of any of our Lord's acts in the thirty years from Bethlehem to Bethabara. The Gospels are not biographies of Jesus; they are a collection of faith-promoting accounts from the Savior's ministry that, if believed, will induce receptive souls to come unto Christ and partake of his goodness.

President J. Reuben Clark, Jr.—than whom the Church has produced no greater scholar on all matters pertaining to the life of our Lord—has written a small booklet, less than one hundred pages, *Wist Ye Not That I Must Be About My Father's Business,* in which he traces Jesus' steps from Nazareth to Jerusalem and tells of the sacrifices in the temple; of the slaying of the Paschal lamb; of the eating of the Passover meal; of the Feast of Unleavened Bread; and of the doings of Jesus in the temple courts with the doctors. We have heretofore discussed the offering of sacrifices and the keeping of the feasts, and it is now our purpose, through the eyes of President Clark, to place Jesus in the sacrificial and festive setting of the Passover, in order to determine how much he then knew of his divine mission and the extent of the spiritual insight that already was his.

Joseph, Mary, Jesus, and their fellow worshippers from Nazareth begin their pilgrimage to Jerusalem. "As we think of them moving slowly down into the valley with their donkeys laden with necessary supplies," President Clark says, "picking their way among the boulders that strewed the path, we cannot escape wondering what were the thoughts of Jesus. That He was exceeding wise, the experience in the Temple shows. But was this wisdom earthborn from His studies, or did He have also a spiritual memory that brought to Him a recollection of all that had before happened, and a vision to show what was thereafter to happen along this road to Jerusalem, a road richer in incidents of God's dealings with His children, than any other road on the face of the earth? . . .

"One wonders if, as He came to Nain, He saw a vision of His future miracle of kindness there. . . .

"When He came to the neighborhood of Jezreel, did He see in vision the disastrous defeat of Josiah on the plain of Esdraelon by Pharaoh Necho, at Megiddo, a defeat so terrible and worked so deeply into the Hebrew heart, that John speaks of the great last battle as Armageddon—'the Hill of Megiddo?' Or did He see the earlier conflict in the time of the Judges, when Barak, Deborah the prophetess guiding, defeated Sisera, leading the forces of Jabin, on that same plain of Esdraelon, and did He see again the deed of Jael afterwards? And did there also come before Him the iniquities and tragic fate of Ahab and Jezebel, and the Lord's vengeance worked through Elijah against the priests of Baal, and the flight of Elijah to Carmel, the passing of the Lord

372

before Elijah in the 'still small voice'? For Jesus was the Lord who spoke to and commanded His ancient prophets."

Then, in the course of a recitation of many other great events in Israel's history, President Clark—no longer using questions, but making affirmative declarations—says: "What must have been the feelings of the young Jesus as he looked at this present magnificence and then recalled the past, and (it seems it must be) visioned the future! . . . for we must believe there was with Him a spiritual recollection, a divine knowledge, of the past. . . . As Jesus looked at all these, . . . there must have crowded in upon his consciousness the scenes of the actual events."

As the pilgrims pass Jacob's Well, the question is asked: "As at twelve He now beheld the well, did He vision the future meeting with the woman [of Samaria] and His sermon on the living water?" And finally, as they come near to their destination, President Clark says: "We must believe that Joseph and Mary, and the youth Jesus, of the royal lineage of David, had awaiting them somewhere a joyous welcome from friends honored in the chance to give them food and shelter. One cannot escape the question whether they went on to Bethany, eastward of Jerusalem, for their lodgings, to the home where in the years to come Jesus spent so many happy hours in a home that loved and honored Him.

"Did the youth Jesus know the youth Lazarus, and the maidens, Mary and Martha?

"Or did they go to Bethlehem, where twelve years before the Messiah was born in a manger?"[1]

Jesus Participates in the Passover

In chapter 8 we considered the Mosaic sacrificial performances of Jesus' day, and in chapter 9, the Jewish feasts of that day, including the Feast of the Passover. We need not here repeat the rites and performances—intricate and detailed almost beyond belief—that appertain to their sacrifices and feasts. President Clark, of course, summarizes them in the work from which we now quote. From time to time in the course of his summary, he comes again to the concept, which seems to weigh heavily upon him, that even then, the deacon-age Jesus—scarce younger, however, than Joseph Smith, or Moroni, or Nephi, and perhaps not any younger at all than Samuel, when the Lord used these youths for his purposes—even then he was heir to the visions of eternity on a continuing basis. From various places out of long recitations about the sacrifices and the Passover, we take these words of President Clark:

"One can but ponder what the thoughts of Jesus were as He watched all this preparation for the sacrifice. Had He then the foresight of the preparation for His Last Supper, preceding His own crucifixion, such foresight as He had in the garden when He prayed: 'Father, if thou be willing, remove this cup from me: nevertheless not my will, but thine, be done.' Did He recall the day, generations before, that He gave commandment to Adam to offer sacrifice, when, under His direction, the angel told Adam the purpose of sacrifice: 'This thing is a similitude of the sacrifice of the Only Begotten of the Father, which is full of grace and truth.' . . .

"Again the thought thrusts itself upon us—what could have been the Youth's thoughts as He came into all this? As He crossed the Royal Bridge, did He see the morning of His arraignments; as He came in among the money changers, did He see how He cleansed the Temple of them, first at the beginning and again at the end of His public ministry? . . .

"Again, we can but wonder what thoughts passed through the mind of the divinely begotten Youth as He saw all this, and realized, as He must, that all of it was, in some measure, symbolic of the sacrifice He Himself was to make. His mortal eyes must have been dazzled by the pomp and splendor of it all; His mortal mind could hardly have escaped some confusion. But His spiritual eyes and intelligence must have looked through it all, and have seen to

374

the very foundations of all its meanings—the Fall, the death, spiritual and temporal, the Gospel plan to redeem from the spiritual death, His own atonement to redeem from the temporal death. He knew the truth: 'For as in Adam all die, even so in Christ shall all be made alive.' . . .

"So Joseph and Jesus, tired after a long day of standing on the marble pavement of the Temple—it would be particularly wearisome for country folk—and laden with the lamb for the evening Paschal supper (which Joseph would carry on his shoulder) would prepare to wend their way through the city streets, and it may be out into the country, back to where Mary and the friends with whom they would later eat the Paschal meal were awaiting their return.

"So Jesus, bodily wearied by the long day during which he too may have fasted, trudged alongside Joseph as they left the Temple enclosure on their way to eat the Paschal supper. . . .

"Scholars believe that this was Jesus' first visit to the Passover; but there is nothing in the scriptural record specifically so stating, and the conclusion is apparently founded upon the fact, already alluded to, that at twelve years a boy became 'a son of the law' subject to the fasts and under obligation to attend the feasts.

"On the other hand, we have the fact that Jesus' 'parents went to Jerusalem every year at the feast of the passover,' and if they were so faithful in performing this commandment, one may well assume they would follow the other command of the Lord to instruct their children [more children than Jesus would be involved], at the Paschal supper, in the meaning of the ceremony, and this they could not do if Jesus [and the others] were not present at the Paschal feast.

"So, with all deference to the scholars, one may be bold to suggest that Jesus had several times before partaken of the Paschal meal in Jerusalem, and so, as He now went wearily to their lodgings, He looked eagerly forward to the eating of the satisfying supper, with its accompanying spiritual experiences. For nothing must be eaten after the offering of the evening sacrifice until the Passover meal.

"But here also, as at every incident in this whole ceremonial, one cannot escape pondering how much of the past was in Jesus' mind. . . .

"One cannot forego again wondering what might have passed through the mind of the youth Jesus. Did He know that this day was the pre-anniversary of the day, some twenty-one years thence, when He should be again in parts of these precincts, that He would be hurried and harried from Annas to Caiaphas, then to the illegal gathering of the elders, to the Sanhedrin, to Pilate, to Herod, and back to Pilate, and then to Calvary and crucifixion; did He now know the scorn, the envy, the malice, the murderous hate that drove forward the High Priest, the chief priests, the elders, and all the Council, and indeed the whole maddened multitude in their demand for His crucifixion; did He see Pilate wash his hands before the seething, cursing mass, and hear Pilate say: 'I am innocent of the blood of this just person,' and hear the people shout their own terrible penalty in reply: 'His blood be on us, and on our children'; did He now sense the agony of spirit in the Garden, and of His body on the cross—did He know and see all this which twenty-one years thence was to happen on this very day and, in part, in these very purlieus? Did His own mission, His own destiny, His own sacrifice, His own atonement rise before Him as a vision of Himself, the Son of God? . . .

"Still again we must wonder whether, as the shadows lengthened and the sun sank in the west, while the full moon rose from the Jordan, as Joseph and Jesus again plodded, after another long day, to their lodgings in the city, in Bethany, or it may be in Bethlehem, did the Youth see and know, on this pre-anniversary of a day yet to come, the grief He was to suffer, the spiritual and physical agony He was to endure, the death that was to come to Him, as He was sacrificed as the Lamb of God to atone for the transgression of Adam, for, by the Fall and through the Atonement man was to meet his destiny?"[2]

In their original setting, these quotations from President Clark are interlaced with long descriptions and explanations of the festive procedures followed at the Passover, and the Feast of Unleavened Bread that followed and was in large measure part of the Paschal feast itself. In more than a dozen instances President Clark asks whether or asserts positively that we must believe that the young Jesus—even then, and though but twelve years of age—had past- and prevision of those things which had been in Israel and would be in the life of Israel's Chief Citizen. This approach, so ably followed by him whom we are quoting—though necessarily speculative, as so many of the biographical pronouncements concerning Jesus must be—is an ideal pattern. We shall feel free to walk in the same path as we consider the mortal doings of the Son of an immortal Father.

Jesus, Now Twelve, Teaches in the Temple
(*Luke 2:43-50*)

After the first two days of the feast the pilgrims were free to return to their villages and cities and resume their temporal pursuits. Either then, or when the whole week was past, Joseph and Mary, with their other children and kinsmen, their friends and fellow worshippers, began the journey back to Nazareth. The spirit of rejoicing and exultation poured out through the Passover period rested upon them; there was thanksgiving in their hearts for the testimonies that were theirs, and for the goodness of Jehovah to his people Israel.

But Jesus was not with them. He, now a son of the law—with deliberation; stirred by the spirit of Passover worship of which he had been a part; recognizing in the sacrificial similitudes his own coming sacrifice; knowing his divine destiny; moved upon by the Holy Spirit, who was his monitor and guide—Jesus, unbeknown to his parents, remained behind. Thinking he was in the company, his parents did not miss him until nightfall. Then, anxious, troubled, worried for his well-being, they hastened back to the Holy City. For three long, wearisome days, days of prayer and self-reproach, they sought him—perhaps in Bethlehem and Bethany, and in all the places and among all the people known to him in Jerusalem—and then, in the one place where they should have looked first, in his Father's house, they found him. He was seated among the doctors, the Rabbis, the scribes, the learned teachers, "both hearing them, and asking them questions. And all that heard him were astonished at his understanding and answers."

Jesus was at home in his Father's House. He felt at ease; the spirit of wisdom and understanding rested mightily upon him. We suppose he had many conversations with many people within the sacred walls of the temple. He was on his own home ground, and in these very courts he would yet make some of the most profound and soul-saving declarations ever to fall from mortal lips. And it was now, as it would be then, he was master of the situation.

We wonder what subjects he talked about. The Paschal celebration was on everyone's minds. Did he speak of the Paschal lambs slain in similitude of the sacrifice of the Lamb of God who should take away the sins of the world? Surely Mary, by now, had told him of his birth and of the miracles that attended. Did he ask the wise men of Israel about the Son, born of a virgin, who should reign forever on the throne of David? Surely he felt the divine necessity to begin to let people know of his divine mission. Did he then inquire as to when the Messiah should come and how he should be known?

Truth is sent forth line upon line, precept upon precept, here a little and there a little. We cannot doubt that the youthful Jesus—as Simeon and Anna and the wise men of the East, and all the others, had already done—was himself now beginning to teach and to testify. His formal and legal ministry cannot begin for another eighteen years. For the time being he is to go back to Nazareth and be subject to Joseph and Mary. He is to mature and grow in the Spirit and find favor with God and man. He is to partake of the normal life of Jewish men, doing what they did, enjoying the familial associations that were part of their culture, and gaining all the experiences he would need for the arduous hours of his formal ministry.

We do not even know that he lived all those intervening years in Nazareth; he was surely not subject to Joseph and Mary, eating at their table and sleeping in their house, during his more mature years. Perhaps he dwelt in Bethany, in the city of Mary and Martha and Lazarus, for a time, or in Bethlehem where he first came into this life.

We cannot believe that he was silent all those years. He spoke at twelve; was his tongue then tied until he was thirty? If he felt the need to be about his Father's business as soon as he became a son of the law, would he feel that urgency any less as he continued to mature and grow in wisdom and stature and learn even more of his Father's will?

But back to the temple. Finding him among the learned, teaching and being taught, his parents, strangely, were amazed. Had they forgotten the miracle of his birth, and had they not observed the talents and abilities that so precociously were his? Mary, not Joseph, gently chided: "Son, why hast thou thus dealt with us? behold, thy father and I have sought thee sorrowing." In the family circle, subject to the family discipline of the day, Joseph was deemed to be the father of all Mary's children, Jesus included. Mary here so says; others at a later time will call him, derogatorily, the carpenter's son. There is a sweet family tenderness here in Mary's reference to Joseph as the father of Jesus.

Jesus, however, is now ministering in the temple as his real Father's Son, not as a member of Joseph's household. "How is it that ye sought me?" he asks. "Wist ye not that I must be about my Father's business?" His Father's business is to bring to pass the immortality and eternal life of man, both of which will come to pass through the atoning sacrifice that Jesus will make as the climax of his ministry. But that is twenty-one years away; for now he must return to Nazareth and be subject to those into whose custody he has been placed. Luke says these custodians "understood not the saying which he spake unto them," meaning that even they, though they knew the miracle of his birth and had full knowledge of his true Father, found it difficult to comprehend the greatness of his wisdom and his rapid growth toward the full stature of that man-God status that was his. He was going from grace to grace, from one level of intelligence to another, from a lesser to a higher degree. Soon he would inherit all power in heaven and on earth. His growth, even at twelve, had attained such proportions that it is little wonder Joseph and Mary were amazed and could not comprehend the full significance of his sayings.

NOTES

1. J. Reuben Clark, *Wist Ye Not That I Must Be About My Father's Business?* (Salt Lake City: Relief Society Magazine, n.d.), pp. 9-17.
2. Ibid., pp. 23-70 *passim.*

Chapter 23

JOHN PREPARES THE WAY

Behold, I will send my messenger, and
he shall prepare the way before me.
(Mal. 3:1.)

Prepare ye the way of the Lord, . . . And
the glory of the Lord shall be revealed.
(Isa. 40:3, 5.)

John Receives the Word of God
(Luke 3:1-2)

As the dawn comes before the day, so John comes before
Jesus. The long night of rituals and rites; of performances;
of sacrifices and blood; of bleating sheep cringing near an
altar, awaiting the sacrificial knife; of a law that decrees an
eye for an eye and a tooth for a tooth—the long night of
Mosaic formalisms is drawing to its close.

Faint rays of morning light break forth in the eastern sky.
John is coming from the deserts of Hebron. A voice is crying: 'Prepare ye the way; make His paths straight; the time is
at hand; soon He, whose the kingdom is, shall walk among
us. I, John, am his Elias.' Soon the sun in its splendor shall
rise over the mountains, and the valleys of life shall be

ablaze with that Light which is the glory of Israel, and which shall also lighten the Gentiles.

It is summer time. We are in Judea. The year is A.D. 26. In six months Jesus will begin his ministry, but for now the day belongs to John. All eyes focus on him; for a brief period the kingdom will rest with him alone. He will prepare the way. Six months older than Jesus, John is now about thirty years of age. He will preach and teach and cry repentance for half a year, and then in January, A.D. 27, he will baptize the Son of God in the murky waters of a river that flows from the Sea of Galilee to the Sea of Death and Desolation.

After so doing, he will continue to teach. A month later we shall hear him say he is not the Christ, and still later that Jesus is the Lamb of God. Indeed, for nearly a year after, until November or December of A.D. 27, his voice will still be heard, inviting all who will to follow his cousin who now, in the full blaze of his Messiahship, is everywhere teaching and working miracles. Then he will be imprisoned by Antipas, the evil Herod who had married his brother Philip's wife, and been condemned therefor by the son of Zacharias. Seven or eight months later, in the summer of A.D. 28, John, still in Herod's prison, will send messengers to Jesus to ask, "Art thou he that should come? or look we for another?" (Luke 7:20)—having in mind that those messengers will be converted and thereafter follow Him whose shoe's latchet the Baptist felt unworthy to unloose.

Finally, after languishing for a full year in prison, and in the winter of A.D. 29, we shall see the headsman's ax sever the Baptist's head so that it can be carried on a charger and given to an evil woman, while his spirit goes to the Paradise of God and his innocent blood joins the innocent blood of all the martyrs, to unite with theirs in crying unto the Lord until he avenges that blood on earth.

John came in a day of spiritual darkness and apostasy. The world was ruled by Rome, and Rome was the world. Everything that was carnal, sensual, and devilish was enshrined—it is not too strong a statement to say worshipped—as part of the imperial way of life. Adultery, incest, abortion, all were a way of life among the Romans. There were no accepted standards of morality and decency, and little or no belief in the immortality of the soul. All the gods of all the nations of the empire were reverenced and worshipped in the capital city, and the emperor and others were deified and adored as gods. Sacrifices were offered on the great altar in Herod's Temple to the emperor and for the well-being of the empire. The Jews themselves—in general and as a people—no longer walked in the light that once was theirs. If ever there was a need for a voice to cry out in the wilderness of wickedness, calling upon all men to repent and turn to the Lord, this was the day. If ever there was a voice— prepared in preexistence, schooled in the home of faithful Levites, and tested and made ready in the deserts of Judea— that was prepared to proclaim the word, to mark the way, to say to all, 'This is the path, come and walk therein; here is the Messiah, follow him,' that voice was John's.

Luke identifies the time and describes the day by the simple expedient of naming those who held temporal and spiritual rule over the people:

Tiberius Caesar, an evil and wicked wretch who walked in all the ways of the Caesars who went before and the Caesars who came after, and who ruled with all the despotism of Augustus and reveled in all the vices of Caligula, sat securely on the throne of the world. Rome ruled the world, and the world was wickedness.

Pontius Pilate, an evil Roman underling who chose, knowingly, to send an Innocent Man to the cross, lest Tiberius hear the rumor that Jesus claimed to be the King of the Jews, was governor of Judea. The scepter, now departed from Judah, left the chosen people in Gentile hands, and the Gentile hands strangled the Jewish religion.

Herod Antipas, an evil ruler whose lusts and incestuous life fitted the pattern of the Herods, and who chose to slay the innocent forerunner of the Lord rather than be embar rassed before his court, was Tetrarch of Galilee, and he, ruling in lust and evil, invited a satanic gloom of spiritual darkness to cover his kingdom.

Philip the tetrarch, though a milder and more humane ruler than Antipas, yet carried in his veins the blood of Herod the Idumean, and was a symbol of the worldliness that lay upon Jewish Israel. Though less evil than his brother, his rule was far from that which is inspired from above.

Luke speaks also of "Annas and Caiaphas being the high priests," which is itself an announcement of the spiritual degeneracy of the nation. In olden times high priests were called of God; not so in these days. Annas had been appointed by Quirinius, and we may suppose he had such influence with the Lord as Quirinius was able to confer, which was not enough, however, to keep him from being deposed by Valerius Gratus (Pilate's predecessor), who then named Caiaphas to the presiding position. He was deposed in due course by Vitellius in A.D. 37. Caiaphas was the son-in-law of Annas, and both of them exercised power and influence with the people.

What concerns us above all else as to the coming of John, however, is that he came with power and authority. He first received his errand from the Lord. His was no ordinary message, and he was no unauthorized witness. He was called of God and sent by him, and he represented Deity in the words that he spoke and the baptisms he performed. He was a legal administrator whose words and acts were binding on earth and in heaven, and his hearers were bound, at the peril of their salvation, to believe his words and heed his counsels.

Luke says: "The word of God came unto John the son of Zacharias in the wilderness." Later John is to say: "He that sent me to baptize with water, the same said unto me," such and such things. (John 1:33.) Who sent him we do not know. We do know that "he was baptized while he was yet in his childhood [meaning, when he was eight years of age], and was ordained by the angel of God at the time he was eight days old unto this power [note it well, not to the Aaronic Priesthood, but] to overthrow the kingdom of the Jews, and to make straight the way of the Lord before the face of his people, to prepare them for the coming of the Lord, in whose hand is given all power." (D&C 84:24.) We do not know when he received the Aaronic Priesthood, but obviously it came to him after his baptism, at whatever age was proper, and before he was sent by one whom he does not name to preach and baptize with water.

We know John was in the desert, for a period of trial and testing and training—perhaps not much different from Jesus' forty days of fasting and testing in the wilderness, as he began his ministry—but we do not know much else about his early life. The New Testament is not a biography of Jesus, let alone of John. The idea that our Lord's forerunner was a Nazarite for life, had never cut his hair or married, and that he lived always in the deserts is speculation that cannot be true.

We can think of no good reason why the Lord would send one of his servants off into the deserts for thirty years to prepare him for the ministry. Men are prepared to serve their fellowmen by associating with them and by learning of their foibles and idiosyncracies and how they will react to spoken counsel and proffered help.

It is true John did not drink wine or strong drink; that he went into the desert for a testing period before his ministry; that while there he ate locusts and wild honey; and that he came forth among the people wearing what was in their minds the prophetic garb, raiment woven from camel's hair, held in place by a leather girdle. We suppose this mode of dress was simply to alert the people to his prophetic status, for the period of his ministry was to be short, and he needed to attract as much attention as possible. That he was married, had children, and lived as normal a life as his ministerial assignments permitted, we cannot doubt.

John Preaches Repentance and Baptizes
(Matthew 3:1-6; JST, Matthew 3:29, 32; Mark 1:1-6; JST, Mark 1:4;
Luke 3:3-6)

And so John came as come he must. He came before the Lord, "in the spirit and power of Elias," as Gabriel promised, "to make ready a people prepared for the Lord." (Luke 1:17.) His coming, as Mark has it, was "the beginning of the gospel of Jesus Christ, the Son of God"—meaning that John proclaimed the good news about Christ and salvation; that he laid the foundation and started the work; that he called the first group of true believers; and that, in reality, he set up the kingdom of God—meaning the Church of Jesus Christ—again on earth.[1] John brought the first converts into The Church of Jesus Christ of the Meridian of Time. He laid the foundations upon which the Lord Jesus and the apostles built. He was the messenger, promised by Malachi, who should go before the Lord's face to prepare the way before him. His was the voice, promised by Isaiah, that should say, "Prepare ye the way of the Lord, make his paths straight."

What does a forerunner or an Elias do to prepare a people for Him who shall come after? He calls people to repentance and baptizes them in water "for the remission of sins," which freedom from sin is actually obtained when the repentant person receives the baptism of fire and of the Holy Ghost. This was the mission of John. He acted in the power and authority of the Aaronic Priesthood.[2] A forerunner preaches "the preparatory gospel"; the One who comes after preaches the fulness of the gospel. "The preparatory gospel . . . is the gospel of repentance and of baptism, and the remission of sins." (D&C 84:26-27.) This is the gospel administered by the law of Moses; it was as far as John's authority went.

No one is ever prepared for the Lord while he remains in his sins. The Lord does not save people in their sins, but from their sins. The plan of salvation is designed to enable men to free themselves from sin so they can, as clean and spotless beings, enter the presence of Him who is without sin. No one is ever prepared for the Lord until he confesses and forsakes his sins, until he repents, until he is baptized for the remission of sins. And the fact that John was to prepare "a people" for the Lord means that a people—composed of a host of individuals—had to set their houses in order, be baptized by him, and await patiently the coming of Him who would give them the Holy Ghost. When they received the baptism of the Holy Ghost, sin and evil would be burned out of their souls as though by fire, and being thus clean, they would be fit candidates to be with the Lord—they would be prepared for the Lord.

John, Preaching in Power, Prepares a People
(*Luke 3:7-14; JST, Luke 3:12-14, 17-20; Matthew 3:7-10; JST, Matthew 3:35-37*)

No voice like John's had been heard in Israel since the days of the prophets. Isaiah and Lehi had thundered forth such damning imprecations and spoken with such divine finality. But who for centuries had come forth, as the voice of one crying in the wilderness of wickedness, with such a call for repentance as came from the tongue of John? Here at last was a man who spoke with authority. He came in the Lord's name, speaking as he was moved upon by the Holy Ghost. The Spirit gave him utterance. So persuasive were his words, so compelling his logic, so sound his doctrine, that all Israel flocked together to hear the message. They came from Jerusalem; they assembled from all Judea; they gathered from all the regions round about Jordan. Here was a man, a voice, a message—spoken in the Spirit and with power—that sank into the hearts of men with convincing and converting power. Great hosts confessed their sins and were baptized in Jordan.

Among his hearers, among those who fell under the spell of his voice, were "many of the Pharisees and Sadducees."

387

Even they, feeling the great swell of emotion that accompanied his words, and being swept along by a great tide of popular approval, came to be baptized. But an inspired priest does not baptize an unrepentant person. Baptism is of no avail without repentance, and contrition, and confession, and a compelling determination to walk ever after in a newness of life.

"O generation of vipers, who hath warned you to flee from the wrath to come?" demanded the voice that read the hearts of men and knew of the damning influence of these leaders of the people. His words were scarcely less of a rebuke than would be those of another voice in another day, which would say to the same hypocrites: "Ye serpents, ye generation of vipers, how can ye escape the damnation of hell?" (Matt. 23:33.) But even for these there was this hope: "Repent, therefore, and bring forth fruits meet for repentance," John commanded. 'Repent first, be baptized second, and then will you be fit candidates to receive the Spirit from him who cometh after me.'

And further: 'Think not that ye are above the law of repentance; that ye keep the law of Moses and need not change your lives; that ye will be saved by the rituals and performances to which you have bound yourselves.' "Think not to say within yourselves, We are the children of Abraham, and we only have power to bring seed unto our father Abraham." Think not to say, "We have kept the commandments of God, and none can inherit the promises but the children of Abraham; for I say unto you, That God is able of these stones to raise up children unto Abraham." Know this: God is able "of these stony Gentiles—these dogs—to raise up children unto Abraham." (*Teachings,* p. 319.)

Having invited these self-sufficient, self-righteous, self-saving souls to repent, the incisive and blunt-speaking John then gave them this warning: 'Even if you do not repent and save yourselves, know this: The ax is laid at the root of the trees—the tree of formalism and Mosaic performances; the tree that saves only the seed of Abraham; the tree of dead and evil works; all the trees that cumber the vineyard of the Lord—and every tree which bringeth not forth good fruit is hewn down, and cast into the fire.'

Hearing John's denunciation of their self-appointed leaders, perhaps fearing lest they too might be hewn down and cast into the fire, those who were repentant and had been baptized asked: "What shall we do then?" 'What course is expected of us? How shall we conduct our affairs, lest these evils come upon us also?'

He answers: 'Bear one another's burdens; help the poor; feed the hungry; clothe the naked; live as becometh saints this is all part of your baptismal covenant. He that hath two coats, let him impart to him that hath none, and he that hath meat, let him do likewise.' And to the soldiers, many of whom must have been the Gentile troops garrisoned among them, he counseled: 'Your military rank does not give you the right to be cruel or inhuman to your fellowmen. Do violence to no man, neither accuse any falsely; and be content with your wages.'

Truly, here was a prophet again in Israel.

John Announces the Coming of Christ
(Luke 3:15-18; JST, Luke 3:4-11; Matthew 3:11-12; JST, Matthew 3:34, 38-40; Mark 1:7-8; JST, Mark 1:6)

With such a man and such a message, at this time of Messianic expectancy, it comes as no surprise to read in Luke that "all men mused in their hearts of John, whether he were the Christ, or not." What greater words would one expect from the lips of the Deliverer of Israel than were here being spoken by this John? What more could any man do to set in order the affairs of the earthly kingdom than was being done by this prophet-garbed preacher from the wilderness of Judea? Was he, indeed, the Promised Messiah?

And yet he had said he was a forerunner, an Elias, a voice, one coming before to prepare the way for one greater.

He must say it again, and again and again and again. He was not the Messiah, but he was his kin, and he would become his friend. And as of now, he would do the assigned work: he would prepare the way; cost what it might in time and toil and sacrifice, he would prepare the way. No man must mistake him for the Messiah.

But he must be accepted for what he was; otherwise men would not accept the one of whom he came to testify. "Why is it that ye receive not the preaching of him whom God hath sent?" he asked. "If ye receive not this in your hearts, ye receive not me; and if ye receive not me, ye receive not him of whom I am sent to bear record; and for your sins ye have no cloak."

"I indeed baptize you with water; but one mightier than I cometh, the latchet of whose shoes I am not worthy to unloose." "He shall not only baptize you with water, but with fire, and the Holy Ghost." 'I am not the Messiah, for the Messiah shall baptize with fire; he it is who shall cleanse and perfect the lives of men; he shall sanctify their souls and prepare them for eternal life. He is Christ, the great Judge.' "He shall reap the earth and harvest the ripened sheaves. With the winnowing fan of judgment, he shall separate the wicked chaff from the righteous wheat, gathering the wheat into the celestial garner and burning the chaff in the depths of hell; his threshing-floor is the whole earth." (*Commentary* 1:121.)

John's voice was one of doctrine and of testimony. He proclaimed the divine Sonship of the Coming One, testified that He was to be the Holy Messiah, and invited all men to come unto Him and be saved. And these are the words which he spake:

> *The voice of one crying in the wilderness, Prepare ye the way of the Lord, and make his paths straight.*
>
> *For behold, and lo, he shall come, as it is written in the book of the prophets, to take away the sins of the world, and to bring salvation unto the heathen nations, to gather*

together those who are lost, who are of the sheepfold of Israel;

Yea, even the dispersed and afflicted; and also to prepare the way, and make possible the preaching of the gospel unto the Gentiles;

And to be a light unto all who sit in darkness, unto the uttermost parts of the earth; to bring to pass the resurrection from the dead, and to ascend up on high, to dwell on the right hand of the Father, Until the fulness of time, and the law and the testimony shall be sealed, and the keys of the kingdom shall be delivered up again unto the Father;

To administer justice unto all; to come down in judgment upon all, and to convince all the ungodly of their ungodly deeds, which they have committed; and all this in the day that he shall come;

For it is a day of power; yea, every valley shall be filled, and every mountain and hill shall be brought low; the crooked shall be made straight, and the rough ways made smooth;

And all flesh shall see the salvation of God.

These words, inserted in the ancient record by the Prophet Joseph Smith as the spirit of revelation rested upon him, contain such a wondrous outpouring of light and understanding that they give an entirely new perspective as to how and in what manner the gospel was preached in the meridian of time. John was not, as our King James Version leaves us to assume, taking Isaiah's Messianic utterances relative to the Second Coming and applying them to the First Coming. Rather, he gave an inspired summary of the mission and ministry and work of the Promised Messiah as it pertained to both of his comings and as it affected all men of all nations. The Deliverer will come, not as a Temporal King, but to atone for the sins of the world, to bring salvation to Jew and Gentile alike, to gather Israel, to make possible the preaching of the gospel to the Gentiles, to bring to pass the resurrection, to return in glory to his Father, and to reign with almighty power. Then in the fulness of time he shall come again to administer justice and judgment unto all and to condemn the ungodly for all their evil deeds; and this shall be the day when every valley shall be exalted and every mountain shall be made low.

"And many other things in his exhortation preached he unto the people," for he was indeed a prophet—yea, more than a prophet—and He who followed after, according to the promises, was the Messiah, the very Christ, the One in whom all fulness and perfection dwells. Blessed be John who prepared the way, and blessed be He who came to fulfill all things spoken of him by his forerunner.

NOTES

1. This matter of whether John set up the kingdom and started the Church is so fundamental, so basic to an understanding of how the Lord and his servants operated in the meridian of time, and so little known and understood in the world, that we take occasion here to quote the following extracts from a sermon of the Prophet Joseph Smith: "Some say the kingdom of God was not set up on the earth until the day of Pentecost, and that John did not preach the baptism of repentance for the remission of sins. But I say, in the name of the Lord, that the kingdom of God was set up on the earth from the days of Adam to the present time, whenever there has been a righteous man on earth unto whom God revealed His word and gave power and authority to administer in His name. And where there is a priest of God—a minister who has power and authority from God to administer in the ordinances of the gospel and officiate in the priesthood of God—there is the kingdom of God. . . .

"Where did the kingdom of God begin? Where there is no kingdom of God there is no salvation. What constitutes the kingdom of God? Where there is a prophet, a priest, or a righteous man unto whom God gives His oracles, there is the kingdom of God; and where the oracles of God are not, there the kingdom of God is not. . . .

"As touching the Gospel and baptism that John preached, I would say that John came preaching the Gospel for the remission of sins; he had his authority from God, and the oracles of God were with him, and the kingdom of God for a season seemed to rest with John alone. . . .

"But, says one, the kingdom of God could not be set up in the days of John, for John said the kingdom was at hand. But I would ask if it could be any nearer to them than to be in the hands of John. The people need not wait for the days of Pentecost to find the kingdom of God, for John had it with him, and he came forth from the wilderness crying out, 'Repent ye, for the kingdom of heaven is nigh at hand,' as much as to say, 'Out here I have got the kingdom of God, and you can get it, and I am coming after you; and if you don't receive it, you will be damned;' and the scriptures represent that all Jerusalem went out unto John's baptism. There was a legal administrator, and those that were baptized were subjects for a king; and also the laws and oracles of God were there; therefore the kingdom of God was there; for no man could have better authority to administer than John; and our Savior submitted to that authority Himself, by being baptized by John; therefore the kingdom of God was set up on the earth, even in the days of John. . . .

"It is evident that the kingdom of God was on the earth, and John prepared subjects for the kingdom, by preaching the Gospel to them and baptizing them, and he prepared the way before the Savior, or came as a forerunner, and prepared subjects for the preaching of

Christ; and Christ preached through Jerusalem on the same ground where John had preached; and when the apostles were raised up, they worked in Jerusalem." (*Teachings*, pp. 271-75.)

2. "I went into the woods to inquire of the Lord, by prayer, His will concerning me," the Prophet Joseph Smith said, "and I saw an angel, and he laid his hands upon my head, and ordained me to a Priest after the order of Aaron, and to hold the keys of this Priesthood, which office was to preach repentance and baptism for the remission of sins, and also to baptize. But I was informed that this office did not extend to the laying on of hands for the giving of the Holy Ghost; that that office was a greater work, and was to be given afterward; but that my ordination was a preparatory work, or a going before, which was the spirit of Elias; for the spirit of Elias was a going before to prepare the way for the greater, which was the case with John the Baptist. He came crying through the wilderness, 'Prepare ye the way of the Lord, make his paths straight.' And they were informed, if they could receive it, it was the spirit of Elias; and John was very particular to tell the people, he was not that Light, but was sent to bear witness of that Light.

"He told the people that his mission was to preach repentance and baptize with water; but it was He that should come after him that should baptize with fire and the Holy Ghost." (*Teachings*, p. 335.)

393

Chapter 24

JOHN BAPTIZES JESUS

And I looked and beheld the Redeemer
of the world; . . . and I also beheld
the prophet who should prepare
the way before him. And the Lamb of God
went forth and was baptized of him;
and after he was baptized, I beheld the
heavens open, and the Holy Ghost
come down out of heaven and
abide upon him in the form of a dove.
(1 Ne. 11:27.)

Baptism Anciently

We cannot understand "the baptism of John"—why multitudes flocked to him to receive the sacred ordinance; why even the Lord Jesus insisted on immersion at his hands—unless we know how the law of baptism operated both anciently and among the Jews in his day.

It is commonly believed, as we suppose, that baptism originated with John; that fired with heavenly zeal, he cried repentance, and baptized—by immersion, sprinkling, pouring, or what have you—for the remission of sins; that such was a new beginning, a new ordinance, a new rite that was then accepted by the so-called first Christians, and by them made a part of the new dispensation. Such a concept has little comparison to the truth. There was a man called John; he did preach with heavenly zeal, and he did baptize repentant persons. But he did not originate the ordinance of baptism; it neither began nor ended with the son of Zacharias.

Baptism is an eternal ordinance, an everlasting rite, a continuing requirement in God's kingdom, and it was practiced by the Jews before John ever came on the scene to minister for a short season among men. He was no more the originator of baptism than he was of faith or repentance or sacrifice or any of the other laws in which he believed or the ordinances in which he participated. It is true that the Jews today no longer perform baptisms, just as they have ceased their sacrificial rites, but it was not so anciently, and it had not been so from the beginning.

Baptism and sacrifice both began with Adam. We have seen how the angelic ministrant revealed to him that his sacrificial performances were in "similitude of the sacrifice of the Only Begotten of the Father." (Moses 5:7.) We must also remember that God, "by his own voice," taught Adam about faith, repentance, baptism, and the gift of the Holy Ghost, and "that Adam cried unto the Lord, and he was caught away by the Spirit of the Lord, and was carried down into the water, and was laid under the water, and was brought forth out of the water. And thus he was baptized, and the Spirit of God descended upon him, and thus he was born of the Spirit, and became quickened in the inner man. And he heard a voice out of heaven, saying: Thou art baptized with fire, and with the Holy Ghost." (Moses 6:51-66.)

From that day onward baptism was the great initiatory ordinance into the earthly kingdom. All of the prophets of all of the ages both baptized others and were themselves baptized. Isaiah tells of the whole "house of Jacob" coming forth "out of the waters of Judah, or out of the waters of baptism." (1 Ne. 20:1.) Paul says "all our fathers" were "baptized unto Moses." They "did all eat the same spiritual meat," he says, "and did all drink the same spiritual drink: for they drank of that spiritual Rock that followed them: and that Rock was Christ." (1 Cor. 10:1-4.) From the time Lehi left Jerusalem until the resurrected Lord ministered among his seed six hundred years later, we find the whole Nephite people performing baptisms for faithful and repentant souls.

Whenever the Lord's people on either continent enjoyed the fulness of the everlasting gospel, this means that they had faith in Christ, repented of their sins, were baptized for the remission of sins, and had the gift of the Holy Ghost. Whenever they were restricted to the lesser law, the law of Moses, and thus had only the preparatory gospel, they still exercised faith, sought repentance, and subjected themselves to baptism in water, but were unable to obtain the right to the constant companionship of the Holy Spirit.

Baptism Among the Jews in John's Day

Baptism was an established way of life among faithful Jews in John's day. We do not suppose that all of the Jews of that day were baptized, for apostasy was rife and rebellion was common. But among the chosen seed there certainly were many faithful people who were baptized on the same basis as they offered sacrifices. "The Levitical Priesthood is forever hereditary—fixed on the head of Aaron and his sons forever, and was in active operation down to Zacharias the father of John." (*Teachings,* p. 319.) This is the priesthood that has power to baptize in water. "Zacharias was a priest of God, and officiating in the Temple, and John was a priest after his father, and held the keys of the Aaronic Priesthood, and was called of God to preach the Gospel of the kingdom of God." (*Teachings,* p. 273.) John himself "was baptized while he was yet in his childhood." (D&C 84:28.) It goes without saying that Zacharias and his fellow priests were baptized. We cannot do other than believe that Elisabeth, Mary, Joseph, Simeon, Anna, the shepherds who heard the heavenly choirs, and hosts of others who waited patiently for the Consolation of Israel had also partaken of this sacred ordinance, all before the ministry of John ever began.

Edersheim says that the baptismal ordinance administered by John was not new. "Hitherto the Law had it," he says, "that those who had contracted Levitical defilement were to immerse before offering sacrifice. Again, it was prescribed that such Gentiles as became 'proselytes of righteousness,' or 'proselytes of the Covenant,' were to be admitted to full participation in the privileges of Israel by the threefold rites of circumcision, baptism, and sacrifice—the immersion being, as it were, the acknowledgment and symbolic removal of moral defilement, corresponding to that of Levitical uncleanness." Our knowledge of the real purpose of baptism lets us know that it was not simply to remove Levitical defilement, as such had been defined by the Rabbis, but was in fact for the remission of sins. What the Edersheim statement does is establish the fact that baptism was common among the people before the ministry of John. In this connection, Edersheim quotes this significant passage from the Talmud: "A man who is guilty of sin, and makes confession, and does not turn from it, to whom is he like? To a man who has in his hand a defiling reptile, who, even if he immerses in all the waters of the world, his baptism avails him nothing; but let him cast it from his hand, and if he immerses in only forty seah of water, immediately his baptism avails him." (Edersheim 1:273.) That is to say: Baptism without repentance is of no avail. Even those who wrote the Talmud knew that.

As to how baptisms were performed for proselytes, Edersheim says: "The person to be baptized, having cut his hair and nails, undressed completely, made fresh profession of his faith before what were designated 'the fathers of the baptism,' and then immersed completely, so that every part of the body was touched by the water. The rite would, of course, be accompanied by exhortations and benedictions. . . .

397

"It was indeed a great thing when . . . a stranger sought shelter under the wings of the Shekhinah, and the change of condition which he underwent was regarded as complete. . . . As he stepped out of these waters he was considered as 'born anew'—in the language of the Rabbis, as if he were 'a little child just born.' . . . The past, with all that had belonged to it, was past, and he was a new man—the old, with its defilements, was buried in the waters of baptism." (Edersheim 2:745-46.)

The issue with reference to baptisms performed in the day of John was not whether people should be baptized—no one was questioning that; people everywhere had been and were being immersed in water by priestly administrators for the remission of sins. The issue was: Is John the one sent of God to baptize and thereby to prepare a people for the Promised Messiah. Any baptisms performed by the priests of Aaron, according to the patterns of the past, were ordinances of the old dispensation. And a new day was now dawning, a forerunner of the future was baptizing, an Elias of the Messias was immersing people in water—and the issue was, in Jesus' words: "The baptism of John, whence was it? from heaven, or of men?"

Jesus answered his own question by saying: "John came unto you in the way of righteousness." (Matt. 21:25-32.) And of John, Luke records: "And all the people that heard him, and the publicans, justified God, being baptized with the baptism of John. But the Pharisees and lawyers rejected the counsel of God against themselves, being not baptized of him." (Luke 7:29-30.)

John came as the last legal administrator of the old dispensation; he overthrew the kingdom of the Jews, and he ushered in a new day. He was, as pertaining to the new kingdom, "the only legal administrator in the affairs of the kingdom there was then on the earth. and holding the keys of power. The Jews had to obey his instructions or be damned by their own law." (*Teachings,* p. 276.) It was now his baptism—"the baptism of John"—that counted, not any other. As it was among the Nephites when the Lord took a new dispensation to them, the Jews had to be baptized over again. John was the new head, for the moment, of the earthly kingdom; they must turn to him. He was now baptizing, and it was his baptism that was binding on earth and in heaven.[1]

The Baptism at Bethabara
(Matthew 3:13-17; JST, Matthew 3:42-46; Luke 3:21-23a; JST, Luke 3:28; Mark 1:9-11; JST, Mark 1:9)

All Christendom believes, as we suppose, that Jesus was baptized by John with water taken from Jordan. How and why and in what manner the ordinance was performed is a matter of the widest speculation, and, in many quarters, of almost total misunderstanding. In a great cathedral in Curitiba, Brazil, for instance, there is a stained-glass window depicting the baptism by John of the Lord Jesus. John is standing on dry ground on Jordan's bank; Jesus is standing ankle deep in the water itself; and John is pouring a handful of water from a cup onto the divine head.[2] How much nearer the truth it would be if the picture had been chosen from the following:

Comes now John to Jordan on the crowning day of his life, the day when he, called and appointed and foreordained so to do, shall baptize the Son of God. Jesus is nearing the close of his long journey from Nazareth to Bethabara, to the spot on Jordan where John is preaching and baptizing. It is a clear, calm day; none of the storm clouds that will one day overshadow the Divine Presence have made their appearance; this is a day of peace and divine acceptance, a day when even the Father's voice will be heard by mortal man. Multitudes throng the banks of the Jordan. John preaches, as was his wont; he cries repentance, and the Spirit of the Lord leads confessing and contrite souls to ask for baptism. John stands waist deep in the water, in a cove, where the current is quiet and the water calm. The new converts make their way to him, and one by one he immerses them in the water. He speaks to each soul a few words signifying his authority and the sacred nature of the holy ordinance here performed. The Lord is pleased with the foundations of the kingdom that are being laid.

Other activities occupy their time for a season. John, again on the bank, picks up the train of thought found in his earlier sermons. There are questions and answers. Believers feel fed by the Spirit; their souls are enlarged; it is good for them to be there. Unbelievers feel hate and resentment in their hearts, and animosity and bitterness show forth from their countenances. The crowd is smaller than it was—some have departed for their homes—but a faithful few still hang on every word. There is a momentary lull in the continuing expressions of doctrine and of testimony. One of dignity and majesty appears on the bank; he has come unexpected and unheralded. He steps forth from the throng. John stands still, and a wave of recognition floods his soul. It is He; this is the day; the hour has arrived. All eyes are on the two inspired men. The Holy One speaks: 'I am he of whom thou hast borne witness. I have come to be baptized.'

John is overwhelmed, subdued. In reverential awe he feels unworthy of the honor to baptize such a one. "I have need to be baptized of thee, and comest thou to me?" he says, not quite having prepared himself for the privilege and the vision that are about to be.

Jesus answers: "Suffer me to be baptized of thee, for thus it becometh us to fulfil all righteousness."

Then John goes down into the water; Jesus follows. John, probably raising his right arm to the square, speaks some such words as these:

> *'Jesus, thou Son of the Most High God: Having authority given me by him who called me and sent me and said unto me, Thou shalt baptize the Holy Messiah, even the Lamb of God, who taketh away the sins of the world, I now baptize thee in the name of the Father, and of the Son, and of the Holy Ghost. Amen."*[3]

Then carefully, reverentially, he places Jesus under the water, and brings him forth out of the water—the immersion in the murky waters of Jordan is complete—and, lo, John sees the heavens open and the Holy Ghost descend in bodily form, in serenity and peace, like a dove.[4] The sign of the dove is given, and the voice of the Father—graciously pleased that his Son has been baptized—speaks, and is heard by John's spiritually attuned ears and by the ears of all present who are in tune. It says:

"This is my beloved Son, in whom I am well pleased. Hear ye him."

"Hear ye him!" The Father testifies of the Son; he introduces him to the world; and he commands: *"Hear ye him!"*

Why Jesus Was Baptized

He who was holy—who did no sin, in whose mouth was no guile, whose every thought and word and deed was perfect—even he came to John to be baptized. Why? Not for the remission of sins, for he had none; not to court popularity with the people who revered John, for his message was to stand or fall on its own merit; not because he needed spiritual regeneration, for the Spirit he had with him always but he came to be baptized "to fulfil all righteousness," that is, to accomplish all that was required of him according to the terms and conditions of his Father's plan.

"And now, if the Lamb of God, he being holy, should have need to be baptized by water, to fulfil all righteousness," Nephi acclaimed, "O then, how much more need have we, being unholy, to be baptized, yea, even by water!"

Then Nephi asks how the Lamb of God, he being holy and needing no remission of sins, fulfilled all righteousness by being immersed in Jordan by John. His answer falls into five parts, and Jesus was baptized for these reasons:

1. *To signify his humility before the Father;* to show that "according to the flesh he humbleth himself before the

Father." He is God's Almighty Son; he made the worlds; the sidereal heavens rolled into existence at his word; he has all power in heaven and on earth—and yet, as a perfect pattern of humility, he wades out into a dirty stream, whose waters are scarcely fit for human consumption, and permits a rugged, unpolished man from the desert to immerse him in baptism, because such is the law of the Lord.

2. *As a covenant of obedience;* he "witnesseth unto the Father that he would be obedient unto him in keeping his commandments." He came not to do his own will, but the will of the Father, who sent him. He was no more free of constraint and control than is any man. He walked the course set out for him because it was his Father's will, and he was under covenant, made in the waters of baptism, to do the will of the Father.

3. *To receive the gift of the Holy Ghost;* that is to say, to conform to the law that gave him the right to the constant companionship of that member of the Godhead. As we are aware, this was a formality only in his case, for he being holy and without sin, the Spirit was his companion always. At baptism he simply went through the form that is required for all men, and that he should have done so is manifest by the fact that "the Holy Ghost descended upon him in the form of a dove."

4. *To gain an inheritance in the celestial kingdom;* that is, his baptism "showeth unto the children of men the straightness of the path, and the narrowness of the gate, by which they should enter, he having set the example before them." In other words, though he is the King of the kingdom, though he authors and proclaims his Father's plan of salvation, though he ordains and establishes the laws governing all things, yet he cannot enter the kingdom of heaven without baptism.

5. *As an example to all men;* to mark the course and chart the way; to show them the path they must follow. "And he said unto the children of men: Follow thou me. Wherefore, my beloved brethren," Nephi says, "can we

follow Jesus save we shall be willing to keep the commandments of the Father?" (2 Ne. 31:5-12.)

And so it is that the Lord Jesus is baptized—to save himself and to mark the path in which all others must walk to gain the same salvation. And so it is that the miraculously born son of Zacharias, fresh from communing with the Lord in the desert, leads the Mortal Messiah down into the Jordan and immerses him in the murky water, from which watery womb he shall come forth, receive the gift of the Holy Ghost, and go forth preaching and teaching. And so it is that he shall tread his way up the Holy Mount, on which his Father's voice shall once again be heard to say: "This is my beloved Son, in whom I am well pleased; hear ye him" (Matt. 17:5); and so it is that he shall descend from the mount and continue his ministry, finally submitting to crucifixion at the hands of evil men—all "to fulfil all righteousness."

NOTES

1. A somewhat analogous situation existed in the early days of this dispensation. Some new converts, having been baptized in other churches, felt they did not need to be baptized over again as members of the newly established kingdom of God on earth. In language that is applicable, in large measure, to the Jewish situation, the Lord said: "Behold, I say unto you that all old covenants have I caused to be done away in this thing; and this is a new and an everlasting covenant, even that which was from the beginning. Wherefore, although a man should be baptized an hundred times it availeth him nothing, for you cannot enter in at the strait gate by the law of Moses, neither by your dead works. For it is because of your dead works that I have caused this last covenant and this church to be built up unto me, even as in days of old. Wherefore, enter ye in at the gate, as I have commanded, and seek not to counsel your God." (D&C 22:1-4.)

2. In this same cathedral, in the stained-glass portrayal behind the altar, may be seen Mary, our Lord's mother, sitting as it were on a throne. On either side, with outstretched arms toward her, and holding jointly a crown, stand the Father and the Son. They are placing the crown on Mary's head. About the Holy Virgin flutters a dove, which is, no doubt, intended to be the Holy Spirit.

3. The words of the baptismal prayer have not been the same in all dispensations and for all people. It appears that the words spoken fit the needs and circumstances of the moment. When Alma took Helam into the waters of Mormon, he first cried out, "O Lord, pour out thy Spirit upon thy servant, that he may do this work with holiness of heart." Then, "the Spirit of the Lord was upon him, and he said: Helam, I baptize thee, having authority from the Almighty God, as a testimony that ye have entered into a covenant to serve him until you are dead as to the mortal body; and may the Spirit of the Lord be poured out upon you; and may he grant unto you eternal life, through the redemption of Christ, whom he has prepared from the foundation of the world." (Mosiah 18:12-13.)

4. All four Gospel authors record that the Spirit descended "like a dove"; Luke adds that he also came in "bodily shape"; and the Book of Mormon accounts say he came "in

the form of a dove." (1 Ne. 11:27; 2 Ne. 31:8.) Joseph Smith said that John "led the Son of God into the waters of baptism, and had the privilege of beholding the Holy Ghost descend in the form of a dove, or rather in the sign of the dove, in witness of that administration."

Then the Prophet gives this explanation: "The sign of the dove was instituted before the creation of the world, a witness for the Holy Ghost, and the devil cannot come in the sign of a dove. The Holy Ghost is a personage, and is in the form of a personage. It does not confine itself to the form of the dove, but in sign of the dove. The Holy Ghost cannot be transformed into a dove; but the sign of a dove was given to John to signify the truth of the deed, as the dove is an emblem or token of truth and innocence." (*Teachings,* pp. 275-76.) It thus appears that John witnessed the sign of the dove, that he saw the Holy Ghost descend in the "bodily shape" of the personage that he is, and that the descent was "like a dove."

Chapter 25

THE TEMPTATION OF JESUS

I will prove you in all things, whether
you will abide in my covenant, even
unto death, that you may be found
worthy. (D&C 98:14.)

Lucifer and the Law of Temptation

Jesus, as our evangelical authors tell us, was led by the Spirit into the wilderness to be tempted of the devil. As we shall see, however, he went into the wilderness, as guided by the Spirit, to be with God. Then, after forty days of fasting, prayer, and divine communion—and in connection with certain great spiritual experiences that then came to him—he was visited by the devil who came tempting, enticing, seeking to destroy the house of faith in which Jesus dwelt.

These recitations—that Jesus, the Son of God was tempted—give rise to speculation and wonderment as to how and why and whether he, a divine being, could be tempted. Theologians speculate as to whether he was peccable, that is, capable of being tempted and liable to commit sin, because of his human nature, or whether he was impeccable, that is, not liable to sin and thus one who was free from sin or stain, because of his divine nature. In reality there neither is nor should there be any great mystery here.

405

Our Lord, as a mortal, was subject to the same laws of trial and testing that govern all mortals. An understanding of the laws governing temptation, and the reasons trials exist, will show why, after Jesus went into the wilderness to commune with God, who is the Author of all righteousness, he then came out to face Lucifer, the enemy of all righteousness.

This mortal life is a probationary estate; one in which every accountable soul must be tried and tested; one in which every man must be subject to the wiles and enticements of Lucifer; one in which all men must choose to worship the Lord, by keeping his commandments, or to follow Satan, by living after the manner of the world. Worship God or submit to Satan—succinctly stated, that is all that life is about. The Lord is worshipped when men adhere to his standards and emulate his way of life. "Be holy, for I am holy," saith the Lord. (Lev. 11:45.) The devil is worshipped when men adhere to his standards and emulate his way of life; when they are carnal, sensual, and devilish; when they forget the Lord and live after the manner of the world; "for he seeketh that all men might be miserable like unto himself." (2 Ne. 2:27.)

Men must have a choice; they must be able to choose; there must be opposites; they must have agency; they must be free to worship the Lord or to follow Satan. All this is imperative. It is inherent in the whole plan of salvation. And unless men have the agency to choose to do good and work righteousness—and, in fact, do so—they cannot be saved. There is no other way.

"It must needs be"—that is, it is mandatory; it must be; it is part of the whole system of progression and salvation, and there is no other way to bring salvation to pass—"It must needs be, that there is an opposition in all things." So says Lehi. "If not so," he continues, "righteousness could not be brought to pass, neither wickedness, neither holiness nor misery, neither good nor bad." If there were no opposites, nothing could exist. There can be no light without darkness; no life without death; no heat without cold; no virtue without vice; no sense without insensibility. There can be no righteousness without wickedness; no joy without sorrow; no reward without punishment; no salvation without damnation. If these things did not exist—that is, if there were no opposites; if there were no opposition in all things; if there were no agency; if men were not free to choose one course or another—such would, as Lehi says, "destroy the wisdom of God and his eternal purposes," and, indeed, should such be the case, and it is impossible that it could be, then "all things must have vanished away." (2 Ne. 2:11-13.)

If there is a God, there is also a devil. It is the Lord who invites and entices men, by his Spirit—the light of Christ—to choose the right; it is the devil who invites and entices men to choose evil works rather than good. The enticements of the devil are temptation, and temptation is, and "must needs be," an essential part of the plan of salvation. Through it are provided the allurements and worldly things that men must overcome in order to progress and gain that eternal life which is the opposite of eternal damnation.

Hence, there is—and must be—a devil, and he is the father of lies and of wickedness. He and the fallen angels who followed him are spirit children of the Father. As Christ is the Firstborn of the Father in the spirit, so Lucifer is a son of the morning, one of those born in the morning of preexistence. He is a spirit man, a personage, an entity, comparable in form and appearance to any of the spirit children of the Eternal Father. He was the source of opposition among the spirit hosts before the world was made; he rebelled in preexistence against the Father and the Son, and he sought even then to destroy the agency of man. He and his followers were cast down to earth, and they are forever denied mortal bodies. And he, here on earth, along with all who follow him—both his spirit followers and the mortals who hearken to his enticements—is continuing the war that commenced in heaven.

There is, then, a law of temptation. It involves the Eternal Christ, by whose power Lucifer fell as lightning from heaven, and it involves the mortal Jesus, who was subject to the wiles of the spirit Lucifer as he dwelt as a man among men. And that our blessed Lord came off triumphant on earth as he did in heaven, we all know, for which ministry of triumph and glory we praise his name forever.

Jesus Communes with God in the Wilderness
(Matthew 4:1-2; JST, Matthew 4:1-2; Mark 1:12-13; JST, Mark 1:10-11; Luke 4:1)

After his baptism by John in Jordan at Bethabara, two things happened in the life of our Lord that always come to pass in the lives of those faithful people who find their own Bethabaras and are immersed in their own Jordans by the legal administrators of their day: (1) the Spirit of God descended upon him with power, though in his case that Spirit had ever guided his thoughts and words and acts, and (2) greater temptations confronted him than had ever been the case before.

After baptism of water comes the baptism of fire. After baptism—when converted souls commit themselves to the Lord's cause; when they covenant to forsake the world and serve the Lord—the devil tries even harder to lead them astray. Then it is that they are tested in all things to see if they will abide in the gospel covenant, even unto death, that they may be found worthy of a celestial inheritance.

Also, after his baptism Jesus did what every person who is born of the Spirit should do: he withdrew from the thronging masses of humanity to a place apart to commune with God. Matthew's account, as he originally wrote it, says: "Then"—that is, following his baptism—"Jesus was led up of the Spirit, into the wilderness, to be with God. And when he had fasted forty days and forty nights, and had communed with God, he was afterwards an hungered, and was left to be tempted of the devil." Mark tells us he "was with the wild beasts; and the angels ministered unto him." Nothing more of this forty-day period is recorded, but we

408

cannot do other than conclude it was a time of rejoicing and spiritual refreshment beyond anything ever experienced by mortal man on earth.

Enoch "was high and lifted up, even in the bosom of the Father, and of the Son of Man," and he beheld marvelous visions beyond anything that the mind of man can conceive. He saw all the spirits that God had created, the nations of mortal men, the coming of Christ and his crucifixion, the Second Coming of the Son of Man, the millennial era, and many other things that are not recorded. (Moses 6 and 7.) The brother of Jared talked for three hours at one time with the Lord and learned many of the wonders of eternity, which are so far beyond mortal comprehension that the Lord has not permitted them to be translated in our day. (Ether 2-4.) Moses saw worlds without number and their inhabitants, and confronted and withstood Satan face to face. (Moses 1.) Paul was caught up into the third heaven and saw wondrous things, "and heard unspeakable words, which it is not lawful for a man to utter." (2 Cor. 12:1-4.) Joseph Smith saw the Father and the Son and the vision of the degrees of glory. (JS-H 1; D&C 76; 137.) Great hosts of faithful people, in tune with the Infinite, have seen and heard the mysteries of the kingdom, things that are "only to be seen and understood by the power of the Holy Spirit, which God bestows on those who love him, and purify themselves before him; To whom he grants this privilege of seeing and knowing for themselves; That through the power and manifestation of the Spirit, while in the flesh, they may be able to bear his presence in the world of glory." (D&C 76:114-118.)

If all these things, and more, happened in the lives of the prophets, what should we expect to find in the life of the greatest Prophet? If there are eternal laws by obedience to which men see visions and commune with the Infinite, what glorious communion with heaven should we find in the life of the one who obeyed all the laws ever given to mortals? If the veil has been rent for lesser men, and they have seen inconceivable glories and heard unspeakable words, what should we suppose was seen and heard by the greatest Man? Surely the spiritual stature of the Man Jesus was such that for forty days the lions and wild beasts treated him as they did Daniel. Surely the visions of eternity were opened to his view as they were to Paul and Joseph Smith. Surely he saw all that was seen by Enoch and Moses and Moriancumer. Surely there was purpose and preparation, refinement and testing, growth and development, during this period when our Lord's body was made subject to his spirit. Fasting and prayer and pondering and visions and revelations prepare men for the ministry, and it was no different, except in degree, where the preparation of the Lord Jesus was concerned.

The Temptation
(*Matthew 4:3-11; JST, Matthew 4:5-6, 8-9; Luke 4:2-13; JST, Luke 4:2, 5-6, 9*)

When man is communing with his Maker, he is not subject to temptation; when angels are ministering to him and he is under the spell of their angelic influence, he is not subject to temptation; when the Holy Spirit rests mightily upon him and the visions of eternity are open to his view, he is not subject to temptation. For forty days Jesus pondered upon the things of the Spirit, poured out his soul to his Father in prayer, sought diligently to receive revelations and see visions, was ministered to by angels, and was enwrapt in the visions of eternity—during all of which time he was not subject to temptation. We may also suppose that during this period he was "with God" in the literal sense of the word, and that the Father visited him.

As the period of edification and spiritual enlightenment drew to its close, as the visions and spiritual experiences ceased—except for two that we shall note shortly—and as Jesus prepared to go back into the normal mortal way of life, with angels no longer at his side and his eyes not open to the unending visions of eternity, then the devil came to entice, to trap, to tempt. Three times he tried and three times he failed, after which "he departed from him for a season," or, as it may be rendered, "till a fitting opportunity."

Jesus was "an hungered." For forty days and forty nights no morsel of food entered his mouth, no drop of water wet his parched lips or dripped down his throat. His extended fast left him weak physically. His body cried out for food, and he needed the strength that comes from a full stomach. His spiritual experiences were, for the moment, drawing to their close. The Divine Providence that calls upon men to fast and pray also expects them to end their fasts and cease their prayers and to take care of their physical needs. Men must eat bread or die, and the time had now come for Jesus to break his fast and to eat, perhaps the berries or locusts or wild honey that was available, and to drink refreshing draughts, perhaps from the nearby spring.

But first "the tempter came to him"—and we must assert that this was a personal appearance, one in which the spirit Lucifer, who was cast out of heaven for rebellion, came in person and spoke to Jesus face to face. It was no mere placing of thoughts in his mind, but an open and spoken conversation; "the tempter came to him" and said: "If thou be the Son of God, command these stones be made bread."

Why not? Had not Jehovah provided manna—which is bread from heaven—to all Israel, six days each week, for forty years, lest they die of hunger in the wilderness? Was it not the will of the Father that his Son now eat and regain his physical strength? And if Israel was fed by bread from heaven, when no other food was available, why would not Israel's Chief Citizen receive food in the same way? What would be wrong with duplicating for one day a miracle that had occurred on more than twelve thousand days when Moses and Aaron led Israel from Egypt to the very Jordan in whose waters he had but recently been immersed?

Actually there was no reason, save one, why food should not have been provided miraculously, which shows how devilishly devised the tempting challenge was—and for aught we know it may have been so provided at a later time. The one reason was: Lucifer had made the providing of food for Jesus' hungry body a test of his divinity. "If thou be the Son of God," do this thing. It was as though he had said: 'Cut off your arm and restore it, and then I will believe you are the Son of God and have the power you seem to think you have.' Of course he could turn stones into bread; in less than two months he would turn water into wine in Cana; and not long thereafter, on two separate occasions, he would multiply loaves and fishes so that thousands could eat, which is to say, he would make food out of the elements that surround us.

But here Lucifer was challenging him to glory in his divinity and to prostitute his powers. He was demanding that he prove something that needed no proof. Jesus knew and Satan knew—both had perfect knowledge on the point—that our Lord was the Son of God. There was no need to prove it by turning stones into bread, even though he had the power, and even though the time was at hand when it was proper for him to eat and be filled. Indeed, if he had yielded to Lucifer, turning the stones into bread, it would have indicated a doubt in his own mind of his divinity; it would have shown he felt a need to prove that which needed no proof.

Jesus answered: "It is written, Man shall not live by bread alone, but by every word that proceedeth out of the mouth of God." Of all the inspired words ever recorded by the prophets who preceded him, these few constituted the perfect rebuke to the rebel Lucifer. They are taken from the very sentence in which Moses reminded Israel of the bread from heaven, as it were, with which they had been fed for forty years. "Thou shalt remember all the way which the Lord thy God led thee these forty years in the wilderness," Moses said, "to humble thee, and to prove thee, to know what was in thine heart, whether thou wouldest keep his commandments, or no"—all of which is a type of the fasting and struggle of Jesus for forty days in the wilderness of his fast. Then came to Israel, by the mouth of Moses, the divine pronouncement: "And he humbled thee, and suffered thee to hunger, and fed thee with manna, which thou knewest not, neither did thy fathers know; that he might make thee know that man doth not live by bread only, but by every word that proceedeth out of the mouth of the Lord doth man live." (Deut. 8:2-3.)

That is, even as Israel relied upon Jehovah for their daily bread, lest they die physically, so they must rely upon him for the word of God, which is spiritual bread, lest they die spiritually. Neither temporal nor spiritual bread, standing alone, will suffice; man must eat of both to live; and in the eternal sense, the word of God, which is the bread from heaven in the full sense, is the more important. Those who make the search for earthly bread their chief concern lose sight of eternal values, fail to feed their spirits, die spiritually, and lose their souls. By choosing from the whole Old Testament the very words that show the relative worth of bread from the earth and bread from heaven, Jesus' triumph over Lucifer is complete. He, as the Son of God, chooses the bread from heaven and will find earthly food when his circumstances permit. He is master over the flesh; his appetites will be kept within the bounds set by divine standards.

We now come to one of the two remaining great spiritual experiences that were part of the period of fasting and testing to which Jesus was subject. "Then Jesus was taken up into the holy city, and the Spirit setteth him on the pinnacle of the temple," we learn from the Joseph Smith Translation. The Spirit did it, not the devil; how unthinkable it is that Lucifer would have power to transport the Son of God, or anyone for that matter, to a place of his choosing! He has no such power! Jesus was placed on the appointed pinnacle by the Spirit!

Other prophets had been and would be transported bodily from place to place by the power of the Spirit. Ezekiel was lifted up and carried by the Spirit. (Ezek. 8:2-3.) Nephi "was caught away in the Spirit of the Lord, yea, into an exceeding high mountain," upon which he "never had before" set his "foot." (1 Ne. 11:1.) Mary herself "was carried away in the Spirit," at the time of the conception of Jesus. (1 Ne. 11:19-21.) Nephi the son of Helaman "was taken by the Spirit and conveyed away out of the midst" of those who sought to imprison him, and thus "he did go forth in the Spirit, from multitude to multitude, declaring the word of God." (Hel. 10:16-17.) After Philip baptized the eunuch, "the Spirit of the Lord caught [him] away," and he was carried to Azotus. (Acts 8:39-40.) It is not an unheard-of thing for the Lord, by the power of the Spirit, to transport mortals from place to place; and it would appear that Jesus was to have all the experiences enjoyed in mortality by any of the prophets who went before or who came after, excepting only that he was not translated and taken into heaven without tasting death as some had been and would be.

Why the Spirit took him to the pinnacle of the temple is not stated. Perhaps it was to show him the throngs of worshippers and let him see anew the sacrifices being offered in similitude of his coming sacrifice. In any event, "Then the devil came unto him and said, If thou be the Son of God, cast thyself down, for it is written, He shall give his angels charge concerning thee, and in their hands they shall bear thee up, lest at any time thou dash thy foot against a stone."

Here was a new temptation, more subtle than the first. Lucifer was now quoting scripture, a Messianic prophecy, which must be fulfilled. Perhaps Jesus could control his appetites and overcome the flesh, so be it; but would he dare refuse to conform to a Messianic prophecy? Jesus had chosen, by refusing to turn stones into bread, to put spiritual things ahead of temporal things, and so now Lucifer tempts him with reference to a spiritual matter: If our Lord is choosing to put the things of God's kingdom ahead of the things of this world, then let him cast himself down, for he will then fulfill a scripture and triumph before the people in a spiritual field.

'If thou be the Son of God,' the tempter says, 'then cast thyself down in the midst of the worshipping throng. If thou art the Messiah, surely thou wilt fulfill this Messianic prophecy; how else can it be fulfilled but by you on this occasion? And what a beginning for thy ministry! All men shall hear of the marvelous thing thou hast done! They will flock to hear your message, and you will be able to accomplish what you were sent to do! This is the very thing the Messiah must do to prove his divinity, and it must be done to commence your ministry. If thou be the Son of God, thou wilt surely cast thyself down. Now, do it now; this is the time; this is your great hour!'

Jesus replied: "It is written again, Thou shalt not tempt the Lord thy God." And again the answer was perfect. First, it was his witness that he was the Son of God: 'Thou shalt not tempt me, for I am the Lord thy God. I am the God of Israel; I am the Messiah; I am the Son of God.' Next, his quotation came from a context that forbids asking the Lord to perform miracles to prove he is the true God. Moses said: "Ye shall not tempt the Lord your God, as ye tempted him in Massah." (Deut. 17:1-7.) And it was at Massah that the children of Israel, dying of thirst and perishing for want of water, as they supposed, demanded of Moses that he prove that the Lord was with them by providing water for them and their cattle. It was then that Moses smote the rock and the water gushed out, "because they tempted the Lord, saying, Is the Lord among us, or not?" (Ex. 17:1-17.) For the second time our Lord's victory over Lucifer was total and triumphant. Seductive as the appeal was, he would not yield; his divinity was not to be proved by a plunge from the temple pinnacle, nor was his ministry to be announced by any such dramatic occurrence. He was his own witness, and the people, as in all ages, must come and hear a prophet's voice and choose for themselves whether to believe or to rebel.

After this, "again, Jesus was in the Spirit"—in the second spiritual experience to which we made reference—"and it taketh him up into an exceeding high mountain, and showeth him all the kingdoms of the world and the glory of them. And the devil came unto him again, and said, All these things will I give unto thee, If thou wilt fall down and worship me. Then said Jesus unto him, Get thee hence, Satan; for it is written, Thou shalt worship the Lord thy God, and him only shalt thou serve." Thereupon Satan left him for a season.

In theory this should have been the least of all the temptations Lucifer could make to the Messiah. So here is the great Roman empire with Tiberius at its head; here are armies and navies and palaces and stately buildings; here are legions of men ready to bow the knee or draw the bow at a word from their ruler; here are the cattle and crops and vineyards on a thousand hills and in ten thousand valleys; here is the whole wealth of the whole world, plus all the power that goes with it—what of it?

Why offer a handful of dust, as it were, to him who created the earth, the universe, and the sidereal heavens, and whose destiny is to inherit, possess, and receive all things, and to have all power in heaven and on earth? Why should the Creator of all things be tempted, when a usurper who has momentary control over a few of them offers his handful back in return for obeisance and worship? But this is only the theory.

In practical reality this must have been the crowning test of the three. Jesus was a mortal man, and every mortal has planted in his heart the desire for wealth and power. One of the great purposes of mortality is to bridle this desire and to keep it under control.

Cain slays Abel to gain his flocks and herds; Esau sells his birthright for a mess of pottage; Joseph's brothers sell him to the Ishmaelites for a few pieces of silver; Judas plants the traitor's kiss for thirty pieces of silver; Ananias and Saphira hold back a part of the price of their property, and lose their souls in the process—such has always been the way with mortals. Women sell their virtue for a few baubles;

politicians sell their souls to be elected to office; generals sell the lives of their soldiers to satisfy their vanity; merchants sell their integrity for a few paltry pence—such is the way of the world. And since our Lord's temptations were real and a part of his necessary trials and tests, we cannot do other than suppose that all the kingdoms and wealth and power of Satan's world must have seemed desirable to him. Men have the potential of becoming joint-heirs with him of all that his Father hath, and yet they sell their souls for naught. Why should he be subject to any less testing?

How apt are these words, quoted from Andrewes by Farrar: "There are some that will say that we are never tempted with kingdoms. It may well be, for it needs not be, when less will serve. It was Christ only that was thus tempted; in Him lay an heroical mind that could not be tempted with small matters. But with us it is nothing so, for we esteem more basely of ourselves. We set our wares at a very easy price; he [Lucifer] may buy us even dagger-cheap. He need never carry us so high as the mount. The pinnacle is high enough; yea, the lowest steeple in all the town would serve the turn. Or let him but carry us to the leads and gutters of our own houses; nay, let us but stand in our windows or our doors, if he will give us so much as we can there see, he will tempt us throughly; we will accept it, and thank him too. . . . A matter of half-a-crown, or ten groats, a pair of shoes, or some such trifle, will bring us on our knees to the devil." (Farrar, p. 105.)

Why Jesus Was Tempted

Jesus was tempted—if we may so say—to fulfill all righteousness. It was part of the eternal plan. It gave him the experiences he needed to work out his own salvation, and it prepared him to sit in judgment upon his erring brethren, who, in a lesser degree, are tried and tested as he was.

We have said his temptations were real. Whether we can understand how and why the things he underwent were real and genuine temptations is of no great moment; that we know he was called upon to choose the right in the hardest and most difficult situations ever imposed upon mortals will perhaps suffice. That his temptations were over and above those of any other person is shown from the Messianic prophecy: "Lo, he shall suffer temptations, and pain of body, hunger, thirst, and fatigue, even more than man can suffer, except it be unto death." (Mosiah 3:7.) Of the temptations he suffered, after those of which we have here spoken, and before the trial in Gethsemane, he said to the Twelve: "Ye are they which have continued with me in my temptations." (Luke 22:28.)

Paul, as in so many other matters, is our best New Testament source of doctrinal exposition as to the temptations and sufferings of our Lord. To the Hebrews he wrote:

"It became him, for whom are all things, and by whom are all things, in bringing many sons unto glory, to make the captain of their salvation perfect through sufferings. . . .

"Wherefore in all things it behoved him to be made like unto his brethren, that he might be a merciful and faithful high priest in things pertaining to God, to make reconciliation for the sins of the people. For in that he himself hath suffered being tempted, he is able to succour them that are tempted. . . .

"Seeing then that we have a great high priest, that is passed into the heavens, Jesus the Son of God, let us hold fast our profession. For we have not an high priest which cannot be touched with the feeling of our infirmities; but was in all points tempted like as we are, yet without sin. . . .

"Though he were a Son, yet learned he obedience by the things which he suffered; And being made perfect, he became the author of eternal salvation unto all them that obey him." (Heb. 2:10, 17-14; 4:14-15; 5:8-9.)

The first Adam, yielding to temptation, brought death and sin into the world; the Second Adam, overcoming temptation, brought life and righteousness to men, because he overcame the world. Having been baptized and having come off triumphant in the war with Satan, he is now prepared to go forth on the greatest ministry ever wrought among men.

SECTION III

JESUS' EARLY JUDEAN MINISTRY

JESUS' EARLY JUDEAN MINISTRY

"The word which God sent unto the children of Israel, preaching peace by Jesus Christ: (he is Lord of all:)

"That word, I say, ye know, which was published throughout all Judæa, and began from Galilee, after the baptism which John preached;

"How God anointed Jesus of Nazareth with the Holy Ghost and with power: who went about doing good, and healing all that were oppressed of the devil; for God was with him.

"And we are witnesses of all things which he did both in the land of the Jews, and in Jerusalem." (Acts 10:36-39.)

MANNA

Come drink of the waters of life;
Come feast on the good word of God;
Come drink from the cup of the Lord;
Come eat of his heaven-sent bread.

Come buy without money or price
That meat which gives life to the soul;
And eat at the table where seers
Have spoken the mind of the Lord.

Come drink, saith the Spirit to all;
Drink deep of those waters that fall

Like rain on the parched desert soil
Which heaven sends down for the soul.

Come feast on the manna from heaven
That falls like the dew of the morn;
Come feed in the pastures so green;
Find place with the sheep of the Lord.

Drink deep from the rivers that flow,
Direct from our great Fountain Head;
Rejoice in the waters so pure
Which he sendeth forth among men.

Drink deep of the fruit of the vine;
Eat now for salvation is free;
Drink wine on the lees well refined;
Eat now, for the time is at hand!

—Bruce R. McConkie

Chapter 26

JOHN ACCOMPLISHES HIS MISSION

John saw and bore record
of the fulness of my glory.
(D&C 93:6.)

Two Men Called John

Two men called John sit together on the banks of the
Jordan at the place called Bethabara. Both are devout and
righteous souls who, like Simeon and Anna and many
others, have been waiting for the Consolation of Israel; both
believe the Messianic prophecies and desire to ally themselves with the Deliverer and Savior of whom they speak;
both were foreordained for the ministries that are theirs; and
both have the spiritual stature, acquired long before mortal
birth, to recognize truth and comprehend the mysteries of
the kingdom.

They talk of the hosts of Jews from all walks of life who
are repenting and being baptized for the remission of sins.
They discuss the words of their prophets and the hopes of
their nation. As devout Jews they rejoice that the Promised
Messiah is at hand. They marvel at the miracle wrought but
a short time before in these very waters when one came to
fulfill all righteousness by being baptized therein. They
speak of the opening of the heavens and the descent—in

425

calmness and serenity, like a dove—of the Holy Spirit of God; and their souls vibrate as they recount again the majesty of the occasion when the voice from heaven acclaimed: "This is my beloved Son, in whom I am well pleased. Hear ye him." These are true believers whose names shall be forever enshrined in the hearts of all likeminded souls who come after.

One of these men called John, at this point in their eternal association, is acting as a teacher, the other as a disciple. The teacher is the son of Elisabeth and Zacharias, and his miraculous conception, birth, name, and ministry as the Lord's forerunner were all foretold by Gabriel. He is now just past thirty-one years of age and has been preaching and teaching and baptizing for a year and a half. He is destined to do more teaching, to be imprisoned by Herod, to be slain, and then as a resurrected personage to restore in the latter days the Aaronic Priesthood. The disciple is the son of Zebedee and the brother of James. Probably a young man, scarce out of his teens, he is destined to be an apostle of the Lord Jesus Christ, to serve with Peter and James in the First Presidency, and to write the Gospel of John, the Book of Revelation, and three New Testament epistles. He is to become the Beloved Disciple and the Revelator, to be translated, and also to come again in the latter days, along with Peter and James, to restore the Melchizedek Priesthood.

John the Baptist also is destined to write of the gospel of that Lord whose witness he is, but his account, perhaps because it contains truths and concepts that the saints and the world are not yet prepared to receive, has so far not been given to men. On May 6, 1833, however, the Lord did reveal to Joseph Smith eleven verses of the Baptist's writings, and promised that "the fulness of the record of John" would be revealed when the faith of men entitled them to receive it. (D&C 93:6-18.)

From what has been revealed of the writings of the Baptist, and from what John the Apostle has written in his Gospel, it is clear that John the Apostle had before him the writings of John the Baptist when he wrote his Gospel. John 1:1-38 and John 3:23-36 are quoted or paraphrased from that which was first written by the Baptist, a reality that will be perfectly clear to all as we consider their content and message in detail. We shall now begin such a consideration.

John the Baptist—Our Lord's Witness
(John 1:1-12; JST, John 1:1-10, 15; D&C 93:6-10)

John the Baptist, as we are aware, was "filled with the Holy Ghost from his mother's womb"; "was ordained by the angel of God at the time he was eight days old unto this power, to overthrow the kingdom of the Jews, and to make straight the way of the Lord before the face of his people, to prepare them for the coming of the Lord"; and "was baptized while he was yet in his childhood." (D&C 84:27-28.) This we learn from latter-day revelation. Our New Testament account tells us that the son of Zacharias was in the desert, apart from men, as he prepared for his ministry. John himself speaks of someone who sent him to baptize with water and who told him he would see the Holy Spirit descend upon the Son of God and remain upon him. Jesus said John was a prophet and more than a prophet. As we are aware, he held the Aaronic Priesthood and the keys thereof while in mortality, both of which he restored to Joseph Smith and Oliver Cowdery in modern times.

Now, how much would such a man know about the plan of salvation, about the mysteries of the kingdom, about the divine mission of the one whose witness he was? Surely he would rank with the apostles and prophets of his age in greatness and spiritual stature, and from such fragmentary accounts of his doings and sayings as have come down to us, we are of the opinion that he did.

What visions, what revelations, what rending of the heavens enabled our Baptist friend to write of the Lord Jesus such things as these: "I saw his glory, that he was in the beginning, before the world was"—leading us to surmise that

427

he saw, as Enoch and Abraham and Moses had each seen, a vision of preexistence and the spirits of men there assembled. "Therefore, in the beginning the Word was, for he was the Word, even the messenger of salvation—The light and the Redeemer of the world; the Spirit of truth, who came into the world, because the world was made by him, and in him was the life of men and the light of men."

These words rank with those of the greatest of the prophets. How aptly did John the Apostle distill their meaning in the beginning of his Gospel: "In the beginning was the Word, and the Word was with God, and the Word was God," and so forth; and even how much more profound is the thought as it comes to us as perfected by the Prophet Joseph Smith: "In the beginning was the gospel preached through the Son. And the gospel was the word, and the word was with the Son, and the Son was with God, and the Son was of God." Also: "In him was the gospel, and the gospel was the life, and the life was the light of men; And the light shineth in the world, and the world perceiveth it not."

At this point the Gospel account acclaims: "There was a man sent from God, whose name was John. The same came into the world for a witness, to bear witness of the light, to bear record of the gospel through the Son, unto all, that through him men might believe." John knew and understood the gospel and the plan of salvation. He came, and he knew he came, so that all men might believe in the Son and be saved. The depth and breadth and height of his teachings compare with those of Enoch and Moses and Joseph Smith.

"He was not that light," the account continues, "but came to bear witness of that light, Which was the true light, which lighteth every men who cometh into the world; Even the Son of God." Christ is the Light, the one to whom all men must turn for salvation; the word and the truth that comes from him will save men. All of his prophets, even John, send forth only a reflection of the greater light. "The words were made by him; men were made by him"—meaning as he acted by divine investiture of authority from his

428

Father—"all things were made by him, and through him, and of him," the Baptist said.

"The Word Was Made Flesh"
(John 1:13-14, 16-18; JST, John 1:12-19; D&C 93:11-17)

"And I, John," says the son of Zacharias, "bear record that I beheld his glory, as the glory of the Only Begotten of the Father, full of grace and truth, even the Spirit of truth, which came and dwelt in the flesh, and dwelt among us."

When this vision came and how much more the Baptist saw—and wrote—remains to be revealed. As he preached, month by month, to the throngs that came to him, the visions he had seen and the revelations he had received and the impressions borne in upon his soul by that Spirit which attended him from his mother's womb—all these must have been referred to and explained and quoted to the people. And his beloved disciple John, the future apostle, must have heard them orally even as he later received them on papyrus.

Of Jesus' birth the account now available says: "He was born, not of blood, nor of the will of the flesh, nor of the will of man, but of God." That is: 'Jesus was born, but not as other men are—not of blood—not of a mortal father who had flesh and blood; he was born—not of the will of the flesh—for no mortal appetite or desire was involved; other men are conceived because of the love between parents, but Jesus had no mortal father; he was born—not by the will of man—but because his Eternal Father willed it. As the Eternal Word, he was made flesh to fulfill eternal purposes.'

"For in the beginning was the Word, even the Son, who is made flesh, and sent unto us by the will of the Father," the holy account continues. "And as many as believe on his name shall receive of his fulness. And of his fulness have all we received, even immortality and eternal life, through his grace."

And then, his forerunner John being the last legal administrator of the old Mosaic dispensation and the first administrator sent of God in the new Christian dispensation, how appropriate it is that the revealed record contrasts the two systems. "For the law was given through Moses, but life and truth came through Jesus Christ. For the law was after a carnal commandment, to the administration of death; but the gospel was after the power of an endless life, through Jesus Christ, the Only Begotten Son, who is in the bosom of the Father." We cannot believe other than that all these things were explained and taught on the banks of the Jordan, even as they should be known and taught today.

"And I, John"—it is the Baptist speaking!—"saw that he received not of the fulness at the first, but received grace for grace; And he received not of the fulness at first, but continued from grace to grace, until he received a fulness; And thus he was called the Son of God, because he received not of the fulness at the first. And I, John, bear record"—and here comes the account of what the Baptist saw as he brought the Lord Jesus up out of the waters of Jordan— "and lo, the heavens were opened, and the Holy Ghost descended upon him in the form of a dove, and sat upon him, and there came a voice out of heaven saying: This is my beloved Son." This same John, looking forward to that day when Jesus would be raised in glorious immortality to receive that—and more—which was his before the world was, testified: "And I, John, bear record that he received a fulness of the glory of the Father; And he received all power, both in heaven and on earth, and the glory of the Father was with him, for he dwelt in him."

One other truth, known of old and revealed anew in plainness in our day, we must record: "And no man hath seen God at any time, except he hath borne record of the Son; for except it is through him no man can be saved."

How the cobwebs of the past are swept away when inspired men speak and write! How the fountains of truth pour out the waters of life when prophets of God are available to regulate the flow! How wondrous it is that we know as much as we do of that which was known anciently to two men called John!

And what a perspective it gives us of the mortal ministry of our Lord to know that all these things were known—and testimony was borne of them—even before he started his formal ministry. No doubt Jesus had done much informal teaching over the years, as he did when twelve years of age in his Father's House, and he may even have healed the sick and worked other miracles on special occasions. But his formal ministry, an account of which Divine Providence has preserved for us in the Gospels, began after his baptism, after his temptation, and, be it noted, after his forerunner had testified of him to the full to all who would listen.

Thus, as far as his formal ministry is concerned, at least, before Jesus taught the saving truths of his gospel; before he worked miracles; before he ministered comfort to the comfortless and gave hope to the downcast; before he called apostles and seventies; before any of the great events of his ministry were performed—before all this—the witness had gone forth; the testimony had been born; gospel truths had been taught; the people had been prepared for the Lord; the forerunner had done his work. The time had now come to transfer the responsibility for the kingdom, as it were, from John to Jesus.

John: Our Lord's Elias
(John 1:19-28; JST, John 1:21-22, 26-28)

There was a tradition among the Jews, so we learn from the Talmud, that when the Messiah came he would cry repentance, and the new kingdom would be ushered in by a great movement of reformation. John's preaching was so persuasive—so powerful was the word of testimony that God had given him—that great hosts flocked to him from Jerusalem and all Judea. Believing souls were repenting; baptisms in great numbers were being performed; and a special people was being prepared for a new kingdom. Could

431

this be the Messiah? Was John the one for whom the whole nation had so long waited? If he was not the Messiah, who then was he? And why was he baptizing and setting up a new organization among the people?

Accounts of his ministry—no doubt garbled and confused accounts, for they would have been carried by unbelievers who found fault and who sought to discredit the great movement now sweeping the nation—accounts of his ministry reached the scribes and leaders of Jewish thought. Even the Sanhedrin itself is assumed to have been concerned. These leaders—in effect the false ministers of the false sects of the day—would not deign to go and hear the teachings of an unlearned prophet, one who had not been trained for the ministry. But they would make inquiry; they would send a deputation, chosen from among the Pharisees; they would send priests and Levites to find out what was going on. Indeed, the movement had such popular appeal that they had no choice; they must know who this disturber was, who was disrupting their kingdom and their system of religion and worship.

There was also among the Jews a prevailing doctrine relative to Elijah (Elias), whose coming must precede that of Messiah, and also a prevailing doctrine relative to Elias, who should restore all things—their kingdom and glory and the truths and powers they once possessed. Portions of these doctrines remain to this day among devout Jews who set a special chair for Elijah at their Passover meals. The Jews of Jesus' day had scriptural passages relative to Elias and his ministry that we do not have, but even then their understanding of Elias and his mission was no more accurate than their knowledge of Messias and his mission.

And so the deputation came to John to propound three great questions, which he answered plainly and forthrightly:

1. *"Who art thou? . . . Art thou Elias?"* In answer, "he confessed, and denied not that he was Elias. . . . And they asked him, saying; How then art thou Elias? And he said, I am not that Elias who was to restore all things."

'Yes; I am Elias. I am sent to go before the Lord in the spirit and power of Elias. My mission is to turn the hearts of the disobedient to the wisdom of the just, and to make ready a people prepared for the Lord. I am his forerunner; I hold the priesthood of Elias. But I am not that Elias who was to restore all things; his mission is greater than mine. I am sent to prepare the way for him.'

2. *Art thou that prophet like unto Moses whose coming is promised?* Moses, the man of God, than whom there has not been so great a prophet in all Israel, had left this promise to his people: "The Lord thy God will raise up unto thee a Prophet from the midst of thee, of thy brethren, like unto me; unto him ye shall hearken. . . . [For thus saith the Lord]: I will raise them up a Prophet from among their brethren, like unto thee [Moses], and will put my words in his mouth; and he shall speak unto them all that I shall command him. And it shall come to pass, that whosoever will not hearken unto my words which he shall speak in my name, I will require it of him." (Deut. 18:15-19.)

This, of course, is a Messianic prophecy, and the one like unto Moses was the Messiah and not another, though it was falsely assumed by many, in the day of which we speak, that Moses' words had reference to someone else, identified only as "that prophet." John's answer came in the negative; he was not "that prophet."

3. *Art thou the Christ?* His answer: "I am not the Christ." Further: 'Christ, who is preferred before me, is already among you, and he is the Son of God.'

Having been so answered, the Pharisaic priests and Levites, who had yet to give answer to those in whose employ they served, had yet another question:

"*Why baptizest thou then, if thou be not the Christ, nor Elias who was to restore all things, neither that prophet?*" John answered: "I baptize with water, but there standeth one among you, whom ye know not; He it is of whom I bear record. He is that prophet, even Elias, who, coming after me, is preferred before me, whose shoe's latchet I am not worthy

433

to unloose, or whose place I am not able to fill; for he shall baptize, not only with water, but with fire, and with the Holy Ghost."

And so it is that the way was prepared. John will continue to preach and baptize for nearly a year. But he has now prepared the way; an organized body of worshippers is awaiting the Messiah; John has borne the testimony he was sent to bear; and tomorrow and the day following we shall see him in process, as he continues to teach and testify, of turning over the kingdom to Jesus and of saying to his own disciples: 'Follow thou him!'

Chapter 27

JESUS BEGINS HIS MINISTRY

He went forth ministering unto the
people, in power and great glory; and
the multitudes were gathered together
to hear him. (1 Ne. 11:28.)

"Behold the Lamb of God"
(John 1:29-34; JST, John 1:30-32, 34)

Jesus is back from communing with his Father in the
wilderness; his forty days and forty nights of fasting and
prayer and spiritual experiences have been woven into the
bones and sinews of his very being. He has now resisted the
wiles of Satan, come off triumphant in temptations that were
infinitely greater than any other person could have born, and
overcome the world. He is now prepared to minister—formally and officially, using all his time, talents, and abilities—
among his fellowmen. All that now remains is for his forerunner to make the great climactic pronouncement of Jesus'
divine Sonship, and that the son of Zacharias is now prepared to do.

John has already told the deputation from Jerusalem that
he, the son of Zacharias, is neither the Christ, nor Elias of
the restoration, nor "that prophet" of whom Moses spoke,
who, in fact, had they known it, was the Messiah. He has

also told them that he is Elias the forerunner; that he has come to prepare a people for the Lord; and that the Lord, who is God's Son, the very Christ, now ministers among them, with power not only to baptize in water, as he, John, is doing, but also to baptize with fire and the Holy Ghost. The word has gone to the leaders of the people, and it is official. The deputation has come from the Sanhedrin, and has returned to report. The highest legal body of their people will now discuss the report and be apprised—however they may react—that a legal administrator, who had obvious power and authority, has told them in plain words that the Nazarene is the Messiah.

Our Lord's Elias—standing on the banks of the Jordan at the site called Bethabara, in the presence of Jesus but newly back from the wilderness, and in the presence of all the people—is now prepared to make the formal pronouncement.

What words of preparation and background he used we do not know; no doubt this great and formal introduction was the climax of a persuasive and powerful sermon. But when it came, it was in these words: *"Behold the Lamb of God, which taketh away the sin of the world." The Lamb of God!* He that taketh away the sin of the world! How fitting that John, a priest, who, like his father before him, had offered lambs in sacrifice on the great altar—to atone for the sins of repentant Israel—should now introduce his Master as the Lamb of God, as the one whose coming sacrifice would give efficacy, virtue, and force to all the sacrifices of the past and make freedom from sin available to all men!

This pronouncement—and surely the words spoken were chosen by the Holy Ghost, whose guidance was ever with John—surely this majestic declaration stirred in the hearts of his hearers a remembrance of Isaiah's Messianic teachings about the Lord's Suffering Servant who should come. John may even have quoted from Israel's Messianic prophet, as he had done in announcing that he himself was the voice of one crying in the wilderness: "Prepare ye the way of the Lord, make straight in the desert a highway for our God. . . . And the glory of the Lord shall be revealed." (Isa. 40:3-5.)

The Lamb of God! To be slain for the sins of the world! The Lord's Suffering Servant! The Promised Messiah!

Had not Isaiah said, "He hath borne our griefs, and carried our sorrows"? Were we not promised that he would be "wounded for our transgressions" and "bruised for our iniquities," and that "with his stripes we are healed"? Did not Isaiah say, "The Lord hath laid on him the iniquity of us all," and that "he is brought as a lamb to the slaughter"? The Lamb of God, brought as a lamb to the slaughter!

Does not the Messianic prophecy say, "He was cut off out of the land of the living: for the transgression of my people was he stricken"? Is it not written that "it pleased the Lord to bruise him," and that he should "make his soul an offering for sin"? Was he not to "see the travail of his soul," and to "justify many; for he shall bear their iniquities"? Were not these Isaiah's words: "He hath poured out his soul unto death; . . . and he bare the sin of many, and made intercession for the transgressors"? (Isa. 53.)

Surely John's formal introduction—"Behold the Lamb of God, which taketh away the sin of the world"—crystallized, in the minds of receptive hearers, the whole purpose of four thousand years of sacrifices, all performed in similitude of the sacrifice of the Only Begotten of the Father.

But John also "bare record of him unto the people, saying, This is he of whom I said; After me cometh a man who is preferred before me; for he was before me, and I knew him, and that he should be made manifest to Israel; therefore am I come baptizing with water. And John bare record, saying: When he was baptized of me, I saw the Spirit descending from heaven like a dove, and it abode upon him. And I knew him; for he who sent me to baptize with water, the same said unto me; Upon whom thou shalt see the Spirit descending, and remaining on him, the same is he who baptizeth with the Holy Ghost."

John, having so testified, must now see to it that his dis-

437

ciples—all those baptized by him for the remission of sins—
turn to Jesus and receive the promised baptism of the Holy
Ghost. He must invite his followers to forsake him, as it
were, and follow the one whom he had been sent to introduce.

John's Disciples Follow Jesus
(John 1:35-40)

John, who bore testimony of Jesus, did so for one reason
and one reason only: he was seeking to persuade men to
believe in Christ, to come unto him, to accept him as the Son
of God, and to be saved by obedience to the laws and ordinances of his gospel. When John baptized for the remission
of sins, he was not seeking disciples who would follow him,
except as he guided them to the one who should come after.
Indeed, the very remission of sins that he promised could not
come until they received the Holy Ghost—the baptism of
fire—which burns sin and evil out of a human soul as though
by fire. John's whole purpose was to persuade his disciples to
follow, not himself, but the Lord Jesus whose witness he was.

Thus, on the day after the great pronouncement in which
he introduced Jesus and testified of his divinity, John was
standing, still on Jordan's bank, with two of his disciples.
Jesus walked nearby, and John said to his disciples—
Andrew, the brother of Simon Peter, and John, the future
apostle and revelator—"Behold the Lamb of God!" We do
not know what preceded or followed these words; it may
well be they were accompanied by explanations relative to
John's own ministry—his ministry as the Elias of Preparation—and that also of Jesus, who came as the Elias of Restoration for that day. In any event the two disciples left John
and followed Jesus—which was the whole intent and design
and purpose of John where they and all of his disciples were
concerned.

And this raises a question of great import. Why did
Andrew and John leave their Baptist friend—whose doc-

trines they believed, whose words thrilled their souls, and who had himself baptized each of them in Jordan—to follow another whom as yet they did not even know? What force impels these or any seekers of religious truth to forsake family and friends and possessions and to go they know not where, at the behest of others whom they do not know, but whose words they believe? The answer: they have what we call a testimony; they know in their souls of the truth of the Lord's work; and they are willing to forsake all else to follow the new light that has been kindled in their souls.

What is this thing that we call a testimony? It is the revealed knowledge that Jesus is the Lord; that he is the Son of the living God; that he was crucified for the sins of the world; that he has brought life and immortality to light through his gospel; that his is the only name given under heaven whereby men may be saved; and that his church and kingdom, in whatever age is involved, is the one place where salvation may be found. Such a testimony comes from the Holy Ghost, and from no other source. "By the power of the Holy Ghost ye may know the truth of all things." (Moro. 10:5.)

When the Holy Spirit of God speaks to the spirit within a man—revealing truth, certifying that Jesus is the Savior— the person so blessed has a testimony. This witness comes whenever a person obeys the law upon which its receipt is predicated. "And the Spirit shall be given unto you by the prayer of faith." (D&C 42:14.) When a prophet or righteous man speaks by the power of the Holy Ghost, the Holy Ghost carries his words into the hearts of all who are in tune with the Spirit and bears record to such persons that the words spoken are true. The hearers, thus receiving truth from the Spirit, gain testimonies for themselves. Hence Paul's statement, "It pleased God by the foolishness of preaching to save them that believe." (1 Cor. 1:21.)

And so we find John bearing testimony by the power of the Holy Ghost that Jesus is the Lamb of God, the Savior of the world, whose atoning sacrifice frees men from an eternal burden of sin, and we find Andrew and John—themselves also in tune—receiving the witness in their hearts and knowing for themselves of the truth of what John said. With this knowledge they now have no choice. They must leave John and follow Jesus, for Jesus is the Lord. And so follow him they do.

Jesus, looking upon them, asks, "What seek ye?" They reply, "Rabbi, . . . where dwellest thou?" Jesus says, "Come and see." And they go and abide with Jesus that day, as their question indicates it was their desire to do. What they talked about that day we do not know, but when the day was over they knew, as they had aforetime learned from John, that he was the Messiah. They had determined henceforth to follow him, and they were ready to go out and bear testimony of his divine Sonship and enlist others in his cause.

The transfer of disciples from John to Jesus is now underway; the circle of loyalty toward the forerunner is being enlarged to take in the One who was to come, and we cannot but suppose that thousands of other devout and believing souls left the Baptist to follow the One whom he had baptized.

Jesus Calls Other Disciples
(John 1:41-51; JST, John 1:42, 44)

Now the processes of conversion are beginning. Andrew and John have come into the fold. They know Jesus is the Lord—they have heard his voice and believed his words. Andrew now does what every new convert should do: he seeks out the members of his family so they too may receive the saving truths of the gospel. And so Andrew "findeth his own brother Simon," and says: "We have found the Messias." It is just that simple: there was no long period of growth and development; he did not need to hear many sermons and see many miracles; it is not something that he grew into gradually. Andrew knew whereof he spoke, and he knew it the very day he left John and followed Jesus. 'We have found the Christ; he is the Messiah; God's Son has come; he is the Deliverer; John testified of him; and we now bear record that John's witness is true.'

And so Andrew brought Simon—Simon Peter!—unto Jesus. Jesus said: "Thou art Simon, the son of Jona, thou shalt be called Cephas." This new name—"which is, by interpretation, a seer, or a stone"—forecast what was to be in the life of Andrew's brother, who was destined to be, under the Lord, the chief officer of the perfected church and kingdom, the foundations of which were then being laid. Peter, the Rock and the Seer, who would yet hold the keys of the kingdom of heaven; Peter, to whom the Lord would one day say that the gates of hell should never prevail against the rock of revelation and the seership of eternal vision—Peter has now come into the fold.

Whether Peter was one of the Baptist's disciples we do not know, nor do we know how much of the witness of the Lord's Elias he had heard. Having been found by Andrew and having come to Jesus, he was taught the gospel. His soul was open and he believed the message. He too knew, immediately and by instinct, as it were, of the divine Sonship of him whom he now chose to follow. The completeness and surety of the initial conversion of John and Andrew and Peter is attested to in these words of scripture: "And they were fishermen. And they straightway left all, and followed Jesus." Such is the mark of valiant souls who know whereof they speak. These disciples had testimonies of the truth and divinity of the work from the very day they met and were taught by the Lord Jesus. Thereafter they would be fed spiritually by his teachings and his deeds, but from the beginning they were forsaking all to follow him. Even their daily bread and that of their families must somehow be supplied by other means; they are laying down their nets to commence a work that will make them fishers of men.

On the next day, Jesus and his three disciples go into Galilee to a city called Bethsaida. There Jesus himself finds Philip, and says, "Follow me," which means that our Lord

441

and the others told Philip all that had transpired in recent days. They taught him the gospel, told him of the Baptist's teachings and testimony, and, each in turn, bore personal testimony of Jesus' divine Sonship and of the Messianic ministry that was now commencing. Philip believes, not simply because two words are spoken to him, but because the message of salvation is expounded in plainness and by the power of the Spirit. His bosom burns within him, and he knows as the others know.

What then? Philip, being converted, finds Nathanael—who is believed to be Bartholomew, the apostle—and says, "We have found him, of whom Moses in the law, and the prophets, did write, Jesus of Nazareth, the son of Joseph." Moses and the prophets wrote of the Messiah. Philip has gained his testimony, and he is now bearing it to his friend Nathanael. New converts seek out their friends, that they too may receive the light of heaven that has come into their souls. Philip calls Jesus "the son of Joseph," even as Mary said to the young lad in the temple, "Thy father and I have sought thee sorrowing," meaning that Joseph was assumed by those who knew the family to be the father of Him whose Father was divine.

Nathanael's response quotes a derogatory proverb of the day. "Can there any good thing come out of Nazareth?" he asks. Philip's response is the persuasive comment: "Come and see." Whatever else Philip said, his explanations were sufficiently influential to cause Nathanael to accept his invitation. They go to Jesus, who says of the newly found disciple, "Behold an Israelite indeed, in whom is no guile!"

Reacting quite naturally, Nathanael asks, "Whence knowest thou me?" Jesus' response is an exhibition of the gift of seership, the gift to see and have a complete awareness of events in the past, present, or future that transpire out of sight of the viewer. "Nathanael had undergone some surpassing spiritual experience while praying, or meditating, or worshiping under a fig tree. The Lord and giver of all things spiritual, though absent in body, had been present with Nathanael in spirit." (*Commentary* 1:134.) In answer to Nathanael's question, Jesus says: "Before that Philip called thee, when thou wast under the fig tree, I saw thee."

Perhaps our Lord went on to reveal to the future apostle what had actually taken place under the fig tree; and certainly, as Philip and Nathanael had traveled together to the place where Jesus was, there had been extended discussion of the testimony of the Baptist, of the reactions of Andrew and John and Simon, and of Philip himself. All this, coupled with Jesus' seeric declaration, caused the guileless Nathanael to formulate in words what already he had been phrasing in his heart: "Rabbi, thou art the Son of God; thou art the King of Israel." The fifth new convert had been added to our Lord's entourage as he prepared to go from Bethsaida, on the shores of the Sea of Galilee, to Cana, where he would change water into wine. Nathanael now knew as the others knew of the divinity of Him whom they had chosen to follow.

"Because I said unto thee, I saw thee under the fig tree, believest thou?" Jesus asked of his newest disciple, though in fact that was only the crowning cause of the testimony. Then he gave him this promise: "Thou shalt see greater things than these." He was to see greater things than he had seen under the fig tree, and have a greater manifestation of the gift of seership than Jesus had just shown forth. "Verily, verily, I say unto you," our Lord continued, "Hereafter ye shall see heaven open, and the angels of God ascending and descending upon the Son of man." When and under what circumstances this prophetic utterance was fulfilled, we do not know; we have only the ever-present assurance that all things that this Man ever spake came to pass according to his word.

Jesus here calls himself the Son of Man—not in allusion, as is falsely supposed by the scholars of sectarianism, to his humanity, as inherited from Mary, but he calls himself the Son of Man because God, who is his Father, is a Holy Man. "In the language of Adam, Man of Holiness is his name, and the name of his Only Begotten is the Son of Man, even Jesus Christ." (Moses 6:57.)

All of those whom he has so far called as his special disciples, as his traveling companions, as those who are to forsake all and follow him in his ministry, as those who one day will be called to the holy apostleship—all of these have borne testimony that they know he is divine. They have said he is the Messias; he is the one of whom Moses and the prophets wrote; he is the Son of God; he is the King of Israel. This has been their witness. Now Jesus speaks forth his own testimony of himself. He is the Son of Man, the Son of Man of Holiness, the Son of that Holy Being whom their fathers worshipped in Jehovah's name.

Truly Jesus' ministry has begun. He is teaching the gospel. He is calling disciples to forsake all and follow him. He is accepting their Spirit-born witness that he is God's Son, and he is adding his own testimony that their words are true, saying in his own words, 'I am the Son of Man, the Son of God. Follow thou me.'

Chapter 28

JESUS BEGINS HIS MIRACLES

The Lord Omnipotent . . . shall go forth
amongst men, working mighty miracles,
such as healing the sick, raising the
dead, causing the lame to walk, the
blind to receive their sight, and the deaf
to hear, and curing all manner of
diseases. (Mosiah 3:5.)

Miracles—Their Nature and Occurrence

Jesus is in Cana of Galilee at a wedding feast. At his mother's earnest entreaty he turns water into wine; about one hundred fifty gallons of water become wine of delicious taste and superior quality, excelling whatever else the guests had been drinking.

It is a miracle, the first public miracle of a great ministry of miracles. Shortly, at his word, the lame shall leap, the blind see, and the ears of the deaf shall be unstopped. We shall soon see the sick healed, paralyzed bodies regain their vigor, and lepers cleansed. He will multiply loaves and fishes, calm storms, and walk on water. He will curse a fig tree, restore a severed ear, and even say to a rotting and stinking corpse: 'Arise; be made whole; live again!'

The Lord Jesus—the Lord of life—is going forth to heal

the sick, cast out devils, and raise the dead, and to perform such marvelous miracles that none who know of them—except those who love darkness rather than light because their deeds are evil—can do aught but say: 'Truly, this is God's Son; he is the Messiah. Let us follow him, and he will save us!'

One by one we shall see him perform his mighty works, and—though we know he is God's Son—yet we shall marvel at the deeds he will do. But as a prelude we must be reminded of the law of miracles and tell ourselves anew of the marvelous way in which the Lord always and everlastingly deals with his people.

What then are miracles, and how are they wrought?

Miracles defy full definition; they are manifestations of the power of God in the lives of men. That which was a miracle yesterday may be commonplace today, and some of the most common events are the greatest miracles. Birth and life and existence—these are miracles, and yet few so consider them. Death is a miracle, as is resurrection, and what is a greater miracle than the cleansing of a sin-sick soul through repentance and the receipt of the Holy Spirit?

We ordinarily think of miracles as those signs and wonders and marvels which God does for his people because they have faith in him, and which they cannot do for themselves. More often than not these performances seem to transcend natural laws, though in fact they are always in complete harmony with them, and are simply the manifestations of higher laws not generally known to mortal men.

Miracles are part of the gospel of the Lord Jesus Christ. They are one of the chief characteristics of true believers. Where they are found, there are the Lord's people; where they are not found, there the Lord's people are not. They are the signs that Deity gives to identify those who have faith. Faith is power, the power of God. Unless men have power, among other things, to perform miracles, they do not have faith.

God is a God of miracles; everlastingly, always, and

without exception, he performs miracles among his people. The decree is that signs shall follow them that believe; unless the signs are present, the beliefs involved are not founded on the Rock of Eternal Truth, who is Christ. God is an "unchangeable Being," a Being "with whom is no variableness, neither shadow of turning"—if it were not so "he would cease to be God," which he cannot do. And because he is "the same yesterday, today, and forever," miracles are always found among those who have faith. (Morm. 9; James 1:17; *Mormon Doctrine*, 2nd ed., pp. 506-8.)

Adam, as Michael, took part in the creation of the earth; and what is a greater miracle than to take unorganized matter and so arrange it that life in all its forms and varieties—including man—can dwell on the planet thus provided for mortal habitation? "Through faith [which is power, God's power] the worlds [this world and all others] were framed by the word of God." (Heb. 11:3.)

And if the earth was made by faith; if great mountains and small streams came into being by God's power; if seas and dry lands took their place because of faith; if storms and tempests and all the elements were set in being by the miracle of creation, why not continue to control and govern all these things by the same power? What is more natural than to see Enoch and Moriancumer move mountains and turn rivers out of their courses? Why should we think it impossible for Moses to part the Red Sea so that its waters congeal into walls on the right hand and on the left? Or what question should arise because Joshua stops the sun, or Jesus stills the storm or walks on the water? Where there is faith, all needed miracles are forthcoming.

Melchizedek, while yet a child, closes the mouths of lions and quenches the violence of fire; Moses and Aaron pour out plagues upon Pharaoh and his people, even to the point of slaying the firstborn in every Egyptian family; Elijah calls down fire from heaven to destroy his enemies, and multiplies the meal and the oil of a widow, whose son he raises from death; and so on and so on and so on. All these miracles—

447

and they are but samples of what has been—are performed in the name of Christ, by the power of Christ, because men had faith and because signs always follow those who believe.

And it is so obvious that it scarce needs stating, that if the Lord's prophets are dividing seas and stopping the sun, they are also healing the sick and opening the eyes of the blind. For instance: "There were great and marvelous works wrought by the disciples of Jesus, insomuch that they did heal the sick, and raise the dead, and cause the lame to walk, and the blind to receive their sight, and the deaf to hear; and all manner of miracles did they work among the children of men; and in nothing did they work miracles save it were in the name of Jesus." (4 Ne. 1:5.)

And it also scarce needs stating, so obvious is the fact, that the Son of God in his mortal ministry, sent as he was to labor among men and to save that which was lost, was destined to perform more miracles and work more wonders than any of the prophets who went before or who shall come after. In this, as in all things, he is the pattern.

The Marriage Feast in Cana of Galilee
(John 2:1-2; JST, John 2:1)

Jesus and his disciples—Andrew, John, Simon Peter, Philip, and Nathanael-Bartholomew, five noble souls who one day will be apostles—are in Bethsaida on the shores of the Sea of Galilee. The newly called followers of the Messiah are basking in the glory of his presence and in the new light of testimony that has come into their lives. They are all, both Jesus and the disciples, "called" to a marriage and to a marriage feast in nearby Cana—Cana of Galilee, a little village whose name is everywhere known for one reason and one reason only: our Lord performed his first public miracle there.

The Blessed Mary seems to be in charge of the festive portions of the wedding celebration, but no mention is made of Joseph, giving rise to the assumption that he has now passed on to that paradise where the righteous find peace and rest. John's account says the disciples were called, without indicating by whom or on what authority. Shall we not say—since Jesus' ministry has now begun and nothing must be permitted to interfere with it—that their presence was required, that one or more of them was an essential part of the proceedings that ever thereafter would be remembered for the miracle that was then to occur. Scholars generally feel that some member of the Holy Family was being married, and that Mary was supervising and guiding what went on.

Marriages and all that attended them had a significance and an import among the Jews that bespoke the divine origin of the sacred ordinance. They and their fathers believed that a proper marriage in the house of Israel had eternal implications. In Jesus' day there was a formal betrothal ceremony, after which the parties—as pertaining to inheritance, adultery, and the need for a formal divorce— were considered as married, except that they did not live together as husband and wife until after the later and second ceremony.

Devout persons fasted and confessed their sins before marriage and believed they gained a forgiveness of sins by entering the holy order of matrimony. They even had an allegory among them that "God Himself had spoken the words of blessing over the cup at the union of our first parents, when Michael and Gabriel acted as groomsmen, and the angelic choir sang the wedding hymn." (Edersheim 1:353.)

On the evening of the marriage, the bride was taken in a bridal procession to her husband's home. It was customary for friends and neighbors and onlookers to join the procession. A formal ceremony was performed; a legal instrument was signed; the required washings were performed and benedictions spoken; the cup was filled, blessed, and drunk; and the marriage supper commenced. The marriage feast lasted from a day to a week or more, with a governor of the feast acting as master of ceremonies.

Jesus' attendance at the marriage in Cana and his participation in the marriage festivities—whatever the reason and whatever the part he played—puts a divine stamp of approval upon marriage and its attendant festivities. Those who forbid marriage to any portion of their adherents are not of God. Also, at the very beginning of his ministry, it dramatized the course his ministerial service would take. Whereas John, the last legal administrator of the Old Order, had come fasting, praying, obeying the letter of the law, a prophet of the traditional mien, garbed in garments made of camel's hair—our Lord, the great Prophet of the New Order, came eating and drinking and associating with his fellows in a friendly and easy manner. His was to be a ministry among and with people, a ministry to touch the lives of men in ways in which they had never been touched before. And indeed, where better could he begin his ministry of public miracles than at a wedding feast, and upon an occasion when joy and rejoicing were in every heart?

Jesus Turns Water into Wine
(John 2:3-12; JST, John 2:4, 9, 11)

Every hour of every day somewhere on earth the Lord turns water into wine. By his power, pursuant to the laws he has ordained, men prepare the soil and plant the vine; from the good earth, from the rains that fall, and from the light of the sun, the vine takes nutrient, grows, and bears fruit; men dung it and dig about it and prune it, and the fruit matures and ripens; they harvest the crop and process it in the wine vat; and it comes out as wine on the lees well refined. It is a miracle. He who has given a law unto all things provides the way and the means; the water and the elements that could turn into raisins become wine instead. Life in all its forms is a miracle, and the transmutation, as it were, of one substance into another is a part and portion of earthly existence.

But in March of A.D. 27 in Cana, an obscure village of

Galilee that would not even be known today, had not this event occurred there, the Lord of life—who is the very one who gave a law unto all things, by which they grow and are and change—he who is the Lord Jesus, turned water into wine, in an instant, suddenly as it were, by laws known to him but unknown to us. It was a miracle, the first of his public miracles.

"The miracles of Christ were miracles addressed," Farrar says, "not to a cold and skeptic curiosity, but to a loving and humble faith. They needed not the acuteness of the impostor, or the self-assertion of the thaumaturge. They were indeed the signs—almost, we had said, the accidental signs—of his divine mission; but their primary object was the alleviation of human suffering, or the illustration of sacred truths, or, as in this instance, the increase of innocent joy. An obscure village, an ordinary wedding, a humble home, a few faithful peasant guests—such a scene, and no splendid amphitheatre or stately audience, beheld one of Christ's greatest miracles of power." (Farrar, pp. 127-28.)

At some point in the wedding festivities, apparently after the joyous feast had gone on for some time, "the mother of Jesus saith unto him, They have no wine." That she felt some obligation to the assembled guests none can doubt, and that she expected her Son to do something about it is also clear. Perhaps Jesus himself, at this particular marriage supper, had a personal obligation to look out for the well-being of the guests and see that they wanted for nothing. Eastern hospitality was of such a nature that it would be a matter of great embarrassment to those in charge of the festivities if the needs of the guests went unheeded.

But we are left to surmise what Mary expected Jesus to do, and it is not unreasonable to conclude that she wanted him to use his divine power. She knew God was his Father; she knew of the angelic message sent at his birth, and of the heavenly choirs that sang hosannas to his name; she had heard the testimony of Simeon and Anna in the temple; she had seen the wise men from the East and heard their witness; she knew of the angelic direction Joseph had received; and she had received the gentle rebuke, "Wist ye not that I must be about my Father's business?" when she and Joseph found their twelve-year-old teaching in the temple. Of all this we are certain.

And we cannot avoid the conclusion that between Jesus' twelfth and thirtieth years there were many marvelous and miraculous things of which Mary knew. There is no reason to believe there was a spiritual drought of eighteen years, a period when all that was divine and heaven-guided should be obscured. Nor can we avoid believing that Mary was made aware of the mission and testimony of John—her first cousin once removed, the son of her confidante and counselor, Elisabeth, the one whose birth Gabriel had also heralded.

Surely she would have been told of her Son's baptism—if indeed she was not present—and of the descent of the Holy Ghost upon him, and of the voice from heaven which said: "This is my beloved Son, in whom I am well pleased. Hear ye him." She may already have learned of Jesus' forty days in the wilderness and of the spiritual experiences and the temptations incident to them. And we would suppose that accounts of the conversion of the first disciples had reached her. The five who were with Jesus at the marriage would have sought her out to recount how they knew that the fruit of her womb was, as Philip expressed it, "Him of whom Moses in the law, and the prophets, did write," or as Nathanael testified, "The Son of God ... the King of Israel."

In this setting, how can we do other than suppose that Mary expected her Son to provide the wine that would assure the success of the celebration then under way.

Jesus' reply seems to contain—as did his words as a twelve-year-old in the temple—a mild reproof. "Woman," he said—a form of salutation that was respectful according to the language and customs of the day, a form of salutation that he would again use as he beheld her at the foot of the cross and was lovingly putting her in the care and keeping of his beloved John—"Woman," he said, "what have I to do with thee? mine hour is not yet come." It is as though he said: 'Please, I am no longer placed in your care. No longer am I subject to the guidance of an earthly mother. My ministry has commenced. I am on my Father's business, and I must make the choices. I will determine when the hour is ripe to perform miracles, to preach, to do all that I am sent to do.'

His mother, understanding, knowing him and his ways, aware of their relationship, and receiving his gentle reproof, yet having perfect confidence in him and knowing her request was right and would be granted, said to the servants: "Whatsoever he saith unto you, do it."

Now it was the practice of the Jews—pharisaically imposed and rabbinically endorsed—to wash, for ritualistic and purification purposes, their hands before and after eating and also to wash the vessels used. The regulations and procedures, set out in the Mishnah and Talmud, were burdensome, unrealistic, and detailed. In the house in Cana six waterpots of stone were available for this purpose. Apparently they were empty, but each, when full, may have held as much as twenty-five gallons, making as much as one hundred fifty gallons of water available for the ritualistic performances of that abode.

Jesus said to the servants, "Fill the waterpots with water." They filled them to the brim. "Draw out now, and bear unto the governor of the feast," he said; and they did so.

Tasting "the water that was made wine," and not knowing whence it came, though the servants knew, the governor said to the bridegroom: "Every man at the beginning doth set forth good wine; and when men have well drunk, then that which is worse: but thou hast kept the good wine until now."

We can well imagine the sense of reverential awe that came into the hearts of the revelers as the servants let it be known what Mary's Son had done. And we can suppose that all the villagers wondered and asked, as they heard the account, 'What manner of man is this? We thought he was a carpenter of Nazareth; can he be the Messiah, as some say?' John says that by this act, Jesus "manifested forth his glory; and his disciples believed on him." Miracles follow faith, and miracles strengthen faith.

Jesus turned water into wine. Did he speak out or merely will it so? No matter; it is the deed that counts. He who but shortly before had refused to turn stones into bread to feed his own famished soul, and that for good and sufficient reasons, now provided sweet nectar for others that they might add to their already sated pleasures, as they rejoiced with a bride and a bridegroom in their newfound happiness. Ought we not also to turn the ordinary waters of life—the ritualistic and mundane washings and performances that go with mortality—into the wine of righteousness and joy that dwells in the hearts of those whose lives are purified?

After the wedding feast Jesus, Mary, her other sons, and the five disciples went to Capernaum, where they stayed until time to go to the Feast of the Passover in Jerusalem, which our Lord must needs attend and where his ministry was to take a turn and gain a prominence that none but he could now foresee.

Chapter 29

JESUS MINISTERS AT THE PASSOVER

I am become a stranger unto my
brethren, and an alien unto my
mother's children. For the zeal of thine
house hath eaten me up; and the
reproaches of them that reproached
thee are fallen upon me. (Ps. 69:8-9.)[1]

Jesus Attends the Feast of the Passover
(John 2:12-13)

Our Blessed Lord, after turning water into wine at the wedding celebration in Cana—which was in March of A.D. 27, according to the chronology we are using—chose for himself a city of residence, a home base as it were for the years of his active ministry. That city was Capernaum. Matthew says he "dwelt" there, that it was "his own city." (Matt. 4:13; 9:1.)

We are left to suppose that Mary and her other sons also now lived in this beautiful spot on the shores of the Sea of Galilee; at least they traveled with Jesus from Cana to Capernaum after the wedding feast. We know it was the home of Peter and Andrew, and of James and John, and that it was the place where Matthew sat as a collector of customs. It may be that on the occasion of this visit—for Jesus traveled much and abode in many places during the years of his ministry, and indeed had no permanent place to lay his head—it may be that he stayed with his family members. On later occasions it was his wont to stay with Peter.

Capernaum itself, in the days of Jesus, lay amid the wealth and prosperity of Palestine. The fertility of the plain of Gennesaret was legendary; the district itself was spoken of as "the garden of God" and as "paradise." It was here that Capernaum and numerous other cities, all exceeding fifteen thousand in population, were located. The Sea of Galilee, otherwise called the Lake of Gennesaret, was plied by four thousand boats. Industry, agriculture, and commerce thrived in all the cities there located.

Jesus' choice of Capernaum as the city of his abode placed him in the mainstream of Galilean life, in the midst of a people—part Jewish, part Gentile—where he, as the Light sent forth "to lighten the Gentiles," could fulfill Isaiah's Messianic utterance: 'In the land of Zebulun and of Naphtali, beyond Jordan, in Galilee of the Gentiles, the people that walk in darkness shall see a great light; they that dwell in the land of the shadow of death, upon them shall the light shine.' (Isa. 9:1-2.)

And shine it did, as shine it must, for a short season, following which Capernaum, then exalted to heaven, would be brought down to hell. "For if the mighty works, which have been done in thee," Jesus would soon say, "had been done in Sodom, it would have remained until this day." (Matt. 11:23-24.) Today we do not so much as know the site of ancient Capernaum.

But Jesus' stay in Capernaum on this occasion was brief. John says that "he, and his mother, and his brethren, and his disciples"—including, at least, Peter, Andrew, John, Philip, and Nathanael-Bartholomew—"continued there not many days." It would appear that the whole group of them then "went up to Jerusalem" with Jesus, because "the Jews' passover was at hand." Perhaps Jesus, during his brief stay there, had some opportunity to preach and teach in the streets; certainly any Sabbaths would have seen him in the synagogue teaching doctrine, bearing testimony, and working miracles. But the Passover, and the Feast of Unleavened Bread, which was linked with it, was now to receive the chief attention of the little group. In the year A.D. 27 these festive events covered the period April 11 to 18.

This Passover time—the first of four during Jesus' mortal ministry—was a glorious time of festivity and worship when every faithful male in Israel, if he could possibly arrange it, presented himself before the Lord in the Holy Temple in the Holy City. As the First of the Faithful, Jesus must do his duty and go to worship in his Father's House.

There again, as when first he went up at the age of twelve, and as when he attended during all the years of his preparation, he will mingle with the worshipping throngs and feel the spirit of a people set apart from all nations because they worship Jehovah and sacrifice to his holy name. There, as is his wont, he will keep the feast, eat the paschal lamb, and renew his covenant to serve God and keep his commandments—all in connection with the sacrificial offerings that will be made, legally and officially, by those holding the Priesthood of Aaron.

But this time—with holy zeal, for was it not written, "The zeal of thine house hath eaten me up"?—this time he himself, the future Paschal Lamb, will minister as none others had before done in that house which his Father still owns, but which has been desecrated by designing and sinful men whose hearts are set on money and carnal things rather than upon the great sacrificial ceremonies that would have freed them from their sins.

Jesus Cleanseth His Father's House
(John 2:14-17)

Arriving in Jerusalem to keep the Feast of the Passover, Jesus and his friends found their way to the Holy Temple, as all who came up to the Holy City to worship the King, the Lord of Hosts, at that season must needs do. He and his disciples came to his Father's House, to the House of the Most High God, to the house where all Israel had been commanded to worship the Father in the name of the Son by the power of the Holy Ghost. He and they came to join in worship of the Supreme Being, to place themselves in tune with the Infinite, to renew their covenants, and (in the case of all save the Sinless One who led the group) to receive a remission of their sins through the sacrificial ordinances that would be performed by those legal administrators who sat in Aaron's seat.

His Father's House! Outwardly a house of glory and honor, with solid gold covering the great marble stones of the inner temple building; the great altar of unhewn stones in daily use; the holy place, containing the table for the Bread of the Presence, the golden candlestick, and the altar of incense, in constant use; the veil and the Holy of Holies, into which the high priest went each year to make an atonement for the sins of the people, as it should be—outwardly, in architecture and form and magnificence, his Father's House was, for that day and time, as it should have been.

But inwardly it was full of ravening wolves, as it were, of greedy souls who made merchandise of sacred things, and whose hearts were sealed against the true meanings and purpose of the sacred ceremonies designed for that holy place. It is no wonder that the Shekinah no longer rested in the Holy of Holies, nor would it have done so even if the ark of the covenant—with the tables from Sinai, the Urim and Thummim (as we suppose), the mercy seat of pure gold, and the Cherubim—had been present as of old. It was to this spiritual wickedness that a righteously indignant Son of God now addressed himself.

Having passed through the vendor-crowded streets where hawkers of wares sought to profit from the traveling worshippers; having been enticed to buy salt and oil and wine and all else for sacrifices; having been offered clay dishes and ovens for the Passover lamb; having faced the higher prices made possible by the tourist trade, Jesus and his group came into the outer court, the Court of the Gentiles. There they looked upon a scene of unholy merchandising that desecrated the temple and testified against those who were engaged in its money-grubbing practices. There they saw the moneychangers, those who examined sacrificial animals for a fee, the sellers of sheep, and the hawkers of oxen and doves. The noise and the haggling destroyed every vestige of reverence; the lowing of cattle and the bleating of sheep drowned out the priestly performances nearby; and the filth and stench of the barnyard so overpowered the senses that arriving pilgrims soon lost the desire to worship the Lord in Spirit and in truth. It was a scene of desecration, of physical filth, and of spiritual degeneracy.

Moneychangers in the temple of the Lord! Greed and avarice and sharp dealing replacing the spirit of true worship! True it was that each year all Israel, both Jews and proselytes—women, slaves, and minors excepted—had to pay the atonement money to ransom their souls. This temple-tribute of half a shekel, payable only in the shekel of the Sanctuary, gave rise to a thriving and profitable exchange business. Palestinian, Roman, Grecian, Egyptian, Tyrian, and Persian coins, among others, were in common circulation in the Holy Land. Money-changing involved weighing the coins, taking deductions for loss of weight, arguing, debating, disputing, bargaining, oftentimes using scales of questionable accuracy. Tables piled high with coins of all denominations and nations were the stock in trade of those who charged a fixed fee, and more, in the lucrative enterprise.

For a fee those who brought their own sacrificial animals had them examined at the temple for Levitical fitness. All that was needed for meat offerings and drink offerings was for sale within the sacred walls. Oxen, sheep, and doves could be purchased outright. There is a record of Baba ben

Buta bringing in three thousand sheep at one time for sale in the Court of the Gentiles. Great herds of cattle and tiers of wickers filled with flocks of doves were more the rule than the exception. A courtyard, paved with marble, that could accommodate two hundred and ten thousand people had ample room for the needed sacrificial animals, for those who bought and sold, and for those who weighed and haggled as coins exchanged hands.

Profits earned or extorted through all this sacrifice-related merchandising went both to individuals and to the temple officials. Sums paid for the items needed for meat and drink offerings went directly to the temple; others paid rent for the use of temple space. Even a temple market, referred to as the bazaars of the sons of Annas, occupied part of the space in the court. Annas was, of course, the high priest before whom Jesus would stand in three years during another Passover season. There was considerable popular resentment against the sons of Annas and their temple merchandising. "From the unrighteousness of the traffic carried on in these Bazaars, and the greed of their owners," Edersheim says, "the 'Temple-market' was at the time most unpopular." Because of the prevalent abuses, he says, it is "no wonder that, in the figurative language of the Talmud, the Temple is represented as crying out against them: 'Go hence, ye sons of Eli, ye defile the Temple of Jehovah!' " (Edersheim 1:371-72.)[2]

This popular feeling relative to the merchandising practices that desecrated the temple enables us to see why there was no popular outcry when Jesus drove out the cattle and the money-changers. Aside from the fact that the targets of his indignation had their mouths closed by their own guilty consciences, the cleansing act performed by our Lord seems to have met with popular appeal among the people.

We have no doubt that the eyes of many were upon Jesus when he entered the Temple Court. It was as though the Lord whom they sought had "suddenly come to his temple." He was there in person, the Incarnate Jehovah, not to "purify the sons of Levi" (Mal. 3:1-3), as he would do at his Second Coming, but to drive out both the men and beasts whose filth and dung desecrated the Holy Place.

We are confident that word of his coming had preceded him. John's testimony that Jesus was the Lamb of God had not been borne in a corner. All Jerusalem had heard the word. The testimonies of his own disciples had surely been noised about, and the Galilean pilgrims who came to the Passover would not have hesitated to speak of the water that became wine.

And so, as the center of attraction, with many waiting and wondering what this new Rabbi would do, he who eighteen years before had said, within these same walls, that he must be about his Father's business, now engaged in that business with vigor and vengeance.

Sickened by the stench and the filth, repulsed by the jangling and haggling as paltry coins were exchanged, saddened by the complete absence of spirituality with which the chosen people should have been so richly endowed, the Son of Him whose house these evil miscreants then desecrated "made a scourge of small cords." Then, filled with indignant justice, his righteous anger blazing forth in physical strength, he of whom Moses had said, "The Lord is a man of war" (Ex. 15:3), this Galilean from Nazareth, drove out the sheep and the oxen and those in whose custody they lowed and bleated.

To the keepers of the doves he commanded: "Take these things hence." With force and violence he overturned the tables of the moneychangers, scattering their ill-gotten coins amid the dirt and dung on the marble floor. To those who bought and sold, who haggled in the temple bazaars, and whose hearts were set on laying up treasures on earth rather than in heaven, with a voice of authority he decreed: *"Make not my Father's house an house of merchandise."*

Truly, as Peter and John and Andrew and Philip and Nathanael and all his disciples saw this open and bold ushering in of our Lord's Messianic ministry, they rejoiced in what he did and remembered the Messianic words of Israel's greatest king: *"The zeal of thine house hath eaten me up."*

"My Father's house!" "Thine house," O God, *'for thou art my Father.'* When but a lad of twelve, when a mature man of thirty—during all the years of his life and ministry—Jesus, freely, openly, publicly, to all men, be they devoted disciples or sinning scribes, was bold to announce that God was his Father. Even the cleansing and purifying of the house Herod had built for the Hebrews became an occasion for such a solemn declaration. Jesus was God's Son. He knew it, and he wanted all men to gain the same sure knowledge.

Jesus Foretells His Own Death and Resurrection
(*John 2:18-25; JST, John 2:22, 24*)

Jesus has driven the cattle and sheep from the Court of the Gentiles; the cages of doves have been removed from the sacred site; the coins and scales of the bankers, who contended over the weight of their coins, are lying in the rubble; and the temple bazaars of the sons of Annas the high priest are in shambles. Merchandising in the temple has ceased, and profits are no longer flowing into the pockets of the rapacious and priest-appointed merchants who plied their wares among the Passover throngs. Indeed, their flocks and herds are scattered, their coins lost, and their merchandise destroyed. The loss to individuals and to the temple treasury itself is of giant proportion.

And yet there is no public outcry. No Roman soldiers have come to keep the peace. No one calls for Jesus' arrest. No one even berates him for causing a disturbance or for destroying the property of the merchants. One thing only happens. The leaders of the people and the officials of the temple ask, "What sign shewest thou unto us, seeing that thou doest these things?" There is no resistance, no seeming bitterness over financial loss—just an inquiry as to why he has overstepped his bounds and cleansed the temple when it is their responsibility to regulate all that therein transpires.

Why this mild reaction on the part of those whose property has been destroyed and whose functions have been assumed? We have already noted that there was popular support for the cleansing of the Temple Court; the dealings of the sons of Annas were known by the common people to be corrupt. But there was a greater reason. In the persuasive and well-chosen words of Canon Farrar, it is summarized in these words:

"Why did not this multitude of ignorant pilgrims resist? Why did these greedy chafferers content themselves with dark scowls and muttered maledictions, while they suffered their oxen and sheep to be chased into the streets and themselves ejected, and their money flung rolling on the floor, by one who was then young and unknown, and in the garb of despised Galilee? Why, in the same way we might ask, did Saul suffer Samuel to beard him in the very presence of his army? Why did David abjectly obey the orders of Joab? Why did Ahab not dare to arrest Elijah at the door of Naboth's vineyard? *Because sin is weakness;* because there is in the world nothing so abject as a guilty conscience, nothing so invincible as the sweeping tide of a Godlike indignation against all that is base and wrong. How could these paltry sacrilegious buyers and sellers, conscious of wrong-doing, oppose that scathing rebuke, or face the lightnings of those eyes that were kindled by an outraged holiness? When Phinehas the priest was zealous for the Lord of Hosts, and drove his javelin through the bodies of the prince of Simeon and the Midianitish woman with one glorious thrust, why did not guilty Israel avenge that splendid murder? Why did not every man of the tribe of Simeon become a *Goel* to the dauntless assassin? Because Vice cannot stand for one moment before Virtue's uplifted arm. Base and grovelling as they were, these money-mongering Jews felt in all that remnant of their souls which was not yet eaten away by infidelity and avarice, that the Son of Man was right.

"Nay, even the Priests and Pharisees, and Scribes and Levites, devoured as they were by pride and formalism, could not condemn an act which might have been performed by a Nehemiah or a Judas Maccabæus, and which agreed with all that was purest and best in their traditions. But when they had heard of this deed, or witnessed it, and had time to recover from the breathless mixture of admiration, disgust, and astonishment which it inspired, they came to Jesus, and though they did not dare to condemn what He had done, yet half indignantly asked Him for some sign that he had a right to act thus." (Farrar, pp. 144-46.)

Show us a sign! 'What proof can you offer that you are entitled to cleanse the courts of the temple?' The mere fact that they asked such a question shows that doubt and fear were rising in their minds: 'What if this Man really is the Messiah, as his disciples say?'

But the Lord and his prophets do not perform miracles to prove their divine appointments and priestly powers. Signs follow faith, and faith precedes the miracle. It is a wicked and adulterous generation that seeks for a sign. For them there is only one sign—"The sign of the prophet Jonas: For as Jonas was three days and three nights in the whale's belly; so shall the Son of man be three days and three nights in the heart of the earth." (Matt. 12:38-40.)

That is to say, for the wicked and ungodly, for those without faith, for those who reject the words of the prophets, there is only one sign: *the work itself.* Prophets are known by their fruits. If "the church is built upon my gospel," Jesus said to the Nephites, "then will the Father show forth his own works in it." (3 Ne. 27:10.) There are to be no signs—meaning no miracles or gifts of the Spirit—for unbelievers. They are left to pursue their own course now, but in a future day they shall know that Jesus rose again the third day and is the Son of God. His resurrection is the sign; it proves his divine Sonship and testifies of the power resident in him to cleanse the temple or do all else that his Father commands.

And so, "Jesus answered and said unto them, Destroy this temple, and in three days I will raise it up." The sign of the prophet Jonas! The only sign for wicked men! The sign that proves the work is true when it is everlastingly too late, everlastingly too late for those who seek for signs in a day when they should seek for faith, that signs might follow!

'Crucify me; destroy this body; place me in the Arimathean's tomb; and, lo, in three days I shall rise again, rise in glorious immortality, rise to judgment. This shall be your sign.'

Whether Jesus, in his answer, said more than the bare words quoted by John we do not know; but this we do know: those to whom he spoke, despite their false pretensions, knew exactly what he meant. They knew that to destroy the temple meant to take the life of the Nazarene, and that his promise to "raise it up" in three days meant that his dead body would come forth in immortality on the third day.

It may well be that one of the very reasons Jesus cleansed the temple was so he could say—in this setting, using a figure, and with words that would never be forgotten—that he would be slain and would come forth in the resurrection on the third day. In any event, his spoken word, so dramatically phrased, was not forgotten. Three years later a false witness, hoping to see him crucified on a Roman cross, would testify: "We heard him say, I will destroy this temple that is made with hands, and within three days I will build another made without hands." (Mark 14:58.) And a reviling scoffer, glorying in the agony of our Lord's crucifixion and awaiting the death that all felt was near, taunted the Cleanser of the Temple by saying: "Ah, thou that destroyest the temple, and buildest it in three days, Save thyself, and come down from the cross." (Mark 15:29-30.) And yet again, while his body lay in the tomb, a Jewish spokesman, hearkening back to our Lord's declaration made at this memorable Passover, would say to Pilate: "Sir, we remember that that deceiver said, while he was yet alive, After three days I will rise again" (Matt. 27:63), with reference to which Canon Farrar so aptly says: "Now there is no trace that Jesus had *ever* used any such words distinctly to them; and unless they

465

had heard the saying from Judas, or unless it had been repeated by common rumour derived from the Apostles—*i.e.*, unless the 'we remember' was a distinct falsehood—they could have been referring to no other occasion than this." (Farrar, p. 149.)

And yet their immediate response to Jesus was: "Forty and six years was this temple in building, and wilt thou rear it up in three days?"[3] At this point in the record John says simply: "But he spake of the temple of his body."

After his resurrection—and the sign proving he was God's Son, the sign proving he had power to cleanse the temple, was the fact of resurrection—his disciples remembered the teachings of this day and believed all of the words Jesus had spoken unto them.

At this Passover Jesus performed many miracles, none of which are named or described in the Gospel accounts. John says simply that "many believed on his name, when they saw the miracles which he did." But Jesus, knowing "all things," including the fact that faith founded solely on miracles leaves much to be desired, "did not commit himself unto them." He sought no motley throng who followed because the sick are healed and the dead raised. His disciples must, like Peter, gain the witness of his divine Sonship by the power of the Holy Ghost. And this revealed knowledge was to come to many in the years ahead.

NOTES

1. John quotes the portion of these Messianic words that apply to the cleansing of the temple by our Lord during the First Passover of his ministry. The disciples, John says, saw in them a Messianic prophecy of the zeal of their Messiah toward his Father's House. The further pronouncement—relative to the Messiah's "brethren" and to his "mother's children"—is also of particular note at this time when Jesus has just attended a wedding celebration with his mother and the other children in her family, and when he has traveled with Mary and his brethren from Cana to Capernaum. The words "my mother's children" are a clear promise that Mary would have other children in addition to the Firstborn. It is the Catholic view that those mentioned in the New Testament as being brothers and sisters of Jesus were the children of Joseph by a former marriage and that the Blessed Virgin had but one offspring. To show that this could not be, it is merely necessary to ask: How could Jesus be the heir to the throne of David—through Joseph, as the New Testament genealogies recite—if Joseph had elder sons? Other like questions might be: What became of the motherless brothers and sisters when Joseph and Mary went to Bethlehem and then

466

into Egypt? And why is there no mention of them on such occasions as the Passover trip to Jerusalem when Jesus was twelve? To those who esteem marriage as being ordained of God, and who, with Paul, believe that "marriage is honourable in all, and the bed undefiled" (Heb. 13:4), there is nothing indelicate or inappropriate in the Mother of the Son of God having other children by Joseph, her legal and lawful husband.

2. Of special interest is this further comment of Edersheim: "These Temple-Bazaars, the property, and one of the principal sources of income, of the family of Annas, were the scene of the purification of the Temple by Jesus; and in the private *locale* attached to these very Bazaars, where the Sanhedrin held its meetings at the time, the final condemnation of Jesus may have been planned, if not actually pronounced." (Edersheim 1:372.)

3. It is April of A.D. 27, and forty-six years have already gone into the building of Herod's Temple. It will not be completed until A.D. 63, just seven years before the soldiers of Titus will tear it apart, stone by stone, as they acquire the gold that now covers the marble blocks.

Chapter 30

NICODEMUS VISITS JESUS

Marvel not that all mankind, yea, men
and women, all nations, kindreds,
tongues and people, must be
born again; yea, born of God, changed from
their carnal and fallen state, to a state
of righteousness, being redeemed of God,
becoming his sons and daughters;
And thus they become new creatures;
and unless they do this, they can in nowise
inherit the kingdom of God.
(Mosiah 27:25-26.)[1]

Jesus' Ministry Divides the People

Our Friend and Brother, the Lord Jesus—and blessed be
he—has now spent about two months in his active and
formal ministry among men. As nearly as we can tell—and
this is the chronology followed by President J. Reuben
Clark, Jr.—Jesus was baptized by John in Jordan in January,
A.D. 27; his forty days of fasting, prayer, and worship in the
wilderness were in January and February (possibly continuing into March); probably he began to teach and call dis-

ciples (Andrew, Simon, and others) in February, not later than in March; and in March in Cana came the first public miracle, the changing of water into wine. Now it is Passover time, April 11-18, and the place is Jerusalem, the Holy City.

Our Lord has driven from the Temple Court the sacrificial animals, probably numbering in the thousands; has used a scourge of small cords upon the carnal men who made merchandise in his Father's House; and has extended his own arm of healing to bless and cure many—and all Jerusalem is aware of the miracles he has done. Up to this point in the scriptural accounts there is no record of what he has said in any sermon or of what he did in the performance of any miracle, except the one in Cana. All this now is to change.

Perhaps he began his ministry when he was baptized by his kinsman; perhaps it was when he overcame temptation and viewed the wonders of eternity while in the wilderness; perhaps it was when he taught and called disciples. No matter. But when he openly confronted the priestly powers of the whole nation; when he announced that God was his Father, and that he would be slain and rise again the third day; and when he confirmed—proved, if you will—his right so to act and teach by performing many miracles, then his ministry became the matter of chief concern to all the people in all Palestine. No longer were his deeds done in a corner. No longer could anyone say: 'He is only a Galilean, a Nazarene, someone from a place out of which ariseth no prophet.'

At this Passover Jesus made his ministry the thing that would be uppermost in all minds for the three long years of that ministry, until the fourth Passover, when he would crown his work in Gethsemane, at Golgotha, and before an open tomb.

At this Passover, Jesus divided the people. He began the process of assembling the goats, to be damned, on his left hand, and the sheep, to be saved, on his right.

At this Passover, he incurred the undying enmity of the rulers of the people. Ever thereafter they would plot and scheme and seek to defame his character and mission and to bring about his death.

But at this Passover also, people began to flock to his standard because of his gracious words and his mighty miracles. Many began to believe the reports they had heard of a voice from heaven at his baptism; of a miracle performed in an obscure Galilean city; of disciples who testified openly that he was David's Son, the one of whom Moses and the prophets had written, the Promised Messiah.

And this brings us to Nicodemus—a Pharisee, a ruler of the Jews, one of the Great Sanhedrin—who came to Jesus by night to learn about this new Rabbi whose miracles bore testimony that he had divine power. In effect Nicodemus wanted to investigate the gospel in secret, lest his associates turn against him and his worldly influence wane. His discipleship does not compare with a Peter, who drew his sword in the Master's defense, or of a Thomas—unwisely and somewhat slanderously referred to as Doubting Thomas— who was willing to face persecution for the cause, and once said to the others of the Twelve: "Let us also go, that we may die with him" (John 11:16); or a Stephen, who was stoned to death for saying he saw 'the heavens opened, and the Son of man standing on the right hand of God" (Acts 7:51-60).

But at least he came, and it is apparent that he thereafter believed in Christ and supported the gospel cause. Indeed, as Edersheim says: "It must have been a mighty power of conviction to break down prejudice so far as to lead this old Sanhedrist to acknowledge a Galilean, untrained in the Schools, as a Teacher come from God, and to repair to Him for direction on, perhaps, the most delicate and important point in Jewish theology. But, even so, we cannot wonder that he should have wished to shroud his first visit in the utmost possible secrecy. It was a most compromising step for a Sanhedrist to take. With that first bold purgation of the Temple a deadly feud between Jesus and the Jewish authorities had begun, . . . and it needed not the experience and wisdom of an aged Sanhedrist to forecast the end." (Edersheim 1:381.)

We are left to assume that following his interview with Jesus, the processes of conversion continued to operate in the life of Nicodemus. On one occasion, when the officers of the Sanhedrin excused themselves for their inability to arrest Jesus, Nicodemus asked his fellow rulers: "Doth our law judge any man, before it hear him, and know what he doeth?" (John 7:45-53.) And after Joseph of Arimathea had obtained the body of the Crucified One, Nicodemus "brought a mixture of myrrh and aloes, about an hundred pound weight" (John 19:38-42) for use in preparing the body for burial.

Jesus Teaches: Fallen Man Must Be Born Again
(John 3:1-12)

John tells us that Nicodemus came to Jesus by night, and we are left to assume the meeting took place in a house owned or occupied by John in Jerusalem.[2] If so, the interview may well have taken place in the guest chamber on the roof, which would have been accessible via outside stairs. John was either present or Jesus recounted to him what was said. The scriptural account is clearly a digest and recitation of the chief points made in what has come to be called our Lord's first great recorded discourse.

"Rabbi," said Nicodemus in a solemn and respectful way, "we know"—perhaps indicating that he and others of the Sanhedrin had like feelings—"that thou art a teacher come from God." This pronouncement is in effect a testimony. It was clear to every unprejudiced mind that Rabbi Jesus was more than an ordinary teacher. He came from God! "For," Nicodemus continued, "no man can do these miracles that thou doest, except God be with him." If only all his fellow Sanhedrists, and the people generally, had known and remembered this simple test. Those who work miracles of the sort performed by Jesus bear the stamp of divine approval. And if a man both raises the dead and says he is the Son of God, it must of necessity be so, for a dishonest man could not wield the power that says to a decaying corpse: 'Arise and live again, because I will it.'

Jesus' answer was blunt, concise, and apparently not responsive, leading to the assumption that Nicodemus had more to say than has been preserved in the holy record. "Verily, verily, I say unto thee," Jesus said—and note that our Lord is not quoting scripture, not speaking in the name of another as the prophets of old did, but is speaking in his own name, as the Author of truth—"I say unto thee," he says, "Except a man be born again, he cannot see the kingdom of God."

Man must be born again; he must receive the promptings of the Spirit; he must turn from darkness to light; he must die as to carnal things and live again as to the things of righteousness; he must rise from spiritual death and go forth in spiritual life—all this if he is to "see" the truth; if he is to gain a testimony; if he is to know where the truth is and the course he must pursue to gain peace here and eternal reward hereafter.

If ever there were a people or a nation in need of spiritual rebirth, it was the Jewish assemblage of Jesus' day. If ever there were those in darkness who needed the light of heaven to shine in their souls, it was these children of the prophets who now dwelt in the shadow of death. If ever there were a kindred or a kingdom that needed to rise from the degeneracy of the present, as they sought for the glory of the past, it was those among whom God had sent his Son. And as that Son turned the early events of his ministry into a *cause celèbre,* which would come to the attention of all Israel, he chose to speak of being born again. One man must be born again to see the kingdom of God. All men must receive the spiritual rebirth if the people and the nation are to bask in the light of divine favor as had their fathers.

Nicodemus, himself a teacher and a leader of the people,

one who should have been guiding them toward the spiritual rebirth they so much needed, should have known they could not save themselves by continuing in the Herodian course of darkness and rebellion. If the people were to rise again to the heights attained by some under Moses and Joshua, and in the days of Samuel and of David and of Isaiah, they must once more live in the Spirit as the ancients had. If the Shekinah was to rest visibly in the Lord's Holy House, as it did in the days of Moses and Solomon, there must once again be people fit and worthy to enter the divine presence. But Nicodemus did not know; as an appointed teacher of spiritual truths, he himself was in spiritual darkness. "How can a man be born when he is old?" he asked. "Can he enter the second time into his mother's womb, and be born?"

To these foolish questions, which showed a complete lack of understanding of the great moral issues involved, Jesus gave the eternal reply that has been the basis of salvation for men and nations in all ages. Again he spoke solemnly in his own name: "Except a man be born of water and of the Spirit, he cannot enter into the kingdom of God."

Such is the plan of salvation for all men in all ages. Adam fell and brought death—both temporal death and spiritual death—into the world. The effects of his fall passed upon all men; all die temporally, and all are subject to spiritual death. Spiritual death is to die as pertaining to the things of the Spirit, as pertaining to things of righteousness. If men are to live again as pertaining to the things of righteousness, they must receive a spiritual rebirth.

Beginning in the days of Adam, the Lord's word has gone forth among his people "that all men, everywhere, must repent, or they can in nowise inherit the kingdom of God, for no unclean thing can dwell there, or dwell in his presence." By the mouths of Adam and Enoch and prophets in all ages, these words of the Lord have been taught, "That by reason of transgression cometh the fall, which fall bringeth death, and inasmuch as ye were born into the world by water, and blood, and the spirit, which I have made, and so became of dust a living soul, even so ye must be born again into the kingdom of heaven, of water, and of the Spirit, and be cleansed by blood, even the blood of mine Only Begotten; that ye might be sanctified from all sin, and enjoy the words of eternal life in this world, and eternal life in the world to come, even immortal glory."

In all ages past the Lord's people had been taught these things, and to them had been appended this divine proclamation: "This is the plan of salvation unto all men, through the blood of mine Only Begotten, who shall come in the meridian of time." (Moses 6:57-62.)

We suppose that Jesus taught these wondrous truths to the inquiring Sanhedrist, either in the same or similar words. Such a doctrine is the natural prelude to the testimony he was about to bear of himself, that as the Only Begotten of the Father he had come to bring salvation. We do know that he said, "That which is born of the flesh is flesh," meaning that people are born into this world of water and blood and the Spirit, and so become of dust living souls; and we do know that he said: "And that which is born of the Spirit is spirit," meaning that men must be born again of the Spirit if they are to be alive as to spiritual things, and therefore qualify for that spiritual or eternal life reserved for the faithful. And that this second birth, this rebirth, this birth into the kingdom of heaven, is through the waters of baptism, comes by the power of the Holy Ghost, and is possible because of the cleansing power of the blood of Christ is apparent to all. Hence, Jesus says, "Marvel not," Nicodemus, "that I said unto thee, Ye must be born again." The doctrine is so basic, so fundamental, so much at the bedrock of the house of salvation, that he and all men must believe and understand it if they are to gain the promised rewards.

"The wind bloweth where it listeth," Jesus continued— perhaps as they felt the cool refreshment of the night breeze as it gusted and whispered through the dark streets of Jerusalem—"and thou hearest the sound thereof, but canst not tell whence it cometh, and whither it goeth"—for such is the way with the gentle zephyrs, who knoweth their source or their destiny. Then came the gospel verity that grew out of the illustration: "So is every one that is born of the Spirit."

"How can these things be?" Nicodemus asked. 'How can the water of baptism, and the Spirit of the Lord, and the blood of the Only Begotten, constitute a birth into the kingdom of heaven? How can the serene and calm influence of the Spirit—the still small voice, as it were—descend, as from nowhere, upon a human soul?'

"Art thou a master of Israel, and knowest not these things?" comes the reply. 'Art thou an appointed teacher, a guide and a light to the people, a member of the Great Sanhedrin itself, and thou knowest not that spiritual rebirth is the very beginning of righteousness, and that until men are born again they are not so much as on the path leading to eternal life?' Was there just a touch of irony in our Lord's response?

Then in tones of solemn adjuration, as it were, the greatest Rabbi of them all bore testimony of the truths taught by him and by his disciples. "We speak that we do know," he said—as with all the prophets, they were sure of the truths they proclaimed—"and testify that we have seen; and ye receive not our witness." Only those who are alive spiritually can comprehend the deep and hidden meanings of those things spoken by the power of the Spirit; the light may shine in the darkness, but those who choose darkness rather than light comprehend it not.

"If I have told you earthly things, and ye believe not, how shall ye believe, if I tell you of heavenly things." 'If I have told you the simple, basic truths about being born again; if I have told you the first principles—faith, repentance, baptism, and the receipt of the Holy Ghost—and ye believe not, how shall ye either believe or understand if I tell you the "wonders of eternity," "the hidden mysteries of my kingdom," the "things which eye has not seen, nor ear heard, nor yet have entered into the heart of man"?' (*Commentary* 1:142.)

Jesus Testifies: I Am the Messiah, the Son of God, the Only Begotten
(John 3:13-21; JST, John 3:13, 18, 21-22)

If all men everywhere must be born again; if they must be born of water and of the Spirit and be cleansed by the blood of the Only Begotten; if they must put off the natural man and become new creatures by the power of the Holy Ghost; if they must taste the good things of the Spirit; if they must believe in the Messiah and accept him as their Savior— all to the end that they may enjoy the words of eternal life here and now and be inheritors of eternal glory hereafter— then the great questions are: Who is the Messiah? Where shall he be found? How is he to be recognized? And what must men do to accept him?

Jesus has a ready answer, the one and only true answer, which he now vouchsafes to Nicodemus. "No man hath ascended up to heaven," he says, "but he that came down from heaven, even the Son of man which is in heaven." Here, then, is one of the "heavenly things" that none can see but those whose spiritual eyes are open, and none can hear but those whose spiritual ears are attuned to the Infinite. It is: 'I am the Messiah, who has come down from heaven. I am the Son of Man of Holiness who is in heaven; and I shall yet ascend to be with God who is my Father.' And if we look upon Nicodemus with a critical eye because he failed to grasp the infinite wonder of this heavenly truth, how much more shall we despair for the hosts of sectarians who, with the New Testament scriptures before them, fail to accept the Son as the Only Begotten in the full and literal sense of the word.

"And as Moses lifted up the serpent in the wilderness," our Lord continues, "even so must the Son of man be lifted up: That whosoever believeth in him should not perish, but have eternal life."

Moses, in the wilderness, when the Lord sent "fiery serpents" among them, so that many people in Israel were bitten and died, made a serpent of brass and put it upon a pole. Then all who were bitten by the poisonous creeping things and who looked, in faith, upon the brazen serpent, lived; the others died. Why? Because Moses was commanded of God so to do, and the thing was an ordinance in Israel—an ordinance performed in similitude of the fact that the Promised Messiah would be lifted up upon the cross, and all who looked to him in faith would live; the others would die. Nephi the son of Helaman, speaking of Moses to his Hebrew brethren, asked: "Did he not bear record that the Son of God should come?" In answer, this ancient American prophet said: "As he [Moses] lifted up the brazen serpent in the wilderness, even so shall he be lifted up who should come. And as many as should look upon that serpent should live, even so as many as should look upon the Son of God with faith, having a contrite spirit, might live, even unto that life which is eternal." (Hel. 8:13-15; Num. 21:4-9.)

Eternal life—life in the highest heaven; the kind of life enjoyed by Deity himself; life reserved for those who receive, inherit, and possess all things—this glorious type and kind of everlasting existence comes to those who believe in the Son of Man! How is it brought to pass? In answer Jesus speaks what is considered by many to be the most glorious and wondrous single verse of scripture ever to fall from the lips of God or man: *"For God so loved the world, that he gave his only begotten Son, that whosoever believeth in him should not perish, but have everlasting life."*[3]

God so loved the world! The Father sent the Son! He is the Only Begotten! Believe in him and gain eternal life! "For God sent not his Son into the world to condemn the world; but that the world through him might be saved." Salvation is in Christ. "He who believeth on him is not condemned; but he who believeth not is condemned already, because he hath not believed on the name of the only Begotten Son of God, which before was preached by the mouth of the holy prophets; for they testified of me."

How could Nicodemus or anyone misunderstand these

teachings? Our Lord is speaking in the early days of his ministry. He is using plain, simple, and forceful language. The doctrine is strong. No parables are involved; nothing is hidden with imagery or in similitudes. He is saying plainly that men must believe in him; that he is the Son of God, the Promised Messiah, the Only Begotten of the Father, the One of whom Moses and the prophets testified. He is saying that men must repent and be baptized in water; that they must receive the companionship of the Holy Spirit and be born again.

It is plain and clear beyond question. Why, then, do not men believe? He answers: "And this is the condemnation, that light is come into the world, and men loved darkness rather than light, because their deeds were evil. For every one that doeth evil hateth the light, neither cometh to the light, lest his deeds should be reproved. But he who loveth truth, cometh to the light, that his deeds may be made manifest. And he who obeyeth the truth, the works which he doeth they are of God."

Jesus has spoken. These are his words. This is his testimony of the doctrine taught and of his own divine Sonship. We shall see these truths accepted by many, and this witness borne by his disciples, as we follow the feet of the Son of God along the dusty lanes of Palestine, and as we hear his voice speaking in private to his disciples and in public to all men.

How glorious is the Voice from heaven!

NOTES

1. These words, more definitive and expressive even than those spoken to Nicodemus, were spoken by the Spirit Lord Jesus to Alma the son of Alma, about a hundred years before our Lord's mortal birth. They are preceded in the Book of Mormon account by Alma's declaration: "I have repented of my sins, and have been redeemed of the Lord; behold I am born of the Spirit." (Mosiah 27:24.) Alma had, of course, been baptized of water in his youth, and the occasion of which he here speaks was the actual receipt by him of the Holy Spirit, without which no man ever receives the new birth.

2. Such ownership is inferred from John 19:27.

3. Similarly, our Lord "so loved the world that he gave his own life, that as many as would believe might become the sons of God." (D&C 34:3.)

478

Chapter 31

JOHN (THE BAPTIST) AND JESUS MINISTER IN JUDEA

Believe on the Lord Jesus Christ, and
thou shalt be saved. (Acts 16:31.)

Jesus Preaches and Baptizes in Judea
(John 3:22; 4:1-3; JST, John 4:2-4; Matthew 4:12; Mark 1:14; Luke 4:14)

Jesus came to Jerusalem at Passover time—when all Israel was present, either in person or through appointed representatives—to announce publicly and officially, before the rulers and the people, that he, the Promised Messiah, was now among them and that his ministry had commenced. With thunderous and righteous indignation he cleansed the temple and proclaimed his coming death and resurrection, thus affirming that he himself was the Messiah who had life in himself because God was his Father. All this he did openly and before all the people, and we cannot doubt that his acts and deeds were known to most of the two and a half to three million people who crowded into the city and its environs at this most sacred time.

To selected souls—Nicodemus and his own disciples among them—he spoke even more plainly. Men must be born again; repentance and faith in Christ are essential to salvation; he had come down from heaven to atone for the sins of the world; it was of him that Moses and all the

479

prophets had spoken; he was God's Son, the Only Begotten of the Father. It was there, spoken in plain and clear Aramaic. He had announced his divine commission and had done it in the spiritual capital of Jewish Israel. It was done formally; he spoke officially; his voice was the voice of his Father; and his words would stand as a witness in time and in eternity.

Having so done, our Lord's work in Jerusalem, for the moment, was accomplished. With the departing pilgrims, who would carry an account of his doings and sayings to the chosen seed everywhere, he and his disciples also left the Holy City. Their destiny: the villages and cities of Judea, from Beersheba and Moladah in the south, to Masada and Engedi on the Dead Sea, to Joppa in the northwest and Jericho in the northeast. Their mission and purpose: to preach the gospel of the kingdom and to baptize repentant souls. For how long? For nine full months, until December of A.D. 27, at which time—having, as Peter expressed it, preached "throughout all Judea" that "word which God sent unto the children of Israel" (Acts 10:34-43)—he and his disciples went through Samaria (where the conversation at Jacob's Well took place) and into Galilee.

It is not our good fortune to possess a day-by-day account, or even a week-by-week or month-by-month summary, of what Jesus did and said in the days of his flesh. We are sure that his waking hours were filled with wise words and good deeds, his sleeping hours with the dreams of heaven and the visions of eternity, for he was serving on a mission. He was sent by his Father to preach the gospel, heal the sick, and perform the ordinances of salvation. To those whom he has called in these last days, his instructions are: "Thou shalt send forth my word unto the ends of the earth. Contend thou, therefore, morning by morning; and day after day let thy warning voice go forth; and when the night cometh let not the inhabitants of the earth slumber, because of thy speech." (D&C 112:4-5) We cannot assume that he imposed any less standard than this upon himself during his own ministry. But it is only an isolated word here and a healing miracle there that has been preserved for us by the evangelical authors.

As to the early Judean ministry, John says only that "Jesus and his disciples"—and they must by now have included more than Peter, John, Andrew, Philip, and Nathanael; perhaps women also were among them—"tarried" and baptized in "the land of Judea." Nine months gave them time to tarry long enough in each locale so that all those who dwelt there would hear the word and be accountable for their reaction to it. No doubt many of the seeds sown would be harvested by the apostles and seventies as they thereafter went forth proclaiming the same gospel and baptizing by the same power.

After naming "all Judea" as the place where Jesus "published" the glad tidings of salvation, Peter tells "how God anointed Jesus of Nazareth with the Holy Ghost and with power: who went about doing good, and healing all that were oppressed of the devil; for God was with him." (Acts 10:37-38.) The early Judean ministry thus would have been like the later great Galilean ministry, concerning which we know far more, as shall hereafter appear.

Whenever the gospel is preached by legal administrators having power and authority from on high; whenever ministers possess the power of the priesthood and are guided by the Holy Spirit; whenever those professing to be apostles and prophets do in fact hold these high and holy callings, they always both preach and baptize. Jesus was no exception. He preached the gospel and baptized repentant souls.

Jesus performed baptisms in water for the remission of sins, and he did it on the same basis and in the same way that his forerunner John performed the same sacred ordinance. When John first came, baptizing by immersion in the river Jordan, he taught that the one who was coming after him—the one mightier than he; the one whose shoes the Baptist was not worthy to bear—that such a one would baptize with the Holy Ghost and with fire.

481

This baptism of fire and of the Holy Ghost, which the Son of God was destined to perform, is not the baptism of which we now speak; such was to come and did come later. While Jesus was with the disciples, he did not give them the gift of the Holy Ghost, so they could have at that time the constant companionship of that member of the Godhead. It was after he ascended to his Father—it was, in fact, on the day of Pentecost—that the Holy Spirit descended in power upon those whom Jesus had called out of the world and into his earthly kingdom. But at this time, in the early days of his early Judean ministry, Jesus and his disciples performed the same baptismal ordinance that John the Baptist was still performing. One of the things this means is that Jesus had already conferred the priesthood upon his newly called disciples.

And so we find our evangelist friend, John, commenting upon the events of that day in these words: "When therefore the Pharisees had heard that Jesus made and baptized more disciples than John, They sought more diligently some means that they might put him to death; for many received John as a prophet, but they believed not on Jesus.[1] Now the Lord knew this, though he himself baptized not so many as his disciples; For he suffered them for an example, preferring one another."[2]

John Continues to Baptize and Prepare the Way
(John 3:23-26; JST, John 3:27)

It is now a full year since John the Baptist began his public ministry; since he cried repentance in the wilderness of Judea; since he reprehended the Jewish multitudes, calling them a generation of vipers; since he immersed repentant souls in the Holy River, promising them a remission of their sins and the future receipt of the Holy Ghost under the hands of Him whose forerunner the Baptist was. It is a full year since the Lord's forerunner first bore public witness that the mighty Messiah would soon walk among them, and that he would baptize them with the Holy Ghost and with fire.

It is now at least six months—probably seven, and possibly eight—since the son of Zacharias baptized the Son of God. And it is five or six months since the appointed Elias bore fervent witness that Jesus was the Lamb of God, which taketh away the sins of the world. And during all this time the promised forerunner has continued to prepare the way for the Promised Messiah.

There is nothing incongruous or unexpected in finding the one who was to prepare the way continuing to prepare a people for their Lord until that day when the one of whom the witness was borne had been identified in every mind as the one who should come. John was expected to continue to invite repentant persons to forsake the world and come unto that Christ whose witness he was. And John was doing just that. He was preaching and baptizing at Aenon near Salim— a location now unknown to us—"because there was much water there," and all valid baptisms must be performed by immersion.

Jesus and his disciples were baptizing in Judea, no doubt in many locations, for all Judea was hearing the word from the mouth of the one whose word it was. John's influence as a figure of public renown, as the center of a great national movement of popular appeal, was on the wane; that of Jesus was waxing great; and though many still came to John, multitudes flocked to Jesus.

Two reasons identify the basis for this shift in public opinion: the word of truth and salvation was with the Source of truth and the Author of salvation, as it should have been; and when John made converts, he sent them to Jesus. Whereas the forerunner had once baptized in the name of Him who should come and had made ready a congregation to receive the Lord, he now baptized in the name of Him who had come and invited his converts to join the congregation of his Leader. The converts were Christ's. The gathered sheep belonged to the Shepherd. John claimed no personal preference. He was a servant, and his glory was to serve the Master.

But it is not surprising to find some of John's disciples feeling that their teacher was deserving of more attention and honor than he was receiving. And so, when a dispute arose between them and "the Jews"—or as the better translations read, "a Jew"—"about purifying," they took the matter to John. It seems clear that the dispute involved the purifying power of baptism and whether John's baptism actually brought remission of sins.

To a caviling, disputing, contentious theologian of that day, an obvious point of debate would have been: How can John's baptism be for the remission of sins when those who receive it must have a second baptism of the Holy Ghost so that sin and evil and dross will be burned out of their souls as though by fire? How are men actually purified by baptism? Is baptism in water for the remission of sins, or is the purifying power of the Holy Spirit needed to cleanse a human soul? However the contention was phrased, John's disciples called it to the attention of the Baptist, saying: "Rabbi, he who was with thee beyond Jordan, to whom thou bearest witness, behold, the same baptizeth, and he receiveth of all people who come unto him." With these words the stage is set for John to bear one of his greatest witnesses of the one whose way he prepared.

John Reaffirms His Witness of Christ
(*John 3:27-36; JST, John 3:32-36*)

Comes now the blessed Baptist—the son of Zacharias and Elisabeth, named John by the angel Gabriel; our Lord's forerunner and witness, who also immersed him in Jordan—to bear, as far as our scriptures record, his final glorious testimony of Jesus. He will continue as a free man to speak and baptize for another four or five months, until November or December of A.D. 27; then he will be imprisoned by Herod. He will languish in the dungeons of Machaerus for more than a year, perhaps fifteen months, before Herod's headsman, at the word of almighty Antipas, will send him to a martyr's grave, from which he shall come forth, with Christ, to receive glory and honor in the kingdom that is prepared.

We can be sure that wherever he met people, and as long as he had breath, his burning witness of one greater than he was given freely, boldly, and with prophetic zeal. We know that he sent disciples to hear Jesus while he himself was restrained in the dungeons of the fortress where Herod had chosen to imprison him. But what he is now to say is his last witness to find place in the scriptures that have come to us. He whose "little light" is being "swallowed up in the boundless Dawn" (Farrar, p. 156), this stern and impassioned prophet from Hebron and the Judean deserts, speaking by the power of the Holy Ghost—which gift he possessed from his mother's womb—is opening his mouth to bear one of the most eloquent and powerful testimonies to find place in Holy Writ.

Whether he answered his disciples' queries about the purifying power of baptism, we do not know, nor does it matter. Many revelations unravel the baptismal mysteries, and many prophets have expounded upon the purifying power of the Holy Ghost. Let the disputants search the scriptures and find their answers. But there was only one Baptist, sent—as the voice of one crying in the wilderness of doubt and disbelief—to prepare the way before the Son of the Highest. John must be true to his trust and bear the witness that was his alone to proclaim. And the acceptance of that witness would provide answer for all lesser problems and solve all doctrinal controversies. Thus with the voice of testimony and of doctrine the Baptist proclaimed:

A man can receive nothing, except it be given him from heaven. Ye yourselves bear me witness, that I said, I am not the Christ, but that I am sent before him. He that hath the bride is the bridegroom: but the friend of the bridegroom, which standeth and heareth him, rejoiceth greatly because of the bridegroom's voice: this my joy there is fulfilled.

'I, John, came only as the promised Elias, but he came as the holy Messiah, of whom all the prophets have testified. Each of us has received only as the Father has given unto us—he to be the Lamb of God who taketh away the sin of the world, I to announce his coming and to prepare the way before him. It is not given to me to do his work, for he, as the Son of an immortal Father, is greater than I. Ye yourselves are witnesses that I have always said I was not the Christ, only his forerunner. He is the Bridegroom; I, his servant, am as the friend of the bridegroom, the one sent to make arrangements for the wedding. My reward is to be near him, to hear his voice, to know my mission was successful; in this my joy is full.'

He must increase, but I must decrease. He who cometh from above is above all; he who is of the earth is earthly, and speaketh of the earth; he who cometh from heaven is above all.

'His mission is beginning, mine ending; he must increase, I decrease. My counsel is: Forsake me; follow him; he is the Light of the world who teaches the truth and makes salvation available to all men. He is the Lord Omnipotent who, coming from his Father in heaven, is superior to all men; I am as other men, of the earth.'

And what he hath seen and heard, that he testifieth; and but few men receive his testimony. He who hath received his testimony hath set to his seal that God is true.

'But though he is the very Son of God, and though he carries the very message his Father sent him to deliver, yet few men receive his testimony. Those who do believe his witness and obey his counsels, however, have a seal placed upon them; they are sealed up unto eternal life in the everlasting kingdom of the Father.'

For he whom God hath sent, speaketh the words of God; for God giveth him not the Spirit by measure, for he dwelleth in him, even the fulness.

'And the Son, whom the Father hath sent, speaks the words of the Father because the Spirit of God is not apportioned to him; he enjoys it in full measure, and it is by this means that the Father dwelleth in him. Yea, and the Father loveth the Son and hath given all things into his hands—all power, all wisdom, all truth, all judgment, and the fulness of every godly attribute.'

The Father loveth the Son, and hath given all things into his hand. And he who believeth on the Son hath everlasting life; and shall receive of his fulness. But he who believeth not the Son, shall not receive of his fulness; for the wrath of God is upon him.

'Now those who believe in Jesus as the Son, who believe so fully and completely as to abide in his counsels, shall have everlasting life, even exaltation in the highest heaven of the Father's kingdom. They shall then receive of his fulness, even all power, both in heaven and on earth, and the glory of the Father shall be with them, for he shall dwell in them. But those who believe not on the Son shall fail to gain eternal life and shall not receive of his fulness, for the wrath of God is upon them.' (*Commentary* 1:147-48.)

Such is the last recorded witness of the one chosen from all the spirit hosts of heaven to prepare the way before the Son of God, to bear record of his divine Sonship, to invite all men to flock to his standard that they might be saved with him in the kingdom of his Father.

Herod Imprisons John

(*Matthew 4:12; 14:3-5; JST, Matthew 4:11; Mark 6:17-20; JST, Mark 6:21; Luke 3:19-20*)

There is no New Testament account of any act or word of either Jesus or John from the summer of A.D. 27, when the Baptist bore his wondrous witness, to November or December of that year, when Herod Antipas reached forth the Roman arm of power and imprisoned the son of Zacharias. We know only that Jesus and his disciples were tarrying and teaching in the villages and cities of Judea, and we must assume that John also continued his labors with unwearying diligence.

Herod the Great—an Idumean Jew; a Jew as to religion, a pagan as to practice; the mad monster who ordered the slaughter of the Innocents in all the coasts of Bethlehem; a polygamist who had ten wives—passed on both his murderous proclivities and his religious superstitions to his son Herod Antipas, who governed Galilee and Perea in the days of John and Jesus. Lechery and lust were a way of life with the Herods, and Antipas, like his father before him, felt free to take and reject wives at will. Divorcing his first wife, he married Herodias, the wife of his half-brother Philip (not Philip the tetrarch). Herodias, the mother of Salome by Philip, was a granddaughter of the original Herod, and so married, in turn, her uncle Philip and her uncle Antipas. Under Jewish law the marriage of Herod Antipas and Herodias was scandalous, incestuous, and adulterous, and was so viewed by the people.

Herod Antipas, conceived in sin, reared in the household of sin, himself the servant of sin, trumpeted his sinful lusts before all Israel by endorsing and practicing—openly and defiantly—the abominations of adultery and incest. Such a course could not go unreproved. John the Baptist had been sent to cry repentance; he had power to baptize for the remission of sins; and a Herod on his throne was no different from any man. All men—high or low, kings and slaves, Jews and Gentiles, everyone—must repent or they will be damned, and all men are entitled to hear the warning voice from the lips of a legal administrator.

If John commanded the publicans to exact no greater taxes than they were appointed to collect; if he commanded the soldiers to do violence to no man, to accuse none falsely, and to be content with their wages; if the common people were called to forsake lesser sins, how much greater is the need to rebuke the ruler in his palace who flaunts the sanctity of the moral law and the holiness of the family unit!

There is nothing in the prophetic nature that admits of the fear of men, whether they be kings on their thrones or generals before their armies. As Samuel rebuked David before his armies, and as Elijah called down curses upon Ahab and Jezebel in the house of the king, so John must confront Herod Antipas and his ill-gotten marriage partner. They must needs be called to repentance.

And so, apparently in a face-to-face encounter, the voice sent to cry repentance in a wilderness of sin, the voice of John, reproved Herod for all the evils he had done, and also said: "It is not lawful for thee to have thy brother's wife." The gauntlet had been hurled; the issue was set; Herod and Herodias must repent or be damned. John was a legal administrator, and he had delivered his message.

Herodias demanded the death of John, and Herod agreed. But in the providences of the Lord, there were yet further tests and added spiritual experiences for the forerunner of the Son. At a future time, Herodias, Salome, and Herod—an unholy trio—would gape upon the severed head of the Baptist as it was paraded before the drunken nobles of Herod's court. But for now, the Baptist had yet to drink the dregs of the bitter cup that an all-wise Father had placed in his hands. He must drain the cup and do all he was sent to do; he must yet suffer to the full for the testimony of Jesus. He must languish for more than a year in the dungeons of Machaerus.

Thus, when Herod "would have put [John] to death, he feared the multitude, because they counted him as a prophet," and so the decree, for the present, was one of imprisonment only. Not only did Herod fear the multitude, but he also personally feared John. He knew that John "was a just man, and a holy man, and one who feared God and observed to worship him." There must have been some stirring in Herod's soul, some desire to rise above the iniquities of his court and to live by higher standards, for the record says that when he heard of John, "he did many things for him, and heard him gladly." How often it is that adulterers and sinners of the vilest sort, knowing in their hearts that their course is evil, turn to religion of one kind or another, seeking to find peace of mind of some sort. Yet how often, as with Herod, the seeds of repentance die in the stony soil of sin where they are first sown.

Why was John imprisoned? It was with him as with all the prophets. Satan sought to silence his tongue, by death if possible, by imprisonment in any event; and the Lord permitted that evil one to triumph for a season, as part of the refining processes that would cleanse and perfect the life of his servant. The Baptist's imprisonment was "but a part of that merciful fire in which He is purging away the dross from the seven-times-refined gold of a spirit which shall be worthy of eternal bliss." (Farrar, p. 220.)

From an earthly perspective, three motives appear for the course Antipas chose to take. For one, with the fires of conscience burning at her vitals, and having an implacable hatred against one who had held her up to popular contempt and ridicule, Herodias sought his imprisonment and death. For another, and Josephus is the source of this view: "The Tetrarch was afraid that his absolute influence over the people, who seemed disposed to carry out whatever he advised, might lead to a rebellion. This circumstance is also indicated in the remark of St. Matthew, that Herod was afraid to put the Baptist to death on account of the people's opinion of him." (Edersheim 1:657.) And finally, there can be little doubt that pharisaic intrigue played its part. The Pharisees, those masters of deceit and of opposition to revealed truth, opposed Jesus and had broken with John, who bore witness of Jesus. The clear inference is that they used their persuasive powers to make Herod their tool of terror against John, just as they would make Rome their weapon to crucify the one greater than John, when the Lord Jesus was led as a lamb to the slaughter. (Edersheim 1:657-58.)

"To St. John Baptist imprisonment must have been a deadlier thing" than to most of the suffering seers and prophetic messengers who fell into like dungeons of despair, "for in the free wild life of the hermit he had lived in constant communion with the sights and sounds of nature, had breathed with delight and liberty the free winds of the wilderness. To a child of freedom and of passion, to a rugged, untamed spirit like that of John, a prison was worse than death. For the palms of Jericho and the balsams of Engedi, for the springing of the beautiful gazelles amid the mountain solitudes, and the reflection of the moonlight on the mysterious waves of the Salt Lake, he had nothing now but the chilly damps and cramping fetters of a dungeon, and the brutalities of such a jailor as a tetrarch like Antipas would have kept in a fortress like Makor [Machaerus]. In that black prison, among its lava streams and basaltic rocks, which were tenanted in reality by far worse demons of human brutality and human vice than the 'goats' and 'satyrs' and doleful creatures believed by Jewish legend to haunt its whole environment, we cannot wonder if the eye of the caged eagle began to film." (Farrar, p. 220.) Such is the eloquent language of Farrar.

From our vantage point, however, we know that the eye of the caged eagle did not begin to film. Rather, a wondrous and glorious event took place that brightened the caged eagle's eyes and enabled him to see out of the darkness of the dungeon, and beyond the confines of the earthlike prison, whereon all pilgrims from God's presence dwell for a moment. The veil was rent; the heavens were opened; angelic ministrants from the courts of glory hied themselves to the prison called earth, and to the dungeons of Herod, to speak peace to the weary and tried soul of the one who prepared the way before the Son of God. In majestic simplicity, the inspired record says: "And now Jesus knew that John was cast into prison, and he sent angels, and, behold, they came and ministered unto him."

Jesus did it! John was not forgotten by him. No more are any of those who suffer for his name's sake. Though heaven's Lord dwelt in a tabernacle of clay, yet the angelic legions were subject to his will, and he—in his love and in his pity and in his mercy—sent some of them to his friend and forerunner.

We cannot doubt that the heavens were rent after John had overcome the world. Faith precedes the miracle. After John had risen in his own mind from the bottomless pit of despair, he was prepared to ascend on angelic wings to heights beyond the skies.

His mortal work was done. As with Joseph and Hyrum in Carthage Jail, one thing only remained to be done: the sealing of his own testimony with his own blood. And that, as we shall hereafter see, was destined to be.

Prophets die that prophets may live, and through it all souls are saved and God is glorified. So be it.

NOTES

1. "That is, they accepted John as a prophet in an emotional, unreasoning way, much as the world today believes in the prophets of old. If they had accepted John in the full gospel sense, they would have also believed in Jesus as the Messiah, for such was the burden of John's message to them." (*Commentary* 1:148.)

2. Jesus was the great Exemplar—in the life that he lived, the teachings he taught, the miracles he wrought, the ordinances he performed; indeed, in all things that pertain to life and godliness. Without question he also performed all other gospel ordinances. We know he ordained the members of the Twelve. (John 15:16.) President Joseph Fielding Smith suggests that Peter, James, and John received their endowments from Jesus on the Mount of Transfiguration. (*Doctrines of Salvation* 2:165.)

Chapter 32

JESUS TAKES THE GOSPEL TO SAMARIA

Unto him that keepeth my
commandments I will give the mysteries
of my kingdom, and the same
shall be in him a well of living water,
springing up unto everlasting life.
(D&C 63:23.)

Jesus Journeys to Sychar in Samaria
(John 4:4-6; JST, John 4:2, 6-7)

"I must needs go through Samaria," Jesus said to his disciples, as he and they prepared to leave Judea and go to Galilee. Having embittered the Pharisees with his bold doctrines to the point that "they sought more diligently some means that they might put him to death," and knowing that his mission in Judea, for the moment, was completed, Jesus chose to go back to Galilee, to the land of his youth, to the rugged and hilly homeland where friends and kinsmen dwelt, there to launch his great Galilean ministry.

But why take the dangerous and robber-infested route through Samaria? It was the Jewish practice to go the long way around, through Perea, for the Samaritans were a hated race whose customs were abhorred and whose traditions were shunned. True, "the direct road to Galilee ran through the half-heathen country of Samaria," but this "road was proverbially unsafe for Jewish passengers, either returning from Jerusalem or going to it, for it passed through the border districts where the feuds of the two rival peoples raged most fiercely. The paths among the hills of Akrabbim, leading into Samaria, had often been wet with the blood of Jew or Samaritan, for they were the scene of constant raids and forays. . . . The pilgrims from Galilee to the feasts were often molested, and sometimes even attacked and scattered, with more or less slaughter; each act of violence bringing speedy reprisals from the population of Jerusalem and Judea, on the one side, and of Galilee on the other; the villages of the border districts, as most easily reached, bearing the brunt of the feud, in smoking cottages, and indiscriminate massacre of young and old." (Geikie, p. 361.)

Why, then, did Jesus feel compelled to go through Samaria? Superficially, some have supposed it was to avoid Perea, that part of Palestinian soil which was subject to Herod Antipas, who had now imprisoned John, and who—thanks to pharisaic intrigue—apparently opposed Jesus for himself and because he was the friend and colleague of the Baptist. Perhaps with Herod's soldiers on the alert to arrest for treason any who gathered followers—whether religious or political—there were perils connected with Perean travel, and they may have been, in Jesus' case, more serious than those through Samaria. We must conclude, however, that Jesus, though merely en route to Galilee for a greater work, chose to utilize his time and to bear witness of his divinity to the Samaritans. That is, Jesus went to Samaria to preach the gospel, to tell that spiritually benighted race that he was the Messiah whom they sought, and that salvation is in him. His message is the same for all people, Jew and Gentile alike, and the Samaritans were a racial mixture, half-Israelite and half-Gentile.[1] They must hear his voice; the Everlasting Word must speak to them in person.

As to the religion of the Samaritans, it was "a spurious Judaism," Edersheim says, "consisting of a mixture of their former [pagan] superstitions with Jewish doctrines and rites." They had once built their own temple on Mount Gerizim, and they claimed their own high priest and their own priestly administrators. "In the troublous times of Antiochus IV. Epiphanes, the Samaritans escaped the fate of the Jews by repudiating all connection with Israel, and dedicating their temple to Jupiter. . . . In 130 B.C. John Hyrcanus destroyed the Temple on Mount Gerizim, which was never rebuilt." (Edersheim 1:396-98.)[2]

The Samaritans were a half-Jewish, half-heathen race who practiced a form of worship of Jehovah and who looked for a Messiah who was to come. Their religious sensitivities were not so highly refined as were those of the Jews, but they were nonetheless children of the Father of us all, and his Son chose to preach the gospel of salvation to them beginning in Sychar.

And so our Lord and his missionary companions go from Judea to Samaria—from northern Judea, where he and they were teaching and baptizing, to Jacob's Well near Sychar, a distance of some twenty miles. Their travels are through a rugged, hilly area; even in December the Palestinian weather is hot. Jesus is thirsty, hungry, weary.[3] He rests in the shade of the alcove that protects the well while his disciples go another half mile or so into the city to obtain food.

Jesus Offers Living Water to All Men
(John 4:7-15; JST, John 4:11, 15-16)

Jesus is alone on ground hallowed by the feet of the great patriarch Jacob, who is Israel and whose descendants are the chosen people, of whom Jesus is one. Here is the parcel of ground that Jacob gave to his son Joseph; here is the well— seven or eight feet in diameter and one hundred fifty feet deep—that the father of all Israel dug to provide life-giving draughts to his family and cattle. On either side are Ebal and Gerizim, mountains of ancient fame, and nearby is the tomb of Joseph, whose bones were carried out of Egypt.

What ponderings as to the past, and what meditations of the present and the future, our Lord now has on this sacred spot, we can only surmise.

His moment of solitude soon ends. A woman of Samaria—alone and unattended, carrying a pitcher on her head, with a long cord to lower and raise the vessel—comes to draw water from her ancestor's well. Jesus speaks. "Give me to drink," he says. And, be it noted, to have the very conversation that he is now commencing is one of the chief reasons he chose to travel through Samaria, as he made his way to his homeland of Galilee.

"How is it that thou, being a Jew, askest drink of me, which am a woman of Samaria?" the woman responds, "for the Jews have no dealings with the Samaritans." To give drink to a thirsty traveler was, in that day and in that part of the earth, a cardinal rule of proper human conduct. To drink water is to live; to thirst for its life-giving properties is to die. All people in Palestine, Jew and Samaritan alike, gave water to their neighbors as the need arose. But the woman here is so taken back by the request of a Jew that she hesitates to comply with a basic rule of their society.

Time was when the Jews cursed the Samaritans in their synagogues, refused to accept them as proselytes, accused them of worshipping idols, said that to eat their bread was like eating swine's flesh, and taught that they would be denied a resurrection. Even Jesus spoke of a Samaritan as a stranger, or more accurately, an alien. These feelings were not now so intense, as witness the fact that the disciples were then in Sychar to obtain Samaritan food, but much of the old hatreds remained. Why then was this Jew asking a Samaritan for a drink?

"If thou knewest the gift of God"—the gift of his Son ("For God so loved the world, that he gave his only begotten Son, that whosoever believeth in him should not perish, but have everlasting life"—John 3:16)[4]—"and who it is that saith to thee, Give me to drink; thou wouldest have asked of him, and he would have given thee living water."

Living water! "For the thirsty and choking traveler in a desert wilderness to find water, is to find life, to find an escape from agonizing death; similarly, the weary pilgrim traveling through the wilderness of mortality saves himself eternally by drinking from the wells of living water found in the gospel.

"Living water is the words of eternal life, the message of salvation, the truths about God and his kingdom; it is the doctrines of the gospel. Those who thirst are invited to come unto Christ and drink. Where there are prophets of God, there will be found rivers of living water, wells filled with eternal truths, springs bubbling forth their life-giving draughts that save from spiritual death." (*Commentary* 1:151-52.)

For the sin-laden woman of Samaria, Jesus' words have little meaning. Her spiritual understanding is dimmed almost to darkness because she has chosen adultery as a way of life. "The things of God knoweth no man, but the Spirit of God. . . . The natural man receiveth not the things of the Spirit of God: for they are foolishness unto him: neither can he know them, because they are spiritually discerned." (1 Cor. 2:11-14.) Her response can deal only with literal water; the things of the Spirit are beyond her comprehension.

"Sir, thou hast nothing to draw with," she says, "and the well is deep: from whence then hast thou that living water?" As though living water could be found in a dead well! As though spiritual things can be understood by a carnal mind! "Art thou greater than our father Jacob, which gave us the well, and drank thereof himself, and his children, and his cattle?" Her claim to prophetic ancestry but dramatizes the reality that even the wicked and ungodly have religious instincts that they seek to satisfy by forms of worship that do not interfere with their carnal courses.

The stage is set, all is in readiness, and the Master Teacher is now prepared to teach the perfect lesson, to deliver the message of how salvation comes to thirsty and water-hungry mortals. They must drink the draughts of eternal truth; these only will give life to the spirit; these eternal wells, full of eternal water, will make available eternal life. As the parched and swollen tongues of desert travelers are refreshed with water drawn from the wells of earth, so the thirsting spirit lives again when living water is poured into the soul. Hence, Jesus' answer is:

Whosoever shall drink of this well, shall thirst again; But whosoever drinketh of the water which I shall give him shall never thirst; but the water that I shall give him shall be in him a well of water springing up into everlasting life.

But the woman, still blinded by her sins, fails to hear the message. Still thinking only of the things of this world, as is the way with carnal people, she says: "Sir, give me this water, that I thirst not, neither come hither to draw."

Jesus Invites Men to Worship the Father
(*John 4:16-24; JST, John 4:26*)

Jesus taught the woman of Samaria that she must come to him and receive the living water that refreshes and enlivens the spirit and leads the spiritually refreshed person to eternal life. His teachings were beyond the level of her spiritual understanding. She remained in darkness. He now uses her to find other truth seekers for him, and he does it by shocking her with a demonstration of his divine power, so that, perchance, even yet she will come to an understanding of the message he is sent to deliver. "Go, call thy husband, and come hither," he directs. "I have no husband," she replies. Jesus says, "Thou hast well said, I have no husband: For thou hast had five husbands; and he whom thou now hast is not thy husband: in that saidst thou truly."

A light begins to dawn. This is no ordinary man; not only does he speak of a strange water, living water, but he also reveals those things which can only be known by divine power. "Sir, I perceive that thou art a prophet," the woman says.

This, then, is her opportunity. This Jew is a prophet; he

can solve the centuries-old dispute between the Samaritans and the Jews. True Israelite worship centers in a temple. Jerusalem has its House of Herod with its great altar and its Holy of Holies; the Samaritan temple on Mount Gerizim was destroyed more than one hundred fifty years ago. Now, here at the foot of that Samaritan place of worship, the woman ventures to say: "Our fathers worshipped in this mountain; and ye say, that in Jerusalem is the place where men ought to worship."

"Woman, believe me," comes the response, "the hour cometh, when ye shall neither in this mountain, nor yet at Jerusalem, worship the Father," which is to say: The places where men built the temples of the past shall no longer be the only centers of approved worship. The old order changeth; there ariseth a new covenant, a new gospel; the temples of the future are the bodies of the saints;[5] and the sacrifices of the future are a broken heart and a contrite spirit.[6] The true believers of the future shall worship in all places and at all times, not just when sacrificial fires burn on Gerizim and in Jerusalem.

"Ye worship ye know not what." Samaritan worship was a strange intermixture of pagan and Israelite doctrine. Centuries before they had added the worship of Jehovah to the worship of their numerous idols; now this higher form of worship had become the dominant force in their way of worship, and their rituals and performances were dominantly Mosaic in nature, but still their worship was both Jewish and pagan all wrapped in one.[7]

"We know what we worship," Jesus continued, "for salvation is of the Jews." As between Jerusalem and Mount Gerizim; as between the Jews and the Samaritans; as between a people who accepted all of the Old Testament, and another that believed only the Pentateuch; as was the case with the Samaritans—the Jews were right and the Samaritans were wrong. The Jews knew what they worshipped, and such knowledge was not had by the Samaritans. Jesus had no hesitancy in telling would-be worshippers that their system of religion was wrong. Though the Jews were apostate, as a people, yet they did have the scriptures; they did search the writings of the prophets; their priests were still legal administrators; they had the knowledge of God to a degree; and salvation was to come through them to the world. Their Messiah was to be the Savior of the world. And so Jesus, the foundation again having been laid, makes the great proclamation:

But the hour cometh, and now is, when the true worshippers shall worship the Father in spirit and in truth: for the Father seeketh such to worship him. For unto such hath God promised his Spirit [not God is a Spirit, as our King James Version erroneously records]—*And they who worship him, must worship in spirit and in truth.*

Jesus Saith: I AM THE MESSIAH
(John 4:25-30; JST, John 4:28)

We know that there is a God in heaven, who is infinite and eternal, from everlasting to everlasting the same unchangeable God, the framer of heaven and earth, and all things which are in them; And that he created man, male and female, after his own image and in his own likeness, created he them; And gave unto them commandments that they should love and serve him, the only living and true God, and that he should be the only being whom they should worship. (D&C 20:17-19.)

Praise ye the Father. Worship the Father. Come unto the Father. He is God above all. Worship him in spirit and in truth. Such is his will. But do it in and through Christ who is the Messiah.

The number one truth—in all eternity—is that God is our Father, the Creator of us and all things, whom we must worship in spirit and in truth to gain salvation. Jesus has now, at Jacob's Well, proclaimed this eternal verity. It is the beginning of all true religion.

The number two truth—in all eternity—is that the Son of

God is the Messiah, the Redeemer, through whose atoning sacrifice immortality and eternal life are brought to pass. Having testified of the Father, our Lord must now bear witness of the Son. The woman, still not comprehending the pearls of great price that are dropping from the mouth of a Jew, says: "I know that Messias cometh, which is called Christ: when he is come, he will tell us all things."[8] She could not believe this unknown Jew; if only the Messiah would come, if only he were here, all problems would be solved!

> *Jesus said unto her, I who speak unto thee am the Messias.*

She had his witness of the Father; now he bore record of himself. He knew who he was. In the temple when but twelve years of age, he had so certified, in the statements about his Father's business. He had accepted the testimonies of John the Baptist and of his disciples. Nicodemus had heard him refer to himself as the Only Begotten of the Father. He was the Messiah; he knew it; and he knew it was his mission so to testify to all who would hear, whether they were receptive or, as this Samaritan woman, had sealed hearts and unbelieving blood.

How much else Jesus said to this woman we do not know. At this point in the dialogue, John's account says the disciples returned from Sychar with food to eat. They marveled that Jesus talked with the woman—a conversation that he and not she had initiated, for it violated the customs of the day for a Rabbi to speak in public with a woman, to say nothing of a Samaritan woman, and least of all a woman of easy virtue. Yet their reserve was such and his command of the situation so complete that none asked, "What seekest thou: or, Why talkest thou with her?"

With the arrival of the disciples, the woman left, leaving, in her excitement, her water pot. In the city she said to the men, "Come, see a man, which told me all things that ever I did." No doubt her report was a great exaggeration, but Jesus may well have told her other things about her life than those which pertained to her marital state. She had heard him say he was the Messiah, and so she said to the people in the city: "Is not this the Christ?"

"Then they went out of the city," as Jesus had planned and foreseen, "and came unto him." He had preached to one unreceptive person with such power and effect that he now had a congregation of many receptive souls, all anxious to hear the marvelous message about which one of their own number spoke so positively.

"He That Reapeth Receiveth Wages"
(*John 4:31-42; JST, John 4:40*)

After the woman, whose name we do not even know, departed for Sychar, the disciples made ready their food. When it was offered to Jesus, he said: "I have meat to eat that ye know not of," which caused the disciples to ask one another: "Hath any man brought him ought to eat?"

To this Jesus said: "My meat is to do the will of him that sent me, and to finish his work." The preaching of the gospel; the spread of eternal truth; the establishment of the earthly kingdom; the onward rolling of the great cause of truth and righteousness among men—these become the work, the all-consuming passion, of those who are endowed with power from on high. It becomes their meat and their drink; it takes all their strength; it embraces every waking word and thought. Those who are called to divine service are expected to serve with all their hearts, might, mind, and strength. Temporal needs sink into oblivion. The work becomes their meat and drink and breath and life. Jesus' meat was to do the work of his Father.

Now the multitudes are arriving. "Say not ye, There are yet four months, and then cometh harvest?" Jesus asks. That is, it is late December, possibly early January, and in four months the barley harvest will begin in Palestine. But as Jesus had spoken of living water and spiritual meat, he is now speaking of a harvest, not of barley, but of human souls.

"Lift up your eyes, and look on the fields; for they are white already to harvest." Surely this was a sample of what the prophet Joel had foreseen: "Put ye in the sickle, for the harvest is ripe," he said, as he spoke of the "multitudes in the valley of decision" (Joel 3:12-14), the hosts of men who must decide whether they will be gathered with the Lord's harvest into his kingdom or be left for the day when the tares and the grain that are not harvested shall be burned.

"And he that reapeth receiveth wages, and gathereth fruit unto life eternal," Jesus continued, "that both he that soweth and he that reapeth may rejoice together." The Lord pays his servants. Those who sow and those who harvest in his fields receive wages. They receive eternal life for themselves in that kingdom which is eternal; such a reward is the wages that are provided.[9]

"And herein is that saying true, One soweth, and another reapeth. I have sent you to reap that whereon ye bestowed no labor; the prophets have labored, and ye have entered into their labors." The work of saving souls is a great cooperative enterprise: one sows and another reaps. Isaiah and the prophets foretold the coming of a Messiah and the setting up of his earthly kingdom; they sowed the seeds of faith in the hearts of all who should read and believe their words, and the disciples who were with Jesus in his ministry reaped in the fields planted by their fellow servants of old. The Nephite prophets sowed the seeds of faith and righteousness in the Book of Mormon, and we go out, in our day, to reap the harvest, so that we and our Nephite brethren can rejoice together in that great day when all are safely gathered into the Eternal Granaries.

Jesus preached to those who thus came out to hear him, and he went, at their importuning, into the city, where he abode two days ministering among the people. Many believed because of the testimony of the woman. "And many more believed because of his own word," and they testified: "We have heard him ourselves, and know that this is indeed the Christ, the Saviour of the world."

Truly, the gospel was preached in Samaria. Seeds were sown and a harvest reaped. And at a later date, apostles and seventies and other missionaries would yet reap in the same fields. Jesus' stay there lasted only a few days, but the results of his ministry shall endure to all generations. And we cannot but hope that the woman who first met him at the well of the ancient patriarch was among those who forsook the world, had their sins washed away in the waters of baptism, kept the commandments thereafter, and received an eternal inheritance with the saved and exalted of all ages.

NOTES

1. "When the Ten Tribes were transported to Assyria more than seven centuries before the Christian era, Samaria was repeopled by heathen colonists from other Assyrian provinces. These pagan peoples, intermixing somewhat with scattered remnants of Israel, founded the race of despised and hated Samaritans of Jesus' day. As a nation, they claimed Jacob as their father and maintained they were inheritors of the blessings of the chosen seed. Their religion, partially pagan in nature, accepted the Pentateuch, but rejected the prophets and the psalms. In the day of Jesus they were friendly to Herod and Rome, but bitter toward the Jews, a feeling fully reciprocated by their Jewish kindred." (*Commentary* 1:151.)

2. "The political enmity and religious separation between the Jews and Samaritans account for their mutual jealousy. On all public occasions the Samaritans took the part hostile to the Jews, while they seized every opportunity of injuring and insulting them. Thus, in the time of Antiochus III they sold many Jews into slavery. Afterwards they sought to mislead the Jews at a distance, to whom the beginning of every month (so important to the Jewish festive arrangements) was intimated by beacon fires, by kindling spurious signals. We also read that they tried to desecrate the Temple on the eve of the Passover; and that they waylaid and killed pilgrims on their road to Jerusalem. The Jews retaliated by treating the Samaritans with every mark of contempt; by accusing them of falsehood, folly, and irreligion; and, what they felt most keenly, by disowning them as of the same race or religion, and this in the most offensive terms of assumed superiority and self-righteous fanaticism." (Edersheim 1:399.)

3. "Here we view one of the most human scenes of the Master's whole ministry. The Lord of heaven, who created and controls all things, having made clay his tabernacle, is physically tired, weary, hungry, and thirsty, following his long journey from Judea. He who had power to draw food and drink from the elements, who could have transported himself at will to any location, sought rest and refreshments at Jacob's Well. In all things he was subjecting himself to the proper experiences of mortality." (*Commentary* 1:151.)

4. Farrar, p. 159, footnote 2; Edersheim 1:399-403; Luke 17:18.

5. "Know ye not that ye are the temple of God, and that the Spirit of God dwelleth in you?" (1 Cor. 3:16.)

6. "And ye shall offer up unto me no more the shedding of blood; yea, your sacrifices and your burnt offerings shall be done away, for I will accept none of your sacrifices and your burnt offerings. And ye shall offer for a sacrifice unto me a broken heart and a contrite spirit." (3 Ne. 9:19-20.) "Present your bodies a living sacrifice, holy, acceptable unto God, which is your reasonable service." (Rom. 12:1.)

7. We might liken Samaritan worship to that of the Aztecs or the Mayas, after those ancient peoples had been conquered by Cortez and the other Spanish generals. Their conquerors imposed Christianity in the form of Catholicism upon them, and the result was

a strange admixture of religious form and thought, which over the years has taken on more and more of the basics of Catholicism and less and less of the paganism of the past.

8. With the Samaritans it was as with the Jews, they anxiously awaited the advent of the Messiah. "They looked for the coming of a Messiah, in Whom the promise would be fulfilled, that the Lord God would raise up a Prophet from the midst of them, like unto Moses, in Whom his words were to be, and unto Whom they should hearken. Thus, while, in some respects, access to them would be more difficult than to His own countrymen, yet in others Jesus would find there a soil better prepared for the Divine Seed, or, at least, less encumbered by the thistles and tares of traditionalism and Pharisaic bigotry." (Edersheim 1:403.)

9. "For behold the field is white already to harvest; and lo, he that thrusteth in his sickle with his might, the same layeth up in store that he perisheth not, but bringeth salvation to his soul." (D&C 4:4.) "Whoso desireth to reap, let him thrust in his sickle with his might, and reap while the day lasts, that he may treasure up for his soul everlasting salvation in the kingdom of God." (D&C 6:3.)

INDEX

Aaron, 245, 248
Aaronic blessing in synagogue worship,
195-96
Aaronic Priesthood: advent of, 60-61;
perfection came not by, 147; offices in,
247-48; holds power to baptize in water,
396
Abraham, 26; God's covenant with, 56-67,
215-16; reminder of promises made to,
146; seed of, all who receive gospel
become, 157 n. 3, 216; saw Christ's day,
281 n. 1; covenant of circumcision made
with, 334
Adam, 26; fall of, 36; true worship began
with, 50-51; blessed his righteous
posterity, 65 n. 3; offered sacrifices,
125-26; became presiding patriarch,
214; had fulness of gospel, 228-29; kept
book of remembrance, 269; baptism of,
395
Adam-Ondi-Ahman, 65 n. 3
Aethrogs, or tree boughs, 175
Agency, 22-23, 406-7
America, events in, attending Christ's
birth, 342-43, 346-47
Andrew, 47, 440-41
Angel: taught Adam how to worship, 51,
126; announced coming of Christ,
301-2; appeared to Zacharias, 308-10;
appeared to Mary, 318-19; appeared to
Joseph, 332; warned Joseph to flee to
Egypt, 362
Angels: hierarchy of, 311-12 n. 5; come to
impart God's word, 317; appeared to

shepherds, 347-49; ministered to John
the Baptist in prison, 491-92
Animals, selling of, in temple courtyards,
459-61
Anna the prophetess, 46, 355
Annas, 247, 384
Antiochus, 287-88
Antipas. *See* Herod Antipas
Apocrypha, 273
Apostasy: two components of, 229; of
Israel, 233-34; among Jews in Christ's
day, 234-39; is result of
unrighteousness, 237
Ark of the covenant, 101, 150
Athanasian Creed, 31-32 n. 2
Atonement: Christ worked out, 7-8;
reconciled man to God, 37; sacrifices
pointed to, 127; through sacrifice, 134;
Day of, 137-40; was Christ's most
important purpose, 141-42; necessity of,
152-53
Authority: John the Baptist had, 384,
398-99; Holy Ghost accompanies those
with, 481

Baal, 231
Balaam, 358
Baptism: for the dead, 122 n. 3; is symbolic
of Christ's death, burial, and
resurrection, 125; for remission of sins,
386-87; did not begin with John the
Baptist, 394-95; of Adam, 395; among
Jews, 396-98; is worthless without
repentance, 397; by immersion, 397-98;

INDEX

God is revealed through, 5; mortal
experiences of, 5-7, 38-39; was God's
Son, 6, 314; worked out infinite
atonement, 7-8; invites men to learn of
him, 8; man's knowledge of, is limited,
12-13, 20; invites men to come unto
him, 16-17; set perfect example, 18;
foreordination of, 26, 36, 284-85;
godhood of, 27-30; advanced by
obeying laws, 35; detailed prophecies
concerning life of, 38-40; millennial
reign of, 44-45; lived Mosaic law, 68;
second coming of, 117-22; will reign
over Israel, 120; all things bear record
of, 124; fulfilled Mosaic law, 127,
151-52; came into world to die, 140-41;
was in God's express image, 142; as
High Priest, 143-44; intercessory prayers
of, 148; taught in synagogues, 197-99;
taking name of, upon oneself, 216-17;
was born to Jewish family, 217, 219-20;
rejection of, was necessary, 236; earthly
ministry of, 282-85, 295-96; came to
overcome world, 289; received not
fulness at first, 299, 367, 430;
preparation of, for ministry, 299-300,
370; coming of, should be announced
by angels, 301-2; genealogy of, 315-16;
Gabriel announces pending birth of,
318-19; parents of, 330; birth of, 343,
345, 429; signs accompanying birth of,
346-49, 359; date of birth of, 349-50 n.
2; meaning of name of, 352;
redemption of, according to Israel's law,
352-53; Simeon and Anna testify of,
354-55; physical growth of, 367-68;
possible feelings of, on journey to
Jerusalem for Passover, 372-76; was
found in temple, 378; had to be about
his Father's business, 379-80; John the
Baptist prophesied of, 390-91; baptism
of, 400-403, 430; was capable of being
tempted, 405-6; was hungry in desert,
411; divinity of, needed no proof, 412;
Satan tempted, to cast himself down
from temple, 414-15; Spirit carried, to
mountain, 415; Satan tempted, with
wealth of world, 416-17; reasons for
tempting of, 417-19; glory of, John the
Baptist beheld, 429; events preceding
formal ministry of, 431; formal

introduction of, by John the Baptist,
435-36; John the Baptist testifies of,
437-38, 485-87; disciples left John the
Baptist to follow, 438-40, 483; calls his
disciples, 440-44; turns water into wine,
450-54; dwells in Capernaum, 455-56;
travels to Jerusalem for Passover,
456-57; drives moneychangers from
temple, 461; spoke of raising temple in
three days, 464-66; beginning of formal
ministry of, 468-70, 479; Nicodemus'
visit to, 470-71; men must believe in, to
be saved, 478; preached throughout
Judea, 480-81; performed baptisms,
481-82; declares himself as Messiah,
501; meat of, was to do God's will, 502
Jesus Christ, teachings of: understanding
setting of, 12; on being born of water
and the Spirit, 473; on living water,
496-98; on harvest of souls, 502-3
Jethro, 55
Jews: prophets of, 40-41; looked for
Messiah as temporal deliverer, 43-44;
many, recognized and worshipped
Christ, 46-47; true worship among, 62;
rejected Christ, 64; had form of
godliness but denied power, 109;
importance of temples to, 113-14;
converted to Mormonism, shall rebuild
temple, 116; feasts of, Christ used,
158-159; Sabbath observance among,
201, 205-11; four centers of worship
among, 204-5; family life among,
217-18, 222-26; education of, 223-24;
apostasy among, in Christ's day, 234-39;
ancient, beliefs of, 241-42; divisions
among, as to beliefs, 244, 276-77; brief
secular history of, 286-88; subjection of,
to Roman rule, 292-94; Christ
ministered and taught among, 296;
baptism among, 396-97; marriage
customs of, 449-50. See also Israel
John the Baptist: recognized Christ, 47;
was Christ's forerunner, 302-3; Gabriel
announces birth of, to Zacharias,
309-10; leaped in his mother's womb,
323; birth of, 333; naming of, 335;
ministry of, 382; had authority from
God, 384, 398-99; underwent period of
testing in desert, 385; laid foundations
for Christ's work, 386-87; many flocked

511